The Michigan Historical Reprint Series

Reprints from the collection of the University of Michigan University Library

This volume is produced from digital images created through the University of Michigan University Library's preservation reformatting program. The Library seeks to preserve the intellectual content of items in a manner that facilitates and promotes a variety of uses. The digital reformatting process results in an electronic version of the text that can both be accessed online and used to create new print copies. This book and thousands of others can be found in the digital collections of the University of Michigan Library. The University Library also understands and values the utility of print, and makes reprints available through its Scholarly Publishing Office.

For access to the University of Michigan Library's digital collections, please see http://www.lib.umich.edu.

The Scholarly Publishing Office seeks to disseminate high-quality, cost-effective scholarly content through both print and electronic publishing. Information about the Scholarly Publishing Office can be found at http://spo.umdl.umich.edu.

The Scholarly Publishing Office
the University of Michigan
University Library

A PRACTICAL TREATISE

ON

BUSINESS.

"There is a tide in the affairs of men,
Which, taken at the flood, leads on to fortune;
Omitted, all the voyage of their life
Is bound in shallows and in miseries."

A PRACTICAL TREATISE

ON

BUSINESS:

OR HOW TO

GET, SAVE, SPEND, GIVE, LEND, AND BEQUEATH

MONEY:

WITH AN

INQUIRY INTO THE CHANCES OF SUCCESS AND CAUSES OF FAILURE IN BUSINESS.

BY EDWIN T. FREEDLEY.

ALSO,

PRIZE ESSAYS, STATISTICS, MISCELLANIES,

AND

NUMEROUS PRIVATE LETTERS FROM SUCCESSFUL AND DISTINGUISHED BUSINESS MEN.

Twentieth Thousand.

PHILADELPHIA:
LIPPINCOTT, GRAMBO & CO.
1853.

PHILADELPHIA:
STEREOTYPED BY GEORGE CHARLES.
PRINTED BY T. K. & P. G COLLINS.

PREFACE.

"The wisdom touching negotiation, or business, hath not been hitherto collected into writing, to the great derogation of learning and the professors of learning. * * For if books were written of this, as the other, I doubt not but *learned men, with mean experience, would far excel men of long experience without learning, and outshoot them with their own bow.*"—Bacon's *Adv. of Learning*.

It needs no long experience, I think, to convince any one that men engaged in active business need all the information they can get to manage their concerns with success; nor does it require a world-wide observation to discover that not a few purchase their knowledge at the price of their fortune and reputation. Impressed with this conviction, I determined, some months ago, to take advantage of the leisure accidentally afforded me to see what landmarks had been set up, and to know how much could be learned respecting a matter so important as business, by means less costly and more pleasant than the severe teachings of experience. On looking through the records within my reach, I found a good deal that I considered valuable, and which I was satisfied that all who are engaged in business do not know, though doubtless many know the whole of it and much more. It seemed to me that, by separating that which was useful and practical from the mass of irrelevant matter with which it was mixed up, and arranging it in an interesting and instructive shape, with the addition of some facts entirely within my own possession, I could do some service to those for whom I entertain a higher respect than for any other class of men in the world—I mean the active, intelligent business men of the country—and especially to those who are fitting themselves for business pursuits. Whether the attempt is a happy one,

I cannot say. It is a hazardous undertaking for an unpractised hand to attempt authorship at any time; and on subjects like this, it is doubly hazardous.

My claims to the indulgent consideration of those whose attention I necessarily solicit by the act of publication rest mainly on the fact that the number of books on the principles of money-making is few—none to serve as models—and that more are wanted; and upon the fact that I honestly entertain the opinion, however mistaken it may be, that those who favor this humble treatise with a candid and an unprejudiced perusal will not find that their time and money have been totally thrown away. The value of books of this kind does not consist solely in what they state, but also in what they may suggest, so that a wide-awake man stands a chance of having an idea suddenly darted into his mind by which he may materially and essentially improve his fortune, or increase his happiness. What is called TACT, which makes so large a figure in the conversation of the world, and which is certainly a powerful instrument of success, is nothing more than quickness of perception, united to promptitude of action. It is the result of possessing a variety of practical ideas, and confidence in their correctness. The sources whence these ideas may be obtained are, first, a fertile brain: secondly, actual personal experience in the affairs of life: and, thirdly, the experience and views of others, analysed and made our own by study.

"In the outset, then, we apprise the reader," to use the language (which is especially true of this work) of the author of the chapter on speculation, "that, inasmuch as one man's wisdom or experience would be a very insufficient guide in this great search for truth, WHICH HAS A BIG BAG OF MONEY AT THE END, we have not undertaken to rely on our own acquired skill in money-making, but have made free with the knowledge of others. The principles, the facts, the maxims, and the judgments we design to set forth are partly original, and partly compiled. Few men have written books without saying something wise on the subject of money-getting, and what we have learned from divers sources respecting this matter" may be found in the following pages. This work embraces, *besides what is original,* and besides numerous extracts and interesting letters to the author from Hon. John Freedley, Hon. Horace Greeley, J. W. Scott, P. T. Barnum, and others, a most excellent and interesting prize essay on farm management, by J. J. Thomas, which will give to those who read only to increase their stock of general knowledge more information on the best mode of managing a farm than many farmers possess; an excellent original essay, the True Man of Business, by Hon. Horace Greeley, written for this work : How to Get Rich by Speculation, by a merchant of Boston, originally written for the *Boston Courier;* the most valuable part of Taylor's celebrated essay of Money, never before republished in this country; and some valuable statistics and miscellanies, for a part of which I am indebted to Mr. Hunt, proprietor of *Hunt's Merchants' Magazine,* which is the most valuable periodical for the business man ever published in any country.

Hoping that this treatise, though humble, contains some hints that will be of value to those for whom it has been prepared, and that those of its friends who believe that it will do good, notwithstanding its faults, will take some interest in its circulation, I leave it in the hands of a generous public.

PHILADELPHIA, *June* 14, 1852.

CHAPTER IV.

GETTING MONEY.

CHAPTER V.

GETTING MONEY BY FARMING.

CHAPTER VI.

GETTING MONEY BY MERCHANDISING.

CHAPTER VIII.

HOW TO GET CUSTOMERS.

CHAPTER IX.

THE TRUE MAN OF BUSINESS.

CHAPTER X.

HOW TO GET RICH BY SPECULATION.

CHAPTER XI.

GETTING MONEY—*Continued.*

INTEREST, BANKING, PRIVATE BANKING.

CHAPTER XII.

GETTING MONEY BY INVENTIONS, PATENT MEDICINES.

CHAPTER XIII.

HOW TO BECOME MILLIONAIRES—OPINIONS OF MILLIONAIRES

CHAPTER XIV.

LOSING MONEY—CHANCES OF SUCCESS—CAUSES OF FAILURE.

LETTERS AND MISCELLANIES.

LEGAL ADVICE AND USEFUL SUGGESTIONS FOR THE PURCHASERS OF THIS BOOK.

A PRACTICAL TREATISE ON BUSINESS.

CHAPTER I.

BUSINESS—INTRODUCTORY.

"THE philosophy which affects to teach us a contempt of money does not run very deep; for, indeed, it ought to be still more clear to the philosopher than it is to the ordinary man, that there are few things of greater importance. And so manifold are the bearings of money upon the lives and character of mankind, that an insight which would search out the life of a man in his pecuniary relations would penetrate into almost every cranny of his nature. He who knows, like St. Paul, both how to spare and to abound, has a great knowledge; for, if we take account of all the virtues with which money is mixed up—honesty, justice, generosity, charity, frugality, forethought, self-sacrifice, and of their correlative vices, it is a knowledge which goes near to cover the length and breadth of humanity, *and a right measure and manner in getting, saving, spending, giving, taking, lending, borrowing, and bequeathing, would almost argue a perfect man.*"—TAYLOR'S *Notes from Life.*

OUR subject is Business, and our first inquiry is, *What is Business?*

Business, in one sense, means employment or serious engagement, in distinction from trivial transactions. In its ordinary acceptation, it implies employment, in some *useful* affairs, for the purpose of profit or improvement. It is also a general term for all the occupations that engage the daily time, attention, and labor of mankind; but, in strictness, it should be confined to those which require skill and attention more than physical labor. It is a word that is derived from the German, and, in its primary sense, it signifies "seeing or closely inspecting." In the Latin, it denotes self-denial of ease—nego otium, *negotium*—I deny myself all pleasure and self-indulgence for the sake of business.

Man is a compound of body and mind. His nature is a complexity of the animal and the spiritual; of the physical and the intellectual. The gratification of his material wants is the object of business; science and literature aid his intellectual growth. The business man cultivates, manufactures, gathers together, and distributes those things by which the body is cherished or adorned; the scholar originates, collects, and furnishes food for the mind. Whether the office of the latter be more important to society than the former is an inquiry as useless as whether the mind is superior to the body, both being essential to the existence of a human being. A body, without a mind, is the definition of a corpse; a spirit, without a body, is a frightful spectre. In determining a man's conduct and destiny, too, the body has frequently as much influence as the mind, and he who aspires to be master of his actions must pay a due attention to the regulation of both. "Falstaff would have been as abstemious at the banquet as a hermit, and as firm in the battle as a hero, if he could have but gained over the consent of his belly in the one case, and of his legs in the other. He that strives for the mastery must join a well disciplined body to a well-regulated mind; for with mind and body, as with man and wife, it often happens that the stronger vessel is ruled by the weaker, although, in moral as in domestic economy, matters are best conducted where neither party is unreasonable, and where *both* are agreed."

What is the end of Business? We answer, happiness. The acquisition of property is subordinate to this end. Money is valueless, except as it will satisfy wants. Business is a source of happiness in several ways. Its pursuit engages, invigorates, and enlarges the mind; its usefulness promotes self-respect; its results, if successful, increase the power of doing what the head conceives and the heart desires.

The history of our race is the record of a long, fruitless chase after happiness. Men have traversed the whole cycle of imaginary good in search of it; they have sought it in glory, ambition, fanaticism, pleasure, action, repose, science, philosophy, at the bloody shrines of paganism; on the sands of Asia, beneath the banners of the Cross; in the lap of luxurious indulgence; in the cloisters of monks; at the confessional of the Jesuit; yea, they have invoked the Seven Spirits to teach them happiness; but, like the rémorse-stricken hunter of the Alps, have been answered, "It is not in our essence—in our skill." Philosophy was summoned, at an early day, to point out the way. For more than a thousand years, she preached to men to elevate their minds above all physical comforts; to contemn all useful improvements; to seek their happiness in the study of abstract science and metaphysical speculation; but, alas! it was impossible to "solve insoluble enigmas," or attain unattainable frames of mind. About the sixteenth century, a different doctrine was promulgated. The multiplication of human enjoyments, and the mitigation of human suffering, were held up as the only aim worthy of philosophy; and the invention of things useful, as the highest exercise of intellect. In less than two centuries, results have been realized that have outstripped human belief, as they have surpassed human experience. The progress of the age is a term as familiar in the lonely cabins of the West, as in the Academy of Sciences. And, in so far as happiness depends on the earnest, energetic engagement of the mind in any pursuit; on personal freedom; on good laws; on increased duration of life; on the mitigation of pain; on improvements in the healing art; on facilities of locomotion and correspondence; on the comforts and conveniences of life, this new philosophy has contributed greatly to the happiness of mankind.

It is a matter of deep regret that so many of those who are fitted by nature and education to be profitable instructors of mankind have so often seen proper to speak disparagingly of those employments which are embraced in the term business. Sordid, low, base, selfish, grovelling, are the mildest epithets they have used when speaking of industrial pursuits; and a harsh necessity, from which men should escape as speedily as possible, is the best apology they can make for them. "A mere merchant! a mere man of business! who would be content with such a designation? What respect can one feel for such a character?" says a distinguished divine, who makes

$3500 per annum out of his moral and religious sentiments This is the spirit of that old philosophy which, like those "Roman matrons who swallowed abortives in order to preserve their shapes, took pains to be barren for fear of being homely." It is to be regretted, because it tends to lower the character of business pursuits in the public estimation; and many who engage in them will think of nothing but accommodating themselves to the course of conduct pointed out, and laying the blame of their selfishness and misconduct on the business, when in justice it should fall upon themselves. Why should business pursuits be stigmatized as low? In the literature of all countries and of all ages, idleness has been held up as the parent of vice. "A busy man," says a Turkish proverb, "is troubled with but one devil, an idle man with a thousand." "Men are usually tempted by the devil," runs a Spanish proverb; "but an idle man positively tempts the devil." But if idleness were a virtue, it is impracticable. Mind cannot exist inactively; it must be engaged in something good or evil, while the body is awake. The body, too, is framed for action, and, without it, sinks speedily into decay. In what, then, can body and mind be better engaged than in some one of those employments which, while they afford both an agreeable exercise, at the same time cure the ground of the curse which fell upon it, and cause the earth to "breathe and bloom again with the flowers and fruits of Paradise?" What will more contribute to general or individual happiness? Is it religion or knowledge? Religion is an essential element of happiness. Without it, a man cannot enjoy any real happiness, though he may have the intellect of a Milton, and the wealth of a Crœsus. The happiness of an irreligious man who, nevertheless, believes in the existence of a Great First Cause—in the immortality of the soul—in the truth of the Christian revelation—is that of the criminal under sentence of execution, or of him who stands totteringly on the edge of an abyss into which a breath of wind may plunge him. He feels the weight of an impending doom—he has no resource in affliction—no consolation in adversity. But religion, though indispensable, is not all-sufficient for happiness in this life. Man was not created to spend his whole time in fasting and prayer. A recluse, it is said, living in the early ages of Christianity, betook himself to a cave in

Upper Egypt, which, in the time of the Pharaohs, had been a depository of the mummies, and there lived to pray, to converse with the spirits of the dead, to mortify himself, eating only dates, and drinking only the water of the Nile. At length, becoming weary of life, he prayed one day more fervently than ever, and then, sinking exhausted into a profound sleep, there appeared to him a vision of an angel in a dream, commanding him to rise, and cut down a neighboring palm-tree and make a rope of its fibres, after which the angel promised to appear to him again. Upon awaking, the hermit instantly resolved to obey the vision, and, travelling for many days from place to place, in search of an axe, he found himself happier than he had been for many years. His prayers, though shorter and fewer than those he had been accustomed to offer, out-measured them in fervor and effect. Having returned with the axe, he cut down the tree, and with much labor and assiduity for a long time prepared the fibres to make the rope, and, by daily occupation, after some weeks he had completed the command. According to promise, the celestial visitor that night appeared again, and said: "Dominico, thou art now no longer weary of life, but happy. Know, then, that man was made for labor as well as for prayer, the one being not less essential to his welfare than the other. Arise in the morning, take the cord, gird up thy loins, go forth into the world, and let it be a memorial to thee that God expects from man, if he would be happy, a course duly adjusted both to his animal and to his spiritual nature."

Knowledge is a source of happiness. Every advance in intelligence that brings man in closer communion with the source of all true knowledge—every new faculty discovered or called into willing activity—every idea that gives a clearer comprehension of the mysteries of the visible world, or the still greater mysteries of the human mind—is an increase of happiness. But knowledge, without purity of heart, is a snare; and knowledge that cannot be applied to usefulness promotes wretchedness and temptation. "A man intellectually cultivated must be either a patient saint, or a gloomy misanthrope, if placed by the selfishness of society, or his own will, in such a position that he cannot profitably or happily apply his knowledge. He may be able to interpret the eloquence of nature, and look out amongst the stars with a feeling of the infinite glories of heaven, but yet he lies buried in the earth with all his burning thoughts. He feels the darkness, the uselessness and rottenness of death, because he lives in the consciousness of all that might have been for him, and ought to have been for him but that, although awakened into earnestness by the urgencies of his own nature, and by the affected officiousness of artificial teachers, he is still left to shift for himself, though imprisoned in poverty, as if in cold iron, stone, and gloom. Such is the lot of many a classic mind, to whom 'the ploughman whistling o'er the lea' is a prince. And the reason of this misery is in the fact that the knowledge which has nothing to do with daily employments, induces pride, false or unnatural taste, and makes the world a wilderness, because the heathen gods have been banished, and the vale of Tempe requires tillage, that its inhabitants may eat. And all kinds of education are equally maddening that do not give vigor and liberty to human sympathies, or induce a disposition to labor, and make demand for it. There is no happiness without action: and he who, from the state of his mind or the style of his ideas, or the mismanagement of monopolists, cannot get to work, might as well be palsied, or in the penitentiary. Nothing but the strong hold on the right hand of God, as the vindicator of the oppressed, and the omnipotent opener of prisons and graves, can comfort the man who knows and wills, and cannot act."*

A man who desires to make a wise disposition of his time, should so regulate it as to give each of these great sources of happiness—religion, knowledge, and business—its proportionate share of his attention, and not allow his mind to become absorbed in any one of them to the exclusion of the others. It is a union that is eminently practicable, and the result will be happiness. The idea that an energetic devotion to business in its time and place is incompatible with a high degree of moral culture or intellectual ability, is entirely erroneous. On the contrary, a man must possess great strength of moral principle and an enlarged intellect to carry on an extended business with a reasonable hope of success.

* Moore's "Man and his Motives."

Business is, in truth, a test of virtue, a fiery furnace to principle. He who passes his days in studious ease, holding converse with the spirits of the great dead, or meditating on abstract truths, and sees life only through the windows of his study, knows nothing of trial, or danger, or temptation. He may be a swindler, or a forger, or a murderer like Webster, and never suspect it. But no man can spend many years in business without developing his character to his own conscience at least, if not to the knowledge of the world. If he is a man of weak wit, he will become an habitual liar; if a man of lax moral principle, he will become a rogue, and consequently a bankrupt. If his conscience tells him that he is still a man of moral uprightness, he need fear no other trial. Let him who desires to test the strength of his principles, or improve his moral nature by wholesome discipline, embark in trade. Let him who considers himself a skilful arbitrator or adjudicator of nice questions in morals or metaphysics, place himself in a position where, every day of his life, he must adjust those in which he himself is an interested party. Let him who thinks himself a proficient in moral or mental arithmetic, try calculating a problem in which his liberty, his home, his fortune, are involved. Let him who is firmly convinced from study and reflection, that business does not call for intellectual ability, that "any fool can get money," embark his all in some credit business; and if he does not pray, before the fourth of November, that whole hecatombs of dead authors may bury him from the sight of living men, we will reconsider our opinion. That trade is a severe trial to virtue—too severe for the endurance of all men—is no proof that it is unfavorable to moral growth. Life is a probation, and business may be designed as a means of perfecting the moral nature. But it *is* a proof that science and religion should come down from their "starry heights," and aid the poor sons of toil in their daily trials—that wisdom should make known not general principles merely, but rules that will be applicable to individual cases as they arise. It *is* a proof that preachers should preach a practical religion, and teachers teach a practical knowledge.

The *social* progress of mankind and physical improvement of the world, are entirely dependent on the accurate discovery and universal dissemination of those principles that make industry productive and business successful. The steam-engine has been called a democrat. We would call it a radical reformer. It is destined to achieve as grand results in the moral and political world as it has in the material—to annihilate evils, as it has annihilated distance.* There is no great social evil, that I can think of, that will not disappear when the laws that make industry most productive are understood and applied to practice. The condition of the poor in our large cities, none can reflect upon without sorrow. But are there not millions of acres of uncultivated land in the globe? Are there not hundreds of thousands of farmers who would be richer men if they employed more labor? Circulate, then, a knowledge of the true principles of business; convince farmers that labor will and must pay, and soon the demand for labor will be greater than the supply. There will be agents in all the large cities, whose business it will be to procure laborers for the country. One tenth of the additional income that men might have, if they were wise in their

* *Extract from Cist's Cincinnati in* 1851.—"The time consumed in seeding, tending, and harvesting the cereal crops, embraces about one-half the year: if not in idleness, then, during the remainder of it, the laborer has to seek other employments than on the land. The grain crop is sown and gathered during the months of April, May, June, July, August, September, and part of October; this includes corn. The cotton crop is seeded in the spring, and gathered during the late fall and winter months. Now, let the great reduction take place which I predict in the cost of locomotion; let the passage between this city and Charleston come down, as I predict it will, to five dollars, and to intermediate points in the same proportion; and let the time consumed in the trip be within my estimate, say thirty-six hours to Charleston, *who will gather the cotton crop? What becomes of slavery and slave labor, when these northern hordes shall descend upon the fair fields of the sunny South?* No conflict, no interference with Southern institutions need be apprehended; the unemployed northern laborer will simply underwork the slave during the winter months, and, when the crop is gathered, return to his home. It is known that the labor required to gather the cotton crop, as compared with that to plant and tend, is as about four to one; that is, one man can plant and tend as much as four can gather." "The English harvest is gathered by Irish laborers, many hundreds and thousands of whom cross the Channel every year for that purpose."

business pursuits, would support all the unfortunate poor in the United States, and perhaps the world.

Our main reliance, in the *moral* progress of mankind, is found in those means which aim at the elevation of the business character. When men discover the great truth that no man is wise or safe but he that is honest; when they perceive clearly that virtue and knowledge will improve their chances of success in this life, and promote their present as well as future happiness, they will not neglect the acquisition of knowledge, nor delay the practice of virtue. There is an identity of interest, a mutual dependence, an intimate relationship between all things that are good, and business prepares the way for the favorable reception of truth—as Truth, Virtue, and Knowledge are the best friends of business. Idleness is a foe to virtue, and business conquers idleness. Poverty is an evil: but, in the house of the industrious man, "want may look in, but dares not enter." Charity is a virtue, and business gives the means as well as the disposition to be charitable. Public spirit is a virtue, and it flourishes best where trade is most respected. Honesty is a virtue, and the more nations are commercial, the more honest they are in their dealings. Patriotism is a virtue, and it exists in its purest vigor where men are free to get property, and where laws protect property. War is an evil;—it is the same "man-slaying, blood-polluted, city-smiting god" now as in the days of Homer; and we believe the genius of Commerce alone can effectually stay the ravages of the sword. Commerce, an important branch of business, extends civilization, equalizes the comforts of life in all parts of the globe, circulates valuable discoveries in the arts and sciences, and stimulates invention. It is favorable to establishments of learning and religion, and every where it is identified with improvement—improvement in mind and manners—"improvement in arts and letters—improvement in knowledge, in morals, in legislation, in laws, in liberty; and in all improvement it has led more than it has followed; it has been the pioneer much more than the fellow and companion of human advancement and civilization."

But it is needless to defend industrial pursuits from the attacks of the censorious, or enlarge upon the benefits they have conferred upon society. We have full faith in the truth of the popular notion that poverty is an evil, and wealth a blessing; but, at the same time, we hold that individual wealth is a reward too uncertain of attainment to be made an object of primary consideration. No one who has become very rich can say, in strict truth, that he "made his own money;" for no other man, by doing exactly as he did, will arrive at the same goal. Wealth may be compared to those birds that smell the hunter afar off, and fly from his approach, while sometimes an ordinary traveller may knock them down with his cane. The first great step in life is to form rational ideas of happiness—ideas worthy of immortal beings. We have the lamp of the world's experience and the Book of Wisdom to guide us, and we need not err. Independence is certainly attainable by adhering to the laws of trade; a reasonable degree of happiness is attainable by the right management of business; but all that can be done by any one towards acquiring wealth is to place himself in the way of favorable junctures, and make himself ready for their approach; to descry opportunities at a distance, and keep his eye steadily upon them—watch all the motions that make towards them—and when the time comes, to lay fast hold, and never let go; and, secondly, not to turn aside the favorable train of circumstances that may have been laid for him, by his own wilfulness, imprudence, or unskilfulness. All that can be done by books, and it is all that need be done, is to aid the judgment in distinguishing appearances, and to collect together those principles which have generally resulted in good fortune, and those which have led to ruin. A *moderate* desire of gain is indispensable to the coolness of judgment which can decide upon the probability of events or appreciate principles. And he who thus consults his true happiness will find favor in the sight of his Creator, who delights in the happiness of his creatures; will be preserved from many dangers and temptations; and will probably find that those means which he has taken to promote or secure his happiness have at the same time contributed to his worldly prosperity.

It is the design of this humble treatise to open the field of business to the view of those who have only a general notion of it; and, if possible, to contribute something that will make men more successful in the attainment of happiness, and, so far as it depends upon themselves, in the acquisition of wealth.

CHAPTER II.

BUSINESS EDUCATION—CHOICE OF A BUSINESS.

"It is the great advantage of a trading nation that there are few in it so dull and heavy, who may not be placed in stations of life which may give them an opportunity of making their fortune," says Addison, truly : but, while any one may be a man of business, who is legally competent to make a contract, and while all can find in a flourishing community stations suited to their talents and disposition ; to carry on an extended business successfully, requires powers of thought, and capabilities of endurance, and a vigor of constitution that few possess. Business is a "death potion" to many ; and a more unhappy situation than the incongruity between the business and the capacity, can scarcely be imagined. It is a life-long torment, for which there is hardly a remedy, as a change of business or profession seldom succeeds. The world argues that he who has failed in his first profession, to which he had devoted "the morning of his life and the spring-time of his exertions," is not the most likely person to master a second. It is proper, therefore, to glance at the best *temperament* for a man of business—the *most suitable education*—and suggest a few thoughts that should have influence in the *choice of a business or profession.*

I. It has been frequently remarked—and a late author* has expressed it the most forcibly—that the best temperament for great affairs is "a combination of the desponding and the resolute ; or, as I had better express it, of the *apprehensive* and the *resolute.* Such is the temperament of great commanders. Secretly they rely upon nothing and upon nobody. *There is such a powerful element of failure in all human affairs, that a shrewd man is always saying*

* Companions of my Solitude.

to himself, What shall I do, if that which I count upon does not come out as I expect! This foresight dwarfs and crushes all but men of great resolution."

These are wise words. He who has an abiding confidence in his good fortune—who is sure that all will end well—that it matters little what he does, the result will be favorable—has the most happy disposition; but it is not a temperament that fits him for great deeds. And a man who wants resolution to try, to try again, will be certain never to do even moderate deeds. A combination of the apprehensive and the resolute is especially necessary in the pursuit of wealth. Fortune is proverbially fickle; business success cannot be guaranteed; and he who suffers his mind to dwell upon his future greatness—who indulges in visions of magnificence and power, and allows the love of money to become closely entwined around his heart—will be tempted to overleap himself, or be lulled into a fatal security from which he will awake to find his happiness gone forever with his dreams. But the true business man thinks not of the end; as there is a "powerful element of failure in all human affairs," he will probably fail; but he is *determined to try*, and will leave no stone unturned that will give probability of success. His thoughts are on the *means*, and not on the *end;* he wishes to hear of the dangers of the road, and the means by which they can be escaped, and not flattering tales of doubtful success. If he fail, as fail he may, he has a reserve at hand which he can fall back upon, without being bankrupt in happiness as well as fortune.

II. An education that can be called practical must be directed to two objects—the *cultivation of the senses*, and *the discipline of the mind* by such studies as will also be useful in themselves. It is needless to remark how important a part the *senses* perform in dealing with material objects. They are the instruments by which experiments are to be observed, and discoveries to be made; and in trade, perhaps one-half of the superiority which some manifest over others is to be ascribed to greater accuracy of taste, smelling, sight, or feeling. Who has not been struck with admiration at the accurate observation of the Indian by which he can retrace his steps in the most trackless wild? Who has not felt it would be an advantage to possess the blind man's acuteness of touch? "Mankind," says Dr. Hook, "have by their ingenuity wonderfully assisted the sense of sight and hearing, and have prolonged to age the advantages of youth, but it remains for them to bring their senses to the highest state of perfection and activity by judicious cultivation. It is worth remarking that even common artisans, not distinguished by any superiority of intellect, have, by exercise and patience, brought some of their senses to a degree of perfection truly astonishing. The *exercise of the senses is naturally pleasurable to children*, and may, therefore, be easily promoted and improved, and in distinguishing smell, colors, taste, and the touch of various things, the pupil will soon become expert if he have a *sufficient supply of visible and tangible objects on which to exert his attention.*" This is a subject, then, which should receive the attention of parents; and in childhood, instruction may be combined with amusement.

The *discipline of the mind* is a work of longer time, and more difficult attainment; but cultivation will effect it. The mind is naturally like a colt, wild and ungoverned. It must be broken to the bit, and familiar with the rein. The great cardinal powers, Attention, Abstraction, Perception, Memory, Judgment, are in a great degree dependent for their growth and power on culture. This constitutes the great difference between the reason of man and the instinct of brutes. They arrive at a certain point in knowledge, and there stop. The beaver displays no more originality in the construction of his dam in our Western forests now than he did before Columbus landed on our shores. The swallow builds her nest no more skilfully now than she did before the flood. But the human intellect is susceptible of unlimited improvement, and makes the accumulated knowledge of the past the starting-point of future discoveries.

It is fortunate that those studies which best discipline the mind are, in themselves, eminently practical and useful. The Physical Sciences, Natural Philosophy, Mathematics, Chemistry, unfold and exercise the mental powers to habits of attention, method, and right trains of reasoning, and at the same time instruct how to investigate the powers of nature, the properties of material bodies, their action one upon another, and explain the qualities of those substances which the Creator has intended for the use and happiness of man. The excellent Dr. Barrow says of the mathematics: "They effectually exercise, not vainly delude, nor vexatiously torment studious minds with obscure subtleties, but plainly demonstrate every thing within their reach, draw certain conclusions, instruct by profitable rules, and unfold pleasant questions. These disciplines also enure and corroborate the mind to a constant diligence in study; they wholly deliver us from a credulous simplicity, and most strongly fortify us against the vanity of scepticism; they effectually restrain us from a rash presumption, most easily incline us to a due assent, and perfectly subject us to the government of right reason."

It may be worthy of remark that the most of those who have been distinguished in practical affairs have also been noted for their love of mathematical studies. Bonaparte was an eminent example. Even the classical Everett, notwithstanding his love of the ancient founts of poetry and eloquence, is compelled to admit that in England it has been observed of the study of the law—though the most difficult parts of its learning, with the interpretation of the laws, the comparison of authorities, and the construction of instruments would seem to require philological and critical training; though the weighing of evidence and the investigation of probable truth belong to the province of the moral sciences, and the peculiar duties of the advocate require rhetorical skill—yet "that a large proportion of the most distinguished members of the profession has proceeded from the University, that of Cambridge, most celebrated for the cultivation of mathematical studies."

Chemistry should receive especial attention in a course of practical education. As the profits in the old channels of business become more and more reduced by competition and other causes, we must look to Chemistry to discover new mines of wealth; as fertile land becomes scarcer, we must look to Chemistry to teach us how to cultivate the field and the garden so as to secure the utmost in quantity, and the best in quality, of their inestimable productions. The annals of one of the early revolutions in France furnish a remarkable instance of the resources of Chemistry in times of difficulty. The ports of France were blockaded; her commerce, on which she depended for her supplies of saltpetre, was interrupted; her manufactories were idle, and her soldiers useless for want of ammunition In this distress, the ministers called upon the chemists to devise some means of relief, and they quickly informed them of the immense quantities of saltpetre which nature had deposited in her bosom; and that animal and vegetable substances, the refuse of cow-houses and aviaries, would yield still greater quantities.

Of languages, the *German* and the *Spanish* are the most likely to be useful. The German emigration into this country is immense. As many as five hundred emigrants arrive in one day at the port of New York, and in the year 1847, *fifty thousand* landed at that one port. These men become American merchants and mechanics. Pennsylvania and Ohio number their German citizens by hundreds of thousands. They are generally noted for their frugal habits, prompt payments, and their custom is desirable. Many a man who has become wealthy can ascribe his early success to the sole advantage of possessing a knowledge of the German language. And, as the public mind is now earnestly attracted towards Cuba, Mexico, California and the South American provinces, and it may fall to the lot of any one to go there, it will not be an unwise precaution to acquire a knowledge of the *Spanish* language.

How to obtain a practical education—is a question that admits of but one answer. "Every thing is bought with a price:" and the price of an education is vigilance and self-labor. Journeymen of the rarest skill cannot do the work. Mind acknowledges no master but Will; it attains its maximum of strength by one process only—*intense* thought. Every one whose mind is disciplined to obedience and stocked with knowledge holds his acquisitions by the best of titles, and can call it emphatically his own work. Self-cultivation, therefore, is the only cultivation worthy of the name.* Books, teachers, schools, colleges are only *means*

* I may, perhaps, frequently take occasion to furnish extracts from private letters of the Hon. John Freedley, deceased, late member of Congress from the Fifth Pennsylvania Congressional District. Mr. F. began life with no advantages of a school education, and with no capital but his "head and hands." By self-cultivation he accomplished his mind to a degree perhaps unsuspected by any but his intimate friends; and his capital he turned to

that render the work less difficult—they surround the student with an intellectual atmosphere that prepares the mind to receive

such advantage that, in less than thirty years of active life, without indulging in hazardous speculation, he accumulated a fortune of near $300,000. He will therefore perhaps be considered good authority in a work of this kind. The following is an extract from one of his letters written several years ago: "Resolution is omnipotent; with proper industry, and action, and effort, there is no limit to advancement. 'Tis not well to sit down with folded arms and point to your past works—*onward* is the word in self-cultivation. Although the last effort was commendable, the next must be better, and the next again better. The arts and sciences, rhetoric and logic are wide fields for study, but a wider field is man and the business of man. By this, however, I do not wish to be understood as recommending to you so wide a field of study. Your books, according to the prescribed course, deserve your first attention. These require your attention during the hours of study; but in your hours of pastime, of recreation, and of pleasure, is the time to look into the world, with a determination to turn every moment to account, to profit by every passing incident, with the old philosopher's motto, 'Higher, for ever higher.' The observant student must and will attain the highest elevation his intellectual and physical powers are capable of. By this latter expression you will understand me as entertaining the opinion it is not every one that is capable of reaching the highest pitch of human acquirements. There must be *soul* and a body suited for it. There must be intellectual and physical strength. There must be a foundation to raise the superstructure upon. A puny and effeminate body never can contain the soul of a Milton, or have the Herculean intellect of a Locke, or of a Shakspeare, or of a Webster. The body, however, as well as the intellect, is susceptible of cultivation. Physical exercises are as necessary as mental ones. Firmness of purpose, and a fixed resolution which does not vary, never go hand in hand with effeminacy of body. I will finish this part of my subject at present by a quotation, which I wish you to commit to memory, and never forget: 'He that resolves upon any great end, by that very resolution has scaled the great barriers to it; and he who seizes the grand idea of self-cultivation, and solemnly resolves upon it, will find that idea, that resolution burning like fire within him, and ever putting him upon his own improvement. He will find it removing difficulties; searching out, or making means; giving courage for despondency, and strength for weakness.'

"It is also reasonable for every one to believe that he is not a mere nonentity for whom there is no course chalked out or duty prescribed, but rather to entertain the belief that he is destined, under Providence, to fill impressions, and they place within his reach materials which may aid his progress. In the education of a business man, it must never be forgotten that his future life will be a life of *action* and not of study. Great care must be taken that the health be not impaired in a strife for useless honors—that the feelings be not suffered to grow over sensitive in recluse contemplation—nor the mind lose its spring and elasticity under a load of cumbersome and unpractical learning. A collegiate education therefore cannot be recommended. It is even a matter of great doubt in the minds of many observing men, whether colleges—those venerated and highly-lauded alma-maters—have not directly and indirectly ruined a greater number of their sons than they have ever benefitted. It has been said that one-fourth of the students in college leave them with impaired health: full one-half are too sensitive to bear the rude jostlings of the world: and perhaps two-thirds of the balance have some defect that will seriously mar their happiness and usefulness. Certain it is that he who has passed this ordeal with his health unimpaired—his intellect unwarped, and his morals unscathed, is a man of extraordinary mental and moral power. Yet how many parents spend money which they can ill spare, to unfit their sons for all future usefulness; and how many sons are compelled to start in the world with the presumption at least against them, that they are unfit for practical affairs.* A

some appointed duty, and that there is a guardian spirit to whose admonitions proper deference is to be paid, and hence to consider all 'partial evil as universal good.' The idea conveyed by this line of Pope has been to me a source of much consolation through life. It teaches us to consider all disappointments as preservations from hidden snares; all adversity as chastenings for our general good. Some of the greatest men that ever lived have had strong faith in signs and omens, and in the decrees of Fate. But I will not enter further, at present, into this mysterious field."

* Extract from a private letter of the Hon. John Freedley, dated Nov. 21, 1846: "These diplomas are sometimes of service to a man, but very often a positive injury. Where there is intellect to raise a man above the vanity and self-conceit which such gewgaws are apt to inspire, a diploma is of service. I think Webster, Kent, Spencer, and most of the men who have distinguished themselves in high stations in our country are graduates. Even Ewing and Corwin, who earned their money by chopping wood for the fur-

counting-house is the business man's college. When the youth has finished his course of preparatory education at a school or private seminary under the charge of an able instructor, who teaches as much by *conversation* as by a prescribed course, he should go into a counting-house, whatever may be his future occupation. It is there that he will learn order, method, obedience, and acquire a knowledge of life and the business of life; it is there that he will learn the value of time and the value of money—two very important things to know. The Hon. George S. Hilliard has drawn a graphic picture with a somewhat different view, intended as a source of consolation to those who are deploring their fate that they cannot attain a collegiate education; but we use it to show the advantage of a counting-house over a college education. "Two youths, for instance, of the same age leave school at the same time, and one enters college and the other goes into a counting-house. And let us suppose them equally conscientious and equally disposed to make the best of their opportunities. The collegian works hard, and learns much, and acquires distinction; but in the mean time he has perhaps lost his health, for, as far as my observation goes, I should say that one-quarter, at least, of the

naces after they arrived to age, to obtain for themselves the means of getting an education, worked on until they were able to graduate. But then such men act with their diploma as though they had it not. They lay it on the shelf, and fall to work. They know it is of no use to them except as an auxiliary to their own exertions. These were men of physical powers who could undergo fatigue, and were capable of performing much mental and bodily labor. They by habitual industry so disciplined their minds as to be enabled to fix their entire attention on whatever was the object of their study, and thus constantly and intuitively to acquire knowledge as it were in a stream, and retain it. But these are men one in a hundred—not so with the other ninety-nine. They will point to their diploma as the ultimatum of their wishes—as their certificate of learning and gentility—'tis this that is to feed and clothe them—'tis this that makes labor unnecessary to them; and the plodding and drudgery of office, necessary to success in a profession, as beneath them: and hence he, with less learning and without a diploma, but who works, plods, and attends to every thing that pertains to his business, will generally leave them far in the rear. To these a diploma is rather a positive injury than a benefit, because it puffs them up, and causes them to be 'too big for their breeches.'"

young men educated at our colleges leave them with impaired health. From the recluse life he has led, he is likely to have awkward manners, and an unprepossessing address. From not having been trained to self-control, he is perhaps impatient of contradiction and needlessly sensitive. He is probably conceited, possibly pedantic, and pretty sure to want that sixth sense which is called *tact.* He knows much of books, but little of men or life, and from mere confusion of mind, incurs the reproach of weakness of character. On the other hand, the lad who enters a counting-room finds himself perhaps the youngest member of a large establishment; and whatever of conceit he may have brought from the village academy is soon rubbed out of him. He learns to obey, to submit, and to be patient: to endure reproof without anger, and to bear contradiction with good-humor. He is obliged to keep his wits about him, to decide quickly, to have accurate eyes and truthful ears, to learn that there are just sixty minutes in an hour, and just one hundred cents in a dollar. He is compelled to bear and to forbear, to resist temptation, to struggle down rebellious impulses, and to put on the armor of brave silence. The hours of his day come freighted with lessons of self-reliance and self-command, and the grain of his character grows firm under the discipline of life." A counting-house education will be of advantage to every man, whatever his future occupation may be. To farmers it will teach business habits and attention to accounts, which will give them increased interest and success in their business. To the mechanic it will teach order, system, management, the practical value of book-keeping, and remedy many of their deficiencies. To the professional man, it will afford a clearer insight into the practical operation of business affairs, and give them facilities in obtaining practice.* The time spent in the counting-

* "A lawyer in a commercial city must not only be a merchant, a mechanic, a navigator, a seaman so far as navigation and an acquaintance with the different parts of a vessel are concerned, but must also be able to read, speak, and translate the different languages in use in the different parts of the commercial word. *No man can try a case and do it justice unless he is perfectly master of the matter to which the dispute relates.* Hence I have observed that those persons who have spent some time in business, either mercantile or mechanical, previous to studying law, *generally succeed best in obtaining practice.*"—*John Freedley.*

house should, of course, vary with circumstances. A youth designed for mechanical pursuits should spend probably a year; a farmer, one winter. It is generally noticed that, at the end of six months, countrymen get deathly homesick; that is the time for them to leave, and they will never hanker after city life more. A merchant should spend some two years in a counting-house after he has completed his preparatory course, and then go to one of our law schools, and devote some time to the study of mercantile law. A knowledge of the law will always be beneficial, and he will derive the additional advantage of association with the first minds of the country, and may form friendships that will be serviceable to him in his subsequent career.

A *moral* education need not be dwelt upon. Parents who read books for information, and teachers who are fit to be intrusted with the management of the young, need no arguments on this subject. This is especially a work of self-cultivation; no principles can be called temptation-proof, but those which are the result of logical conviction, and for which repeated sacrifices have been made. Facts in the subsequent pages will speak on this subject more forcibly than arguments.

It is of immense advantage to a young man, during minority, to have constant and familiar intercourse and correspondence with a man who is practised in affairs, and capable of communicating his knowledge. It is a privilege which should be valued almost above all others by those who possess it. The pupils of the Jesuits were noted for greater presence of mind in conversation, a more ready recollection of their knowledge, and were more men of the world than youths brought up by any other preceptors, and this acknowledged superiority was ascribed to the fact that each pupil was allowed a certain number of hours of conversation with his superiors. An ability to communicate varied and practical knowledge by conversation is a qualification that specially fits a man to be a teacher, and it should not be overlooked in the selection of a teacher. In addition, parents who are unfitted, or too busy to discharge their share of this duty, should select a suitable man whose business it would be to advise in the choice of books, solve the student's doubts and queries, direct his observation, converse and correspond with him during his school and business apprenticeship. A man of sound judgment and some experience should be selected; but it is not necessary that he should be distinguished for any particular success in his own affairs, for such men cannot be had, and, if they could, they would very probably be incompetent for the office. It is a singular fact that those who are the most distinguished for success in their own undertakings are the poorest of all advisers for others; while many who are keen in the originating of plans, and advising others, seem to lose their power when they come to act for themselves. There are two great classes of men in the world—men of action and men of contemplation. The former can do a thing when they are told how, and the latter know how it should be done, but cannot do it. It is very rarely that these two qualities are united in one person; and I believe that, in nine cases out of ten, the idea of those speculations and undertakings for which men have got the most credit, came to them at second-hand—they acted, while others were debating; hence it is not the most successful whose opinions are always the most valuable. To those who have no special advantages, we say, *cultivate your senses—observe keenly—discipline your mind, especially by mathematical studies—search after and seize hold of every valuable fact—be a constant reader of useful books*—and the glory of your triumph will be in proportion to the difficulties you have overcome.

III. When parents have not chosen a pursuit for the young man, and circumstances do not plainly reveal to him his true path the *important duty of choosing a business or profession* falls upon him, and the great question, "What shall I do?" comes into his mind with a force and power that will probably be remembered in all subsequent time. "The most important thing in life is the choice of a profession," says Pascal; and I am sure it is an embarrassing one to him who is sensible of its importance. It is a choice that must be made at an early age, with few guides to direct, and in a matter in which but few directions can be given.

Our first hint is in the language of an author quoted before. 'Be not over choice in looking out for what may exactly suit you; but rather be ready to adopt any opportunities that occur. Fortune does not stoop often to take any one up. Favorable opportunities will not happen precisely in the way you imagined. Nothing does. Do not be discouraged, therefore, by any present detriment in any course which may lead to something good." The first question to be settled is, what is the object in choosing a business at all? We answer, to attain independence. What is independence? He who can make something more than his necessities require him to expend is as independent as the richest of the land, and generally far more happy. How can independence be attained with the greatest certainty? No man is sure of being able to make more than his necessities will require him to expend but he who is able to perform a day's labor. A trade is a sure road to independence. "He that hath a trade hath an estate, and he that hath a calling, hath an office of profit and honor." Among the ancient Jews, every one, however well educated, was brought up to a trade. At Sparta, there was a law declaring every one who refused to support his parents, when in want, infamous; but, if the father had neglected to bring up his son to some trade, the son was not bound to maintain his father, although in want. We may add that all kinds of regular business pay equally well in the long run to those who have the ability to carry them on: and that all useful employments by which a man can earn an honest living, are equally respectable in the estimation of every sensible person. "There is but one way," says Dr. Lyman Beecher, "of securing universal equality to man—and that is, to regard every honest employment as honorable, and that for every man to learn, in whatsoever state he may be therewith to be content, and to fulfil with strict fidelity the duties of his station and to make every condition a post of honor."

Our second hint is *suffer not fancy to overrule the judgment* in the choice. It has been observed that the history of the bar shows that those who have become the most eminent in the law had at first the greatest distaste for it. Where a man is equally adapted to two or more kinds of business, fancy may decide the choice—but it is a quality too evanescent in itself to control the judgment.

Our third and main rule is, let there be a correspondence between the prominent feature of the mind or character, and the prominent *requisite of the business.* Know thyself, and know something of the business beforehand. Every occupation has some leading, essential quality which its follower must have, or success is impossible. The great cardinal powers of business, as they may be called, are *strength*—*ingenuity*—*good address*—and *strong nerve or enterprise.* Some occupations require only one of these—others require a combination of them—and others, again, require a combination of some one of these essentials with other qualities, to carry them on with honor and success.

I. The occupations in which the essential requisite is *physical strength* are those of day-laborers, butchers, and farmers. A farmer will succeed best who possesses mental cultivation of the first order; but still, the leading requisite of the business is physical strength, without which he cannot discharge its duties. A strong, healthy boy will soon learn the art of killing and dressing an animal. Strength is also requisite to the success of a bookbinder and a wheelwright.

II. The occupations whose leading requisite is *mechanical ingenuity* are generally called trades. A tailor, shoemaker, or brushmaker need have but little ingenuity; but trades in general require a large share of it in combination with strength, mathematical skill, and other qualifications. A machinist must have ingenuity, skill, and a considerable degree of physical strength. A carpenter must have strength, ingenuity, great skill, and an aptitude for mathematics and drawing. A stone mason must possess the same, with perhaps greater power of endurance. A jeweller must have ingenuity, good taste, steadiness, application, and a capacity to resist temptation. A clock or watchmaker must possess ingenuity, a fair education, and a persevering disposition. A cabinet-maker must have an aptitude for and a knowledge of drawing, good taste, and ingenuity. A chemist must possess ingenuity, a liberal education, retentive memory, and a persevering disposition.

III. *Good address* presupposes some education, a genteel person, and an obliging disposition. It is the leading requisite in all trading pursuits, and is the basis of successful storekeeping. United with fondness for books, the boy may become a bookseller; with fondness for music, a music-seller. An apothecary must possess good address, a good education, a retentive memory, and a cheerful, compassionate disposition. An auctioneer should have good address, memory, a quick eye, and shrewdness.

IV. Strong nerve, in its ordinary acceptation, is necessary to the surgeon, dentist, and probably many others. It is also used as synonymous with resolution and enterprise. It is the prominent requisite in all kinds of speculation, and, when combined with every other great and good quality, makes the merchant, the professional man, the author, (?) and the statesman.*

We need not mention the professions. They do not fall within the scope of our plan, as they are not, and should not be, money-making pursuits. No class of men in the world, considering the amount of capital expended in their education, and the amount of labor in their profession, are so poorly paid as professional men. It has been said, with emphasis and truth, that merely to obtain wealth, a man would be more likely to succeed, to begin with a wood-saw and an axe, than with an education which cost him ten years' hard labor, and all the money he could borrow. Lawyers sometimes get large fees, but they are "few and far between." Their average income throughout the United States does not exceed fifteen hundred dollars per year, and the majority in the profession get less than that; a few get a great deal more, while many get nothing at all. Divines have one secular advantage; they can sometimes marry advantageously. Women have an idea that they make good husbands, and, hence, with address, they may obtain serviceable fathers-in-law. But the professions should be chosen from other considera-

* I intended to compile a table of occupations, which I must defer to a more "convenient season," if it ever comes. I will merely remark that the average wages of journeymen, in mechanical employments, are about $9 a week; that tailors, shoemakers, and blacksmiths do not get, on an average, so much as this; and that hatters, jewellers, watch-case makers, and printers, get more. No one should think of starting a *mechanical business in large cities with less than one thousand dollars capital.* The average wages of operatives in iron works, in the United States, is 97 cents a day; in Pennsylvania, the average is $1 06. The average wages of males, in cotton factories, is 70 cents; of females, 37½ cents. In Pennsylvania, males get 65 cents, and females 33 cents, on an average. In woollen factories, males 82 cents, and females 44 cents. In the Pennsylvania woollen factories, the average wages of males is 74 cents; of females, 30 cents

tions than to obtain wealth. They are a splendid field for the exercise and display of intellect, and the gratification of philanthropy. The only worthy motive in choosing a profession is a strong desire to ameliorate the condition and amend the follies of mankind,—of which the reward is to be the consciousness of a life well spent—but to do this, previous independence is indispensable. "How absurdly those parents act," says Collyer, "who, having no fortune to give to a son, bring him up to be an attorney's clerk, and thus force him to be contented with an income more precarious, and not much more certain, than that of a journeyman tailor, or to become a nuisance to society by being a poor, pettifogging attorney, an employment equally base, scandalous, and injurious to society." It is to be regretted that so many young men, who could fill other stations with honor and respect, are now rushing pellmell into the professions, without aim or object, apparently taking it for granted they were born qualified, as Minerva sprang full-fledged from the brain of Jupiter. Experience must be their schoolmaster.

CHAPTER III.

HABITS OF BUSINESS, WHAT ARE THEY?

WHEN we have chosen our business wisely—when we have become initiated in its mysteries, and our apprenticeship is drawing to a close—the great question that will frequently recur in our after life, What shall we do? stares us in the face a second time. Shall we attempt business on our own account, or work awhile for another already established; and how shall we be able to attain the best situation? We solicit advice from our friends, and they tell us that the world will ask us two questions, which we had better ask ourselves beforehand. *Are you master of your business? and have you habits of business?* The former is presumed; but what is meant by habits of business? Habits of business include six qualities. *Industry, arrangement, calculation, prudence, punctuality,* and *perseverance.* Are you industrious? Are you methodical? Are you calculating? Are you prudent? Are you punctual? Are you persevering? If so, you possess what is known by the familiar term, Habits of Business. It is not the possession of any one of these qualities in perfection, nor the occasional exercise of them by fits and starts, as it is called, that will constitute a man of business; but it is the possession of them all in an equal degree, and their continuous exercise as habits, that give reputation and constitute ability. The difference in men and their success may be attributed, in a measure, to a difference in their business habits; and many a man has made his fortune with no other capital than their superior cultivation. In fact, a large capital and excellent opportunities, without them, will only provoke greater disaster, and a more wide-spread ruin. Perfection in most things is unattainable; yet men have attained to a greater degree of perfection in the cultivation of these qualities than in almost any thing else; and, at all events, it is certain that he who "aimeth at the sun, though he may not hit his mark, will shoot higher than he that aimeth at a bush."

Industry is the energetic engagement of body or mind in some useful employment. It is the opposite of the Indian's maxim, which says, "It is better to walk than to run, and better to stand still than to walk, and better to sit than to stand, and better to lie down than to sit." Industry is the secret of those grand results that fill the mind with wonder—the folios of the ancients, the pyramids of the Egyptians, those stupendous works of internal communication in our own country that bind the citizens of many different States in the bonds of harmony and interest. "There is no art or science," says Clarendon, "that is too difficult for industry to attain to; it is the gift of tongues, and makes a man understood and valued in all countries and by all nations; it is the philosopher's stone, that turns all metals and even stones into gold, and suffers no want to break into dwellings; it is the North-west passage, that brings the merchant's ships as soon to him as he can desire; in a word, it conquers all enemies, and makes fortune itself pay contributions." The tendency of matter is to rest, and it requires an exercise of force or of will to overcome the *vis inertiæ*. When a thing should be done, it must be done immediately, without parleying or delay. A repeated exercise of the will, in this way, will soon form the habit of industry.

Arrangement digests the matter that industry collects. It apportions time to duties, and keeps an exact register of its transactions; it has a post for every man, a place for every tool, a pigeon-hole for every paper, and a time for every settlement. A perfectly methodical man leaves his books, accounts, &c., in so complete a shape on going to bed that, if he were to die during the night, every thing could be perfectly understood. Jeremiah Evarts is represented to have been a model of industry and arrangement. A friend says, "During years of close observation in the bosom of his family, I never saw a day pass without his accomplishing more than he expected; and so regular was he in all his habits, that I knew to a moment when I should find him with his pen, and when with his tooth-brush in his hand; and so methodical and thorough that though his papers filled many shelves when closely tied up, there was not a paper among all his letters, correspondence, editorial matter, and the like, which he could not lay his hands on in a moment. I never knew him search for a paper; it was always in its place." Some manifest this habit at an earlier age than others, and apparently exercise it with less difficulty; but any one with attention may acquire it.

Calculation is the mind of business. A readiness in calculation gives a man great advantages over his less experienced neighbor; and many a man has brought his fish to a bad market from inability to calculate quickly and accurately. To attain the habit of quick calculation without the aid of a slate and pencil, Dr. Alcott recommends that the learner seize on "every circumstance which occurs in his reading, where reckoning is required, and, if possible, stop at once and compute it. Or, if not, let the place be marked, and, at the first leisure moment, let him turn to it and make the estimates.

"Suppose he reads of a shipwreck. The crew is said to consist of thirty men, besides the captain and mate, with three hundred and thirteen passengers, and a company of sixty grenadiers. The captain and mate, and ten of the crew, escaped in the longboat.—The rest were drowned, except twelve of the grenadiers, who clung to a floating fragment of the wreck, till they were taken off by another vessel. Now is there a single person in existence, who would read such an account, without being anxious to know how many persons in the whole were lost? Yet nine readers in ten would *not* know, and why? Simply because they will not stop, and use what little addition and subtraction they possess.

"Long practice, it is true, will render it unnecessary for an individual to *pause*, in order to estimate a sum like that above mentioned. Many, indeed most persons, who are familiar with figures, might compute these numbers while reading, and without the slightest pause; but it certainly requires some practice. And the most important use of arithmetical studies, except as a discipline to the mind, is to enable us to reckon without slates and pencils. He has but a miserable knowledge of arithmetic who is no arithmetician without a pen or pencil in his hand. These are but the ladders upon which he should ascend to the science, and not the science itself."

But calculation as a business habit is not limited to arithmetic. It deals with principles as well as figures, and frequently arrives at principles by means of figures. It deduces the value of economy, and distinguishes between a true and a false economy. It shows that a man who spends a dollar and a half in hiring a horse, and also the greater part of a day to purchase six or eight bushels of wheat at a sixpence a bushel less than he must have given nearer home, is not so economical as he may have imagined. It satisfactorily demonstrates that honesty is the best policy, and that a rogue is a fool. I cannot comprehend the force of that philosophy which excludes calculation as an unworthy process of arriving at a right course of action. A maxim, that is true, can be proved to be so by any test; and in considering a principle, a man should choose that means which ordinarily yields him the greatest certainty of conviction. There is nothing debasing in reducing every thing to a rigid system of calculation; and principles that will not bear it are not sound. A man takes advantage of confidence to perpetrate an act of villainy; is he a wise man or a fool? How does his account stand? On the debtor side is found the confidence of the community, which would have supported him for life, lost; his family disgraced; his happiness embittered; his soul endangered, and much more. On the creditor side is found a temporary advantage gained, and the balance is largely against him. The man who *killed* his goose to get at the golden eggs has not been handed down to us as a very wise man; and Solomon says, "He that getteth riches, and not by right, shall leave them in the midst of his days, and at his end shall be a fool." Policy, right, reason, and revelation, all harmonize.

Prudence is defined to be wisdom applied to practice. As this is one of the most important of qualities, and the most difficult to describe, we subjoin the various definitions of prudence, and some general rules that may be serviceable. Under prudence are comprehended that discreet suiting and disposing as well of actions as words in their due place, time, and manner. It is principally in reference to actions to be done, and due means, order, season, and method of doing or not doing. A man exhibits the highest prudence who places himself in such a position that, whether the pru ciples he acts upon prove true or false, he secures a happy issue to his actions. In a case where the probabilities on the one hand somewhat preponderate the other, yet if there be no considerable hazard on that side which has the least probability, and a very great apparent danger in a mistake about the other, prudence will oblige a man to do that which may make most for his safety. It is always prudent in matters of importance to conceal intentions, or we may be anticipated by others; and it is generally prudent to conceal motives, letting only friends have a key to our hearts as to our garden. It is prudent to withhold confidence from an entire stranger, and in some disagreeable cases it is prudent to do nothing. "When a prudent man," says Chesterfield, "gets into that predicament that he must ask himself more than once what he shall do, he will answer 'Nothing.' Where reason points out no good way, or at least none less bad than the other, he will stop short and wait for light. A little busy mind runs on at all events—must be doing, and like a blind horse fears no danger because he sees none." "I think a prudent man," says Plutarch, "ought not to permit any thing at all to trust to fortune, but to trust some things to his wife, some things to his servants, and some things to his friends, while he is employing his reason about such matters as are most proper for him, and of greatest concernment." Prudence is the result of judgment. Judgment is an original faculty of the mind which God has given to supply the want of certain knowledge, and by which a man takes a proposition to be true or false without perceiving demonstrative evidence in the proofs. A total want of judgment cannot be supplied by art; but, where the faculty exists, it may be cultivated to an extraordinary degree of accuracy.

Partnership, marriage, and the proper time or age for commencing business are important subjects for the exercise of judgment. In any remarks on these subjects, I desire to be understood as expressing my individual opinion, and not well-settled truths, as my range of facts is limited.

Partnership is prudent or not according to the nature of the business and the relative situation of the parties. It is prudent in an extended business where each partner will have separate and distinct duties, or where it is necessary for them to be in different places, without a constant supervision of the others. It is prudent in cases where one furnishes capital and the other knowledge, good character, and activity. It is generally prudent for clerks to take an interest in well-established houses in which they have been employed when they can, and it is prudent for the merchants to give them an interest when they have shown themselves to be *worth a salary of a thousand dollars a year.* But it is imprudent to form an ordinary partnership to carry on a small business, where every transaction would be likely to come under the supervision of both. It is imprudent to enter into partnership with a *covetous man, or a very passionate man,* or an *obstinate man,* or a *revengeful man,* or a *familiar crony,* or a *man involved,* unless it be a limited partnership, in the case of a creditor, with a view of escaping greater loss. And, in general, it may be said to be imprudent where the business can be managed with a reasonable degree of success without it.

"The trust reposed in copartners," says a distinguished commercial lawyer, "notwithstanding all precautions, is wholly indefinite and unlimited. And when one thinks of forming a connection of copartnership with another, he should ask himself if he is willing to trust him with the power to ruin him; for such and no less is it. He will, therefore, be careful to consider not only his business capacity as a man of shrewdness, of skill, of experience, but will need to look into his social and moral qualities. Is he a man of good temper, with whom difficulties will not be likely to occur? Is he placable, one who will not lay up the memory of an accidental slight, of a heated expression, or of an unreasonable wrong, which you have done every thing in your power to redress? Is he a man keen in the pursuit of his own interest? Will he listen to any candid views adverse to his own? Will he in a difference between you be willing to unite with you in consulting mutual friends as mediators? Are you sure of his principles? Do you know his associates? All these are questions not merely of taste and curiosity, but entering into the very essence of your decision as to a partner."

Marriage is a matter in which there is so little "demonstrative evidence in the proofs," that, if it were generally entered into on prudential grounds, it might be considered a test of judgment. The apostle Paul intimates that it matters little whom, or from what considerations a man marries, the result will be all the same; and mankind frequently take that view, believing that possibly they will have leisure enough to repent it. "But and if thou marry, thou hast not sinned: and if a virgin marry, she hath not sinned. Nevertheless, such shall have trouble in the flesh: but I spare you." 1 *Cor*. vii. 28.

But, though it may often demand a seer's power to divine the character of the wife in that of the girl, and however willing men may be to sacrifice themselves, if need be, on the altars of the blind god—I deem it a duty to offer one suggestion, for the consideration of those who, in this predicament, have one of their five senses yet in a healthy condition—and that is, that they strive at least to ascertain whether their choice be *meddlesome*, or *desponding*, or *extravagant*. A sprinkling of ugliness, and a spice of temper—a tinge of vanity, and occasional attacks of folly, are trifles; but he, whose wife is always meddling and never understanding—or forever croaking evil, and doing nothing to avert it, or unceasingly crying give, give, and never economizing, must either fold his arms in listless despair, or with an iron will summon a supreme contempt for her and her wishes, her words and deeds. Neither horn of the dilemma is a pleasant one, and in relief, we give the following picture drawn for the model wife of a statesman, but which will answer equally well as a mirror in which the model wives of accomplished business men may see themselves reflected. "The wife of a statesman's choice should be sound in health, and of a light and easy temper, neither jealous herself nor giving cause for jealousy; neither going much abroad, nor requiring her husband to be more at home than his avocations will permit; fresh in her feelings, and alert as to her understanding, but seasonable in the demonstration of either, and willing at all times to rest contented in an intelligent repose."

The proper time or age for commencing business on one's own account is a mooted question. It is imprudent in any one to embark in business without that moderate capital ordinarily required in the business. It is imprudent in a young man to accept a loan from a money-lender, giving his friends as security, in order to get that moderate capital. *But suppose that the friends of a young man who is of age and out of his apprenticeship, propose to furnish him the necessary capital to set up business, is it prudent in him to embark?* I will merely express a few of the arguments on both sides, and leave it to the exercise of the individual judgment. A good deal undoubtedly depends on the previous education, and the extent of his knowledge. On the one side it is stated that experience is a relative term; a man at twenty-one has frequently more knowledge, than many men of forty. Knowledge, not experience, is the one thing needful. Experience is only one of the ways of arriving at knowledge. "Wise men are instructed by reason; men of less understanding by experience; the most ignorant by necessity, and beasts by nature." The mind is a thing of impulse, of quick penetration; it acquires its knowledge of life by bounds and flights. In war, literature, and statesmanship, the greatest exploits of the most renowned men have been performed at an early age. Hannibal crossed the Alps before he was twenty-four. Alexander the Great died at thirty-three; Byron wrote Childe Harold at twenty-one. Bonaparte was first consul before he was thirty. "Of all the great human actions ever heard or read of," says Montaigne, "of what sort soever, I have observed, both in former ages and our own, more have been performed before, than after the age of thirty; and oft-times in the very lives of the same men. May I not confidently instance those of Hannibal, and his great competitor, Scipio? The better half of their lives, they lived upon the glory they had acquired in their youth; great men, 'tis true, in comparison with others: but by no means in comparison with themselves."

On the other side, we have the general observation of mankind, that those who have been most successful in business, have generally begun life with "an axe and a tow-shirt," and worked themselves gradually up. We have the facts that Girard was a poor man at thirty, and even at forty; that Rothschild did not get his capital of £20,000 till after he was thirty years old: that at thirty Astor had not made his first $1000, which, he says, was harder to make than all the others. We have the assertion of men who have spent twenty years in their avocation, that, although they thought themselves wise when they began, they were exceedingly ignorant. We have the knowledge that an energetic prosecution of business makes large draughts on the physical constitution; and the assertion of medical men that the frame does not harden till thirty; and, lastly, we have the example of our Saviour, who, although able to confound the doctors at twelve, did not commence his ministry till he was thirty years of age. Now, when doctors disagree, who shall decide? I will merely remark, that a man who has, or can obtain, a good situation, should not abandon it from slight reasons; that the task of the employed is easier than the employer; and that the reputation of doing business on one's own account is a consideration too trifling to influence a wise man's decision.

Punctuality is the hinge of business. It is a virtue that all men reverence in theory, but all do not carry into practice. We like a punctual man because he respects his word, and has a regard for our convenience: we dislike an unpunctual man, because he interferes with our plans, consumes our time, causes uneasy feelings, and impliedly tells us that we are not of sufficient importance, in his estimation, to make him prompt. Punctuality has reference to time engagements, money engagements, and engagements for work. It is a quality that is usually found in connection with other good qualities, as the want of it argues the absence of other essential habits. A want of system, defective calculation, and imprudence in making promises when the probabilities of fulfilling them are very uncertain, are frequent causes of want of punctuality. To be unpunctual is sometimes considered a mark of consequence by little great men, but truly great men have always thought differently. Blackstone was punctual, and could never be made to think well of any one notoriously defective in this virtue. Lord Brougham, while a kingdom seemed to be resting on his shoulders—who presided in the House of Lords and the Court of Chancery; who gave audience daily to barristers, and found time to be at the head of at least *ten* associations which were publishing works of useful knowledge—was so punctual that, when these associations met, he was uniformly in his place in the chair when the hour of meeting had arrived.

In the complexity of business affairs, it is not always possible to be punctual in all things; but it is always possible to avoid the infliction of trouble and uneasiness. In payments of money, creditors generally compel their debtors to fix a time of payment, and these promises are made, and understood to be made, conditionally on the fact of having the money at the time, which is not always the case. When this occurs, a punctual man will not keep his creditor in suspense as to the cause, or put him to the trouble of calling to ascertain it; but *will give him timely intimation of the fact by sending him a note or an agent, or calling himself, and renew the promise.* A man who does so, though he fails a dozen times in the same transaction, is more worthy of credit than the clown who, besides keeping you out of your money, consumes your time, and causes uneasy and unhappy feelings.

Perseverance is the last of the business habits that we have to notice. It means the steady pursuit of a plan, whether good or bad; but it would be very unwise to persevere in a plan which conscience or practice had proved to be bad. In actual life, where there are so many different pursuits, and different ways of doing the same thing, it means steadiness in the execution of whatever plan is determined upon. Burgh makes mention of a merchant who, at first setting out, opened and shut his shop every day, for several weeks together, without selling goods to the value of two cents, who by the force of application for a course of years rose, at last, to a handsome fortune. But I have known, he says, many who had a variety of opportunities for settling themselves comfortably in the world, yet for want of steadiness to carry any scheme to perfection, they sank from one degree of wretchedness to another for many years together, without the least hopes of ever getting above distress and pinching want. There is hardly an employment in life so trifling that it will not afford a subsistence, if constantly and faithfully followed. Indeed, it is by indefatigable diligence alone that a fortune can be acquired in any business whatever.

The accomplished William Wirt says, "That the man who is

perpetually hesitating which of two things he will do first, will do neither. The man who resolves, but suffers his resolution to be changed by the first counter-suggestion of a friend—who fluctuates from opinion to opinion, from plan to plan, and veers like a weathercock to every point of the compass, with every breath of caprice that blows, can never accomplish any thing great or useful. Instead of being progressive in any thing, he will be at best stationary, and, more probably, retrograde in all. It is only the man who carries into his pursuits that great quality which Lucan ascribes to Cæsar, *nescia virtus stare loco*—who first consults wisely, then resolves firmly, and then executes his purposes with inflexible perseverance, undismayed by those petty difficulties which daunt a weaker spirit, that can advance to eminence in any line."*

Did you ever know any body," says the lamented Neal, "to stick to *any* kind of business, no matter how unpromising, ten years at most, who did not prosper? Not one! no matter how bad it might be in the beginning—if he stuck to it earnestly and faithfully, and tried nothing else, no matter how hard he found it sometimes to keep his head above water, still, if he persevered, he always came out bright in the long run—didn't he?—whatever it might have been at the beginning, at the end of ten years he had made a business for himself."

These are the qualities that are included in the term Habits of Business. There are many others which give value to character and accomplishment to mind, but these are *essential* to the successful prosecution of business. They are as necessary to the clerk as to the employer—to the mechanic as to the merchant—to the professional man as to the mechanic—to the man of genius as to a dull man. With them, a man of the most ordinary abilities

* The magnetic needle and the weathercock have always been favorite illustrations of unsteadiness, but it seems to me they are examples of steadiness also. The mind of a business man may be allowed to vibrate, for that the needle does; but, like the needle, it must still be constant; it should veer like a weathercock, with changing times and circumstances, but, like a weathercock, it should always show which way "the wind blows."

may hope to realize a competency for himself, and, with favorable circumstances, perhaps a fortune. Without them, a man of the most brilliant genius, though he may rise speedily and dazzle for awhile, will as suddenly dart into an oblique course, and sink into oblivion. Fortunate is he who acquires them early.

CHAPTER IV.

GETTING MONEY.

"To catch Dame Fortune's golden smile,
Assiduous wait upon her,
And gather gear by every wile,
That's justified by honor;
Not for to hide it in a hedge,
Not for a train attendant;
But for the glorious privilege
Of being independent."

ST. JAMES says, "If a brother or a sister be naked, and desti tute of daily food, and one of you say unto them, Depart in peace, be ye warmed and filled; notwithstanding ye give them *not those things which are needful to the body, what doth it profit?*" And how can we give without first getting? Or what excuse can there be for not having, when we might get? To get money,* then, seems to be a religious duty, as well as a necessity and a right, and needs no other vindication.

To be charitable to the destitute is also a religious duty. But to be independent ourselves, and have the ability to be charitable to others, it is necessary to have a surplus. No one, then, has any moral right to limit his exertions by his wants. It is reasonable for every one to consider himself as destined, under Providence, to discharge some duty, or fill some station, in which money may be a valuable means; and as a reward for continued, energetic exertion, there is a pleasure attached to the process of accumulation. It by no means follows that, because one man gets more than the necessaries of life, others must want them. The earth is an inex-

* I use the word money in its popular sense.

haustible mine, in which, if I and my neighbors work four hours a day, we may probably get sufficient for our daily wants; but, if I continue to work longer than they do, or more skilfully, I will probably get more. The claims of the weak and the unfortunate to assistance are equally binding upon us all—those that have a surplus, and those who have not; but with my surplus, if I choose, I can have the happiness of relieving my co-laborers from their support. The *getting* of money, and the proper *use* of money, are distinct subjects, and must not be confounded. It is right that every man should get all the money he can under proper limitations, and it is also incumbent upon him to make good use of it, in conformity with the dictates of reason, and the commands of his Creator.

"To get all we can, and keep all we get," is a doubtful natural right, and certainly only applicable in a state of nature. In civilized life, there are *limitations* upon the right of getting, and restrictions upon the right of keeping. As population increased, it may be reasonably presumed that the good old rule—

> "The simple plan
> That they shall take who have the power,
> And they shall keep who can,"

did not answer well in practice, and men, for the better security of that which they possessed, consented to limit their right of indiscriminate acquisition by certain rules; and upon this consent are founded, and these rules are called, the *laws of the land.* The Creator of both world and man has been pleased to aid men on their journey to happiness, by the revelation of his will; and, in so far as it relates to the acquisition of property, the natural right of accumulation is still further limited by his will, which may be termed the *moral law.* As business became complex, it was found that the laws of the land were too general, and the obligations of morality too weak, to induce right action in all cases; and it was necessary to establish still another limitation, with the severest of all penalties to an unimbruted mind, the discountenance of *honorable men.* Hence, a man has the right, and it is his duty to get all the money he can, consistently with a due obedience to the *laws of the land*, the *moral laws*, and the *laws of honor*.

The laws of the land, or human laws, comprehend all those rules of conduct which originate in the wisdom of man individually or collectively considered, and which are designed to regulate their behavior to one another in society, and which are enforced by human authority and worldly sanction. They are rules of conduct, proceeding from the will of those who by nature are on a level with the rest of mankind, but who have the consent of the others to govern them for their temporal or political good. Every law has two branches, the one *declaratory*, and the other *penal;* the former defines the rights to be observed, or the wrongs to be eschewed, and the other signifies what penalty shall be incurred by those who disregard these rights, or commit these wrongs. Hence, there are *two* ways by which a conscientious man can obey a law that has no other sanction than the power of civil authority; the one is by observing the declaratory part of the law, and the other is by disregarding that, and suffering the penalty, in either case, the law is obeyed and satisfied. Human laws, as they proceed from men no wiser than ourselves, are full of imperfections; and he who has no other standard of morality than the laws of the land may be, and probably is, a villain.

Moral laws are of higher origin and greater force. They are identical with the will of God, as learned from two sources: first, express revelation; and, secondly, the light of nature, or tendency of any action to promote or diminish the general happiness. Where the Great Creator has expressly made known his will, "it sure becomes the creature" to obey. "Thou shalt not steal," is a plain command, and plainly forbids one mode of getting money. But where his will is not so plainly manifest, we must inquire of our reason, in order to determine whether an action we are about to do be right or wrong in view of morality, *what would be the effect on the general happiness of mankind, if such action was generally permitted?* God has plainly designed the happiness of his creatures, as may be seen in the construction of the world and of man. "If he had wished our misery, he might have made *sure* of his purpose, by forming our senses to be so many sores and pains to us, as they now are instruments of gratification and enjoyment; or by placing us amidst objects so ill suited to our perceptions as to have continually offended us, instead of ministering to our refreshment and delight. He might have made every thing we tasted bitter; every thing we saw loathsome; every thing we touched a sting; every smell a stench; and every sound a discord." Whatever, therefore, would tend, if generally done or allowed, to increase the happiness of mankind, is in conformity with His will, and whatever would produce evil, or inconvenience, or misery, is a violation of the moral law. Here we arrive at the foundation of the obligation of contracts. Hence, I am obliged *to keep my word, to perform my promises, to execute my contracts;* because, if generally disregarded, there would be an end to confidence, which is essential in all the relations of life, and to the existence of happiness.

The obligation of promises is to be measured by the expectation which the promiser voluntarily and knowingly excites; and, therefore, Moral Philosophy, which is one of the interpreters of moral law, has deduced a rule governing the construction of contracts, which is that—

Whatever is expected by one side, and known to be so expected by the other, is to be deemed a part or condition of the contract.

Incidental to this, and included in it, there are two other rules which are of daily and hourly application in the business of life. The first is, *that the seller is bound in conscience to disclose the faults of what he has to sell.*

The buyer expects a certain article, or an article of a certain quality—and the seller knows that he expects it; hence he is bound to furnish such an article, or make known its faults. The man who advances a direct falsehood, in recommendation of an article, is called a cheat. He who conceals faults which he knows it possesses, acts from the same motive, viz., to procure a higher price than he could otherwise expect, and the effect to the prejudice of the buyer is precisely the same. This is a just and a practical rule, for it is obligatory on all alike, from the manufacturer to the retailer, and on all who buy and sell.*

The second rule is that the price which the seller asks or charges for his merchandise is impliedly the market price. "Where there exists no monopoly or combination," says Paley, "the market price is always a fair price; because it will always be proportionate to the use and scarcity of the article."

"Whoever opens a shop, or in any manner exposes his goods to public sale, virtually engages to deal with his customers at a market

* The temptations to a violation of this rule in trade, and many of the complaints of cheating, arise from two causes—a want of ability on the part of the merchant, and a want of honesty on the part of the consumer. A defective buyer is strongly tempted to sell, as he buys, an inferior article for a better. There is an unfortunate idea abroad that "off-handedness" is a sign of a smart business man. Sellers like this quality in buyers, as it saves them trouble and gives them chances; and they always praise it. There are some men whose first thoughts are the best; but there are others, slower in conception, who affect it; and frequently find their tongues are more "off-hand" than their wits. They go off "half cock'd" in buying, and must cheat in selling, or lose. Those who are careless in buying should be careful to deal with reputable houses, who make it a point to consult the interest of the buyer, as much as to get his money.

Consumers are not always honest. Persons go into a store, and inquire for a certain article; it is shown them, and a fair price asked. At once they object, and try to get it for three-fourths its value. Probably an article worth about what they offer is shown them, leaving them to infer that it is as good as the other: they take it, and think they have got a great bargain. When they discover the difference, they complain loudly about being cheated. Is this cheating? It is an admitted exception to the rule in the case of a person who buys a horse at public auction without warranty, when it is usual to warrant, and I am disposed to consider this as another. The buyer in both cases has a compensation in the price, and the fact of its being a bargain is always sufficient to excite suspicion, and put him on his guard. This habit in customers has led some men to impose an extra price on their goods, in expectation of falling, and thus to wrong persons who act on a different plan. To avoid trouble and imposition, it seems best not to go a shopping at all; to select reputable houses—*always giving the preference to those who would be essentially benefitted by our custom*—from whom we buy regularly, and with whom we have a fair understanding. The one price system is a good one if rigidly adhered to.

price; because it is upon the faith and opinion of such an engagement that any one comes within his shop doors, or offers to treat with him. This is expected by the buyer; is known to be expected by the seller: which is enough, according to the rule delivered above, to make it a part of the contract between them, though not a syllable be said about it. The breach of this implied contract constitutes the fraud. Hence, a man who disclaims such engagement may set what price he pleases on his property."

There are many interesting questions in casuistry, which scholiasts have propounded and discussed with various conclusions, to which we need not refer; but there is one that originated with Cicero, and, having been treated by nearly all the writers on morals since his day, we cannot omit it without incurring the charge of oddity. A corn merchant of Alexandria arrived at Rhodes in time of great scarcity, with a cargo of grain, and with the knowledge that a number of other vessels laden with corn had already sailed from Alexandria for Rhodes, and which he had passed on the passage; *was he bound in conscience to inform the buyers of that fact?* Cicero decides that he was; Chancellor Kent intimates that he was. Dr. Dewey, in a late work, devotes one or two pages to this question, and decides that he was; but informs us that Grotius, Puffendorf, and Pothier, dissent from this opinion with careful qualifications. Dr. Dewey bases his decision upon the presumption that every man in asking a price impliedly says, that the price asked is in his opinion the fair value of the article—that it is worth it. It is singular that he should make this presumption, inasmuch as he had previously laid down the true doctrine that "there can be no such thing as abstract value. The worth of a thing depends on the want of it." "The value of a thing is the market price of it. This is the only intelligible idea of value, and the only reasonable adjustment of price." Now, market price is the result of competition among buyers, and is constantly fluctuating. In the case of the corn merchant it is to be presumed that he had little to do in fixing the price; that he took what was offered, after fair competition; or in other words the market price at the time of the sale, without regard to the market price some days hence, when the other vessels might arrive. Dr. Dewey states a case. Suppose that the people of Rhodes had been suffering a famine, and this merchant had taken all their disposable property as the price of life, and borne it off, all the while knowing that bountiful supplies were at hand, what should we have said? He answers, that his perfidy would have been equal to his cruelty, and he would have been both a pirate and a villain. But scarcity is not famine. Famine or danger of starvation would have given them the right to take the grain without the owner's leave or any payment at all, except a *fair* restitution when it was in their power. We can imagine many questions that would have had as much effect in depressing the market price as the fact that other vessels might shortly arrive. Suppose that the merchant was "short" of cash; that he must sell; that there was an execution out against him, and the sheriff would be down on him in a few hours; when they could have got the grain at their own price, was he bound in conscience to reveal that fact? This is a question of superior information as much as the other. I can imagine a state of society in which my opinion in both of these cases would be in the affirmative; but it must be remembered that mercantile business is an artificial sphere, which men have created to increase their comforts, and occupy their minds, and in which they have the right to lay down what rules they choose, provided they do not contravene any plain laws of nature or revelation. The golden rule, "Do unto others as you would have them do unto you," is in such cases to be interpreted with a view to established customs in trade. Wisdom consists in adopting such rules as tend to make the business an agreeable pursuit; and I am seriously of opinion that it would promote the happiness of the greater number to do away with superior information in matters of contract altogether; but, while it is allowable by general consent, a man can act honestly in conformity with the rule.

There is another question. Is a man who has failed in business, and been discharged from his legal obligations *by the act of his creditors*, morally bound to pay his old debts whenever he has the means to do so? This is a delicate question, for which no rule can be given that is applicable in all cases. In the event of failure, the debtor is always bound to examine his conscience and see whether he has acted with *fraud, misrepresentation, carelessness, or extravagance*, and if so, he is morally bound, when able, to pay to the uttermost farthing; but if he is satisfied that he has not, I cannot think it would promote the happiness of society to establish the doctrine of moral liability. The majority of those who engage in business, strictly so called, fail at least once in their lifetime, and if there were any obligation resting upon them to pay their *old* debts, and they practically felt its force, the wheels of business would stop, or drag along in heaviness and labor. A load of old debts is more than poor human nature can bear; but a legal discharge, that is not also a moral one, is a mere fiction. There need be no fear of harm in deciding this question in the negative, for honest men alone are interested in its settlement. Rogues care nothing for moral nor legal obligation if they can evade it. We would say, then, that the moral liability to pay debts rests solely on the general moral obligation to perform promises. There is no scriptural injunction that I am aware of, which says, Pay your debts. It is true, St. Paul says, "Owe no man any thing, but to love one another;" but this, if interpreted strictly, would prevent the creation of a debt. Debts being then not more sacred than promises, they follow the general condition of promises. Now, a promise may be *released in conscience as well as at law, and when released is no longer binding*. This is evident. If I promise a man to go to a certain place and he afterwards excuse me from going, I am certainly not bound to go, and it matters not what reasons induced the release, provided it be not compulsory, or caused by any wrongful act of the promisor, for no man has a right to take advantage of his own wrong.

In all cases of credit, where there are no words or acts of *especial trust and confidence*, the relation of buyer and seller, of borrower and lender, is one of mutual promise and mutual risk. The seller impliedly promises to deal fairly, and charges a profit proportionably to his opinion of the risk; and the buyer agrees to make a fair representation of his circumstances, to act with such prudence, and to live with such economy that he may reasonably hope to pay his debts, and where both parties act in good faith, but the buyer is compelled to fail, a full surrender of property is as much as the creditor can ordinarily demand in justice.

Credit originates with men of large capital with a view to increased profit, and partakes largely of the nature of agency. Agency and credit in a commercial community are necessary and eminently beneficial; they should be used in perfect good faith, and guarded by the nicest honor; but where misfortune occurs, it is a misconception of justice that all loss shall fall on the agent and none on the real owner of the property.

But in all doubtful questions of principle, a man must consult his own conscience, and be governed by the decision.

In the majority of failures, I believe there are circumstances known to the conscience of the individual, which render it obligatory upon him to make reparation, and all that I would contend for is that there shall be no universal public rule that will cast a stigma upon those who feel no such obligation. Every man knows with as much certainty as he can know any thing, whether he has a good conscience or no. The very meaning of conscience is the knowledge which the mind has of the true springs and motives that have governed the actions, and the judgment either of approbation or censure which it makes upon them; and it is well to leave a good deal, both in law and in morals, to this judgment of the individual, which he may do or not do, as he sees proper. In laying down principles, there is danger, by asking too much, of losing all. A law that is generally broken or evaded is worse than no law; a moral rule that is impracticable weakens the sense of moral obligation, and leads to a disregard of other rules of vital importance. The creed that would take away from the individual the right of controlling his actions by his judgment, and reduce every thing to a system, like the theory that would deny to energy and skill rewards superior to indolence and ignorance—that would yoke the Arabian steed and the ox in the same plough—is false in policy, and immoral in tendency.

The only limitation upon the indiscriminate acquisition of money that remains to be considered is that of *honor*. In a populous community, where business is complex, and interest powerful, it is necessary to have a court of chancery to law and honesty. This is the object of the court of honor. Its decrees are not written in a code, nor are its proceedings regulated by rules and formulas.

Its seat is in the bosom of nature's noblemen, and its power is manifested in the infinite variety of unwitnessed transactions, and the extended confidence of commercial intercourse. Without honor, commerce must stop at every step to prepare her writings; and suspicion, like a heavy armor, would impede the march of enterprise. "It ought to tempt one," says Chalmers, "to be proud of his species, when he looks upon the faith reposed in a merchant by a distant correspondent, who without one other hold of him than his *honor*, confides to him the wealth of a whole flotilla, and sleeps in the confidence that it is safe. It is, indeed, an animating thought, amid the gloom of a world's depravity, when we behold the credit which one man puts in another, though separated by seas and continents; when he fixes the anchor of a sure and steady dependence on the reputed faith of one whom he never saw; when with all his fears for the treachery of the various elements through which his property must pass, he knows that, should it arrive at the door of his agent, his fears and suspicions may be at an end. We know nothing finer than such an act of homage from one being to another, when perhaps the diameter of a globe is between them; nor do we think that either the renown of her victories, or the wisdom of her counsels, so signalizes the country in which we live as does the honorable conduct of her merchants, or the awarded confidence of those men of all tribes and colors and languages, who look to our agency for the faithfulness of all management, and to our keeping for the most inviolable of all custody."

Honor is the foster-parent of credit. Who would trust his property in the hands of another, looking to the law alone for repayment? Honor is the patron-saint of business. Who would take upon himself the immense load of labor necessary to do business if no man's word could be relied upon? Business would degenerate into petty traffic, and society retrograde into barbarism. Honor is to business men what courage is to the soldier, what zeal is to the advocate, or impartiality to the judge.

A man violates the laws of honor, when he uses information confidentially intrusted to him, to anticipate the informer. A man violates the laws of honor when he takes the advantage of another's unskilfulness, or inexperience, or the technicalities of the law, to impose upon him. A man acts dishonorably when he does not make sacrifices to pay his debts promptly; when he gives his rivals in business a worse reputation than he knows they deserve; when he attempts to raise the market price on another buyer; when he sells below the market-price to get away his neighbor's customers; when he is unmindful of favors; when he does not allow his clerks and dependents to share in his prosperity; and, in all cases, when he does acts which, if thoroughly understood, would tend to lower him in the estimation of his customers, or of any good man.

Merchants! pardon a word of appeal. When the storms of a faithless ocean have sent your ships to the bottom; when markets fall, and hope dies; when the gaunt demon of bankruptcy stares you in the face, grasp hold of the sheet-anchor of honor, and never let go. Write to your correspondents as Francis I. did to his royal mother: "All is lost but honor." The day will succeed the night; the storm will pass by; the sun will shine again; and "the flower will bless the cloud when it hath passed by."

Business men of America! Get money. Get an abundance of it; but get it honorably. Elevate your business. Remember that the more elevated the business character, the more easy it will be to get money. Talk not of the baseness of commerce, or the corrupting nature of business. It is men's willingness to be corrupted that makes them corrupt; it is men's dishonorable actions that cast a stigma upon business. Let each one who believes in the right, take his stand and boldly maintain it. Frown down all tricks; all cunning; all those winding and crooked courses: "The goings of the serpent, which goeth basely upon the belly and not upon the feet." Brand the man, who violates confidence and abuses trust, as a thief. Remember the public credit of this nation is in your keeping. If you are tricky, faithless, and dishonorable, such will be the American character in all parts of the globe. Let your stores, warehouses, and marts be temples consecrated to honor. Inscribe over the doors: "Who comes within these walls is safe." Let it be said of American business men as it was said of ancient Tyre: "Her merchants were princes, and her traffickers the honorable of the earth."

"The fear o' hell's a hangman's whip,
To haud the wretch in order;
But where you feel your *honor* grip,
Let that, aye be your border.
Its slightest touches instant pause,
Debar a' side pretences;
And resolutely keep its laws,
Uncaring consequences."

Having considered the limits within which we may get money, we must now proceed to inquire *how* we shall get it. It may be remarked, in the first place, that all business has its origin in wants, and the object of business is to supply wants. Hence, our first important step would be to discover or fix upon some general want which we could supply on terms as favorable as any one else can do, or, in other words, to choose some regular business, as we are presumed to have done. But, as political economists have satisfactorily demonstrated that all useful employments are equally productive and profitable (for when one is known to pay more than the average rate of profit, hundreds rush into it, and soon reduce it to the ordinary level,) it is a matter of less importance what pursuit we follow, provided we are adapted to it, than how we manage it. A man who can lay by, regularly, $500 a year, will be certain to become a rich man if his life be spared to a reasonable age, while he who makes $10,000 in one year, and loses a larger amount the next, will, very probably, be dependent on the charity of friends for support in old age. A man, in New York, is reported to have made $60,000 by selling lead-pencils about the streets, at a penny apiece, and safely investing his profits, while it is not an unfrequent occurrence to hear of men who commenced life with a capital larger than that, afterwards reduced to the necessity of following a similar employment for a livelihood.

A man *who intends to make money*, not merely to try his chances, must look first to the *safety* of his business. It is a well-ascertained fact that those occupations which are the most *useful* are the safest, and that those commodities which can least be dispensed with, pay, in the aggregate, the largest profits. The demand for them is stimulated by actual want, and grows with every increase of the means of production. It is a comparatively rare occurrence for those who deal in superfluities to get rich, as they are subject to continual losses from changes in the fashions, and a hundred circumstances beyond their control; and Say has truly remarked, "The most fashionable tradesmen are oftenest in the list of bankrupts." Next to the supply of indispensable wants, those kinds of business are the safest which are concerned in the production, manufacture, or sale of articles of general convenience, and on which a *large percentage of profit can be made, though the cost to the consumer is inconsiderable.* Secondly, a man must look to *the safety of his investments.* Land is, undoubtedly, a safe and profitable investment in this country, and the largest fortunes have been made by a rise in the value of real estate. When we reflect that the population of this country is increasing at the rate of three per cent. per annum, and that, in less than half a century hence, within the lives of many of us, this country will contain *one hundred millions* of inhabitants, it requires no gift of prophecy to foresee that land, in good locations, is destined to reach a point which would now seem visionary. But, in making investments in land, or in any thing else, a man must be careful, unless he wishes to become a land-speculator, which is a business no safer, nor more profitable in general, than any other, and which must be managed on the same principles, that he does not withdraw from his business more than the actual surplus profits not needed to insure its future productiveness. Thirdly, a man who intends to make money must understand *the true principles of business.*

As this is a matter of great importance, and not well understood, we may, probably, derive hints that will be valuable in all kinds of business, from a consideration of the best modes of managing a few of the most prominent pursuits.

CHAPTER V.

GETTING MONEY BY FARMING.

"There seem to be but three ways for a nation to acquire wealth. The first is by war, as the Romans did, in plundering their neighbors; this is robbery. The second by commerce, which is frequently cheating. The third by agriculture, the only honest way, wherein a man receives a real increase of the seed thrown into the ground in a kind of continued miracle wrought by the hand of God in his favor, as a reward for his innocent life and his virtuous industry."—Franklin.

Agriculture needs no eulogy. Learned men in all ages, philosophers, statesmen, orators from Cicero to Kossuth, have done themselves honor and "appeased the gods" by laying their good-will offerings on the altars of agriculture. It is enough to know that it is the first-born of civilization, the mother of wealth, and the heaven appointed employment of mankind. I believe it would promote the general happiness of society to inculcate the doctrine that farming is the destined occupation of *all men at birth*, and that he who forsakes it for other pursuits must show substantial reasons for the departure to entitle him to encouragement. A man who possesses eminent mechanical ingenuity had better be a mechanic; he who is thoroughly fitted by nature and education is justified in being a public teacher; and he who is born to be a distributor of the earth's products may be a merchant: but all should show evidences of capability for the pursuit to entitle them to the rewards due only to ability. In agriculture, the Creator has furnished a safe and healthy employment for all men. He has endowed *certain* men with peculiar talents suited to the exceptional kinds of business; those who are diligent or fortunate in the discovery of his will in regard to themselves find success and happiness; those who thrust themselves into employments for which they are unfitted, from unworthy motives, must suffer the penalties of violated law. As a necessary consequence of this doctrine, every one should learn the art of farming first, a knowledge of which would be of great advantage to every poor man at least. But it is not our province to discuss theories. Facts, figures, and certain principles are our boundaries, and we have too much reverence for the law and men's rights "to trespass" on other people's *ground.*

I. *Is farming profitable?* This is a practical question. It is also a relative question, and suggests another inquiry. *What is a good and profitable business?* A man who can lay by regularly from $500 to $1000 a year, over and above all expenses of every necessary kind, may be said to be doing a *good* business; a man who can net regularly any thing over *ten* per cent. per annum on capital safely invested, is doing a *profitable* business. The statements of what has been done in farming are numerous in a scattered shape, and we will only select a few of the least extraordinary.

Joshua Tappan, of Newbury, Essex Co., Massachusetts, in 1842, sold from a plot of ground measuring five acres and one-sixth rods, produce to the value of $\$405\frac{65}{100}$.

A. T. Perkins, in the *Maine Farmer*, says: "I have raised, the past year, from 30 acres of land 700 bushels of potatoes, 80 bushels of barley, 25 bushels of beets, 15 bushels of wheat, 10 bushels of beans, 4 tons of mowed oats, 16 tons of hay, 40 bushels of corn, 20 bushels of carrots, 75 chickens and turkeys, and a great quantity of garden sauce. I have killed one hog weighing 390 pounds, made 400 pounds of butter, kept 3 cows, a pair of oxen, 2 heifers, 2 steers, 8 sheep, and 4 hogs."

J G. Chadsey, of Wickford, Rhode Island, states that he purchased 35 acres of land near that village, which he could neither sell nor rent. He concluded to try farming himself, though he had done nothing at it for forty years; but, as a substitute for experience, he took an agricultural paper. His success is that the land which, seven years ago, would not rent for four per cent. on cost, now pays twenty per cent., after deducting all expenses. Cost of land, $3,050. Produce sold in 1846, $1,116 41. Expenses, labor, taxes, and estimating his own labor at $50, 467\frac{66}{100}$ leaving 640\frac{75}{100}$ as profits, or 20½ per cent., for the use of the land.*

It is estimated by practical men that *one-third of the proceeds* of a farm will amply suffice to cover all the ordinary expenditures, or, in other words, will pay for working, keep the farm in repair, and replace the interest on the capital. Dr. Beekman, Secretary of the State Agricultural Society, states, "that, except in extraordinary cases, one-third of the products will meet all expenses, leaving two-thirds as profits." A writer in the *Genesee Farmer* gives an account of two farms in his neighborhood, which he regards as a sample of the well-managed farms. One contains 86 acres; and capital invested, including farm and stock, is $4500. The proceeds per annum average $1442. Profits (one-third less), $962, or interest at the rate of 21 per cent. Another contains 40 acres; capital, including farm and stock, is $1600. Proceeds per annum 851\frac{49}{100}$. Profits (one-third less), 567\frac{66}{100}$, or 35 per cent. on capital

* This instance suggests two considerations that hold good in many cases that have come within our notice. The first is that men who have acquired their training in other pursuits frequently succeed best at farming. Men, at whom old farmers would raise their eyebrows above their temples, frequently show results, in a few years, that old farmers, by their mode of management, cannot attain in a lifetime. It may be ascribed to two causes. They turn to farming because they have a love for it, and prosecute it with zeal; and secondly, their superior business tact, acquired in other pursuits, gives them an advantage in this also. It is certain that no manufacturing or mercantile business could stand the neglect of advantages and mismanagement that farming is habitually compelled to stand. Those engaged in it would fail the first year.

Another consideration suggested is the practical aid and knowledge to be derived from *books* and *agricultural papers*. A man's individual experience is limited—from books he may derive the experience of thousands. All that is wanted to make fortunes is first the idea, and then energy to follow it up. Books on business are likely to suggest the idea; they stimulate the mind to think, and furnish a healthful excitement that keeps up energy. Books on general business and special business should be read with close attention by every man. They are few in number, and the chances that they will suggest a valuable idea will justify the expense. A book which is valueless to one man may be invaluable to another.

Messrs. Cooper, near Bushwick, Long Island, report to the New York Farmer's Club that their farm of 30 acres, four men to work it, and occasionally extra help, yielded, in one year, gross proceeds $3,498$\frac{25}{100}$.

The farm connected with the House of Industry at South Boston contains 30 acres. The proceeds of the farm for the last year amounted to $5,287$\frac{91}{100}$, being equal to $176 per acre.*

At a legislative agricultural meeting held in Boston, some remarks were made by the Hon. Mr. Calhoun on the profits of farming, compared with other pursuits. The conclusion arrived at was, that farmers, on the average, succeed better than merchants; that if, by way of experiment, one hundred men should go into a city in trade, and one hundred go to farming, at the end of twenty years the hundred farmers would be worth the most money. Mr. Calhoun added: "Here is a foundation that may be built upon with more certainty than any other. Yet young men are rushing into the cities to make their fortunes. It is deeply important that

* Why should one acre yield $176 value, when another equally fertile by nature will only yield ten dollars? Why is a garden richer than a field? We *manure* our gardens well, and our fields lightly. We dig our gardens *twenty* inches deep, and plough our fields *five* inches deep. We cultivate a small patch of ground thoroughly, and scratch over a large space of land superficially. A hankering after much land is a serious drawback to successful farming in the United States, and we believe that if three-fourths of those who have over seventy-five acres of land would sell the excess, and devote their entire attention to the balance, they would find themselves better off. A man had a large vineyard and two daughters; when the one married, he gave her as a dowry one-third of his vineyard, yet he discovered that the remaining-two thirds netted him as much as the whole: when the other daughter married, he gave her a third, and found his profits in the succeeding year larger than they had ever been. A practical farmer says, "I am confident that fifty acres, cultivated in the very best style of modern improvement, will yield more profit than many of your one hundred acre farms now yield." *Manure* and *labor* will do the business. Large farms are a weariness to the flesh.

"A little farm well tilled;
A little house well filled;
A little wife well willed"

are the greatest blessings, of an earthly nature, a man can possess.

the facts stated here and at former meetings, should be deeply impressed upon young men. Mr. Brook says: '15 per cent. may be made on capital by any diligent and systematic farmer.' Hon. John Lowell says, '18 per cent.' All this may be done by farming intelligently. He had wondered that farmers generally got along so well as they actually do in their careless mode of management. For himself he had regained his own health by farming. The open air had restored him."

II. *What management is necessary to make farming profitable?* On this subject farmers would prefer to hear a practical farmer speak; and I am happy to state that one of the best practical farmers in the State of New York has written the best and most interesting prize essay "On Farm Management," *which obtained the premium from the New York State Agricultural Society*, that I have ever read. Those who take little interest in agricultural matters will derive pleasure and benefit from a careful perusal of it, and those who contemplate farming should study it.

ON FARM MANAGEMENT—PRIZE ESSAY.

BY J. J. THOMAS.

THE great importance of performing in the best manner the different operations of agriculture is obvious to every intelligent mind, for on this depends the success of farming. But a good performance of single operations merely does not constitute the best farmer. The perfection of the art consists not only in doing every thing well individually, but in a proper adjustment and systematic arrangement of all the parts, so that they shall be done not only in the best manner and at the right time, but with the most effective and economical expenditure of labor and money. Every thing must move on with clock-work regularity, without interference, even at the most busy seasons of the year.

As this subject includes the whole routine of farming in a collected view as well as in its separate details, a treatise upon it might be made to fill volumes; but this being necessarily confined to a few pages, a general outline, with some remarks on its more essential parts, can only be given.

CAPITAL.—The first requisite in all undertakings of magnitude is to "count the cost." The man who commences a building, which to finish would cost ten thousand dollars, with a capital of only five thousand, is as certainly ruined as many farmers are who, without counting the cost, commence on a scale to which their limited means are wholly inadequate. One of the greatest mistakes which young farmers make in this country, in their anxious wish for large possessions, is, not only in purchasing more land than they can pay for, but in the actual expenditure of all their means, without leaving any even to *begin* the great work of farming. Hence, the farm continues for a long series of years poorly provided with stock, with implements, with manure, and with the necessary labor. From this heavy drawback on the profits of his land, the farmer is kept long in debt; the burden of which not only disheartens him, but prevents that enterprise and energy which are essential to success. This is one fruitful reason why American agriculture is in many places in so low a state. A close observer, in travelling through the country, is thus enabled often to decide from the appearances of the buildings and premises of each occupant, whether he is in or out of debt.

In England, where the enormous taxes of different kinds imperiously compel the cultivator to farm well or not farm at all, the indispensable necessity of a heavy capital to begin with is fully understood. The man who merely *rents* a farm, there, must possess as much to stock it and commence operations as the man who *buys* and pays for a farm of equal size in the best parts of Western New York. The result is, that he is enabled to do every thing in the best manner; he is not compelled to bring his goods prematurely to market to supply his pressing wants; and by having ready money always at command, he can perform every operation at the very best season for product and economy, and make purchases when necessary at the most advantageous rate. The English farmer is thus able to pay an amount of tax often more than the whole product of farms of equal extent in this country.

The importance of possessing the means of doing every thing at exactly the right season cannot be too highly appreciated. One or two illustrations may set this in a clearer light. Two farmers had each a crop of ruta-bagas of an acre each; the first, by hoeing his crop early while the weeds were only an inch high, accomplished the task with two days' work, and the young plants then grew vigorously, and yielded a heavy return. The second, being prevented by a deficiency of help, had to deter his hoeing one week, and then three days more by rainy weather, making ten days in all; during this time the weeds had sprung up six to ten inches high, so as to require, instead of two days, no less than six days to hoe them; and so much was the growth of the crop checked at this early stage that the owner had 150 bushels less in his acre than the farmer who took time by the forelock. Another instance occurred with an intelligent farmer of this State, who raised two fields of oats on land of similar quality. One field was sown very early, and well put in, and yielded a good profit. The other was delayed twelve days, and then hurried; and although the crop was within two-thirds of the amount of the former, yet that difference was just the clear profit of the first crop; so that with the latter the amount yielded only paid the expenses.

Admitting that the farm is already purchased and paid for, it becomes an object to know what else is needed and at what cost, before cultivation is commenced. If the buildings and fences are what they should be, which is not often the case, little immediate outlay will be needed for them. But if not, then an estimate must be made of the intended improvements, and the necessary sum allotted for them. These being all in order, the following items requiring an expenditure of capital will be required on a good farm of 100 acres of improved land, that being not far from the size of a large majority in this State. The estimate will of course vary considerably with circumstances, prices, &c.

I. LIVE STOCK.

The amount will vary with the fertility and products of the land, its quality, and situation with regard to market. The following will approximate the average on good farms taken at the spring of the year or commencement of work:—

3	Horses, at $80	$240
1	Yoke oxen	75
8	Milch-cows at $15	120
10	Steers, heifers, and calves	70
20	Pigs at $3	60
150	Sheep at $2	300
	Poultry—say	5
	Total	$870

II. IMPLEMENTS.

2	Ploughs fitted for work	$20 00
1	Small plough, do.	6 00
1	Cultivator, best kind	7 00
1	Drill-barrow	5 00
1	Roller	5 00
1	Harrow	10 00
1	Fanning-mill	20 00
1	Straw-cutter	15 00
1	Root-slicer	8 00
1	Farm-wagon, with hay-rack, &c.	70 00
1	Ox-cart	50 00
1	Double farm harness	30 00
1	Horse-cart	45 00
1	Horse-cart harness	18 00
1	Root-steamer, or boiler	20 00
1	Shovel and one spade	2 50
3	Steel-plate hoes	2 25
2	Dung-forks	2 25
3	Hay-forks	3 00
2	Hand-rakes	0 25
1	Revolving horse rake	8 00
2	Grain-cradles	8 00
	Carried forward	$355 25

Brought forward	$355 25
2 Scythes	4 00
1 Wheelbarrow	4 00
1 Pointed shovel	1 25
1 Grain-shovel, or scoop-shovel	1 25
1 Pick	1 50
1 Mall and wedges	2 50
2 Axes	4 00
1 Hammer	50
1 Wood-saw	1 50
1 Turnip-hook	75
1 Hay-knife	3 00
2 Apple ladders (for gathering)	1 50
2 Large baskets	1 25
2 Hand-baskets	50
1 Tape-line (for laying off land)	2 00
2 Sheep-shears	2 00
1 Grindstone	3 00
1 Steel-yard, large, and one small	2 00
1 Stable lantern	50
1 Curry-comb, and one brush	75
1 Half-bushel measure	1 00
20 Grain-bags	8 00
1 Ox-chain	3 00
1 Crow-bar	2 00
1 Sled and fixtures	30 00
Total	$437 00

Other articles might be included, as subsoil plough, sowing-machine, &c. A threshing-machine is not named, as it is better to employ itinerant threshers, and save capital. To the preceding amount ought to be added one-tenth the expense of fencing the farm, as fences need renewing at least once in ten years. Every farmer should also be supplied with a small set of carpenter's tools, which would cost about $12, for repairing implements in rainy weather, and other useful purposes. This set should include saw, hammer, augers, planes, adze, mallet, chisel, square, breast-bits,

&c., and by the convenience and economy afforded, would soon repay their cost.

III. SEEDS.

2½	Bushels clover seed	for	10 acres	$15 00
2	" corn	"	" 6 "	1 00
30	" potatoes	"	2 "	7 00
3	Pounds ruta-baga seed		1 acre	1 50
2	" field beet	"	½ "	1 50
2	" carrot	"	½ "	1 00
30	Bushels seed wheat	"	20 acres	30 00
10	" oats	"	5 "	2 50
10	" barley	"	5 "	4 00
	Total			$63 00

IV. LABOR.

Supposing the owner to labor with his own hands, as every owner should, so far as is consistent with a general superintendence of all parts, which would probably amount to one-half the time, he would need besides through the season two men and one boy, and in the winter one man; during haying and harvest, he would require two additional hands. The men boarding themselves, could be had for fifteen dollars per month in summer, and twelve in winter; if boarded, the cost of their meals would make up the deficiency in wages to the same amount. The expenditure needed, then, would be,

2 Hired men, eight months, $15 per month	$240 00
1 " boy, " " 6 "	48 00
Day labor in harvest	32 00
Total	$320 00

V. MAINTENANCE OF ANIMALS.

Cattle and sheep would need hay till fresh pasture, and horses nay, and also a good supply of oats till after harvest. All would be benefited by a liberal feeding of roots, including swine. The amount of all these supplies needed would be about

7 Tons of hay	$42 00
200 Bushels oats	50 00
400 " roots	50 00
Total	$142 00

RECAPITULATION.

Live stock	$870 00
Implements	437 00
Seeds	63 00
Labor	320 00
Maintenance of animals	142 00
Total	$1,832 00

The amount of capital needed the first year, in stocking and conducting satisfactorily the operations of one hundred acres of improved land, several items being doubtless omitted.

If this is a larger sum than the young farmer can command, let him purchase only fifty acres, and reserve the rest of the purchase money which would be needed for the one hundred acres, to commence with on a smaller farm, and he will scarcely fail to make more than on a larger, with every part subjected to an imperfect, hurrying, and irregular management. He may calculate, perhaps, on the return of his crops in autumn, at least to pay his hands.—But he must remember that the first year of farming is attended with many expenses which do not usually occur afterwards; which his crops may not repay, besides supporting his family, and paying his mechanics' and merchants' bills. The first year must always be regarded with uncertainty; and it is better to come out at the end, on a moderately sized farm, well tilled, and in fine order, with money in pocket, than on a larger one, in debt, and hired hands, a class of men not to be disappointed, and who ought not to be, waiting for their pay. There are a far greater number of farmers embarrassed and crippled, by placing their estimate of expenses too low, than of those who swing clear and float freely by a full previous counting of cost.

Size of Farms.—After what has just been said, the cultivator will perceive in part the advantages of moderately sized farms, for men in moderate circumstances. The great disadvantage of a superficial, skimming culture is obvious with a moment's attention. Take the corn crop as an illustration. There are a great many farmers, to my certain knowledge, whose yearly product per acre does not exceed an average of *twenty-five* bushels. There are other farmers, whom I also well know, who obtain *generally* not less than *sixty* bushels per acre, and often eighty to ninety-five.—Now, observe the difference in the profits of each. The first gets 250 bushels from *ten* acres. In doing this, he has to plough ten acres, harrow ten acres, mark out ten acres, find seed for ten acres, plant, cultivate, hoe, and cut up ten acres, besides paying the interest on ten acres, worth from three to five hundred dollars. The other farmer gets 250 bushels from *four* acres at the farthest; and he only ploughs, plants, cultivates, and hoes, to obtain the same amount, *four acres*, which from their fine tilth, and freedom from grass and weeds, is much eaiser done, even for an equal surface.—The same reasoning applies throughout the farm. Be sure, then, to cultivate no more than can be done in the best manner, whether it be ten, fifty, or five hundred acres. A friend who owned a four hundred acre farm told me that he made less than his next neighbor, who had only seventy-five. Let the man who applies a certain amount of labor every year to his farm reduce its dimensions until that labor accomplishes every thing in the very best manner. He will doubtless find that the amount of land will thus become much smaller than he supposed, more so than most would be willing to reduce it; but, on the other hand, the net proceeds from it will augment to a greater degree than perhaps could possibly be believed.

But let me not be misunderstood. Large farms are by no means to be objected to, provided the owner has capital enough to cultivate every part as well as some of our best small ones are caltivated.

As an example of what may be obtained from a small piece of land, the following products of fifty acres are given, and are not more than I have known repeatedly to be taken from good land by several thorough farmers:—

10 acres	of wheat,	35	bushels per acre,	at	$1 00	$350 00
5 "	corn,	90	"	"	40	180 00
2 "	potatoes,	300	"	"	20	120 00
1 acre	ruta-bagas,	800	"	"	10	80 00
6 acres	wint. apples,	250	"	"	25	375 00
6 "	hay,	2½	tons,	"	6 00	90 00
10 "	pasture, worth	. .		. .		60 00
5 "	barley,	40	bushels per acre		40	80 00
5 "	oats,	50	"	"	20	50 00
	Total products of fifty acres of very fine land,					$1,385 00

This aggregate yield is not greater than that obtained by some who might be named, from a similar quantity of land. Good land could be brought to that state of fertility very easily, at a total cost of one hundred dollars per acre, and then it would be incomparably cheaper than many large good farms at nothing; for, while the fifty acres could be tilled for three hundred and eighty-five dollars, leaving one thousand dollars net profits, large poor farms hardly pay the work spent upon them. One proprietor of such a farm declared, "It takes me and my hired man all summer hard at work to get enough to pay him only."

Laying out Farms.—This department is very much neglected The proper disposition of the different fields, for the sake of economy in fencing, for convenience of access, and for a full command of pasture and protection of crops at all times, has received comparatively little attention from our agricultural writers and from farmers.

Many suppose that this business is very quickly disposed of; that a very few minutes, or hours at most, will enable a man to plan the arrangement of his fields about right. But this is a great error. Even when a farm is of the simplest form, on a flat uniform piece of ground, many things are to be borne in mind in laying it out.

In the first place, we all know that the *fencing* of a moderately sized farm costs many hundred dollars. It is very desirable to do it well, and use at the same time as little material as possible. To do this, much will depend on the shape of the fields. A certain length of fence will enclose more land in the form of a *square* than in any other practicable shape. Hence fields should approach this form as nearly as possible. Again, the disposition of lanes is a matter of consequence, so as to avoid unnecessary length and fencing, and occupy the least quantity of ground.

But these rules may be materially affected by other considerations. For instance, it is very desirable that land of a similar quality may be in the same enclosure. Some may be naturally too wet for any thing but meadow or pasture; some may be much *lighter*, and susceptible of ploughing, whilst others are not: some may be naturally sterile, and need unusual manuring with green crops. All these should, as far as practicable, be included each in its own separate boundary. The situation of surface drains, forming the boundaries of fields, may influence their shape; facilities for irrigation may have an essential bearing: convenience for watering cattle is not to be forgotten. Where, in addition to all these considerations, the land is hilly, still more care and thought are required in the subdivision, which may possible require years of experience: but where fixed fences are once made, it is hard to remove them: hence a previous thorough examination should be made. A farm road, much used for heavy loads, should be made hard and firm, and cannot easily be altered: it consequently should be exactly in the right place, and be dry, level, and short; the shape of adjoining fields even conforming with these requisitions; but a road little used should not interfere with the outlines of fields.

*   *   *   *   *   *

In laying out a farm with a very uneven surface or irregular shape, it would be best to draw, first, a plan adapted to smooth ground, as the one just given; and then vary the size and shape of the fields, the distance of the lane from the centre, its straightness, &c., according to the circumstances of the case.

Fences.*—The kind of fence used, and the material for its construction, must depend on circumstances and localities. A good fence is always to be preferred to an imperfect one: though it will cost more, it will more than save that cost, and three times the amount in vexation besides, by keeping cattle, colts, and pigs out of fields of grain. A thriving farmer whose whole land, except a small part with stone wall, is enclosed by common rail fence, with upright cedar stakes, and connecting caps to the tops, finds that it needs renewing once in six years. He accordingly divides his whole amount of fences into six parts, one of which is built new every year. All is thus kept systematically in good repair. Stone walls, if set a foot below the surface to prevent tumbling by frost, are the most durable fence. Hedges have not been sufficiently tried. The English hawthorn is not well adapted to our hotter and drier climate, and though sometimes doing well for a time, is not to be depended on. The buckthorn in New England, and the Newcastle and Washington thorns in Pennsylvania and Delaware, have succeeded finely.

Gates.—Every field on the farm should be entered by a good self-shutting and self-fastening gate. A proper inclination in hanging will secure the former requisite, and a good latch, properly constructed, the latter. Each field should be numbered, and the number painted on the gate-post. Let the farmer who has *bars* instead of gates, make a trial of their comparative convenience, by

* "Strange as it may seem, the greatest investment in this country, the most costly production of human industry, is the common fences which divide the fields from the highway, and separate them from each other. No man dreams that when compared with the outlay of these unpretending monuments of art, our cities and our towns, with all their wealth, are left far behind. You will scarce believe me when I say that the fences of this country have cost more than twenty times the specie there is in it. In many of the counties of the Northern States, the fences have cost more than the farms and fences are worth."—*Burnap.*

taking them out, and replacing them without stopping, as often as he does in one year on his farm, say about six hundred times, and he cannot fail to be satisfied which is the cheapest for use

BUILDINGS.—These should be as near the centre of the farm as other considerations will admit. All the hay, grain, and straw being conveyed from the fields to the barn, and most of it back again in manure, the distance of drawing should be as short as possible. This will, also, save much travelling of men and cattle to and from the different parts of the farm. The buildings should not, however, be too remote from the public road, and a good, dry, healthy spot should be chosen. The dwelling should be comfortable, but not large; or, it should rather be adapted to the extent of the lands. A large, costly house, with small farm and other buildings, is a bad indication of management. The censure of the old Roman should be avoided, who, having a small piece of land, built his house so large that he had less occasion to plough than to sweep.

The barn and out-buildings should be of ample extent. The barn should have space for hay, grain, and straw. It is a matter of great convenience to have the straw for littering stables housed and close at hand, and not out of doors, under a foot of snow. There should be plenty of stables and sheds for all domestic animals. This provision will not only save one-third of the fodder, but stock will thrive much better. Cows will give much more milk, sheep will yield more and better wool, and all will pass through the winter more safely. The wood-house, near or attached to the dwelling, should never be forgotten, so long as comfort in building fires and economy in the use of fuel are of any importance.

A small, cheap, movable horse-power should belong to every establishment, to be used in churning, sawing wood, driving washing-machine, turning grindstone, cutting straw, and slicing roots.

There should be a large root-cellar under the barn, into which the cart may be *dumped* from the outside. One great objection to the culture of ruta-bagas and beets, in this country—the difficulty of winter keeping—would then vanish.

Both barn and house cellars should be well coated, on the bottom and sides, with water-lime-mortar, which is a very cheap and effectual way to exclude both water and rats.

Choice of Implements.—Of those which are much used, the very best only should be procured. This will be attended with a gain in every way. The work will be easier done, and it will be better done. A laborer who, by the use of a good hoe for one month, can do one quarter more each day, saves, in the whole time, an entire week's labor.

Choice of Animals.—The best of all kinds should be selected, even if costing something more than others. Not "*fancy*" animals, but those good for use and profit. Cows should be productive of milk, and of a form adapted for beef; oxen hardy, and fast-working; sheep, kept fine by never selling the best; swine, not the *largest* merely, but those fattening best on least food. A Berkshire, at 200 pounds, fattened on 10 bushels of corn, is better than a "*land pike*" of 300, fattened on 50 bushels.

Having now taken some notice of the necessary items for commencing farming, it remains to glance a little at

Soils, and their Management.—Soils are of various kinds, as heavy and light, wet and dry, fertile and sterile. They all require different management in a greater or less degree.

Heavy soils are often stronger and more productive than light; but they require more labor for pulverization and tillage. They cannot be ploughed when very wet, nor so well when very dry. Although containing greater or less portions of clay, they may be distinguished, as a class from lighter soils, by the cloddy surface the fields present after ploughing in dry weather, by their cracking in drought, and by their adhesiveness after rains.

Sandy and gravelly loams also contain clays, but in smaller quantity; so that they do not present the cloddiness and adhesiveness of heavy soils. Though possessing, generally, less strength than clay soils, they are far more easily tilled, and may be worked without difficulty in wet weather. They do not crack or break in drought. Indian corn, ruta-bagas, and some other crops, succeed best upon them. Sandy soils are very easily tilled, but are generally not strong enough. When made rich, they are fine for some succulent crops.

Peaty soils are generally light and free, containing large quantities of decayed vegetable matter. They are made by draining low and swampy grounds. They are fine for Indian corn, broom corn, barley, potatoes, and turnips. They are great absorbers, and great radiators of heat; hence they become warm in sunshine and cold in clear nights. For this reason they are peculiarly liable to frosts. Crops planted upon them must, consequently, be put in late, after spring frosts are over.

Corn should be of early varieties, that it may not only be planted late, but ripen early.

Each of these kinds of soil may be variously improved. Most of heavy soils are much improved by draining; open drains to carry off the surface-water, and covered drains, that which settles beneath. An acquaintance covered a low, wet, clayey field with a net-work of under-drains, and from a production of almost nothing but grass, it yielded the first year forty bushels of wheat per acre, enough to pay the expense, and admitted of much easier tillage afterwards. Heavy soils are also made lighter and freer by manuring; by ploughing under coatings of straw, rotten chips, and swamp muck; and, in some rare cases, by carting on sand, though this is usually too expensive for practice. Subsoil ploughing is very beneficial both in wet seasons and in drought; the deep, loose bed of earth it makes, receiving the water in heavy rains, and throwing it off to the soil above, when needed; but a frequent repetition of the operation is needed, as the subsoil gradually settles again.

Sandy soils are improved by manuring; by the application of lime, and by frequently turning to green crops. Leached ashes have been found highly beneficial in many places. Where the subsoil is clayey, which is often the case, and especially if marly clay, great advantage is derived from shovelling it up and spreading it on the surface. A neighbor had twenty bushels of wheat per acre on land thus treated, while the rest of the field yielded only five.

MANURES.—These are among the first of requisites in successful farm management. They are the strong-moving power in agricultural operations. They are as the great steam-engine which drives the vessel onward. Good and clean cultivation is, indeed, all important; but it will avail little without a fertile soil; and this fertility must be created or kept up by a copious application of manures; for these contribute directly or assist indirectly to the supply of nearly all the nourishment which plants receive. It is these which, produced chiefly from the decay of dead vegetable and animal matter, combine most powerfully to give new life and vigor; and thus the apparently putrid mass is the very material which is converted into the most beautiful forms of nature; and plants and brilliant flowers spring up from the decay of old forms, and thus a continued succession of destruction and renovation is carried on through an unlimited series of ages.

Manures possess different degrees of power, partly from their inherent richness, and partly from the rapidity with which they throw off their fertilizing ingredients, in assisting the growth of plants. These are given off by solution in water, and in the form of gas; the one as a liquid manure, which, running down, is absorbed by the roots; and the other, as air, escaping mostly into the atmosphere, and lost.

The great art, then, of saving and manufacturing manure consists in retaining and applying, to the best advantage, those soluble and gaseous portions. Probably more than one-half of all the materials which exist in the country are lost, totally lost, by not attending to the drainage of stables and farmyards. This could be retained by a copious application of straw; by littering with sawdust, when saw-mills are near; and, more especially, by the frequent coating of yards and stables with dried peat and swamp muck, of which many parts of our States furnish inexhaustible supplies. I say *dried* peat or muck, because, if it is already saturated with water, of which it will often take in five-sixths of its own weight, it cannot absorb the liquid portions of the manure. But, if it will absorb five-sixths in water, it will, when dried, absorb five-sixths in liquid manure, and, both together, form a very enriching material. The practice of many farmers shows how little they are aware of the hundreds they are losing, every year, by suffering this most valuable of their farm products to escape. Indeed, there are not a few who carefully, and very ingeniously, as they suppose, place their barns and cattle-yards in such a manner, on the sides of hills, that all the drainage from them may pass off out of the way into the neighboring streams; and some one mentions a farmer who, with pre-eminent shrewdness, built his hog-pen directly across a stream, that he might, at once, get the cleanings washed away, and prevent their accumulation. He, of course, succeeded in his wish; but he might, with almost equal propriety, have built his granary across the stream, so as to shovel the wheat into the water when it increased on his hands.

The loss of manure, by the escape of gas, is often very great. The proof of this was finely exhibited by Humphrey Davy, in an experiment performed by filling a large retort from a heap of fermenting manure, and placing the beak among the roots of some grass. Nothing but vapor left the vessel, yet, in a few days, the grass exhibited greater luxuriance around the beak of the retort than any of the surrounding portions. Hence the superiority of unfermented manures; the rich portions are not yet lost. And hence, too, the importance of preventing this loss by an immediate application, and ploughing into the soil, and also by mixing it in composts with muck, peat, swamp mud, and even common earth, in a dry state—and of preventing its escape, from stables and yards, by a daily strewing with dried peat, lime, or plaster.

The superiority of unfermented manure has just been mentioned, which is by many doubted. But the very facts on which these doubts rest only prove its efficacy; for, they say, "I have always found fresh manure to be attended with little effect the first year, while it yet remains fresh; but afterwards, when fermentation and decay had taken place, the benefit was great and striking." But here is the proof at hand that, not until the rich, soluble, and gaseous parts had well penetrated and been absorbed by the soil, was their powerful and invigorating influence exerted upon the growing plants. Fresh manure is generally in a state not readily mixed with soils. It is thrown into large lumps over the surface, some of which are ploughed in, and others not; but none of them prove of immediate use to the crops. But, on the other hand, fermented manure, from its ready pulverization, admits of an easy admixture. Let fresh manure be thoroughly ground down, and worked into the soil by repeated harrowings, and two or three ploughings, and its influence will be like magic.

Swamp muck has often been spoken of as manure; but those who expect great and striking results from its application will be disappointed, as the writer has been. Even with ashes, it is much less powerful than stable manure, not only because it possesses less inherent richness, but because it has less soluble parts, and, consequently, imparts its strength more slowly to growing plants. But this quality only makes it the more enduring. By decoction in water, vegetable mould loses a small portion of its weight by solution; but, if the remaining insoluble part is exposed to the air and moisture a few months, another part may be again dissolved. Thus, peat, muck, and all decayed vegetable fibre, become a slow but lasting source of nourishment to plants.

But it is when shovelled out and dried, to be mixed with farm-yard manure, as a recipient for its evanescent parts, that peat or muck becomes pre-eminently valuable. Some parts of the State abound with inexhaustible supplies in almost every neighborhood; many land-owners have from twenty to a hundred thousand cubic yards on their farms, lying untouched, while half-starved crops are growing in the adjacent fields. There are whole counties so well supplied with it that, if judiciously applied, it would, doubtless, double their aggregate products.

All neat farming, all profitable farming, and all satisfactory farming must be attended with a careful saving of manures. The people of Flanders have long been distinguished for the neatness and excellence of their farms, which they have studied to make like gardens. The care with which they collect all refuse materials which may be converted into manures, and increase their composts, is one of the chief reasons of the cleanliness of their towns and residences; and were this subject fully appreciated, and attended with a corresponding practice generally, it would, doubtless, soon increase, by millions, the agricultural products of the State.

But there is another subject of scarcely less magnitude. This is a systematic

Rotation of Crops.—If manuring is the steam engine which propels the vessel, rotation is the rudder which *guides* it in its progress. Unlike manuring, rotation does not increase the labor of culture; it only directs the labor in the most effective manner, by the exercise of judgment and thought.

The limits of this paper do not admit of many remarks on the principles of rotation. The following courses, however, have been found among some of the best adapted to our State:—

I. 1st year—Corn and roots, well manured;
2d year—Wheat, sown with clover-seed; 15 lbs. an acre;
3d year—Clover, one or more years, according to fertility and amount of manure at hand.

II. 1st year—Corn and roots, with all the manure;
2d year—Barley and peas;
3d year—Wheat, sown with clover;
4th year—Clover, one or more years.

III. 1st year—Corn and roots, with all the manure;
2d year—Barley;
3d year—Wheat, sown with clover;
4th year—Pasture;
5th year—Meadow;
6th year—Fallow;
7th year—Wheat;
8th year—Oats, sown with clover;
9th year—Pasture or meadow.

The number of the fields must correspond with the number of the changes in each course; the first needing three fields to carry it out, the second four, the third nine. As each field contains a crop each, in the several successive stages of the course, the whole number of fields collectively comprise the entire series of crops every year. Thus, in the list above given, there are two fields of wheat growing at once, three of meadow and pasture, one of corn and roots, one of barley, one of oats, and one in summer fallow

Operations in the Order of Time.—The vital consequence of doing every thing in the right season is known to every good farmer.

To prevent confusion and embarrassment, and keep all things clearly and plainly before the farmer at the right time, he should have a small book to carry in his pocket, having every item of work for each week or each half month laid down before his eyes. This can be done to the best advantage, to suit every particular locality and difference of climate, by marking every successive week in the season at the top of its respective page. Then as each operation severally occurs, let him place it under its proper heading; or, if out of season, let him place it back at the right time. Any proposed improvements can be noted down on the right page. Interesting experiments are often suggested in the course of reading or observation, but forgotten when the time comes to try them. By recording them in such a book, under the right week, they are brought at once before the mind. Such an arrangement as this will prevent a great deal of the confusion and vexation too often attendant on multifarious cares, and assist very essentially in conducting all the farm work with clock-work regularity and satisfaction.

In reviewing the various items which are most immediately essential to good farm management, some of the most obvious will be—capital enough to buy the farm and to stock it well; to select a size compatible with these requisites; to lay it out in the best manner; to provide it well with fences, gates, and buildings; to select the best animals, and the best implements to be had reasonably; to bring the soil into good condition, by draining, manuring, and good culture; to have every part under a good rotation of crops; and every operation arranged so as all to be conducted systematically, without clashing or confusion. An attention to all these points would place agriculture on a very different footing from its present condition in many places, and with most farmers. The business, then, instead of being repulsive, as it so frequently is, to our young men, would be attended with real enjoyment and pleasure.

But in all improvements, in all enterprises, the great truth must not be forgotten, that success is not to be expected without diligence and industry. We must sow in spring, and cultivate well in summer, if we would reap an abundant harvest in autumn.—When we see young farmers commence in life without a strict attention to business, which they neglect for mere pleasure, well may we in imagination see future crops lost by careless tillage—broken fences, unhinged gates, and fields filled with weeds—tools destroyed by heedlessness, property wasted by recklessness, and disorder and confusion triumphant; and unpaid debts, duns, and executions, already hanging over the premises. But, on the other hand, to see cheerful-faced, ready-handed industry, directed by reason and intelligence, and order, energy, and economy guiding the operations of the farm—with smooth, clean fields, and neat, trim fences—rich, verdant pastures, and fine cattle enjoying them; and broad, waving meadows and golden harvests, and waste and extravagance driven into exile, we need not fear the success of such a farmer; debts cannot stare him in the face, nor duns enter his threshold.

It is such enterprise as this that must place our country on a substantial basis. Agriculture, in a highly improved state, must be the means which, next to the righteousness which truly exalts a nation, will contribute to its enduring prosperity. All trades and commerce depend on this great art as their foundation. The cultivation of the soil and of plants was the earliest occupation of man. It has, in all ages, been his chief means of subsistence; it still continues to furnish employment to the great majority of the human race. It is truly the great art of peace, as during wars and commotions it has languished and declined, but risen again, in strength and vigor, when men have lived at peace with each other; it has then flourished and spread, converted the wilderness into life and beauty, and refreshed and adorned nature with embellished culture. For its calm and tranquil pleasures—for its peaceful and healthful labors—away from the fretful and feverish life of crowded cities, "in the free air and beneath the bright sun of heaven"—many, who have spent the morning and noon of their lives in the anxious cares of commercial life, have long sighed for a scene of peace and of quietude for the evening of their days

CHAPTER VI.

GETTING MONEY BY MERCHANDISING.

I WILL use the term Merchants in the subsequent pages in the Parkerian sense, meaning men who buy and sell; who buy to sell, and sell to buy the more. They fetch and carry between the other classes. They are distributors; they are the merchants. Under this name I include the whole class who live by buying and selling, and not merely those conventionally called merchants to distinguish them from small dealers. This term comprises traders behind counters, and traders behind desks; traders behind neither counters nor desks. There are various grades of merchants. They might be classed and symbolized according as they use a basket, a wheelbarrow, a cart, a stall, a booth, a shop, a warehouse, a counting-room, or bank. Still all are the same thing—men who live by buying and selling. A ship is only a large basket; a warehouse, a costly stall. Your peddler is a small merchant going round from house to house with his basket to mediate between persons; your merchant is only a great peddler sending round from land to land with his ships to mediate between nations.

The Israelitish woman who sits behind a bench in her stall on the Rialto at Venice, changing gold into silver and copper, or loaning money to him who leaves hat, coat, and other *collaterals*, in pledge, is a small banker. The Israelitish man who sits at Frankfort-on-the-Maine, changes drafts into specie, and lends millions to men who leave in pledge a mortgage on the States of the Church, on Austria, or Russia, is a pawnbroker and money-changer on a large scale. By this arithmetic, for present convenience, all grades of merchants are reduced to one denomination—*men who live by buying and selling.*

We will examine first

THE PRINCIPLES AND PROSPECTS OF TRADE.

"Man, they say, is a trading animal—the only one. The wants of each individual are more numerous and varied than his faculties and capacities devoted to supplying them. Each producer of necessaries or comforts naturally produces a superabundance of whatever he grows or fabricates, and exchanges it for a competence of other wares or staples adapted to his wants. The grain-grower has a large surplus of grain, but requires nearly every thing else; the pin-maker consumes perhaps a dollar's worth per year of his own products, and four hundred and ninety-nine dollars' worth of other people's, obtained by the sale of his own. And as man rises in the scale of civilization his wants are increased and diversified. He labors more, produces more, exchanges far more. The lowest savage may produce or gather a hundred dollars' worth per annum, and exchange ten dollars' worth of it for other necessaries or comforts; while the population of the United States or Great Britain produce at least five hundred dollars' worth to each able-bodied man, whereof two-thirds at least is exchanged by producers with each other, and with the producers of foreign lands. And, as man shall continue to rise in the scale of intelligence, industry, efficiency, and comfort, not merely the amount but the proportion of each man's products exchanged for those of others, must continue to increase. The aggregate of exchanges of property is probably now expanding throughout the world at the rate of ten per cent. per annum, though the annual increase of population is less than three per cent.

But while the aggregate of exchanges is rapidly increasing, the profits of the exchanges tend steadily to diminish. It is the interest of the producers of all classes and climes to effect their exchanges with each other as directly and simply, at all events as cheaply, as possible. It matters little to the producers, as a whole, whether prices be low or high, if they be justly proportioned. If A, being a farmer in 1815, received a dollar per bushel for his corn, and bought the broadcloth for his coat at five dollars per yard, and now can get just such broadcloth for two dollars and a half, while his corn will bring but fifty cents per bushel, he is neither better nor worse for the change, all other things being equal. But if in 1815 he paid five bushels of corn for a yard of broadcloth, while the maker of the cloth received but four bushels, and now he gives the like five bushels per yard, but the maker receives four bushels and three pecks of corn, or their full equivalent, for every yard of cloth he turns off, then there has been a real improvement in the condition of the producers of cloth, if not of corn also. And, as intelligence is diffused, and knowledge is brought to bear upon the most intimate and homely relations of life, the cost of making exchanges, in other words, the charges and profits of non-producing traders, must and do decrease continually.

But this by no means proves that trade is poorer, nor that traders, as a class, do worse than formerly. It only proves that the number of traders cannot and does not increase in proportion with the increase of trade, without subjecting them to the necessity of taking smaller and still smaller profits. Every year the number of producers, and of customers of others' products increase, as also the aggregate of products exchanged. Every year the construction of canals, railroads, harbors, steamships, and other facilities of transportation and traffic, impels greater and still greater production, with a still larger extension of commercial exchanges. The neighborhood in the Ohio Valley, which was clad in homespun, and did not pay ten dollars to each person for all its purchases from others half a century since, now wears the fabrics of Old and New England, and is a liberal patron of the spice growers of both the Indies, the tea of China, the coffee of Brazil, and the fish of Newfoundland, probably paying thirty dollars per head for the products of other industry than its own, although the average range of prices is about half what it was in 1800. Trade has greatly increased, is increasing, and is bound to increase even more rapidly than it has ever yet done.

It is idle, therefore, to say that commerce is ruined, prostrate, because overdone. It is only the possibility of making fortunes by trade, with no decided capacity for the vocation, that is vanishing. The time is at hand, if not already upon us, when the mercantile is to take rank with the most intellectual and arduous of the liberal professions. The merchant of the next age must be a genius—a financier—a man born to be an efficient and beneficent distributer of the bounties of nature, of the products of human labor. If he lack these essential characteristics, let him aspire to be any thing else rather than a merchant, for his own sake and that of others. An incompetent doctor may live, though his patients should not; a poor lawyer may damage his clients, yet pocket their fees; a thick-headed merchant must inevitably ruin both himself and his trusting friends. The chances that he may blunder on and dodge bankruptcy for years have grown less and less until they are very nearly extinguished.

It is idle and mischievous to hope for large profits henceforth, save in rare, exceptional cases. The general diffusion of intelligence, and improvement of the facilities for direct exchanges between producer and consumer, render extensive and regular trade on the old basis of small sales and large profits impossible. If the flour-dealers of New England, the coal-dealers of New York, the shoe-dealers of Ohio, will not supply their customers at moderate prices, they provoke competitors to supplant them; or, this failing, they incite consumers to combine and buy at wholesale a cargo of flour, of coal, of shoes, for themselves. Any serious attempt to restore the old system of sales on long credits to doubtful customers, but at such high prices as will compensate for the risk and delay of payment, would only serve to impel the consuming classes to withdraw more and more of their custom from traders as a class, and effect more and more of their exchanges by agencies and arrangements of their own. The practical choice of the mercantile class lies not between large and small percentages on their sales, but between small ones and none.

But small advances on cost do not imply small profits.—On the contrary, there never was a time when larger profits are realized than may be now. Let us suppose, for example, that New England annually consumes ten thousand tons of Western bacon, and that the quantity so consumed is annually increasing. Now, if any Boston merchant at home can manage to become the channel of interchange between the producers and consumers of half those hams at an average net profit of 2 per cent., assuming the hams to be worth $150 per ton, that merchant or house would clear $15,000 annually on bacon alone. So with flour, groceries, and every thing else.

These, then, are the essential bases of a profitable and safe trade in the future; first, ability to supply the public demand on as favorable terms as any one else can offer; secondly, universal knowledge of the fact, and assurance that it may be relied on. Let a Boston dealer in flour, or meats, or cloths, or any thing else be able to supply New England with whatever he deals in at the lowest possible rate, and let all New England be assured of the fact that he can and *will* do so, and his fortune is made. No matter though his average net profit should range even below 1 per cent., his annual income must exceed his necessary expenses by thousands of dollars.

The merchant, therefore, who aims to succeed in business must aim at these two points: first, to be sure that he can satisfy a wide demand for the articles he deals in on the lowest practical terms; secondly, that every body within the proper scope of his business is made aware of his ability, and confident of his disposition to do so. These points attained, he has only to do his business properly as it comes in upon him, and his fortune is secure."

Having thus settled upon the general principles and prospects of trade, we shall proceed to consider in detail: First, *What constitutes ability to supply a public demand?* Secondly, *How to get customers? and* Thirdly, *The characteristics and duties of the merchant, or the true man of business.*

THE FIRST REQUISITE OF ABILITY IS A KNOWLEDGE OF THE BUSINESS.

Every business that is worthy of the name has two departments: its *science* to be understood by study, and its *art* to be acquired by practice. A knowledge of both is especially necessary to the complete education of the merchant. The number of good practical business men who have failed within the last fifty years is sufficient to show that the science or principles of business has not received the study and attention which it deserves. A knowledge of the theory of a profession gives stability to character, a disposition to act within known laws, checks the temptation to sacrifice principle for a temporary end, and throws around the dull details of practice an air of intellectuality that is exceedingly attractive to an ingenious mind. It does more. It gives wisdom in practice, and traces out consequences by the light of experience. What is science? "To know while any thing is taking place what *must* follow; in other words, to know the necessary consequence of what is going on at the present moment—that is science. To know, when any thing has occurred, what *must* have preceded; in other words, to know the necessary antecedents of what has occurred—that is science." It is the extracted essence of facts—the logical result deduced from repeated experiments.

Observation, *conversation*, and *reading* are the sources from which a knowledge of the theory of a profession is to be derived, The first two will furnish facts, while books will furnish facts and principles. The wisdom, touching negotiation or business, has not been entirely collected into writing, even at this day, though much has been done in late years—and the student of mercantile science is compelled in a degree to depend upon his own sagacity. He must, therefore, never forget that he has two eyes, two ears, and one tongue. He must be continually on the watch for ideas which may give him a clue to that labyrinth in which few have travelled safely, and thousands have been lost. Books on general or special business should be his vade mecum. They should be owned, read, and re-read. They contain the experience of men who have gone over the same or a similar road; or the thoughts of others as to its places of safety and of danger, based on the united experience of many. They cannot fail to furnish valuable hints; and may suddenly dart into his mind an idea that will be worth to him thousands of dollars. Books of history, facts, and principles, are always valuable. They deserve to be held in higher estimation by practical men than they are. They stimulate the mind to think, and suggest safe expedients in doubtful circumstances. There is unquestionably an analogy between all the various pursuits of mankind—between war and speculation—between statesmanship and the management of public bodies; and it has been remarked that those who have been distinguished for success in business are of the same stamp as those who are eminent in the walks of literature and science.

Every man and every store should have a library of select practical works. But many books are not desirable. It is the man of few books and much thought who wields power. A distinguished writer remarks that he never felt afraid to meet a man who has a large library. Those books should be selected which have a tendency to excite ideas in the mind of the reader, and to arouse the mental energies into action, and which afford deeper and clearer views of life and the business of life. Books are the sources from which the student should draw his first knowledge of his profession; and he should continue to draw from this fountain through life. "What you read to-day will soon be gone—expended or forgotten; and the mind must be continually filled up with new streams of knowledge. Even the ocean would be dried up, were the streams to be cut off which are constantly flowing into it. How few read enough to stock their minds. And the mind is no widow's cruise which fills with knowledge as fast as we empty it. 'It is the hand of the diligent which maketh rich.'"

But the knowledge of the *science* of his profession will not constitute any one *master of the art.* He must know not only how his trade should be performed, but how to perform it. He has a *habit* to acquire—a practical power and facility in the application of principles. This is a work of time, and the result of progressive drilling and repeated effort. This is especially true of the mercantile profession, and to this end an apprenticeship is necessary. In London, it is customary to pay a fee for being taught almost any trade or calling. It varies from $50 to $3,000. In mercantile business the fee is usually from $500 to $1500, according to the business, character of the house, and the means of the party applying. In the United States, apprentice fees are not customary. But they are given, in rare instances, for special reasons, as I have heard of the sum of $500 being paid for the opportunity to learn the art and mysteries of the silk business.

One of the most important objects to be acquired during apprenticeship, if not the most important, is a *judgment of the value of goods.* A man must possess this knowledge to do justice to his customers and to himself; and to avoid cheating and being cheated. The want of it will blast his reputation, and defeat the best laid plans for success. It is a defect that cannot be concealed. A shrewd seller will detect it in a buyer as quickly as an old banker will ferret out an accommodation bill; and, unfortunately, there are few who will not take advantage of it. He must, then, sell what he buys, an inferior article, for a better, and this is a sure way to get a bad name and drive away custom. It is a knowledge that can only be acquired, to perfection, in youth. A judgment taken in early is seldom lost, as a judgment taken in late is seldom good. Here the cultivation of the senses, of which I have before spoken, is especially valuable; here the Indian's habits of close observation, the blind man's acuteness of touch, are aids to fortune.

In the dry-goods business, a *retail store* is a better school, in which to attain this knowledge, than a wholesale house. The wholesale merchant buys of the manufacturer under a warranty, and the principal bone of contention is the price. He sells again to the retailer, with the same warranty, or the retailer may choose or reject, without stating reasons, so that the observer, however attentive, may learn nothing. In a retail store it is different. The frugal housewife, who may be a customer of the retailer, is not so taciturn and credulous; warranties will not satisfy her; she "wants a patch to try;" and if soap, boiling, and half a day's hard labor will change it, she triumphantly returns it in vindication of her foresight. This may be called positive evidence. Besides this, there are a hundred observations and objections made by different customers, in a retail store, which one person would never think of, and which the young man who is desirous of improvement should use as suggestions for examination. He knows the first cost of the goods; he sees what gain or what loss is made; he is led to inquire into the reason of the difference; sees where they are deficient, and if he is careful in his observations, he is naturally led to have a good judgment of their value.

Book-keeping, *business correspondence*, and their adjuncts, are of essential importance in a mercantile education. They are now regarded as such, and no deficiency need be noted. Books have been called the tradesman's repeating-clock, to tell him how he goes on. The system of book-keeping by double entry is, perhaps, the most beautiful one in the wide domain of literature or science. Were it less common, it would be the admiration of the learned world.

The object of speech or writing is to convey our thoughts so that another may understand them. Business correspondence should be plain, clear, and concise. Fine writing is ridiculous; verbose writing is tedious; while the terse, curt style, which some use, is affected. The accomplished business man should make it a point to familiarize himself with the peculiar technical terms of art which are found in every trade or calling, while he should avoid using those of his own profession when writing to men in a different occupation. Singular mistakes have occurred from a want of this understanding. I will mention one: "A brick-maker, being hired by a brewer to make some brick for him at his country-house, wrote to the brewer that he could not go forward unless he had two or three loads of *Spanish*; that otherwise his brick would cost him six or seven chaldrons of coal extra, and the bricks would not be so good, and hard neither, by a great deal, when they were burnt. The brewer hereupon sends down two cart-loads, with about twelve hogsheads or casks of molasses, which frightened the brick-maker almost out of his senses. The case was this: The brewers formerly mixed molasses with the ale to sweeten it, and abate the quantity of malt, molasses being at that time much cheaper, and this they called Spanish, not being willing their customers should know it. Again, the brickmakers, all about London, mix sea-coal ashes or laystal stuff as we call it, with their clay, and by that shift, save eight chaldrons of coals out of eleven, to the burning of 100,000 bricks in proportion to what other people burn them with; and these ashes they call Spanish; but neither the brewer on the one hand, nor the brickmaker on the other, understood any other of it than as it related to his separate business."

The object of apprenticeship is to understand a special business *thoroughly*. A man cannot be said to understand a business thoroughly, unless he is acquainted with its remote as well as its immediate connections. He must not only be a good judge of the article in which he deals, but he should know where they are manufactured, of what, and the manufacturer's prices, how bought at first hand, the best markets to buy and to sell in, the rate of duties, &c. This information it is sometimes difficult to acquire, but "where there is a will there is a way." It is necessary in order to buy right. In importing houses, it is a customary thing to see men swallow down a story that an article cost $2 50, to import which cost, probably, $1, and then again haggle about the price of another article which is offered at less than cost of importation. To be entitled to the distinction of understanding a business *thoroughly*, he must be able to judge, too, at all times, from his own resources—that is, independently of his neighbor's opinion—of the condition and prospects of his business in all its relations. If this be true, which I think the majority will admit, I will not hazard the popularity of this book by mentioning the number of those who *do* understand their business *thoroughly*. That there is a lamentable deficiency in this respect, is evidenced by those extraordinary fluctuations in price so often witnessed, and by the fact that panics can frequently be manufactured at will by speculating men, whenever sufficient time has elapsed after a previous one, for traders to become frightened at their own prosperity. How often have we witnessed fluctuations in the price of articles, for which none could account! How often, when the political and commercial skies appeared as calm as a summer's day, have we suddenly heard the cry of hard times rung out, and felt the reality follow, for which the wisest could not assign a rational cause! Why is this? What are called *crises* in the commercial world are, in my opinion, the result mainly of two causes; a want of accurate knowledge among the majority of trading men respecting the true condition of things; and, in addition, the consciousness of a general disregard of prudence in extending liabilities far beyond capital. Consequently, when a few influential speculators, seeking, perhaps, more lucrative investments for their money, aided by a few respectable newspapers, begin their dire forebodings, followed by stout asseverations that their predictions have come true, fear seizes hold of men's minds, and they create the ruin they would fain avert. Fluctuations in prices must and will occur—money will be at certain times less abundant than at others—but the laws that regulate supply and demand, if left to the operation of natural causes, or such as could be foreseen by all if all were attentive observers, are as regular as the ebb and flow of the tides. Did each trader, then, fortify himself by an accurate knowledge of the business in which he is engaged, all the arts of speculators in the country could not produce a sudden nor extraordinary rise or fall in the prices of his merchandize. Did each business man cease the petty retailing of his neighbor's opinions as facts, as well as maintain at all times, or rather without regard to times, a prudent proportion of liabilities to capital in the management of his business, all the inventions and croakings of the stock-jobbers of the world could not produce a panic. "Among the innumerable and troublesome ills of life," observes the Dry Goods Reporter, and we commend these remarks to the consideration of merchants as a matter of vital importance, "that of slackness, or a want of promptitude in our business, stands pre-eminent. A common feeling prevails among men of every variety of trade, more especially those termed the dry goods branch, that the opinion of our neighbor in business, relative to the condition of the market for purchasing and selling, will enable us to better judge of the greatest profit and loss. This, to a limited extent, may be true; but only true to the man who has no other sources of information. It is the want of a system in such people's method of doing business—a careful concern troubles them relative to paying out a few shillings for information which, in many instances, would add hundreds of dollars to their profits. There is true merit in the determination to keep our expenses within a reasonable limit, but still there is manifest danger of damming up, with avarice, some streams that would mingle and swell the tide of accumulation. If there is any one worthy of success, in the purchasing and selling pursuits, it is, and must reasonably be, the man who looks into the resources—the outgoes and incomes of the branch of business that sways his investments. The manufacturer is accustomed to make a calculation of the cost of raw material, of the labor bestowed, the waste in manufacturing, the transportation, commissions, and the numerous little expenses attending the production and sale of the article he designs to fabricate. The mechanic and artist work by fixed rules—and there is, as a general thing, so much intelligence among the two classes mentioned, that they can inform you of the cost and amount at all times of every article they produce; and this it is that enables them to transact their business with such success. It is a fact, sustained by abundant proof, in nearly all manufacturing towns, that the mechanics are the wealthiest citizens. We speak of them as a body—we do not intend to advance the idea that they, as individuals, hold the greatest amount of wealth; nor do we think to introduce the jobbers—but allude more particularly to the retailers. The reason we assign for the existing evil, is a want of system and self-reliance. Let that trader, who has sunk the last twelve months as many hundred dollars, lean no longer upon the opinions of a few, who regulate his purchases and post him up, on the condition of the large markets. The means are abundant for a perfect analysis of the whole trade, both on a small and a large scale; by watching closely the amount of importations and the exports, we may know at all times the bulk and styles in the markets—and from the weekly auction sales of New York, Boston and Philadelphia (through which beats the pulse of the market,) we may calculate upon the absolute demand and surplus of goods. We ourselves might spend the whole week in the market, inquiring the prices of A. B and C, and return to our sanctum as lean as we went out; but when we strike at the resources of the producers, the manufacturer's orders, and trace through the domestic and importing avenues the amount of goods coming forward, we have a source of information which is tangible and entirely reliable. Such sources cultivate self-reliance—induce men to think and act upon a sure basis. The loss and gain may be calculated upon to a single farthing. We can only add, that a correct knowledge of any branch of business in which we engage will secure prosperity, if promptly attended to."*

* Among the sources of reliable statistical information may be mentioned, the two principal commercial magazines of the country—the *Mercnant's Magazine* of New York, and *De Bow's Review of the Southern and Wtstern States*, conducted by J. D. B. De Bow, Professor of Political Economy, &c., in the University of Louisiana, and published at New Or-

But even this knowledge is not enough to complete the education of the accomplished business man. He should understand more than his special business. "I have taken," says Bacon in a letter, written when he was only thirty-one, to his uncle, Lord Burleigh, "I have taken all knowledge to be my province." A merchant should take all business to be his province. He should have a familiar acquaintance with one or more kinds of business, akin to his own, and a general acquaintance with all trades and business. In the course of a lifetime, he will be called upon to deal frequently with men out of his line, and without this acquaintance he cannot deal advantageously or satisfactorily. And again, wars, embargoes, inventions, and excessive competition may cause a falling off of his special business; and he who possesses this knowledge can more readily adapt himself to another business than one who has neglected this precaution. When Napoleon's laws and decrees so seriously deranged the commerce of England, pressing necessity forced the merchants, to advise that every one should make himself master of two trades.

Having completed the usual term of apprenticeship, and laid the foundation of a business education, to be perfected by experience, the next grave question that will occur to a young man will

leans. The former is well known to the mercantile community; but the latter, though extensively patronized, and a standard authority at the South, has not received from the merchants of the North that support which an enlightened regard to their own interests would seem to demand. The statistical information embodied in its pages respecting the staples of the South and West, which form the basis of a great part of all our leading commercial transactions, is immense. More than three large volumes have been published upon COTTON alone, and more than a thousand pages upon SUGAR. In point of literary merit too, it is unsurpassed. The leading articles have been written with a vigor of thought and purity of style not excelled, if equalled in the annals of commercial literature, and the intellectual tastes fostered by them are exceedingly favorable to mental growth and worldly prosperity. Mr. De Bow, I have learned, will shortly publish a condensation of all the important papers, articles, and statistics, that have appeared in the twelve published volumes of his Review, in *three*, to be entitled; "The INDUSTRIAL RESOURCES OF THE SOUTHERN AND WESTERN STATES," and I sincerely trust that no intelligent merchant will overlook the advantages he will enjoy, in possessing this vast repository of reliable and valuable information.

be whether he shall embark in business on his own account, or seek a situation in the employ of another. The two main points that will govern his decision in this matter, will be the *amount of his capital*, and the *probable amount of his sales and net profits.*

CAPITAL.—This, in a broad sense, means labor accumulated in such form as to facilitate future production. In a commercial sense, it means the stock of merchandise, or money which an individual or company originally puts into the business, or that part which an individual contributes to the trading stock of a partnership when it is *first* formed. Mercantile transactions are so varied in nature and extent that no certain amount which an individual should possess can be suggested. The only rule that can be given is, *that the capital should be adequate to the business—that it should be increased in proportion to the business, or the business be kept down to a level with the capital.*

No one is justified in starting a business without the moderate capital usually required to carry it on, trusting to accommodations and credit for success. It has been stated that four-fifths of the men who are wealthy commenced business on borrowed capital.—This may be true, but it was actually capital—borrowed for no definite period, or such length of time that it could be paid out of the profits of the business, and not from the sales of stock. No one who has tried doing a business without a suitable capital, even if he has succeeded, will advise another to attempt it. It involves an amount of anxiety, a degree of labor, embarrassment, and hazard, which is painful to reflect upon. To do a business altogether on credit requires a fortunate combination of circumstances, to make it successful, that no prudent man would predict.

There are several important questions relating to the management of capital, that deserve consideration. One very important one is, What proportion should capital bear to liabilities in a mercantile business? In other words, how far is it prudent for a man to extend his purchases beyond his actual capital? I have taken considerable pains to learn something on this subject, but cannot boast of my success. In banking, the safe rule has been laid down to be, the proportion of three to one. Gilbart, manager of the London and Westminster Bank, says, in his *Treatise on Banking*, "Although the proportion which the capital of a bank should bear to its liabilities may vary with different banks, perhaps one would not go far astray in saying that it should never be less than one-third of its liabilities. I would exclude, however, from this comparison, all liabilities, except those arising from notes and deposits. If the notes and deposits together amount to more than three times the amount of the paid-up capital, the bank should call up more capital." In New England, the safe limit, as I am informed by David M. Balfour, Esq., is considered to be that of *two* to one. In business, one of the most eminent bankers in Europe has given it as his deliberate opinion that a man should not extend his business to more than *three* times the amount of his capital, and if it be a large business, to not more than *twice* his capital.—I presume, however, that the rule must vary with different kinds of business; but there is a limit in each particular business beyond which it is not prudent to go. A man has the right to risk his own capital, but he has no right to risk the property of others without their consent, and he can only honestly extend his business at any time, so that if his property should suddenly depreciate in value to the ordinary level of low prices, and he should meet with the average percentage of losses by bad debts, and other risks incidental to the business, he would still be able to pay his debts.—Without accurate information on these points, I think that a man whose liabilities are already three times the amount of his capital, should be extremely cautious in extending his purchases, however inviting the speculation may appear; and that in the taking and giving of credit, he cannot calculate with any degree of certainty in being able to meet his payments promptly, except by giving one-third less credit than he takes.*

* Extract from a private letter of the Hon. Horace Greeley, dated April 22, 1852: "The extent to which a trader may innocently involve himself in debt has been discussed by able writers, with varying conclusions. It is manifestly impossible to prescribe any arbitrary rule on this subject. One man may owe three times the amount of his capital, yet be perfectly and impregnably solvent, while another who owes only twice the amount of his capital may fail, and seriously injure his creditors. A farmer worth

Another question is, *How should a surplus capital be invested?* When profits have accumulated, and the business does not demand an immediate increase of capital, or when the entire capital, ordinarily required, is not in use, the balance is called a surplus capital. This should be invested in a good mercantile security, and held as a reserve for use when it may be needed, but I doubt whether all who are engaged in business have a clear conception of *what constitutes a good mercantile security.* I have known frequent instances of great embarrassment arising from a misconception of this point. Many whose lamentations are most mournful when cramped with limited means, as soon as the pressure is a little removed, will invest their surplus funds in such way, that the next news is a protest. Some buy a lot, but, as they quickly discover that a lot without an improvement is an expense, so the sooner they build the better, and they withdraw a part of the capital actually needed in their business, in the forlorn hope of replacing it by increased profits. Others, again, turn land speculators, and buy several lots, or a country seat, paying part cash, giving a mortgage for the balance; or they will engage in an additional business, in either case, their creditors can calculate with considerable certainty that they must shortly renew their notes, or receive a protest. It must be borne in mind that capital is of two kinds, *fixed* and *floating.* The distinction between them is, that all commodities or improvements, for which the owners only receive rent or interest, constitute fixed capital, as houses, land, ships, machinery, &c.; and all commodities, the *entire* cost of which is replaced out of the current income, are floating capital. The former are stationary, yield only income,

but $1,500, may buy a farm worth $5,000, pay $1,000 down, and give a mortgage for the balance, being perfectly solvent in any probable event; while he, who being worth $10,000 should invest $20,000 in shipments to California, might be justly chargeable with reckless and culpable gambling, with other men's property as his stock. The obvious rule is that no man has a right to hazard other men's property, without fairly apprising his creditors of the nature and extent of the risk, and obtaining their consent to the measure. And then, the debtor should be careful that he incur no responsibility that he cannot fully justify to his own conscience, and does not unalterably purpose to discharge."

and are slow of transfer; the latter are constantly circulating, and easily convertible into cash. A reserve capital should always be easily convertible into money, as the exigencies of trade may require, and hence it should always be invested in those commodities which constitute the floating capital of a country, as stocks, merchandise, notes, bills of exchange, &c. There are few men in this country who have more cash than they can advantageously use in their business; and there is always an abundance of good floating securities for temporary investment. Cash, and property, in merchandising, are two different things, as the business of the trader and that of the capitalist are different pursuits. The advice of the Irishman is directly applicable to men in trade, in the management of their cash: "Be aisy, and if you can't be aisy, be as aisy as you can;" and we may add, when you are easy keep easy.

To invest their surplus capital in such a way that it will be a prop and not an injury to their business, is a matter for careful consideration by men in all kinds of business, whether traders, mechanics, or manufacturers; but what constitutes a proper mercantile security is a consideration of the first importance to *produce and commission merchants*, and to all who, being in the practice of making advances on consignments, are especially liable to error on this point. The *London Economist*, some time since, contained the true doctrine on the subject. It is quite legitimate, it says, for a merchant residing at home to advance his capital on produce consigned to him abroad, or for a merchant residing abroad to advance his capital to the producer on the spot, in anticipation of the future sales of the produce prior to its shipment. And it may even be legitimate to make advances on a growing crop, especially when the state of the law admits of an assignment of such property in that state, and secures its delivery, and when the commodity does not require to pass through a manufacturing process before it is ready for market. But beyond this point, it is impossible the merchant can pass without great hazard; or at least without accepting what cannot be called a good mercantile security. Up to that point, the repayment of his capital is guaranteed by the ultimate sale of the produce he holds, either in the form of bills of lading, dock warrants, or bills of exchange, securities representing his advances until the actual capital is again returned to him. But the moment the merchant passes this point in his advances to producers, the moment he lends money for the purchase of implements, or machinery, or land, or its improvements, on the security of the estate or its plant, that moment he has invested his money in a fixed, in the place of floating security, which is inconsistent with his occupation as a merchant, and is calculated to be productive of great danger in the case of pressure in the money market, especially if he is otherwise availing himself much of his own credit in his business. From a neglect of this plain rule in commerce, there have been greater losses sustained than from any other cause. * * * It is not difficult to discover the sort of irresistible means by which houses become implicated in such securities, and get their capital inconveniently locked up. First, a merchant advances on the produce of the planter; next, competition and the urgent requests of the planter induce him to advance on the growing crop before it is in. All experience has proved that the first advance of this kind becomes a precursor of other advances which are necessary to secure the first; until, on the arrival of a period of pressure, the merchant finds that his capital, instead of being available as it was when in proper mercantile securities, is locked up in unavailable securities abroad, and though he may show a large balance of property in his favor, he is reduced to the painful necessity of suspending payment.

PROBABLE SALES.—These can only be arrived at by calculation founded on data exclusively personal. The considerations which should enter into this calculation are agreeably detailed in the following pertinent anecdote, related by the editor of the *Dry-Goods Reporter:* "A young friend of ours called on us the other day in high glee; he was about concluding arrangements with two others to embark in the jobbing trade, and was quite sanguine of brilliant success. As we did not express full faith in his anticipations, he rather chided us for our doubts, whereupon we questioned him a little as to his prospects. At our suggestion, he took pen and paper and put down first all his proposed expenses. We could see that he had not done this before, as he seemed quite startled to find that even at the moderate estimates he had made, the total expenses for rent, clerk hire, and living of the several partners mounted to the snug sum of $8,200. 'Now for the amount of business,' said we. 'Oh, as to that,' he replied, 'we *hope* to sell $300,000 per annum.' 'But what amount of trade do all of you at present influence?' we asked. 'Make now a careful estimate of the business you can rely upon with some degree of certainty.' He did so, and, to his surprise, it did not quite reach $125,000. 'Now what profit can you average upon this?' After some debate, this was set down at 7½ *per cent.* This gave the sum of $9,375. 'Now what shall we call the losses?' These were settled at 2½ *per cent.* on sales, amounting to $3,125, leaving the net income at $6,250 or $1950 *less* than enough to pay his estimated expenses. He left us proposing to show the estimate to his colleagues. He did so, and, after figuring awhile without arriving at any more satisfactory result, they finally abandoned the undertaking. We have no hesitation in saying that if all who are about to embark in trade would thus boldly look at the figures instead of closing their eyes and *hoping* for the best, we should hear of fewer failures among business men, and there would be less complaint that 'trade is overdone.'"

We will presume that *our* friend can make better figures, or that he has a stronger faith *in things not seen*, and the next step is the selection of a

STORE.—The proper situation of a store is a matter of some importance. It should be situated where the principal stores in the same line of business are. It is a great mistake to choose a location in a *city* because there are none others of the same trade in the immediate neighborhood. Good customers make their purchases where the leading stores are, and, by keeping together, all will do better. Fair competition is the life of trade. Apparent opposition yet secret partnership, has frequently made fortunes for both. This is pleasantly illustrated in the following anecdote of personal experience related by a stage-coach traveller :—

"When I was a young man," said he, "I set up in the hat trade, and took a store in London, where there was not a hat store within a quarter of a mile, thinking I should do more where there were no others; but I found that, at the end of the year, all that I made might have been put into the corner of my small eye, and not injured its sight. I sat down, one day, and, after thinking that my lot was a mighty hard one, told my boy that I was going out awhile, and that he must keep a sharp lookout for customers. I went down town, and, looking around, found that two or three hatters were driving a very good trade very near together, and passing in to one store, I found its owner quite a talkative man. We put our heads together, and in the course of a week, the store directly opposite his received my stock in trade, and a coat of blue paint on the outside, while his received a coat of green. The first day I did nothing but stand at the door, and look pouty at the green store, and my friend Blake stood on his steps looking ditto at me. As people came in, I commenced running down the green store, and Blake always run the blue; so between us both we built up a trade that was quite respectable. People having taken sides, and new-comers always purchasing of one or the other, we gradually grew rich, and at the end of some dozen years, we settled up, and I found that opposition, or apparently so, had made my fortune." A retail store should be established on some leading thoroughfare. This has been considered essential to success. It has also been strongly recommended to secure permanency in a situation once fixed upon, by a *lease*. Steady improvements in a retail business are invariably *local*, that is, they follow the stand, and not the man. In a word, says some one, if your business depends upon customers, get them and keep them by staying where you are. Do not listen to the advice which certain officious friends and foolish people are continually in the habit of offering: "Don't hamper yourself with a lease," say they, which being interpreted into any thing intelligible, means, "Don't secure the only means of security." A lease to a trader is what an anchor is to a ship, the only *holdfast* to be relied on.

A store should be *plain*, *light*, and *well-ventilated*. It is not necessary that it be a handsome building; it is not necessary that it be handsomely fitted up. Fine fixtures and expensive ornament are out of place in a business house. It is a useless expenditure of capital, and can only be justified on the plea of custom. In the

European cities, expensive decoration is carried to an unreasonable extent. A pastry-cook's shop in London, with a stock worth one hundred dollars, will spend $1500 in fixtures. It is a practice that should meet with no encouragement in this republican country. It is a device of rich old traders to monopolize a business by throwing obstacles in the way of men with limited capital; and it is a reprehensible device. Marble palaces, granite buildings, pediments, columns, tiled floors, painting, gilding, &c., have a tendency to foster a spirit of extravagance in trade that leads to ruin. These are rarely the ambitious reachings of men who have commenced life with a solid capital, or made their wealth by laudable means. "Live and let live," is their motto. Charities and city improvements in the way of fine *public* buildings, hotels, theatres, museums, banks, parks, absorb all *their* means. Fine stores and fine churches they justly consider as objectionable, the one keeping men out of business, and the other out of heaven.

Light is a consideration worthy of attention in the selection of a store. Customers look upon a dark store with suspicion; they are fearful they may deceive themselves, and frequently leave without purchasing for no other reason. Sunlight is also a matter of economy, as Franklin has conclusively shown, in one of his essays, that it is cheaper than lamp-light, and I presume gas-light. It imparts a cheerful, pleasant appearance to the store, without that artificial glare produced by elaborate ornament, which sensible people always look upon as deceptive, and, what is of more importance still, it promotes cheerfulness of mind in the employees, which is an essential ingredient of politeness. "Light is sweet, and a pleasant thing it is for the eyes to behold the sun."

Light is a desideratum that cannot always be obtained in cities to a desirable degree; but, were it insisted upon more than it is, an improvement would be effected. The counting house should be light. Abundance of light prevents mistakes both in money and accounts, and saves the time that would be employed in the discovery of errors. The desk of the bookkeeper should be placed so that the window will be on his left hand. In a retail store, a capacious double window is very desirable, as it admits of variety and display

Another consideration of especial importance is *ventilation.* Air kills more than the sword, is the translation of a Latin proverb. Medical men have written volumes on the advantages of a free circulation of air, and the unwholesomeness of confined apartments and crowded cities. In such cases, a person afflicted with consumption of the lungs may communicate the complaint to others, as they must inhale the same atmosphere he has breathed out. Ventilation is of importance to the merchant in the construction of his ships, his warehouse, his counting-house, and his residence. It is well known that there are many commodities which a confined air will effect; some change their qualities, others are predisposed by it to decay, and some are actually destroyed. Here is a field for the exercise of science. It is also well known that a free circulation of air is necessary to decarbonize the blood, to preserve the health, and that it will prevent the liability to take cold. Where a store or warehouse is so unfavorably located as not to allow of a natural ventilation, it may be remedied by an artificial circulation.

The treatises of Reid or of Wyman, on this subject, deserve a perusal.

As much of the time of the merchant must necessarily be spent where the air is not in its purest or freest state, *the situation of a residence* is a matter of great importance. The driest situation in a city is preferable to others; a situation whence the water flows, and where the atmosphere is most exempt from surrounding contamination. The vicinage of graveyards, marshy grounds, and stagnant pools should be avoided. Too many trees, with dense foliage, around a dwelling, obstruct the free currents of air, and cause moist and unhealthy exhalations. In the country, the most proper site for building is "in high places and in an excellent prospect;" a dry sandy plat, rather hilly and full of "downs," is preferable to the best soil.

The old physicians recommended that the front of the house should be to the south, and one especially approves "the descent of a hill south or southeast, with trees to the north, so that it be well watered; a condition in all sites which must not be omitted." The best sites for chamber windows, says another, in my judgment, are north, east, south, and which is the worst, west. Lemnius attributes so much to air, and "rectifying of wind and windows," that he holds it alone sufficient to make a man sick or well; to alter body and mind. "A clear air cheers up the spirits, exhilarates the mind; a thick, black, misty, tempestuous, contracts, overthrows. Great heed is, therefore, to be taken how we place our windows, lights, and houses; how we let in or exclude this ambient air. The Egyptians, to avoid immoderate heat, make their windows on the top of the house like chimneys, with two tunnels, to draw a thorough air. Many excellent means are invented to correct nature by art. If none of these courses help, the best way is to make artificial air, which howsoever is profitable and good, still to be made hot and moist, and to be seasoned with hot perfumes, pleasant and lightsome as it may be; to have roses, violets, and sweet-smelling flowers in their windows; a vessel of warm water to evaporate in the room, which will make a more delightful perfume, if there be added orange-flowers, pills of citrons, rosemary, cloves, bays, rosewater, rose-vinegar, benzoin, laudanum, styrax, and such like gums, which make a pleasant and acceptable perfume."

Having made due provision for what may be considered as incidental to the building, it will now become necessary *to arrange the goods*, so as to enable any given number of clerks to discharge their duties with the greatest efficiency, and so as best to attract the public eye. Little can be said on this subject that is applicable to merchandizing in general, as much will depend on the nature and extent of business, and other circumstances. Besides, it is a matter that has been carried to a great degree of perfection. Some of our first-class dry-goods stores are a model of order and method in this respect. Every department in the store is alphabetically arranged. The shelves and rows of goods, in each department, are numbered, and upon a tag attached to the goods are marked the letter of the department, the number of the shelf, and row on that shelf to which such piece of goods belongs. The respective counters are designated by some imaginary color, and the yard-stick and counter-brush belonging to that counter are painted to correspond. Each establishment has a tool-closet, with a small workbench in it, and every tool has its place. All wrapping-paper, as soon as it is brought into the store, is taken into the cellar, where boys cut it into sizes to suit the parcels of the different departments, and carried there. All pieces too small for use are put into a sack, and reserved for sale. The cashier or bookkeeper is responsible for all worthless money that he takes, and is paid an extra sum for this responsibility. Pages are kept to carry the bills and change from the cashier's desk to the customer, so that the salesman is not obliged to leave the counter. The proprietor's desk is on an elevated platform, facing the front, that overlooks every section of the retail department, and from this desk acoustic tubes communicate with every department in the building, by which a person in any part of it, from the garret to the cellar, may communicate with the principal without leaving his station. Every salesman has a small book in which he enters his sales as soon as made, on which his salary is calculated as a percentage, so that, at all times, the proprietor can compare their respective merits and efficacy. These matters may appear trifling; but it is by attention to small things that large fortunes are made

Another subject of great importance is the selection and appointment of

CLERKS.—A man's powers are too limited to carry on an extensive business with his own resources alone, and he is compelled to call in the assistance of others. His selection of coadjutors may make or mar his fortune.

The chief qualifications to be sought for in a clerk, next to ability, are *honesty* and *politeness*. To ascertain the existence of honesty, no positive rule can be given. It is proper "to inquire into the parentage of the candidate. For although honesty and dishonesty do not run in the blood, yet it is probable that religious and virtuous parents have given their children a religious and virtuous education; and a youth who has been accustomed to see examples of excellence at home, will be most likely to exhibit those excellences in his own conduct. A high degree of moral principle is in itself a necessary qualification in a post of trust and responsibility, and it is usually associated with a cultivated and improved state of the intellectual faculties If there be in the character not only sense and soundness, but virtue of a high order, then, however little appearance there may be of talent, a certain portion of wisdom may be relied upon almost implicitly. For the correspondence of wisdom and goodness are manifold; and that they will accompany each other may be inferred, not only because men's wisdom makes them good, but also because their goodness makes them wise. Although, therefore, simple goodness does not imply every sort of wisdom, it unerringly implies some essential conditions of wisdom; it implies *a negative on folly, and an exercised judgment, within such limits as nature shall have prescribed to the capacity.*"*

Politeness of manner, and patience, or a serenity of temper which nothing can disturb, are essential qualifications of a good clerk. An impertinent, impudent, or ill-tempered clerk may drive away more custom than ten good men can bring together. Serenity of temper is a virtue of which all men cannot boast—and probably without serious derogation of their character or abilities; but it is a fundamental constituent in the character of a clerk and a business man. To command the temper is one of the first great lessons to be learned in practical life. Demetrius, King of Macedon, had a petition offered him again and again by an old woman, and always answered he had no leisure. Whereupon the woman said aloud in his presence, "Why, then, give over to be a king." We may say the same to clerks: If you can't be polite and patient, "give over" clerking. Good health and regular exercise are necessary to the maintenance of a serene temper. A tendency to *embonpoint* or fatness is likely to be associated with mildness of disposition. Lean men are not always patient and long-suffering. Cæsar noted this when he said

> "I fear him not; but were my name
> Liable to fear, I know no man I would avoid
> So soon as that *spare* Cassius."

Lean men, however, have generally by far the most talent, and manifest the greatest perseverance in enterprises that afford scope for ability. A breadth between the eye-brows is said to denote calmness; the opposite, perseverance. Impertinence or impudence

* Taylor's "Statesman."

in any one, or to any one, admits of no excuse, and should not be tolerated for a moment. Some of our public offices, transportation companies, &c., occasionally afford disgusting examples of impertinence, and they do themselves great injustice in tolerating it.

Clerks should be faithful to their employers, and employers should concern themselves in the welfare of their clerks. Faithfulness does not consist in the mere doing of things which we are *obliged* to do; but in the performance of acts, and in the exercise of care, which we are *not obliged* to do, and for which we receive no direct remuneration. Many young men seem to think that when they labor at the employment regularly assigned them, it is all that should be expected. It is, probably, all that *is* expected; but a faithful clerk will not, therefore, neglect opportunities, when by a little extra labor—arranging a few parcels of goods, or putting down an item of account—he can do his employer great service. Some houses, I trust they are few, make it a practice to keep their clerks on their feet all the time, engaged at something, whether there is any thing of importance to be done or not. This is a most unwise and unfeeling plan. When the body is wearied and exhausted, it is almost impossible to summon that cheerfulness of spirit which is necessary to please and be pleased. Clerks should have all the rest they can get, without neglecting essential duties. Every store, in my opinion, should have a select library of practical works, to which those who choose can have access. It is a great advantage to business men to have educated and intelligent assistants. We may use the observation of a bank manager, in advocating libraries in banks for the use of clerks: "Their superior knowledge is always useful; the mental discipline they have acquired improves their business habits; and, possessing within themselves a constant source of enjoyment, they are the less likely to indulge in those expensive pleasures which are the usual temptations to neglect and dishonesty." A library has since been introduced into the Bank of England and the principal London banks, for the especial use of the clerks. I think there are stronger reasons for the introduction of a select business library into stores, than into banks. Clerks in stores are usually less constantly occupied than in banks, and are confined for a longer period of time. The time which they can have to themselves should be devoted to physical exercise in the open air, and hence without a library they are likely to miss all opportunity for improving their minds by reading. Gambols or quarrels, in hours of leisure, should be discouraged.

Clerking, at the present day, is not one of the speediest ways to "put money in thy purse." Competition has not only increased the difficulty of obtaining a situation, but has reduced the *average rate of compensation.* It is difficult to say whether it is wise in merchants to allow competition to influence the amount of a clerk's salary or not. It would seem more proper to fix the amount of the salary sufficient to insure contentment in the situation, and require qualifications of zeal and efficiency that will be worth it. Competition should merely enlarge the field for making a proper selection. It certainly is not wise to pay a salary below a standard of living suitable to the sphere of society in which they are expected to move. When clerks are chosen for the amount of trade they can influence, it is sometimes the practice to pay them only a commission on sales. This arrangement rarely lasts long, or ends satisfactorily. The interests of the clerk and the employer are, in a manner antagonistical. It is the interest of the one to sell to every body, and of the other only to good men, and where the latter refuses to ratify a sale which he may think doubtful, the clerk is apt to consider himself defrauded. A certain fixed salary, with a percentage on sales above a certain amount, is generally more satisfactory. Mr. Taylor, in his "Statesman," makes some remarks in relation to the appointment of clerks in public offices which we may apply to mercantile life. "*There is no position so strong as that of a man who stands upon his head:* and if he be not *induced* to the activity of just thinking and clear reasoning, he will hardly be *coerced* to it. Upon the whole, therefore, I would say that what is most conducive to good appointments in the first instance, and thenceforward to deriving benefit from them, is to offer small remuneration to the beginner, *with successive expectancies proportioned to the merits which he shall manifest, and of such increasing amount as shall be calculated to keep easy, through the progressive wants of single and married life, the mind of a prudent man.*"

Clerks should always share in the prosperity of a house, as they must consent to share in its ill fortune. *Gratuities* quicken zeal, strengthen fidelity, and kindle a friendship "which neither heat nor cold, nor misery, nor place, nor destiny, can alter or diminish." Gratuities, kind words, and a manifestation of interest in his welfare, go further towards making a good clerk than a thousand business precepts. They give "a shock of pleasure to the frame more exquisite than Nectarine juice." Harsh words—a display of passion—towards those who, by the nature of their situation can make no defence, are not only galling to a sensitive mind, but often lead to future evils which no opposite influences can counteract.

An old and faithful clerk is a tried friend. He should never be forgotten. I envy not the man who, while accumulating his thousands, increasing in prosperity, forgets those who have borne the heat of the battle with him: I despise the man who, when he retires perhaps to a country seat to enjoy his ease and luxuries, cares not that those who have contributed to his prosperity must seek some meaner court or alley to reduce the expenses of an increasing family. His riches come not by right, and his end will be that of a fool. The munificent charities of Girard are merely the Egyptian spices that embalm the fame of a loathsome carcase, for he forgot the charities due to long service, and buried the heart of the man in the money-bags of the merchant.

Masters, give unto your servants that which is just and equal; knowing that ye also have a Master in heaven.—Col. iv. 1.

CHAPTER VII.

GETTING MONEY BY MERCHANDIZING—Continued

Buying and Selling.—[We hoped to consider this part of our subject with comfortable feelings, but the following picture, drawn by the editor of the *Dry-Goods Reporter*, has given us a "chill."]

"The manufacturer will over-estimate his goods, that his agent may get a good price for them. The commission merchant will misrepresent his stock, or profess to have made a cash advance, when he is all the while chuckling over the sale. He will go out with a sample card of the last case to close an invoice, when he has a few more of the same sort left. He will assert, probably, that he has just sold to A, B, & C large bills of the same kinds of goods, at much higher prices than he is now asking (all of which is imaginary or grossly exaggerated), or that the house addressed (upon which he assumes a very deferential air) is the only house to which he would offer the article in question at so low a rate. The importer will look you full in the face, and assure you that his goods *cost* him *more* than he is asking you; when, for more, you should, in truth, read *less;* or, if he have hold of a very green 'un, will pass off stale goods, which have kept shop most pertinaciously for years, as *new styles* just brought out. The jobber will go from house to house, when he is purchasing, cheapening goods; telling A that B is underselling him, inflicting the same tale on B, with a positive assurance that A has offered him the same goods at less price than B is now asking, and threatening C & D, alternately, to cease buying from them, unless each will do as well by him as he boasts he can obtain of the other. Sometimes, if he has bought a case or bale of goods a little too high, or when he has them at home, his clerks (all of whom are called to give an opinion upon it) think he has paid too much, he will send the bill back, asking a deduction, *saying* he has seen the goods elsewhere at less prices, when the fact is, he has not seen them in any other store, and does not know where else to look for them. The retailer goes about to buy in the same way, repeating many imaginary offers of goods which have been made to him at extra low prices, and which it is a wonder he did not buy, so much does the price seem under the market. And yet, when he comes to sell out those very goods, how oblivious is he of the exceeding liberal terms at which he could have purchased them! How valuable they have become! How *cheap* do the goods look to him now that he pronounced so very *dear* when he purchased them! What romances will he tell about the cost, the colors, or the quality when displaying them to a customer!

"Is that the lowest you can take for these lawns, Mr. Scissors?"

"Yes, Miss, the very best, and a bargain they are; I bought them at auction, where they were closed out at a great sacrifice and I offer them to you *precisely at cost.*"

"But I saw the same goods at Shears & Co.'s at five cents a yard less."

"Not the same goods at all, ma'am; theirs are steam colors; quite an imitation article, and not near so wide as this."

"The lady, being timid as to colors, is at last persuaded to pay the price, and the shopkeeper pockets his fifteen per cent. profit with as much complacency as if he had only drawn out his purse to give a dollar in charity."

If this be an accurate sketch of buying and selling, then Ecclesiasticus is right: Sin *does* stick between the buyer and the seller as a nail between the joinings of stones. If this be true, the man who puts upon his sign, "Fair dealing done here, and no lies told," will make his fortune in a year; for every body must be disgusted with it by this time. Admitting its truth for a moment, what are the consequences? Has not a lie been told without advantage? Have not men bartered their manhood for naught? Has either party reaped any advantage that he would not have obtained by adhering to straightforward truth? It must be so, or we severely reflect on men's intelligence, and argue that they can be induced to buy what they do not want, by any silly tale that a weak brain can invent. The consequences are, then, that these men have needlessly added their influence to diminish the little confidence there is between man and man. They have probably sown the first seeds of deception and dishonesty, which may grow up to be rank weeds, and poison themselves, in the minds of younger men, who are looking to them as examples of business tact, and they have given additional cause for the contempt with which men whose occupations are less useful and noble, but whose standard of honor is higher, regard their profession.

Is lying necessary in buying and selling? This question needs but a short answer; if it is, then buying and selling are sinful, which is absurd. Many of the assertions in bargaining are mere badinage; they are substitutes for want of something better to say, and are generally an indication of poverty of wit. Many of the falsehoods in trade are about irrelevant matters, not pertinent to the bargain. *Cost* is a matter never pertinent to a sale. It is not to be presumed that a man who is in his right mind is selling at cost, and what he paid for his goods is an interesting inquiry of no practical importance. The reasons which make a man anxious to sell are sometimes, but rarely, necessary to be mentioned. Lying seems to be a natural defect in some men, and must be viewed in the same light as the well-known natural propensity for stealing. In others it is a confirmed habit; they have lied so long and so often that it has become a second nature to them. Loquacious men cannot always command the time necessary to stop and recollect the truth. But in no instance is the ability to lie a qualification of a good buyer or an expert salesman.

The chief qualification of a good buyer is, a judgment of goods; of a salesman, a judgment of men. Both should have a special acquaintance with the laws governing sales and contracts.

A good buyer is a man of few words. He posts himself as to the market—goes to the houses at which he usually deals, and which he first selected on account of their reputable character—asks their price—makes his offer as near the market value as he can, without comment on the prices of others; if accepted, the bargain is closed; if declined, he "don't want it," or will look further.

Much comment on the part of the seller he regards as an incentive to be wary, and all pretences to confidential favors, unless proved to be such by undoubted documentary evidence, as a reproach upon his understanding. When the matter is in any wise doubtful, he demands a warrantee or a guarantee, as the case may require, knowing that no reasonable man can object to his securing himself against contingencies.

An expert salesman has a thorough knowledge of human nature, courteous manners, and a ready tact in adapting himself to the various humors of the buyers. He has perfect command of his business, and having purchased with care he has no hesitation in fairly recommending his goods, or warranting them when requested to do so. His great object or aim is, to acquire the *confidence* of the public. To this end, every thing must bend and tend. Truthfulness is a trump card in his hands for this purpose, and he avoids all doubtful or suspicious assertions of favor or sacrifice, even if true, unless he has the documents at hand to prove their truth. He rarely mentions the cost of his goods, knowing well that his customers do not expect him to sell without a profit, or fearing they would disbelieve him, which would destroy confidence. He has a quick appreciation of the wants of his customers, and does not comment with equal praise on all kinds or styles of goods to all persons; but catches at the fancy of the buyer, and presses delicately upon that; or, if it is an injudicious choice, he points out its defect, and produces a more suitable article, and thus inspires confidence. He does not treat his lady customers with an impertinent familiarity, nor does he worry any one who is not disposed to buy at the time with over-ardent solicitations; but he tries to leave upon their minds such an agreeable and favorable impression that they will be sure to call again.*

* A lady friend of ours, who is *au fait* in matters of shopping, seems to intimate, in a private letter, that all who profess to be salesmen are not masters of their business. We publish an extract, "for account of whom it may concern."

"Some stores in —— Street are noted and avoided, for the impertinently familiar manner which the clerks think proper to adopt towards their lady customers. When a lady goes into the store in search of some article that

There are certain fundamental maxims ever present in his mind, and his creed runs in a manner after this fashion :—

I believe that the life of business is profit; and, as a general rule, I will not make sales without profit. "To sell low for cash, never mind profits," is not my maxim.

I will sell to a punctual man at less profit than to an unpunctual one; and on a short credit, lower than on a long one.

I will use every precaution with a stranger that I would wish to have done, should he turn out to be a villain, and yet treat every man as an honest man until he proves him to be otherwise.

Discretion in speech is more than eloquence.

"There is commonly less money, less wisdom, and less good faith, than men do account upon," is an Italian proverb, and I believe a true one.

It is not all that can be sold to a customer that is well sold, but only what he can conveniently pay for. A past due-bill is a detest-

she is in want of, as soon as the gentleman sees her, he comes forward, makes a grimace, pulls up his shirt collar, runs his fingers through his hair, and assumes an air of easy familiarity that is quite refreshing to look upon. It is true he may not have much sense, but then he has a wealth of smiles; indeed, to listen to his conversation with his victimized customer, a bystander might come to the conclusion that he was proprietor of the establishment, and the lady had made the article in question a mere excuse for a morning call; this is annoying, but in this case one can leave the article, and walk out; but there is one retail store in this city that is a perfect trap—once in, it is impossible to get out; if the article does not suit you, you are worried and talked at; if you attempt to move towards the door, you are run after and brought back; if you tax your genius to give a most unmistakably minute description of what you *do* want, the reply is, 'Oh, yes, madam, in the back store; if you will walk back, we have exactly the article you describe.' And so they get you further in; after looking about on the shelves, they profess to have found the object of their search, and down comes the very opposite of any thing you ever wished to possess. After making half a dozen fruitless attempts to reach the street door, and being each time perseveringly caught and brought back, you give it up, and become submissive and willing to buy any thing they wish you to, making at the same time a firm resolve—as you see your money going for things you don't know what to do with—that if you live to be as old as Methuselah, you will never enter that store again."

able object, and goods not paid for are not sold, but thanklessly given away.

I believe that rich dress, decisive tones, and confident airs are frequently assumed for sinister purposes; and I will always regard those who make a practice of talking about religion and duty on all occasions, in an affected and forced manner, with a degree of suspicion.

A sudden, bold, and unexpected question is a point of cunning in some men to entrap an unwary answer; while others seek to draw the attention from the main point of the negotiation by amusing tales and entertaining stories, as a counsellor and secretary did, "that never came to Queen Elizabeth of England with bills to sign, but that he would always first put her into some discourse of estate that she might the less mind the bills."

Another article of his creed is to treat all men with courtesy; to give cause of offence to no man, knowing that there is none so mean that cannot do a tradesman an injury. "The least fly hath a spleen, and a little bee a sting. An ass overwhelmed a thistle-warp's nest: the little bird pecked his galled back in revenge; and the humble bee, in the fable, flung down the eagle's eggs out of Jupiter's lap. Bracides, in Plutarch, put his hand in a mouse's nest and hurt her young ones; she bit him by the finger. 'I see now' saith he, 'there is no creature so contemptible that will not be revenged.' 'Tis *lex talionis*, and the nature of all things so to do. If thou wilt live quietly thyself, do no wrong to others."

In fine, he is a philosopher and a great man.

In buying and selling, it is customary *to make discounts on merchandise*, and it is necessary to have a clear understanding of their effect. There is an essential difference between addition and subtraction, which, in this instance, is not always perceived. Thus, 20 per cent. added to $100 will make a $120; but 20 per cent. taken off $120 will not leave $100. If A buys $100 worth of goods for $80, and B. buys them for $70, how much per cent. cheaper does B buy them than A? 12½ per cent. We know an instance, says the *London Economist*, of a very deserving man being ruined by a miscalculation of discounts. The article manufactured he at first supplied to retail dealers at a large profit of about 30 per cent. He afterwards confined his trade almost exclusively to large wholesale houses, to whom he charged the same price, but under a deduction of 20 per cent., believing that he was still realizing 10 per cent. for his own profit. His trade was very extensive; and it was not till after some years that he discovered the fact that, in place of making ten per cent., as he imagined, by this mode of making sales, he was only realizing 4 per cent. To £100 of goods he added 30 per cent., and invoiced them at £130. At the end of each month, in the settlement of accounts, amounting to some thousands of pounds, with individual houses, he deducted 20 per cent., or £26 on each £130, leaving £104 net for every £100 value of goods at prime cost, in place of £110, as he all along expected. It is by far the simplest and best plan to conduct transactions at net prices, or subject only to such moderate discount as may fairly apply to an early in place of distant payment.

Another matter of the first importance in merchandising *is the length of credit* that is given. It will astonish any one who has never examined the subject, *how small profits on short credits will accumulate, in comparison with large profits on long credits. One thousand dollars* turned over every four months, at 10 per cent. profit, will amount, in six years, to $\$5,559\frac{91}{100}$. The same sum turned over every six months, at the same profit, will amount, in six years,

to	$4109	89
Do. every 12 months, at 10 per cent., in 6 yrs.,	1771	56
" 18 " " " "	1464	10
" 2 years, " " "	1331	00
One thousand dollars, turned over every 2 years, at 20 per cent. profit, will in 6 years amount to	1728	00
Do. every 18 months, " " "	2073	60
" 12 " " " "	2985	98
" 6 " " " "	8916	10
" 4 " " " "	26623	33

Thus a man may make a profit of only $728, or a profit of over $25,000 from the same capital, in the same time, and by selling at the same percentage of profit, with merely a difference in the length of credit which he gives. This is a subject that needs no argument, as every one can satisfy himself as to his own interest by his own calculations.

A merchant must *obtain information of the means and standing* of those who desire credit. This is no easy task, and many men seem to have given it up in despair. Some, having no faith in human testimony, will sell to no one on credit, whom they have not known from long personal acquaintance; while others, with the same belief, take the opposite course, and sell to every one who wishes to buy, trusting to Providence for a safe deliverance from all their fears. One source of information is from houses from whom the parties applying formerly purchased. This information may be defective, as it has been known that men have recommended a bad customer to credit, in order that he might obtain from others the means to pay themselves. Other sources of information are from parties in the same trade, and from customers in the same place. Another source is the *Mercantile Agency*.—Its professed object is to collect reliable information in relation to the home standing and character of men engaged in business throughout the country, and embody it in records for the convenience of those who choose to pay for access to it. If the system could be made infallible, or in other words, if their correspondents were omniscient men, above all favor or prejudice, I should regard it with unquestionable favor. But this unfortunately cannot be. Their reports are not infallible, as satisfactory evidence has repeatedly demonstrated. Hence, what man whose credit is his bread, does not feel anxious to know whether he has been misrepresented or not? Hence too, the foundation of the generally just prejudices against these agencies. As an additional means of information either for confirming previous reports or for suggesting further inquiry, it is no doubt worth to subscribers more than the amount of the subscription money; but an imperious sense of duty impels me to say that all who believe in the golden rule should watch it with the most jealous scrutiny. It is a system that is fraught with danger. In its infancy it may be harmless and comparatively accurate; but, should it grow to maturity, and be generally relied upon, the credit of the mercantile community, which is its life and soul, would be in the hands of a few men, self-constituted umpires, and their unknown and irresponsible agents, subject to the errors of ignorance and mistakes of carelessness, with no guaranteed exemption from the influence of private malice, favoritism, bribery, or corruption.

The main source of information is to see the man and hear his statements. This, like other means of information, will sometimes fail, but generally the appearance and manners of a man will show his character. A man who is not worth a dollar is frequently more worthy of credit than another who has the nominal possession of thousands. Losses almost always occur in trusting to property and reports, and not to men. "If you have a doubt whether a customer be tricky or honest, speculative or prudent," says an old banker to his fellow-craftsmen, "be guided by the first impression—we mean the impression produced by the first interview. In nine cases out of ten the first impression will be found to be correct. It is not necessary to study physiognomy or phrenology to be able to judge of the character of men with whom we converse on matters of business." It is a good plan to expect that strangers desiring credit should be introduced by some person to whom they are personally known, and the character of the introducer for pru dence and good management should not be overlooked in judging of his friend. Where the reference is good, and the impression on the first interview favorable, it would be an excellent custom to have what might be called a Representation or Information book, in which the party should be requested to make a statement of his business and affairs, and this statement would, in my opinion, be more accurate, in the majority of cases, than the report of any one else. Were it made a general rule, it would be done as a matter of course, and few who are trustworthy would object, though some would no doubt be disposed to "skulk" a statement of their personal expenditures. We believe that it would materially improve the credit system to repeal the law for the collection of debts, and increase the penalties for false representation. It has been said that if a man cheats you *once* it is his fault, but if he cheats you *twice* it is *your* fault.*

* "An individual, possessed of a moderate amount of money, commences

We have remarked in this chapter that both buyer and seller should understand *the law of sales and contracts*, and we have recommended, in a former part of this work, that every one who expects to enter upon an extensive business should spend some time at a law school in the study of Mercantile Law. This is necessary in order primarily to escape litigation, and secondly, to have the law on your side when dealing with litigious scoundrels, of whom, unfortunately, the supply is greater than the demand. Experience has conclusively convinced me that it would be positive economy for every man whose contracts are at all complicated, in fact, whose business is not of the simplest kind, to choose at the outset of his career an able attorney, with whom to consult and advise before concluding any important undertaking. The younger members of the profession are not to be overlooked in this choice, for though they have of course less experience than others, they are more laborious in research, and careful to advise on the safe side. There are many able attorneys, I have no doubt, who would be willing to hold harmless of litigation all who follow their advice, for a very

business in some thriving town. He comes to one of our wholesale markets, and with one or two commendatory letters, but particularly with his money, he soon becomes acquainted; at first but limited; but he has ouly to manage his trumps (his money) with a little tact, and his acquaintance will very soon extend. At first he purchases cautiously, and meets his obligations promptly, always managing to have his goods carefully packed and marked scientifically, and placed on the street several days before he removes them,

> 'Like books and money
> Laid in show
> As nest-eggs
> To make clients lay.'

And he succeeds. He soon becomes known as a man of promptness and capital, and doing a dashing business: and such a business he does do; for the motto at home is sell low for cash, never mind profits. His acquaintance is courted; he is bedrammed, bedinnered, and besuppered. Every thing goes on swimmingly, and finally he buys largely, goes in deeply, makes one grand manœuvre—a most prodigious swell, and then judiciously and profitably explodes."—*Cin. Price Current.*

These are the "suckers" our *boring* friends sometimes catch.

moderate annual sum, and it would be essentially wise to employ them. They are generally men who can see as far through a mill-stone as the miller himself, and a conversation with them will frequently remove the film by which anxious cupidity sometimes obscures the sight. To save men from lawsuits is the noblest office of their profession.

Contracts of sale may be in writing or not, and are of two kinds, *express* or *implied.* The essential legal requisites of a complete and valid contract, as laid down by the jurists are, a person able to contract—a person willing to contract—a thing to be contracted for—a good and sufficient consideration—clear and explicit words to express the contract or agreement—and the consent of both the parties contracting. Equity will sometimes interpose when some of these requisites are wanting, but they should be borne in mind by all.

Infants, married women, idiots, and lunatics from the time of the finding of the inquisition, are not as a general rule able to contract. A person who signs an obligation while in a state of gross intoxication, may annul it. A sale by a person who has no right to sell is not valid against the claim of the rightful owner, and a sale of stolen goods is in no case valid. The proper owner may take them wherever he finds them, even when the party holding them has paid the full value for them; but, in the exercise of this right, he must avoid committing a breach of the peace.

The thing sold must have an actual or *potential* existence, and be capable of delivery, otherwise it is not a contract of sale, but a *special* or executory agreement. If A sells B a horse, or a house and lot, and it turns out that the horse was dead at the time, or the house burned down, though the fact was unknown to both parties, the contract is void.

Consideration is necessary to the validity of all contracts not under seal, and the only exceptions are bills of exchange and negotiable notes, after they have been exchanged and have passed into the hands of an innocent indorsee in the usual course of trade before maturity. The immediate parties to a bill or note, and the indorsee of a bill over-due, equally with parties to other contracts, are affected by want of consideration. A valuable consideration is one that is either beneficial to the party promising, or to a stranger, or some trouble or prejudice to the party to whom the promise is made.

Mutual consent is a requisite. Where the negotiation is conducted by letter, the contract is complete when the answer containing the acceptance is dispatched by mail or otherwise, provided it be done with due diligence after the proposal, and before any intimation is received that the offer is withdrawn. On the other hand, if A makes an offer to B, and gives him a specified time for an answer, A may retract at any time before the offer is accepted, because the consent of both parties is necessary to make it a contract. (See *Kent's Com.* vol. ii. for a fuller exposition of the above principles.)

The moment that both parties have assented to the terms, the moment that one has said, "I will pay the price demanded," and the other has said, "I will receive it," the *right of property* vests in the buyer, *and the risk of accident is with him*, though he does not acquire the *right of possession* until he pays or tenders the price, unless by the terms of the contract it is otherwise provided (6 Dana, 48). Where the goods are sold on a credit, the buyer has a right to possession without tender of price, unless he becomes insolvent before he has them actually in possession. On intimation of this fact, the seller has the right to retain them, or stop them on the way, called in legal phrase stoppage *in transitu.*

When the contract has been completed in terms, it is the duty of the seller to deliver the goods, that is, place them in the buyer's power, so that he may remove them without rightful interference (on performance of the conditions precedent by the buyer), and comply with his warranties, express or implied. It is the duty of the buyer to perform his conditions precedent, which are to tender the price in the absence of a special stipulation, and if they were to be paid for by note or bill, he must tender one. But the word bill is not held to mean an *approved bill,* that means a bill to which no reasonable objection can be made. A seller is not legally bound to furnish change, though the custom is such that he would find it his interest to do so.

The seller must comply with his implied or express warranties. When a man sells goods that are in his own possession, he *impliedly warrants the title*, and must make it good in case of difficulty. When, however, he sells goods that are in the possession of another, and does not expressly warrant the title, the rule of *caveat emptor* applies, and the buyer must run the risk. When the seller is manufacturer of the goods, a warranty is implied in the contract of sale, that the goods shall be reasonably fit and proper for the purpose for which they were bought, and of at least medium quality or goodness. If they come short of this, the buyer can return them, after he has had a reasonable time to inspect them. And it has likewise been held that this rule is not so limited, but extends to all cases where the buyer relies on the skill and judgment of the seller.

Express warranties have been thus defined : every affirmation at the time of the sale of personal chattels or goods is a warranty, *provided it appears to have been so intended.* Mere affirmations or representations, whether oral or written, mere expressions of judgment, opinion, or belief do not, however, constitute a warranty ; it must be an assertion upon which *he intends that the buyer shall rely, and upon which he does rely.*

What would be sufficient evidence of this intention is a matter of so much nicety, that the buyer who relies at all on the warranty should always insist on express words and a direct engagement.

If there be no express warranty, and the goods be present to the parties, and no fraudulent representations be made by the seller, the purchaser will have no remedy after executing the contract, if the goods turn out to be of bad quality, unsound, or of different kind or denomination from what they were thought to be by the parties. Thus, in a case where the purchaser, being present, bought an article as Braziletto-wood, and described as such in the advertisements, invoices, and bill of parcels, which turned out to be peachum-wood—comparatively worthless—(but the fact was not known to the seller), it was decided that the purchaser had no remedy. He must attend to those qualities which are within the reach of his observation and judgment.

But it is also a general rule that each party is bound in every case to communicate to the other his knowledge of material facts, provided he knows the other to be ignorant of them, and they be not open and naked, or equally within the reach of his observa tion. For instance, a horsejockey is not bound to disclose the fact that the horse is blind—because it is within the observation of the buyer to see it; but the seller of a ship, knowing of a latent defect which the buyer could not by any possible attention discover, is bound to disclose it, or the sale is void on account of fraud.—Fraud vitiates all contracts.

In some of the States, the statute for the prevention of frauds and perjuries requires that all agreements—embracing contracts for the sale of goods—*not to be performed within one year*, shall be in writing and signed by the party to be charged, or his agent duly authorized; but, irrespective of this, it is unquestionable policy to reduce to writing all contracts, especially where performance does not immediately follow the agreement, as where weighing, or measuring, or counting is necessary before the bill of parcels can be rendered; because, in these cases, there is some conflict in the law, I believe, as to who holds the right of property during the intermediate period. At all events, the party affirming an absolute sale must satisfy the jury that it is such, which he may not be able to do without some memorandum in writing—signed by the party to be charged; and this will also prevent differences of opinion, which, though honest, are not the less vexatious. But care must be taken, in reducing contracts to writing, that they be full, and contain all the material facts, and not leave any of them to the verbal understanding of the parties—because the law will not admit verbal or parol evidence to supply, explain, or contradict a written agreement. Parol evidence is only admissible when it goes to contradict, not the terms of writing, but to defeat the whole contract as fraudulent or illegal. All matters of negotiation, antecedent to, or outside of the writing, are regarded as merged in the written agreement.

These are a few of the leading legal principles that govern contracts of sale. In consulting elementary works on the law by non-professional readers, it must always be borne in mind that every word has a meaning, and where *if*, *but*, *unless*, *provided*, occur in the stating of a general rule, it must not be supposed that they were introduced for literary ornament. They have invariably an important significance, and mean either an essential requisite or an exception to the rule.

In the application of these general rules, courts frequently give them a liberal construction, and *imply contracts* without the terms being known or expressly agreed upon by the parties. Thus, if A desires B, a storekeeper, to send him a piece of linen, without specifying price, and B sends the linen and charges it at eighty cents a yard, the law implies that A agreed to pay for it, if the price be not unreasonable, as much as if he had given such a promise in writing. When a man employs workmen, without agreeing on a price, the law implies that he agreed to pay what their services were reasonably worth. Upon the same principles of justice, it will make an individual into whose hands money, belonging to a third person, should chance to be paid, or a cargo of merchandise delivered, a trustee for such third person, and also implies that a promise has been made to pay over the money, or the value of the goods on proper demand by the real owner. In some cases, if I expend money for the use and benefit of another, and in all cases, where it is done at his request, the law presumes that he agreed to refund, though we said nothing about it. If A inadvertently pays the debt of B to C, and afterwards, on discovering the mistake, demands a return of the amount, C would be compelled to refund —the law assuming that he agreed to do so, in the event of mistake. Commission merchants, transportation companies, &c., impliedly agree with every man who intrusts them with goods that they will exercise such care over them as a man of ordinary carefulness would take of his own property.

We cannot better conclude our suggestions on buying and selling than by quoting Lord Bacon's observations on negotiating. They should be committed to memory, partly for use, and partly for protection against their superior use by others. "It is generally better to deal by speech than by letter; and by the mediation of a third than by a man's self. Letters are good when a man would draw an answer by letter back again; or when it may serve for a man's justification afterwards to produce his own letter; or where it may be danger to be interrupted, or heard by pieces. To deal in person is good, when a man's face breedeth regard, as commonly with inferiors; or in tender cases, where a man's eye upon the countenance of him with whom he speaketh may give him a direction how far to go; and generally, where a man will reserve to himself liberty either to disavow, or to expound. In choice of instruments, it is better to choose men of a plainer sort, that are like to do that is committed to them, and to report back again faithfully the success than those that are cunning to contrive out of other men's business somewhat to grace themselves, and will help the matter in report, for satisfaction sake. Use also such persons as affect the business wherein they are employed, for that quickeneth much; and such as are fit for the matter, as bold men for expostulation, fair-spoken men for persuasion, crafty men for inquiry and observation, froward and absurd men for business that doth not well bear out itself. Use also such as have been lucky and prevailed before in things wherein you have employed them; for that breeds confidence, and they will strive to maintain their prescription. It is better to sound a person with whom one deals afar off, than to fall upon the point at first; except you mean to surprise him by some short question. It is better dealing with men in appetite, than those that are where they would be. If a man deal with another upon conditions, the start of first performance is all which a man can reasonably demand, except the nature of the thing be such, which must go before; or else a man can persuade the other party that he shall still need him in some other thing; or else, that he be counted the honester man. All practice is to discover, or to work. Men discover themselves in trust, in passion, at unawares; and of necessity when they would have somewhat done, and cannot find an apt pretext. If you would work any man, you must either know his nature and fashions, and so lead him; or his ends, and so persuade him; or his weakness or disadvantages, and so awe him; or those that have interest in him, and so govern him. In dealing with cunning persons, we must ever consider their ends, to interpret their speeches; and it is good to say little to them, and that which they least look for. In all negotiations of difficulty, a man may not look to sow and reap at once; but must prepare business, and so ripen it by degrees."

Insurance.—As soon as goods have been purchased or received on consignment, they should be insured. Insurance is regarded by the late ethical writers as an obligation of moral duty in all cases where the interests of creditors are endangered through neglect of it. They reason in this wise: A merchant who trades on borrowed capital is not honest if he endangers the loss of an amount, which, if lost, would disable him from paying his debts. A man who possesses a $1,000, and borrows a thousand, cannot virtuously *speculate* so extensively as that, if disappointed in his prospects, he would lose twelve hundred. The *speculation* is dishonest whether it succeeds or not—because it is risking other men's property without their consent. Upon the same principles, they argue, it is unjust not to insure in all cases where, if the houses or goods were destroyed by fire, the trader would be unable to pay his creditors: and the injustice consists, not in the actual loss, but in *endangering* the infliction of loss. There are but two ways, they conclude, by which the claims of rectitude can be satisfied: the one is by insurance; and the other is by informing the actual owners of the want of it, and let them run the risk. Be this as it may, the charge is trifling—and not to be compared with the comfortable feeling of security that results.

It is probable that all men feel it to be their duty to insure: the cause of neglect is generally procrastination. It is postponed from day to day, until by and by a sense of security arises, and they begin to calculate how much they have saved by not insuring, and then abandon the idea altogether: others, who are cramped for money, think they cannot conveniently spare the premium. Let all remember that delays are dangerous. It is only men of large property, like Girard, or Longworth of Cincinnati, who can *afford* to neglect insuring: with them the occasional loss of a house or two would not amount to so much as the premium of insurance on all their property. Men of limited property cannot do this: they should insure not only their houses, but their goods—not only their dwellings, but the furniture in them.

Some care, however, must be taken in the selection of an office. In all parts of the country there are good and bad, honorable and dishonorable offices; and in making a choice, the attention should be directed particularly to inquire, as far as possible, how they have settled their losses with men of limited influence. The great complaint against insurance offices of all kinds is a disposition to resist the payment of policies by quibbles and litigation. Men of extensive influence, and those who will be likely to make a noise, may never have an opportunity to observe this trait, but attention to the law proceedings in courts will show that men of less influence have frequently just cause of complaint. Offices that manifest the faintest indications of a disposition of this kind should be marked with ink as black as that which Benton used to expunge the resolutions of censure against General Jackson. It is their business, or it should be, to take risks against every thing but fraud, and then they should receive the universal support of the community.

INSURANCE ON LIFE is a device of man—some say of the devil—since Solomon made the smart remark that "there is no new thing under the sun." It is an older invention than the mercantile agency, and a good deal better. It was in 1706 the first life insurance office, the Amicable, commenced business amidst many prophecies of failure, and loud denunciations that it was flying in the face of Providence. Its plan was to insure all, the young and old, the sick and the sound, at one uniform rate of £5 per cent. per annum, and £7 per cent. entrance money, and it succeeded. Other offices soon followed in England and in other parts of Europe—but the French, to maintain their usual consistency of character, decreed it unlawful, "because it is an offence against public decency to set a price upon the life of a freeman, which is above all valuation."

The system of life insurance is now firmly established in Europe, and is rapidly growing into favor in the United States. Its advocates in this country have had the field of argument, in a measure, to themselves, until lately a banker* from the North, "of eager search and dauntless soul," has pointed out to the people that their profits, like the footprints around a slaughter-house, should admonish those who are entering that the current inward exceeds greatly the

* A. B. Johnson, Esq., of the Ontario Branch Bank, Utica.

current outwards. He states that a man twenty-five years of age, who insures his life for $5,000, for which he pays an annual premium of eighty dollars, will pay in twenty-four years some thirty dollars more than his family will receive at his death, and if he lives to seventy-five years of age, will have paid in principal and interest some $35,000. For this reason, among others, he argues that a man should deposit the premium in Savings' Institutions. This would be undoubted policy, if we could be certain that we would live twenty-four or fifty years longer—but without that certainty, a man of small means *endangers* the future happiness and comfort of his family, when he might avoid it, in case he should die within the next year, or the next ten years. But, aside from this, by insuring in a *mutual* insurance office he will certainly not lose any such sum, and may gain in the way of profits and bonuses even a greater sum.

Savings' Institutions and Life Insurance Companies are both valuable and commendable, and it is prudent to avail one's self of both. Let the man who thinks he should leave his family $10,000 at his death insure his life for $5,000, and whenever he pays the premium on that, deposit a similar amount in a Savings' Bank, and, in any event, he will be certain to leave his family above destitution. The objections to a sole reliance on these banks are, that they do not provide against early casualties; require an immense deal of fortitude in pinching times to add to the deposits, or to keep from drawing them out and using them; and they have a tendency to produce a close and miserly disposition. Life insurance is free from these objections, and is unquestionably good, I think, in principle; but it also needs inprovement in practice, and greater safeguards by law.

There are three kinds or classes of Life Insurance Companies. The first and oldest is the proprietary or Joint Stock Company. They are established in the same manner as other joint stock companies, have an actually paid up capital, insure for certain fixed sums, without any participation in the profits, which are divided among the proprietors of the capital stock. Their peculiar advantages are, the security of the subscribed and actually paid up capital, and where not limited by State legislation, also the private wealth of the individual partners. If incorporated, however, the individuals are not liable beyond the amount of their stock, unless expressly made so in their charter or by-law. The Massa- husetts Hospital Life Insurance and Trust Company, of Boston, is a proprietary or Joint Stock Company, and was established in 1818, with a capital of $500,000, divided into 5000 shares. No stockholder is liable beyond the amount of instalments remaining unpaid on his shares.

The second class may be termed the mixed—they are joint stock companies with a paid up capital; but, instead of giving merely fixed sums to the insured at the termination of life, they, after paying the stockholders simple annual interest, and setting aside a contingent fund, divide the balance of the net profits among those who have taken out policies for life, and generally in the proportion of one-third to stockholders and two-thirds to policy holders. They combine the advantages of security of capital and a participation in the profits. Of this kind is the Girard Life Insurance Annuity and Trust Company of Philadelphia, which makes assurance on the life "of a healthy person, not engaged in any hazardous occupation, and residing within the settled limits of the United States, north of the Southern boundary of Virginia and Kentucky, or within the settled limits of the Two Canadas, Nova Scotia, and New Brunswick."

The other kind is the *mutual,* which is similar in principle and organization to the Mutual Fire and Marine Insurance Companies. The act of incorporation usually prescribes that the company shall not issue a policy until a certain sum, say $500,000, is subscribed, the *premium* on which is their capital. In mutual offices, the whole profits, after deducting expenses, and a proportion for a guarantee fund, is divided among those who are holders of policies for life. Every one insured is, during the existence of the policy, a partner in the concern, and is mutually insurer and insured. Though they have no previously paid up capital, experience has thus far proved that they are equally secure with the others, every one insured having an interest in its prosperity; and they possess, in an eminent degree, the ingredients of popularity and usefulness. Of this kind there are many; and to mention an excellent one, we name the Mutual Life Insurance Company of New York.

In selecting an office, care must first be taken as to its security, and its reputation for good management, which is the main thing; and then particular care must be taken in answering the questions in regard to the diseases which you have had, that nothing be omitted, whether it be material or immaterial. It is better not to insure at all, than, after paying premiums for years, your family finds the policy void, after your death, on account of some omission or misstatement. I would advise every one who is not well posted in legal significations, before he signs a policy, to consult his own private attorney, as he ought to do in every important transaction. I say, *his own* attorney, and not a stranger, for a great number in the profession are secretly in the interest of the Insurance companies, and receive a commission on all the policies they influence. By doing so, you may probably escape signing or taking a policy containing a provision like the following "The company will pay a stipulated sum within three months after death, *provided* every statement, declaration, and all testimonials and documents addressed to or deposited with the company, in relation to the insurance, shall be found *to be, in all respects, true.*" Now, "all testimonials and documents addressed to or deposited with the company," embrace, besides your own statement, the statement of your friend to whom your have referred, the statement of your physician, and the statement of their own medical adviser, all of which you have never seen, nor do you know what they contain. These statements are then held as *warranted,* and taken as the basis of the contract; so that the policy shall be void, if any *important information* has been omitted.

They do not take it upon *themselves* to prove the misstatement or omission; but if they merely take a fancy to object to payment, your family, or whoever may be the owner of the policy, cannot recover unless *they* can prove, to the satisfaction of the jury, after you are dead, that you had *not* at any time, from infancy upwards, all or any of the diseases or symptoms of disease mentioned in the proposals. They throw the burden of proving every thing, though they have the documentary evidence in their possession, upon the claimant of the insurance, and he is placed in the absurd position of having to prove the affirmative of a negative proposition.

This is a common provision, I believe, in London insurance offices; but I am advised that it is not common in American policies. It is true that all generally settle their losses with liberality, and competition increases the security in this respect; but no wide awake man should take a policy that will extend throughout years with no stronger guarantee than the liberality of an incorporation. The few policies which I have seen make the truth of one's own statement the basis of the contract, which is more reasonable; but insurance offices, of *all kinds*, should adopt the principle of the London Indisputable, which is that every policy issued by the company "shall be indefeasible and indisputable, and the fact of issuing the same shall be considered sufficient evidence of the validity of the policy." Those offices, if there are any, that adopt this principle, should, other things being equal, receive the preference.*

We must now leave the first division of our subject. We must consider ourselves prepared to supply a public demand, and inquire *how we shall get customers.*

* "A short rule for ascertaining the expectation of life, according to the Northampton tables, is to take the age from the number 86, and then divide by two." Thus a man 40 years of age will live upon the general average 23 years, for 86 less 40 is 46, which, divided by two, leaves 23. The expectation, at birth, is 25 years, and at one year 32. These are exceptions to the rule. The value of a policy, in case the insured wishes to sell, is considered worth about one-third of the whole amount of premiums that have been paid.

CHAPTER VIII.

GETTING MONEY BY MERCHANDIZING—Continued.

HOW TO GET CUSTOMERS.

In the progressive stages of civilization, men have held many erroneous ideas, and have been chargeable with much folly, but I am not aware that at any time, or in any age, they considered it sufficient to place themselves in one of the "main grooves of human affairs," and wait for fortune. Mercantile men certainly have never entertained the idea that all that is necessary, in order to do business, is to open a shop or store and stock it with merchandise. To take some means to inform the public of the nature of their business, and solicit their patronage, has ever been a matter of primary importance. In the middle of the seventeenth century, the shopkeepers of London made known their business *vivâ voce.* The masters or proprietors would take a turn before their doors, crying out, "What d'ye lack, sir? what d'ye lack madam?" and then run over a list of the commodities they dealt in, and when tired, the task was assumed by the apprentice, thus making the city a Babel of strange sounds.

This democratic era was succeeded by the age of signs, which genius soon improved and ornamented by all imaginable devices. Painting, gilding, boars' heads, flying dragons, and flying swans, were conspicuous emblems. As the capabilities of the printing-press were developed, shrewd men saw in it a chance to "universalize their sign-board;" they saw they could place upon it not only their name and number, but a full account of their stock, and their range of prices; they saw that they could challenge the attention not only of those who passed by their store, but of men in all places, and at all times. The present is the era of advertising,

Advertising is the best mode of *drawing* buyers that I can suggest. By means of it men can sell articles that are valueless, *and make fortunes by it;* why should not those who have valuable articles to dispose of? An extensive system of advertising is invariably resorted to by those who have trash to dispose of, and it succeeds; how much easier, then, to sell a useful and valuable article? *Advertising* and *politeness* are the main levers to get customers. Advertising will draw them, ability to fill their orders will satisfy them, and politeness will induce them to buy.

ADVERTISING.—" To the merchant or dealer who is sure of his ability to fill orders on the most favorable terms, the attainment of an adequate publicity is the matter of primary concern. If his circle of trade is properly the county in which he lives, then he should take effectual measures to let every family in the county know what he sells, and on what conditions. It is idle to speak of the cost as an impediment. He might as well object to the cost of sheltering his goods from bad weather, protecting them from thieves, or dealing them out to customers. All the other cost of his business is incurred without adequate motive or return, so long as the essential element of his business is neglected or scrimped. If his location and his stock only entitle him to expect the custom of his own township and neighborhood, then he should incur the expenses of fully informing that locality. Just so with the wholesale merchant who aspires to a custom coextensive with his State, his section, or the whole Union. If he is prepared to satisfy so wide a demand on favorable terms, the expense of apprising those whom he desires for customers of the nature of his business, the character of his stock, the range of his prices, and the reasons why he should be dealt with, is one which he cannot refuse to incur without gross incompetency and ruinous prodigality. By thus refusing, he increases his expenses for rent, lights, fuel, clerk hire, &c., from one-half per cent. to three, five, and in some cases ten per cent. on his aggregate sales, and renders it morally impossible that he should sell at a profit, and at the same time sell as cheaply as his more enterprising and capable rivals. In effect, he confesses defeat and incapacity, and retreats to the rear-rank of his vocation.

Some men who know enough to advertise are yet so narrow as to confine their advertisements to journals of their own creed or party. If they do not choose to trade with any but men of like faith, this is wise; but if they desire to have the whole public for customers, it is otherwise.

"There is a large class who delight to shine in newspapers and placards as wits and poets, and announce their wares in second-hand jokes, or in doggerel fit to set the teeth of a dull saw on edge. If their object is notoriety or a laugh, this is the way to attain it; but if it be business, it would seem better to use the language of business. Leave clowns' jests to the circus, and let sober men speak as they act, with directness and decision The fewest words that will convey the advertiser's ideas are the right ones.

"Men of business are hardly aware of the immense change which a few years have wrought in the power of a public press. A few years since, a circulation of three thousand copies was a very large one for a daily paper. Now there are journals issuing forty to fifty thousand copies daily, while lists of ten to twenty thousand are frequently and rapidly increasing. As a general rule, an advertisement in a paper now will meet the eyes of four to ten times as many persons as a like announcement would have done twenty years ago. It is easy to place one where it will meet the eyes of one hundred thousand persons within two days, or, by using half a dozen papers, to challenge the attention of half a million of persons. When it is practicable to attain such publicity at the cost of a few dollars, and when some actually *do* attain it, how can those who neglect it expect to build up a new business? An old one may subsist until its customers gradually drop off by death or removal; but he who would build up a business now, must be 'like the time,' and improve the advantages it offers. Foremost among these is the facility now so cheaply afforded for general advertising. To neglect it is like resolving never to travel by steam nor communicate by telegraph. It is to close one's eyes to the light and insist upon living in perpetual darkness. An individual may do this at his own cost; but a community—a class, will never act so insanely; and he who neglects the advantages of advertising, not only robs himself of his fair advantages, but bestows the spoils on his wiser rivals."

POLITENESS is also a powerful lever in the hands of an able man. In the course of a business lifetime, there are many opportunities for the merchant to enlarge the circle of his friends by leaving a favorable impression on the minds of strangers. Strangers frequently call into stores to get some information which is interesting or beneficial to themselves, and this is a golden opportunity. A shrewd, polite man will invariably satisfy their inquiries with manifest good will, to the best of his ability—a fool will invariably think himself too busy, when there is no immediate prospect of gain. As the life of the merchant is the favorable opinion of the public, a shrewd man will seize hold of every opportunity to add to his troop of friends—a fool will make a neutral his enemy.

Politeness has been defined *to be the art of showing men, by external signs, the internal regard we have for them.* It indicates a good heart and a wise head. It is not limited in its expression to set forms or ceremonies, nor can it be learned by any system of rules. The same wisdom that appreciates its value will direct in the choice of the external signs by which to manifest it, and form the manners.

Mankind are naturally polite. There is nothing so graceful in its gestures and winning in its ways as an unspoiled child. It seems to be the private mark of the great Creator, stamped on the infant's brow by the manufacturer's own hand, to tell the world that he is of the family of man. Its import is understood in every language, and in every clime. But, like any other private mark, men may scratch it off, and make themselves beasts—they may counterfeit it, and make themselves fools, or they may set it off, polish it, exhibit it, and make themselves gentlemen. Politeness has a great affinity with nature. It is oftener found "in lowly sheds, with smoky rafters, than in tapestry halls, and courts of princes." Men in cities are liable to become impolite. They are liable to contract a contempt for their species. They become acquainted with their vices, and familiar with their miseries, and soon lose that internal regard and reverence which one human being should have for another. The cultivation of the mind and of the heart will check this tendency; and I regard it no small commendation of a mercantile life that it demands a close attention to the forms of politeness, even if the essence be wanting. Motives are inscrutable to mortal ken, and the man who shows he is desirous of pleasing another may charitably be presumed to have some internal regard for him. The merchant of the present and the next age must be a polite man. The boors have had their day. Henceforth, they will only succeed where gold dollars can be picked up as the Israelites did the manna. Competition in less fortunate places will drive them to their proper vocation of tending swine.

Politeness is never a trifle, and there are no trifles in business. Small things may produce mighty consequences. Every one who has risen to eminence from an humble station can, if he will take the trouble, point to the precise period in his life when a change was unexpectedly wrought in his favor; and, if he examines closely, he will find it associated with some trivial circumstance, or caused by some humble instrument. One morning a poor old soldier called at the shop of a hair-dresser, who was busy with his customers, and asked relief, stating that he had stayed beyond his leave of absence, and, unless he could get a lift on the coach, fatigue and severe punishment awaited him. The hair-dresser listened to his story respectfully, and gave him a guinea. "God bless you, sir!" said the veteran, astonished at the amount. "How can I repay you? I have nothing in the world but this," pulling out a dirty piece of paper from his pocket; "it is a recipe for making blacking; it is the best that was ever seen; many a half guinea I have had for it from the officers, and many bottles I have sold; may you be able to get something for it to repay you for your kindness to the poor soldier!" That dirty piece of paper was the recipe for the renowned Day and Martin's blacking; and that hair-dresser is the now wealthy Mr. Day, whose manufactory is one of the ornaments of London, and whose palace in Regent's Park rivals in magnificence the mansions of the nobility.

> "There *is* a tide in the affairs of men
> Which, taken at the flood, leads on to fortune;
> Omitted, all the voyage of their life
> Is bound in shallows and in miseries."

It is a wise ordination of Providence that we cannot foresee the golden moment of opportunity, so that we may plant ourselves on the rock of principles which the wisdom of ages has built up, and that we may at all times hold ourselves in readiness to embrace opportunity. Were it otherwise, we would have no present interest to act prudently, and could afford to indulge in negligence.

It is well always to remember that relations in business are continually changing. The stranger of to-day may be the creditor of to-morrow; and the harsh creditor of one week may be an unfortunate debtor in the next. Banks sometimes shut down, and a oan would be convenient. A better than Shylock might answer to the man who considered it unnecessary to be polite to strangers and inferiors

> "You spurn'd me such a day; another
> You called me dog; and for these *courtesies*
> I'll lend you thus much money."

It is a matter of daily observation that the Jews are more successful in money-getting than any other people. As rich as a Jew, is a proverb. How to account for this—to what cause to ascribe it—has no doubt been a puzzle with many. If the following statement be correct, there is no difficulty in accounting for it: "The politest people in the world are not the French, the English, the American, the Italian, nor the German, but the Jewish. For the Jews are maltreated and reviled, and despoiled of their civil privileges, and their social rights: yet are they every where polite, affable, insinuating, and condescending. They are remarkable for their industry and perseverance; indulge in few or no recriminations; are faithful to old associations; more respectful of the prejudices of others than these are of theirs; not more worldly-minded and money-loving than people generally are; and every thing considered, they surpass all nations in courtesy, affability, and forbearance. Few persons excel in address a bright and polished Jew. There is no rusticity among that people." Whether the representation be correct or not, we scarcely know; but it is certain that, by doing likewise, we would be on the high road to success.

Politeness is not inconsistent with firmness. It is only the polite man who dares at all times to refuse doing that which his judgment condemns. "Most men," says Lord Clarendon, "are slaves because they cannot pronounce the monosyllable 'No.'" A polite man may pronounce it, whenever he chooses, with less danger of offence than a rude man's "yes."

Politeness is not *inconsistent with a proper degree of spirit.* When we have to deal with a bully, resistance is our only alternative. Any sign of deference or submission will only provoke increased rudeness. A polite man never undervalues himself. He that suffers himself to be ridden, says Burton, or that, through pusillanimity or sottishness, will let every man baffle him, shall be a common laughing-stock to flout at. As a cur that goes through a village, if he clap his tail between his legs, and run away, every cur will insult over him; but if he bristle himself up, and stand to it, and give a counter-snarl, there's not a dog dares meddle with him; there is much in a man's courage and discreet carriage of himself.

Politeness is not *inconsistent with religion.* It is a mistaken notion that some professors of religion seem to have, that bluntness is a mark of sincerity. Young men frequently complain that they take advantage of interviews on business to read moral lectures, and enforce doctrinal points. As I am not of the brotherhood, I will merely commend to their attention an observation of Brother Sharp's, in Discourse VIII. vol. v.: "As for our Saviour, he was a person so far from being morose or reserved in his carriage or a lover of singularity; so far from setting up a way of conversation of his own making, distinct from the way he found in the world, that he was the most free, obliging, civil, and, if I durst use the word, I would say the most *complacent* person that ever appeared in the world." A careful observance of his Sermon on the Mount will make a polite man.

Politeness has no identity with foppery, prudery, pomp, or affectation. These are its counterfeits. The choice of the external signs of manners is, as was said before, a matter for the exercise of individual wisdom. Polite men have not always the most finished manners, nor are those who have the latter always polite. In forming the manners, what is borrowed from study or observation must be adapted to the natural character, or it will not set well.

That which is eminently becoming in one man is the opposite in another. Manners are best taught in childhood and youth, and when acquired later, are rarely perfect. But care must be taken that the mind be not confused by many rules, nor overwhelmed by minute observations. Chesterfield wrote three volumes on the graces to his son, and, as might have been expected, he made a very awkward booby of him. To have the desire of pleasing always uppermost in the mind, is the main thing. He who manifests a desire to please, under all circumstances and to all men, is a polite man, whatever may be his manners. But the latter are by no means to be despised, and he who possesses them in perfection, or can attain them, is a fortunate and well-armed man.

The Rev. John Todd, in his work to students, gives some hints for the cultivation of politeness that are worthy of attention.

His *first* rule is, that "*Good-humor is essential to politeness,*" and by good-humor he says he means "the habit of being easily pleased." It must arise from kind feelings within, and it may be an encouragement to know that every exercise of these kind feelings will surely increase them; so that what is begun as a duty will soon become a pleasure. "We all know that outward expressions of kindness have no value any further than as they are an index of the feelings within; but it is a kind provision of Providence that even the outward expression of kindness has a tendency to cultivate the feelings of good-will."

2. *That the cultivation of the conscience will increase your politeness.*

"The very spirit of the gospel is that you love your neighbor as yourself; and all know that is true politeness: so that, when you see an impolite man make great pretensions to religion, you give him credit for having probably deceived himself. You may now be able to think of a man who is notorious for being wicked. Look at him, and see if he be not far from being a man of politeness. Look again, and see if his wickedness did not first commence at the point of being impolite towards men; for impudence towards men will almost invariably lead to disrespect of God, so that he who begins by throwing aside kind and proper feelings towards his fellows will most assuredly end in despising the commands of his Maker.

The best way, then, to become a man of politeness is to begin with the heart, to act on the principle of making every one as happy as in your power, because you would have all others do so to you."

3. *Cheerfulness is essential to a polite man.*

"A gloomy melancholy man can never think of much except himself. He cannot forget so important a personage to attend to you. He may have cause for all his bad feelings, sufficient to excuse them; but you cannot count any of them as being very kindly towards others. For the purpose of appearing cheerful, you must really feel so; and to feel cheerful, you must be in good health. No one can feel cheerful with a severe toothache upon him, or while turning and tossing under a burning fever. Your health must be good, and kept good by a frugal diet, and a regular course of exercise. It is impossible for the mind to be cheerful, and the spirits buoyant without this. No man ought to undertake to pass himself off in company, or expect to render himself even tolerably agreeable, for a single day, unless he has prepared himself by some suitable exercise. The cheerfulness and buoyancy of a hunting party is proverbial; it is owing to the fact that they are all taking an agreeable exercise without having an object before them of importance enough to do any thing more than barely excite them. There is no real life but cheerful life; therefore, valetudinarians should be sworn, before they enter into company, not to say a word of themselves until the meeting breaks up."

4. *The cultivation of friendship will add to your politeness;* for, so far from rendering the heart selfish by giving warm affections to a few choice friends, it will become more generous towards others." "He that has no one to love or to confide in, has little to hope. He wants the radical principle of happiness; and he who wants this, will in vain strive to be a happy man, or to confer happiness upon others."

The propriety of dwelling upon this subject so long may be questioned, but its importance must be my excuse. Politeness is an important agent in getting money, and, what is better still, it makes business an agreeable occupation. When business men neglect politeness towards each other, the world will be a bear-garden, and business a treadmill. It is the life, animation, beauty, poetry of business, that gives it all its flavor. It is a virtue, too, that needs, and will bear extension. *Merchants are polite enough to customers who buy goods, and to those who pay money, but all are not always polite to inferiors, and to those who come to receive money.* The man who cannot bear dunning should not run in debt, and the man who is insulting, when dunned, should feel the virtue of the law. Clerks are polite enough to their superiors in power, but they are not always polite to strangers who ask them for information within their knowledge. But the main deficiency in politeness is found in what are called the lower and the higher classes. Professional men are rarely polite. They seem to rely upon their character and talents for success, and hence despise the small courtesies of life. Let a stranger go into their offices, and ask some slight information, and it is ten chances to one that he will receive a satisfactory reply. Literary men are not always polite. This may probably be one reason why so many in both these classes are as poor as church mice. No station, rank, or talents can ever excuse a man for neglecting the civilities due from man to man. When Clement XIV. ascended the papal chair, the ambassadors of the several States represented at his court waited on his holiness with their congratulations. As they were introduced and severally bowed, he also bowed to return the compliment. On this the master of ceremonies told his holiness that he should not have returned their salute. "O, I beg your pardon," said he; "I have not been pope long enough to forget good manners."

It is well to remember that the end of business is happiness, and all that we gain on the road is so much clear gain. Much of life is necessarily passed in business pursuits, and all have an interest in making its transactions as pleasant and agreeable as possible.

> "To know
> That which before us lies in daily life
> Is the prime wisdom; what is more, is fume
> Or emptiness, or fond impertinence,
> And renders us in things that most concern us
> Unpractised, unprepared."

The third and last part of our subject, "The characteristics and duties of the merchant or the true man of business," is treated of in the following chapter by the Hon. Horace Greeley, whose able essay on advertising, which we have given before, made me solicitous to obtain his views for the benefit of my readers, and who, so far as my experience goes, may be cited as a pattern of the true business courtesy, as he is an example of industry and self-cultivation. Mr. Greeley may entertain notions on matters purely speculative with which we cannot accord, but none can deny him eminent sagacity in the management of his own business, sincerity of purpose, moral uprightness, and a remarkable vigor of thought and expression. He may think that the whole machine of society should be taken apart and remodelled, while we think it only needs some repairs to work capitally well; but this does not affect the value of his judgment on the proper mode of making the repairs, if that is the course determined upon. In the following original and excellent $50 prize essay, written for this work, he has shown how men may make their business more successful, and at the same time benefit their fellow men, and we solicit for it a candid and attentive perusal, in the hope that, if the judgment approves, correct sentiments will beget correct conduct.

CHAPTER IX.

GETTING MONEY BY MERCHANDIZING—Concluded.

THE TRUE MAN OF BUSINESS.

"As a nail sticketh fast between the joinings of the stones, says Ecclesiasticus, "so doth sin between buyer and seller." The writer does not mean to assert this as an unvarying fact, but to indicate a general tendency. There *is* temptation, there is peril to integrity, in the position and attitude of a trader; and this danger should be pointed out so that it may be avoided. It is a fearful thing to stand face to face with the fact that, if I were only able to buy such a one's property, or sell him mine, before he could receive the news brought from Europe by the last steamship, my fortune would be made. It must be hard for a merchant to know that if to-day's telegraphic dispatches would only embody the news, even though false, of a killing frost throughout the cotton-growing region, or the conflagration of all the mercantile quarter of New Orleans, he would be solvent and wealthy, while in the absence of such tidings he must inevitably suspend payment. Mercantile integrity is subjected to trials of which the farmer or artisan lives and dies in happy unconsciousness—trials none the less real that we all know how false and fleeting is the success or deliverance achieved through wrong-doing. For ages, for centuries, men have repeated, parrot-like, the axiom that "Honesty is the best policy;" yet how many profoundly realize its truth? How many really believe that a man in pecuniary difficulty who might extricate himself by a night of fortunate gaming would be most unwise in consenting to do so? It is so easy to be superficially honest, in the absence of any strong temptation to knavery, that a great many who are ingrained rascals have never yet suspected the fact.

A youth launches gayly and hopefully on the sea of active life, and sails smoothly on its placid bosom, impelled by gentle, favoring gales, unthinking of peril and unsuspecting the neighborhood of adversity—what can he learn from such a voyage? In the absence of danger, what is proved by his freedom from fear? Blest with abundance and ease, what merit is there in his refraining from deception and robbery. And thus it chances that very much which passes current for honesty is only undeveloped or undetected knavery.

Integrity is the corner-stone of the character of the true man of business, in whose absence the whole edifice topples to its ruin. It is quite possible, nay, it is notorious, that dishonest men have acquired wealth by traffic; but they are exceptions to the general rule, and their success, hollow and unreal at best, was a consequence of some good quality they possessed, and not of their lack of the best quality of all. If twenty have succeeded out of one hundred merchants who have traded in any county, or in any particular block in some city, at least fifteen of them would prove, on a careful scrutiny, to have been more upright and conscientious than the great mass of their less fortunate rivals. Vainly shall a man hope to live and thrive by buying and selling after his neighbors, his customers, have learned by sad experience that his word is not reliable—that his representations of the cost or quality of his wares are not to be trusted. Of two persons of equal capacity, who have been ten years in trade, one having acquired therein only experience, with the decided confidence of his neighbors and a fair circle of dealers and customers, while the other has amassed some twenty thousand dollars, but at the cost of a reputation for slipperiness and dishonesty, the latter is this day the poorer man, as time will clearly establish.—Nothing is more common, or more fatal than the grasping of an advantage at the cost of ten times its value; and he who has traded out his neighbor's good opinion is pretty certain to die a poor man, however high the price for which he sold it.

But integrity, though indispensable, is not all-sufficient as a basis of the true mercantile character. The true merchant must be impelled to his vocation by a conviction that therein can he best serve

God by blessing mankind. The merchant is an intermediate, an electric wire, a channel of intercourse, between producers in different sections, climes, or countries. Since it is certain that the heat of the tropics, germinates and ripens many useful plants which could never mature under the skies of the temperate zone, while even the polar regions contribute many things to the sustenance and comfort of man which could not be advantageously produced elsewhere, the honest and capable exchanger of the diverse products of these varying latitudes is a common benefactor. Though not literally a producer, he is essentially and practically so, by enabling each customer to satisfy his legitimate wants more cheaply and thoroughly than he otherwise could do, and thereby inciting to greater activity and efficiency in production. Without commerce, many who now earn and enjoy the material comforts of civilization would rest contented with the few, rude, and scanty devices and satisfactions of barbarism. Commerce increases both the impulses toward and facilities for perpetual progress in the useful arts, whereof intellectual progress is the natural counterpart and concomitant. The merchant, therefore, whose sole attachment to his calling is a sordid lust of gain, coupled with a belief that he can acquire property faster or easier by exchanging others' products than by directly producing himself, is most unlikely to honor his vocation, or even to be eminently successful in the ranks of its votaries.

Assuming, then, that integrity, with an earnest conviction that this is for him the path of duty and of philanthropy, should form the bases of the character and career of a true merchant, let me proceed to indicate some of the qualities and capabilities for which he should be distinguished :—

I. He should be *methodical* and *exact* in his calculations and dealings. His promises, however casual their origin or trivial their subject, should be performed to the letter, and he should insist on the like good faith from others, under penalty of never confiding a second time in one who has forfeited his word. The property or interest immediately involved may be of trifling value, but truth is no trifle. The merchant should, as early as practicable, separate his customers and others with whom he deals into two classes—

those whose word is to be implicitly relied on, and the other sort—and thenceforth, treat each class according to their respective merits. To the latter he should say frankly, whenever the proper opportunity presents itself: "I cannot again confide in your word, because you have shown me that you either cannot or will not redeem it. I do not judge you; but, if I trust at all, it must be some one who fulfils his promises at whatever inconvenience or sacrifice." By this course, he will perpetually and strongly inculcate the advantages of probity and fidelity, and thus conduce to their increase and diffusion.

II. He should inflexibly set his face against any system of *loose, general credit* on goods purchased for consumption. Credit is an excellent, a most beneficent device; but, like most good things, is susceptible of the greatest abuse. A poor young man, qualified to manage a farm or conduct some mercantile business, seeks credit for his farm or his stock, and perhaps for some share of his seeds and implements; though every man should earn something by working for others before running in debt for the outfit of an independent business. The merchant who sells largely may very well require credit for some part of his new stock, if he has taken notes which he cannot readily turn for the old one. But neither farmer, mechanic, nor any body else should run up bills from week to week for food and clothing, but should make a point of paying for his subsistence as he may require it. The neglect of this rule is one main cause of the prevalence of extravagance, over-trading, and general insolvency, frequently resulting in mercantile bankruptcy and general revulsion. The humble cultivator who owes for half his farm and cannot turn off more than two or three hundred dollars' worth of produce per annum, out of which one hundred dollars must be paid as interest on his debt, is often tempted, by the facility of obtaining credit, to buy silks and satins for his wife and daughters, broadcloth and fine boots for his sons, or allow them to buy such for themselves on his account, when he can by no means afford such expenditures. It is the duty of the true merchant to resist and correct this tendency, by insisting on prompt payment for all purchases except under peculiar circumstances. Cash should be the general rule; credit the rare exception. The poor man who has encountered some sudden and severe calamity, such as the burning of his house or the destruction of his crops by hurricane or flood, may very properly be proffered credit for a season at cash prices; so may the poor widow whose children, this year at school, will be earning wages and able to help her next season. But in all ordinary cases the merchant, if only from a patriotic regard for the general well-being, should inflexibly refuse to sell on credit, since such selling is, and ever must be, to the uncircumspect majority, a temptation and facility for general improvidence and over-trading.—"Mr. President," said the eccentric John Randolph, interrupting himself in one of his Senatorial diatribes, "I have discovered the Philosopher's Stone!—It consists of four short words of homely English—'*Pay as you go.*'"

III. On the same principle the true merchant will carefully consider, in selecting his goods, not merely whether he can sell them at a profit, but whether that profit, should he accept it, would not be made at the expense of the moral and pecuniary welfare of the community. He might seem to make a large profit on alcoholic beverages, implements of gaming, &c.; but he knows, in the first place, that he has no moral *right* to make money in any such way; and, next, that all the devil's gold that may thus be realized is sure to vanish, like dream-won treasure, even while the hand fiercely clutches it. The merchant who sells intoxicating liquors is burning up his customers for the little fat he can fry out of them, and wasting nine-tenths of it in the process. He gets some twenty dollars clear profit on a pipe of brandy, and uses up, by selling it, a customer, out of whom he had made fifty dollars a year, and who, falling into intemperance and insolvency, does him out of two hundred dollars or so charged on his books. Thus, all traffic which panders to vicious appetites is ruinous to the legitimate business of the dealer, and every dollar of profit he secures by it costs him ten, twenty, or thirty; but, even if such were not the fact, he has no right to seek gain through the enlargement of Satan's kingdom. The end of his mortal existence is quite other than that. He is here to do good and not evil—to erect barriers to the spread of vice, and not to facilitate and profit by its diffusion. He may, indeed, have a good *opportunity* to secure gain in this way; but to argue thence that he has a *right* to do so, is to sanctify the treachery of Judas, and proclaim his earning of the thirty pieces a "fair business transaction."

IV. But the merchant's virtue should be not merely negative and obstructive—it should be positively and actively beneficent. He should use the opportunities afforded by his vocation to foster agricultural and mechanical improvement, to advance the cause of education, and diffuse the principles not only of virtue but of refinement and correct taste. He should be continually on the watch for whatever seems calculated to instruct, ennoble, refine, dignify, and benefit the community in which he lives. He should be an early and generous patron of useful inventions and discoveries, so far as his position and means will permit. He should be a regular purchaser of new and rare books, such as the majority will not buy, yet ought to read, with a view to the widest dissemination of the truths they unfold. If located in the country, he should never visit the city to replenish his stock without endeavoring to bring back something that will afford valuable suggestions to his customers and neighbors. If these are in good part farmers, and no store in the vicinity is devoted especially to this department, he should be careful to keep a supply of the best ploughs and other implements of farming, as well as of the choicest seeds, cuttings, &c., and of those fertilizing substances best adapted to the soil of his township, or most advantageously transported thither; and these he should be very willing to sell at cost, especially to the poor or the penurious, in order to encourage their general acceptance and use. Though he make no profit directly on the sale of these, he is indirectly but substantially *benefited by whatsoever shall increase the annual production of his township, and thus the ability of his customers to purchase and consume his goods.* The merchant whose customers and neighbors are enabled to turn off three, five, seven or nine hundred dollars' worth of produce per annum from farms which formerly yielded but one or two hundred dollars' worth beyond the direct consumption of their occupants, is in the true and safe road to competence and wealth if he knows how to manage his business. Every wild wood or waste morass rendered arable and fruitful, every field made to grow fifty bushels of grain per acre where but fifteen or twenty were formerly realized, is a new tributary to the stream of his trade, and so clearly conducive to his prosperity.

V. For a higher reason than this, but not therefore in ignorance of the fact, he should be a steadfast and liberal patron of religious instruction and worship, of intellectual culture and discipline, of temperance, of agricultural societies, and mechanics' associations, and whatever sensibly conduces either to diffuse and strengthen morality, or to ennoble and increase industry. A community wherein God is not obeyed, and labor is not respected, must seem, to any reflecting man, a very undesirable place for the training of his children. There life can rarely be tranquil and happy; there property can hardly be secure; there the sweets of peace and contentment can scarcely be enjoyed through a series of years. If it were possible for the atheist or the sensualist to be truly wise, he would labor to inculcate and diffuse the great fundamental truths of religion and morality, if from no higher motive than a selfish regard for his own ease and safety. Nations, states, and smaller communities subsist by faith and virtue, and perish through the disintegrating influences of sensuality and vice. That community which has cast off all faith in the invisible and everlasting, and cut down its creed to a mere recognition of the material and the palpable—which realizes only that sugar is sweet, that fire will burn, and that "ginger is hot i' the mouth"—is on the broad highway to destruction, however dazzling its present outward show of prosperity.

VI. The true merchant will be a liberal but discriminating supporter of the press in his locality. He will not feel an obligation to patronize any and every thing that wears the form of a newspaper, but will scan carefully the intellectual ability and moral fitness of those who assume the lofty responsibility of public teaching through the press. He will not encourage the dissemination nor continuance of journals edited by the incompetent or unworthy; but if there be none other than these already in existence in his county, he will combine with men like himself to procure the establishment of such a journal as is needed, or the transfer of one already existing into the hands of some one qualified to guide opinion and dispel mental darkness. Such a journal he will liberally and steadily encourage and support by advertising in its columns at good prices, by urging upon other business men the duty of doing likewise, and by soliciting his customers and neighbors to give it at least their subscriptions, regularly continued and uniformly paid in advance. By pursuing this course, the merchant may do very much toward the diffusion of intelligence, the predominance of sound principles, and the purification of morals. He need not be a political brawler nor habitual agitator on any subject—there is a more excellent way. He may give to an approved and influential journal in his county from two to five hundred dollars' worth of advertising per annum, and procure from others by the power of his solicitations and example, five times as much more; while each name added to the list of its subscribers extends the publicity of his announcements and their potency in enlarging his business. Thus will he exert a noiseless, unintermitted influence in diminishing the kingdom of darkness, extending the sway of virtue, and laying deep and broad the foundations of general and personal prosperity.

VII. The true merchant will not be likely to forget that his essential function is that of an exchanger of products, and not merely that of a seller. In great cities and at certain commercial points, this function is properly subdivided, not merely between buyers of produce and sellers of goods, but usually between many different classes of sellers and buyers; dry-goods, groceries, paints, meats, breadstuffs, &c., &c., being severally bought and sold by dealers in each particular department. It is otherwise, however, throughout a good part of the country, where, from the necessity of the case, the same person is both buyer and seller, and deals in nearly every variety of product exported, or fabric required by the people of his neighborhood. Here the merchant should be not more solicitous to sell goods than to enable his customers readily to pay for them; to which end he should zealously promote every effort by feasible means to increase their facilities of communication with the seaboard, and to bring markets for their products nearer to their doors by there calling into existence new branches of industry, and building up or reviving manufactures. No wise merchant will fear that his trade will suffer by this diversification of pursuits; for abundant experience has demonstrated that *they buy most from abroad who produce most and in greatest variety at home.* Thus, Massachusetts consumes far more (in value) of foreign products per annum than North Carolina or Tennessee, because the wide extension of her manufactures has rendered her industry far more universal, and has, by largely increasing her aggregate of production, correspondingly increased her power of purchase and consumption. Whether by reducing the expense of reaching a distant market, or by bringing a market for their surplus productions much nearer, the merchant who conduces to the essential advantage of his neighbors, his customers, ministers thereby to his own thrift and solid prosperity.

These suggestions might be indefinitely extended, but enough has been said to show that the mercantile is properly a beneficent and liberalizing vocation, and the merchant's true interests are deeply inwoven with those of the community from which he draws his sustenance. The sordid trader may narrow and degrade his vocation into that of a mere money-getter—a shave—a cormorant; but, if so, he does violence to its nature and wrong to its high-minded devotees. If each merchant would but realize what is the true spirit, what are the essential reqnirements, what the beneficent capabilities, of his calling, he could scarcely fail to live worthily and usefully, and transmit an honored name to his children. May the time speedily arrrive when none but the true merchant can find customers whereby to live, and when the knavish, the unprincipled, the rapacious, the vicious, shall be driven into employments where their moral defects, if not thoroughly remedied, shall be less widely influential and less glaringly pernicious! That such a time *will* come, the steady diffusion of knowledge, the prevalence of observation and reflection, render all but inevitable.

CHAPTER X.

HOW TO GET RICH BY SPECULATION.*

THE attributes which constitute greatness in men are bestowed reluctantly on individuals. A good poet is the pet of an age; a great general is the marvel of a century; and a profound speculator a rarer gift than either. Every science has its laws; and when we neglect laws, we are in ignorance. Empiricism disappears, and quackery takes flight when we discover the law of a phenomenon. The laws of speculation are not well understood; indeed, they may in part be considered not well established. Let us attempt the labor of laying down the necessary rules which ought to govern this great art.

And here in the outset we apprise the reader that, inasmuch as one man's wisdom or experience would be a very insufficient guide in this great search for truth, which has a big bag of money at the end, we have not undertaken to rely on our own acquired skill in money-making, but have made free with the knowledge of others. The principles, the facts, the maxims, and the judgments which we design to set forth are partly original and partly compiled. Few men have written books without saying something wise on the subject of money-getting. What we have learned from divers sources respecting this matter may be reduced to the following heads:—

In the first place, be it observed that successful speculation is not in general mere luck, like that of Lord Timothy Dexter, of Newburyport, when he sent the cargo of warming-pans to the West Indies, for, notwithstanding this instance of fortunate miscalculation, Dexter commonly based his speculations upon good calculation and

* By a Merchant of Boston.

foresight. Ignorant as he was of geography, and domestic life in the tropics, he had a knowledge of human nature, and a shrewd instinct in money matters. He studied and calculated; and a fool who proceeds by study and calculation will do better than a wise man who tries to do without them.

In the second place, it must not be forgotten that there is a wide and essential difference between *speculation* and *trade*, two things which are very apt to be confounded together in theory and practice. It is true that trade and speculation meet in State street, but they have in them nothing in common; and although the object of each is a California at home, they search for its discovery by totally different roads. The trader, properly speaking, has nothing to do with business but to stick to it; and as every business must pay, and all sorts of business in the long run are equally profitable, small gains, carefully accumulated, in time realize a fortune. You are surprised that many men fail in business; but be assured that the fault was in the bankrupt, not in the business. Trade of necessity must pay; and, in the long run, the gains must exceed the losses, otherwise there could be no trade.

Reflect on this fact a moment, and then proceed to the discovery, among the retailers in Hanover street, that traders who know their business are unaffected by change in prices; they lose on their goods when prices fall, but they gain when prices rise. "Put that against that," and if your bookkeeping be correct, one in the course of time balances the other.

The speculator is a very different person. Like the last new comet, he acknowledges a law of his own. He *does* concern himself in the rise and fall of prices, for they deeply concern him. The trader depends on customers; the speculator has none. The trader depends upon small but regular gains; the speculator looks to sudden and eccentric enrichment. The world is his market.

No doubt speculation is a lottery, but so is going to California Since the suppression of lotteries in Massachusetts, mercantile speculation, daring, dashing, hazardous, break-neck adventures, have greatly increased, not only in actual amount, but proportionally in comparison with regular trade. The fact is there is a certain quantum of the spirit of wild, and eager, and hazardous adventure ever in the community, and it *will* seek exercise and gratification in some form or other. People who bought lottery-tickets thirty years ago, now buy "fancy stock" in railroads, bales of cotton, bags of coffee, or the promises of such things—go to bed and dream of castles in the air—the same as formerly. *Then,* they paid five dollars for a chance—now, five thousand.

Men, therefore, *will* speculate; though to the uninitiated, speculation has all the risk of lottery dealing. We will attempt for this reason to initiate those who are bent on this course of adventure.

Three things are essential to a successful speculator—*time, capital and courage;* and these are of little avail without judgment. All speculation has reference to a future, in which the question of time is involved. Results are never immediate. Capital—every body knows nothing can be done without that; and if a man wants courage, let him draw a handcart, sell friction-matches about the streets, get in coal, shovel snow, clean boots, or sit in his chimney corner, and wish he had an office under the government: he will never make a speculator; for he ought to be large of faith—a believer in things not seen. Activity is essential to trade; patience in speculation. Nothing is to be done when nothing is to be gained—a maxim which, from the obvious cause of the necessity of keeping customers, cannot always be followed in trade. Watchful ever, must we here "bide our time," the proper time for buying, the proper time for selling; although, no doubt, it is equally necessary to strike, to act decisively, when that time arrives. That, in fact, nothing be done, when nothing should be done, is, in the present instance at least, not so easy to a mercantile man as may be imagined; for a man of business must always be doing, whether at a profit or a loss, while the periods between the buying and the selling point, or one speculation and another, are necessarily long, dreary intervals of idleness, which afford no room for the exercise of the faculties. He is, therefore, apt to take a narrow, peddling view of things, so different from the qualities required in the more abstracted if not higher calling here taken into view.

The time for entering on trade is when things are at their worst, and that is not a bad time to enter on speculation; you may trade in any thing or every thing, but you can *speculate* only in a few things. You should not speculate in axe-handles, wooden bowls, hoop-poles, shoe-pegs, washing-machines, or mouse-traps, because countrymen and mechanics can make them to order in any quantity when they are wanted.

This law applies to all manufactures, except in reference to the raw material; and raw material admits of speculation only when it is affected by the season. The proper objects of speculation are, therefore, agricultural produce of most kinds, flour, cotton, sugar, coffee, tea, &c., which amply suffice the speculator to make a fortune or to lose one.

As you wish to make a fortune, take the necessary means; *study statistics, and attend to great political and commercial changes.* Take a commodity and find out the average price of years, excluding from consideration extreme cases, and when the price has fallen below the average of years, buy. Thus, let us suppose that this commodity is flour, that there has been a great crop of wheat, or that the price has fallen below the average, or, in other words, it has become cheap; if the harvest after all be bad, you gain; if otherwise, it does not follow that you are to lose; sell, and replace your old stock by a new one.

If the depreciation continue, it might perhaps be well in some cases for a person to become a dealer in the article till a bad crop or under-production takes place. In this way it will be observed that he is always to have the same stock or quantity on hand, which he may have, if not entirely, for nearly the same money; and when a bad crop or under-production takes place, his speculation being now ripe, he is immediately to sell out.

An Englishman of some celebrity used to say that the first of his ancestors, of any note, was a baker and dealer in hops, who, on one occasion, to procure a sum of money, robbed his feather-beds of their contents, and supplied the deficiency with unsalable hops. In a few years a severe blight universally prevailed, hops became very scarce, and enormously dear; the hoarded treasure was ripped out, and a good sum procured for hops, which, in a plentiful season, would not have been salable; and thus, said he, "our family *hopped* from obscurity." Hops are said to fail, on an average, every five years—a hint to speculators. The rule laid down in reference to flour, applies equally well to cotton, but—take care of your statistics. Distrust the Carolina and Georgia newspapers. Long as we have lived, we do not remember a season without a dismal story that the "cotton crop had entirely failed at the South."

There are two qualities which principally fit any commodity for speculation: first, frequency in the change of its price, and, secondly, the extent of that change; it being obvious that alteration—a fall as well as a rise—is necessary to the purpose of the speculator, and the extreme of prices is that which he will chiefly look to, or in which he will seek his gain.

Of the two, trade and speculation, which is superior—which the inferior, we apprehend there cannot be a doubt. Speculation, is, in truth, a mere exception in business, arising out of the derangements of trade, or impossibility of adjusting the supply to the demand; yet so far useful to, or coming in aid of trade, as it has a tendency to produce readjustment; to prevent extremes in price, as well that which is ruinously low as that which is excessive, to prevent dearth and famine. For, if a person buys when prices are low, this has a tendency to raise price; as when he brings out a store, and sells when prices are high, it has to lower it.

Trade is steady and uniform, and can be carried on at all times; speculation, on the other hand, only occasionally, or when opportunity offers. There is, therefore, a peculiar certainty which belongs to the former, which does not belong to the latter; and this certainty is the certainty of employment, or the scope for it. The time also required to mature a speculation is not to be forgotten, during which it may be conceived money will often be made in the regular course of trade. As in mechanics, so in speculation, what we gain in force we lose in time. Yet without doubt, occasionally, very large sums are made by opportunities which it requires but a very ordinary share of sagacity to foresee and take advantage of. Such, however, is the variety of productions afforded by commerce, or brought into demand by the necessities and luxuries of man, and the complex state of things thereby occasioned, that when an object of speculation is dismissed, or fails, a wide field exists in which to look out for another, there is, in fact, always something which is plentiful or scarce, that is, at a price below or above the average—namely, grain, or a particular species of grain, cotton, hemp, flax, wool, leather, oils of various kinds—whale, palm, olive, seal, sperm, cod, whalebone, rice, sugar, coffee, tallow, tar, turpentine, saltpetre, indigo, &c.; so that a person may, at any given or particular time, have an opportunity of laying the foundation of a speculation by purchase, or of finishing it by sale; if not the one, at least the other; and the state of things which fits for the one is just as necessary as that which fits for the other. Thus may irregularity be converted into regularity, and that which is in its nature occasional made permanent, or the subject of a continued mode of operation, or one speculation be uniformly succeeded by another.

There is likewise another consideration which occurs here. In general, it requires considerable time to mature a single speculation, and bring it to a successful termination. Now, if a person embark his whole disposable means in any one article, he is in that case not only obliged to wait the issue of this one adventure, according to the fortune of the article, but is during the time precluded from having any thing to do with any other, whatever advantages it may offer. Therefore, if a person be inclined to make speculation a business, it would seem best to invest only a part of his capital in any one commodity, so as to have many speculations afloat at the same time, different in their stages, some, if possible, always commencing, and others falling in, or terminating. By these means it may be brought more nearly to the nature and condition of a regular trade, in which not only is a person's whole capital with some certainty engaged, but an average established, rendering it more uniform and safe. And so considered, it matters not to a speculator whether things rise or fall. When they fall he is to buy, when they rise he is to sell. His only difficulty is when they stand still. Nor is this to be confounded with wholesale trade strictly understood, which is a different thing, and consists in supplying set customers for a regular profit. But how do you know when commodities are highest or lowest?—when they begin to rise or fall? Shall this be your guide? Not without careful reference to elaborate statistics—the lowest and highest averages. When prices are high, of course there is a great demand, and business is brisk: when prices are low, there is little demand,

and business is dull. Hence the temptation in the one case, and the discouragement in the other. Therefore, to be a good merchant or speculator, as to be a good general, nerve is necessary: and the one as well as the other must often act in the face of appearances. He must believe, contrary to what the fabulous first inhabitants of the earth are reported to have done, that the sun will rise again after it has set. Nay, we should say a good merchant must *always* act contrary to appearances, at least to what appears to the generality of mankind. He must buy when no other person will buy; sell when no other person will sell; although certainly, if properly considered, it is most consistent with reason to buy when things are low; to sell when they are high.

The rule, therefore, generally is (the temptation being apparent) to speculate in high prices; that is, to buy when things are high, in the expectation of their rising still higher. In this, indeed, there may often be much gain, but there is always great risk. Therefore, to be safe, the articles must be got rid of immediately that is, soon—whether at a gain or at a loss; if at a loss, to save a greater. And the last holder, in cases of this kind, be it observed, is always a dupe. The conduct described is, indeed a common one, by which we find many ruin themselves, and often throw away the fruits of a long life of industry by a single false step.

Is there any danger of letting people into these secrets? None whatever; for, as Spurzheim said, men are so stupid there is no fear of their ever becoming wise. He, it is said, who has the folly of mankind for an inheritance, has a plentiful estate. The great object of speculation, indeed, being to substitute sagacity for toil, to enable men to live by their wits instead of their labor, the sole efficiency of the first-mentioned quality in one class refers exactly to the want of it in another.

An American trading-vessel, after interloping at a port in Japan, and making the most of her time, was ordered off, as usual, by the government. The Japanese official said to the captain: "You must never come here again; but *when* you do, be sure to bring some more of that fine broadcloth." So we say to all and singular, who shall read the above: "Never speculate; but *when* you do, be sure to mind our rules."

CHAPTER XI.

GETTING MONEY—CONTINUED.

INTEREST—BANKING—PRIVATE BANKING.

INTEREST is the sum paid by the borrower of a sum of money, to the lender, for its use. The rate of interest is dependent on the security of the principal, and the rate of profit which may be made by the employment of capital in industrial pursuits. No person would lend money, on personal security of a doubtful character, at the same rate of interest as on a good mortgage; and where profits in ordinary business are high, interest is also high. The same laws that regulate the price of commodities, or the rates of insurance, govern the charges for the use of money.

The rate of interest is, in fact, the *net profit on capital.* Whatever returns are obtained by the borrower, beyond the interest he has agreed to pay, really accrue to him on account of risk, trouble, or skill, or of advantages of situation and connection. This being so, it is not difficult to perceive that interest is the most *certain* way of getting money that can be named. The men who, to-day, receive the interest of a portion of the capital of the country, will, eventually, if they pursue the same mode of investment, own the whole property of the country. *The young man, twenty-five years of age, who invests a capital of* $10,000 *on mortgaged security, and reinvests the interest, annually, in the same way, at ten per cent. per annum, which is legal in the State of Ohio and some of the other States, will be worth over* $100,000 *at the age of fifty, without calculating any thing that he might save from the labor of his head or hands, over and above what is necessary for his livelihood.*

* Those who are looking through this book for secrets in money-getting may make a note of this. The diligent searcher will find several others.

This will be the net profit of capital; while those who borrow the money with a view of making larger profits, by assuming *risks*, will, most probably, at the same age, find themselves in a worse condition, pecuniarily, than when they commenced. Interest upon money, and the producing or manufacture of articles *necessary* in civilized life, are the only ways of making money that would not be rendered more secure by a guarantee.

Inasmuch, then, as interest is a sure mode of accumulating money, while the profits of industrious undertakings are uncertain, it is a matter of the first importance to a business community that the rates of interest should be kept down. To this end, governments have passed laws fixing certain rates of loans, which it is deemed legal to charge, and illegal to exceed. It is now considered, by an immense number of intelligent men, that these laws have failed in their aim; that their effect is to increase, not diminish, the rate of interest; that they deter the timid from lending when the market rate is higher than the legal, while the bold disregard them, and charge proportionally for the risk; that they are necessarily evaded by circuitous devices, and thus encourage a feeling of disrespect for law; that they are a violation of the fundamental maxim that trade prospers best when untrammelled by legislative enactments, and therefore should be repealed. The repeal of the usury laws is a matter of experiment; the result can now be only conjectural. If the effect would be to lower the rate of interest, and prevent those ruinous fluctuations, by increasing the number of lenders, in times of scarcity, they *should* be repealed; and the arguments that have been adduced by able men in England and America, for many years, are sufficiently strong to justify the experiment. The first usury law, which was passed in England in 1554, had for its object, not to prohibit the lender from charging interest beyond a certain sum, but to authorize him to charge ten per cent. Previous to that, it was considered unjust to charge interest at all. Aristotle argued that, as money could not produce money, no return could be equitably claimed by the lender. This prejudice is still supported by law in Mohammedan countries. Calvin was one of the first who saw and exposed the fallacy of such notions; as Bentham was one of the first who exposed the inefficacy of the usury laws. Subsequent English statutes reduced the rate, first to eight per cent., and then to five per cent. In 1833, the British parliament abolished the usury law in respect to mercantile paper, for a certain period of time, and a recent act continued the exemption until the 1st of January, 1856.*

* Extract from a letter written by the author to a friend on the usury laws: "Antiquity of a usage is no proof of its justice. People frequently acquiesce in established evils, and console themselves by thinking they could not be otherwise. An emperor of Japan thought he would have died of laughter on hearing that the Dutch had no king. The Iroquois could not conceive how wars could be carried on with success, if prisoners were not to be burnt. The Roman law allowed creditors to cut their insolvent debtors into pieces; the Scotch placed them in a pillory; the English imprison them in jail; all of which they thought right, and we think wrong.

"The repeal of the usury laws is a simple matter of policy. Principle has nothing to do with it. If it is once admitted that interest may be taken at all, a uniform unvarying rate of interest can never be justly established. High and low interest are relative terms—what may be high at one place would be low at another. There are hundreds of men in the Western States worth their thousands, who would be penniless to-day had they not been able to borrow money, some dozen years ago, at twenty-five per cent.—'Squatters' have frequently paid a higher rate, and done wisely by so doing. They select their location; capitalists attend the land sales; buy their claims; give them bonds for deeds on payment of double the amount in from two to four years. This is a customary mode of proceeding, and it is one way of evading the usury laws. Many of these tracts are now worth, in their wild state, from $50 to $80 per acre. Interest on borrowed money is generally the cheapest form of credit. Every body knows that goods can be bought in the Eastern cities at from ten to fifteen per cent. lower for cash, than upon a credit of six months. The buyer, with the cash in his pocket, has also the range of the market, which is no mean advantage. Whence did legislators get their wisdom to know what interest all men, under all circumstances, could afford to pay?

"It has been said that several of the new States tried a repeal of their usury laws, and were compelled to re-enact them. The trial was not a fair one; the time of repeal was too short. The attention of capitalists had not been specially directed that way. In Indiana, interested men took occasion to ascribe the ruin of the 'speculating times' to the repeal of the usury laws, when, it was really the principal and not the interest that ruined men: and, in Wisconsin, the time of the repeal was very short. To my personal knowledge, just before these laws were re-enacted, a number of capitalists

The lender and borrower do not, under the present system, meet each other face to face. A dealer in money, usually called a banker, acts as an intermediate party. He borrows of one party, and lends to another; and the difference between the terms at which he borrows and those at which he lends is the source of his profit. Banks are of two kinds; public and private. A public bank is that in which there are numerous partners or stockholders, and they elect from their body a certain number as managers or directors. A private bank is that in which there are but few partners; and these attend personally to its management. The banks of the United States are generally public or joint-stock banks. In so far as they facilitate loans, drawing into active operation small sums of money, and accommodating those who are in need of additional

were arranging plans to invest over a million of dollars in that State, on terms equally as beneficial to the borrower as to the lender. The experiment of repeal should be fairly tried, especially in the Western States; and I believe millions of dollars would flow in from Europe and the East; rates would be comparatively high at first, as they now are exorbitant, and then gradually sink to a general level.

* * * * * * *

"But, banks of circulation, I think, should be restricted in their charges. They create money, and can monopolize money. They are endowed by the legislature with a species of money-manufacturing privileges, which the constitution has placed in the hands of government alone. This high prerogative is justified solely on the ground of public benefit. Their ostensible object is not to make profit for themselves, but to facilitate the trade of the community. Petitioners for a bank charter do not openly solicit legislative interference in behalf of themselves or their friends. This would not look patriotic. Public good is the plea. A clear distinction should, therefore, be made between incorporated banks and individuals. Deriving their sole existence from law, partaking of the delegated powers of government, law should direct their mode of management, nature of business, and amount of profits. A rigid regard to the *public good* seems to require that they should exchange their notes for the notes of individuals, under careful regulations, charging a difference merely sufficient to pay the expenses of management, and, perhaps, that average of losses, which will accrue under the best management, and directors should be paid for attending to the wants of the community. At all events, the extent of their powers should be distinctly defined."

capital to carry on their transactions, they are eminently useful; but to this is added a dangerous feature. They are incorporated by the legislature, with power to issue bills which shall circulate as money, and with limited liability. While there is not enough metallic money in a country to facilitate exchanges, or it is too unwieldy to be generally serviceable, paper money of some kind seems desirable; but the creation of this paper money is a privilege too solemn to be delegated to unofficial and irresponsible individuals. The benefits and evils of the American Banking System, however, are a field too extensive to enter upon; and as it has been made a political question, it is necessarily excluded from consideration, in accordance with our original plan.—Taking things as they are, all that we propose doing is to instruct the uninitiated in a *few* of the ways by which money has been and can be made. In doing so, we will notice the speculative ways first, and the honorable mode afterwards.

The first step with bank speculators is to apply to the legislature for a charter for a bank; say with a nominal capital of $100,000, divided into a thousand shares of $100 each. It is provided in the charter that, as soon as a certain sum shall be paid on each share, the bank shall commence operations. The payment of the other instalments is left to the discretion of the directors. The speculators themselves subscribe for the whole of the stock, and pay the first instalment, say $5, on each share; and the bank commences business, and issues notes perhaps to five times the amount of capital paid in. The notes are then borrowed by the speculators, and, being current as money, they are used in their private speculations. The interest which they pay as borrowers, they receive back again as stockholders; and thus they have a great advantage over their neighbors. The other instalments are arranged by the discounting of stock-notes, and the payments are merely nominal. This is the first way of making money by bank speculations. It is not generally practised; but it has been and can be done.

The second way to make money is to manage the bank so that it will declare a large dividend the first year. If it declares a dividend of ten per cent., the stock will be worth in the market $150 a share. The speculators will then sell the largest portion of their stock at this rate to parties who will not interfere with the bank management, and invest the proceeds in substantial property, retaining enough, however, to keep the control of the institution in their own hands.

Another mode of getting money is to act the part of the syren in the fable; to tempt men of an ambitious disposition by the proffer of loans to extend their operations far beyond their capital and the bounds of prudence; and at the very time when further assistance is most needed, to shut down on them—draw the reins—plunge them in bankruptcy while the managers of the game, or their agents, buy up the valuable pieces of the wreck for a song, and hold for a rise.

Another way is to refuse discounts of unexceptionable paper at their banking office at legal rates, and buy up the same paper, through brokers or agents, at two, three, and four per cent. a month. As corporations have "neither bodies to be kicked nor souls to be damned," there seems to be no present nor future danger of punishment.

Another way of making money through the medium of incorporated paper-money banks is to deal in government stocks. Voltaire gives us some insight into this in one of his letters from Ferney, in Switzerland. "Here I am," he says, "living in a way suited to my habits, and caring but little for to-morrow: for I have a friend, a director in the Bank of France, who writes to me whenever money is to be made in the public funds. Sometimes he writes to me desiring me to sell, because the bank is going to withdraw its notes. At other times he bids me to buy; for we are going to issue a quantity of notes; and so, through the kindness of my friend, I always make money, though living two hundred miles from Paris."

The honorable, safe, legitimate mode of making money by public banking is to discount business paper to the extent of the capital and the average balance of deposits; equalizing loans among the community, and looking rather to the moral character of the parties applying, and their reputation for prudence, than to the extent of their business or the amount of their property.

Private banks are more in accordance with the spirit of the age and republican institutions, than public banks. It is certainly the opposite of that rapidity which characterizes the business movements of the age to have discounts only once or twice a week; and wait perhaps two days for an answer to an application. It is certainly a serious drawback to the full realization of republican sovereignty to be compelled to court the favor and influence of some half dozen directors of an overgrown moneyed institution in order to obtain a loan. Private banks are free from these objections. They discount every hour of the day when they discount at all; and an answer to an application may be had in five minutes. In dealing with a private banker, the applicant deals as with a private trader, to whom it is of as much importance to lend, as it is to himself to borrow. The extent of their business depends in a degree on the disposition they manifest to accommodate their customers. They are responsible in the whole amount of their fortunes; their whole faculties are exerted in the management of their business; and this is the only way that any business can be well conducted.

An able writer has remarked; "All the cities of Europe have furnished eminent examples of the power and usefulness of private capitalists. Unlike banking associations, they combine immense power in the person of a single far-seeing and capacious mind, which is the centre of a large circle of mercantile operations, operating around and depending upon it. While it restrains them from pushing too fast in times of confidence and prosperity, it puts out the hand and supports them in the hour of adversity. It was a remarkable fact on the occasion of a political revolution and change of government in Paris, with the presence of a foreign army, that very few failures occurred among the mercantile classes; because the private capitalists, understanding perfectly the nature of the crisis, instead of partaking in a common panic, and rushing headlong to ruin, as is always the case under such circumstances with corporate institutions, extended liberally and freely their aid to all their customers, carrying them through their obligations as they matured, until the return of the political calm; when business, reviving, brought back their means with safety and profit to all parties. The prevalence of banking corporations in this country has hitherto stifled the growth of this class of citizens, who are emphatically the pillars of the State. They form the only resource of the government, in furnishing forth its armies to beat back the invading enemy, and in supplying revenues which perish with the cessation of commerce. At such times paper banks are crushed with the weight that leans on them. Of late years public banking has been going out of favor, and individual genius and enterprise are rapidly assuming its position. The public are already, in cheap exchanges and superior facilities, experiencing the superiority of individual over corporate bankers."

In London, private bankers do, probably, the largest portion of the banking business of that immense metropolis. They discount bills, receive deposits, and, in some cases, allow interest on deposits. In Scotland, it is customary to receive upon interest even small sums, and also allow interest on the balance of a running account. In our Eastern cities, private banking is not known as a distinct profession, and broking and stock-jobbing by no means compensate for the want of it. In the western States, the business of private banking flourishes to a considerable extent. A deficiency of banking capital, and the demands of commerce called it into existence, and the competition among borrowers for money has made it the *most certain, and perhaps the most profitable business of the West.*

In Cincinnati, of late years, private banks are a marked feature. The capital of the public banks of the sixth city of the Union is little more than one and a half millions of dollars, and their notes, as well as gold and silver, are at a premium, and of course rarely seen. It is easy to perceive that this is a mere "plum" for the directors and their friends, with a slice for the pork merchants. Traders, manufacturers, and mechanics, keep their accounts with private bankers, partly from necessity, and partly from preference The latter usually allow an interest of six per cent. on current deposits, and on special agreement a higher rate is sometimes given. The rates of discount vary from one to four per cent. a month; the average rates in respectable institutions are about one and a quarter or one and a half per cent. a month. It is customary with several of the private banks to make temporary loans to their customers, on individual security, without requiring indorsers. This is a good plan; and we believe that the general establishment of private banks will essentially modify the inconvenient and dangerous system of indorsation, now made necessary by the demands and regulations of incorporated banks.

Private banking is a business that should receive the consideration and examination of capitalists. Those who are about investing large capitals in merchandising would do well to give it their attention. The business is more profitable, in the long run, than merchandising, and far more certain. It is yet in its infancy in the United States, and there is room for the profitable use and employment of millions of dollars. In the West, fortunes can rapidly be made in the business; and, in the Eastern cities, I am satisfied that the establishment of private institutions doing a regular banking business, and perhaps allowing a certain interest on deposits, would meet with ample encouragement. There are many men of large property who are absolutely sick of the present system, and there are hundreds who would cheerfully stand a larger interest than ordinary bank rates, to be sure of discounts at fair rates at all times when they have good paper to offer. The principles of safe banking are now pretty well understood by those who desire to understand them; and, with prudent management, the business is a sure one.

T. S. Goodman & Co., of Cincinnati, stand at the head of their profession. It is, I think, the oldest established house in that city, and has always maintained the deserved respect and confidence of the community. Possessing a solid capital, and without the ambition to do a larger business than prudence will warrant, or the avarice to accumulate wealth rapidly by extortionate charges, they have gradually increased their business and their wealth. Like the Rothschilds, it is a family concern. The senior partner is a gentleman of the old school, and eminently possesses those qualities of courtesy and firmness which constitute a good banker. The wonderful growth of that wonderful city, its rapidly increasing wealth, and their own established reputation, open before them a brilliant destiny.

CHAPTER XII.

GETTING MONEY BY INVENTIONS—PATENT MEDICINES, ETC.

"It will be perceived that the number of *patents*, compared with the number of *applications*, is as three to four, nearly. I have had occasion to remark, in previous reports, that the number of patents cannot increase in proportion to the number of applications. The field of invention, in many of its departments, is limited, and every year must necessarily circumscribe it still more narrowly, leaving little to be invented except what has been invented previously. Although many inventors are familiar with what has been done in those branches of the arts to which their attention has been directed, yet the number of those not thus informed is very great; and as the field becomes more and more occupied, this latter class can do little else than invent what has been previously known, and their exertion and sacrifice must finally end in *bitter disappointment*. The spirit of invention, although laudable in the highest degree, appears to be stimulated, in many cases, beyond a healthy action; and many are *wasting their time and substance* in attempts to improve branches of the arts, with which, in their full extent, they are unfamiliar, and, in so doing, produce what has long since been exploded, or is already in extensive use. As many patentees have been eminently successful, and as a happy hit has sometimes brought wealth and distinction, *multitudes* are induced to follow the example of their inventive predecessors, and ultimately to find themselves less fortunate, if not less capable, than those whom they attempted to rival. The evils arising from a want of information can never be, in any considerable degree, removed. Something can and should be done for the dissemination of knowledge; but knowledge sufficiently comprehensive and minute to guard against the reproduction of things old, and guide uniformly, or generally, to that which is new and useful, has never been possessed by inventors as a class, and never can be possessed except by comparatively few."—*Patent Office Rep.*, 1849–50.

Discoveries in science, and inventions in the arts, are scarcely within our province. They have, however, yielded large fortunes to a few, are prosecuted with ardor by many, and are looked up to by all as the safety-valve when the pressure of competition in regular trade becomes too great. But they are exceptions to business rather than business itself, and should be regarded as such by all who have a disposition for experiment. It is exceedingly imprudent for any one to employ, in invention, any other than his leisure time, without interference with his regular pursuits; or to use, in experiments, any other than his surplus money, no matter how important the results promise to be, in the event of success. The risks are too great. Not one in a thousand proves profitable to the inventor, and many a noble bark has stranded on this rock.

When a new field of invention has been opened by any one, it becomes a common centre into which hundreds and thousands throng, "some to improve on the original, and others to pirate and rob the originator of his just earnings." Improvements, too, succeed each other with such rapidity that one has not time to be fairly tested before it is superseded by another; and thus all fail, or perhaps that which has least merit, but the most capital to advance it, triumphs in the end. Nothing is more despicable than this disposition for trifling improvements, with a view of making money at the expense of the original inventor. A man who desires fame or money should remember that true genius disdains to sail with the crowd in quest of trifling improvements. "True genius is rather ambitious to bring up pearls of its own, than solicitous to polish those of other men." The field of original invention—of wants, and of agencies to supply those wants—is by no means exhausted. In taste, we want a drink a little stronger than water, and less expensive and injurious than wine. In agriculture, we want a machine that will combine the uses of the plough, harrow, and clod-pulverizer in one, leaving the ground loose and free to the genial action of the air, which the present instrument does not. In navigation, we want increased speed in our sailing vessels and ocean steamers. In the world at large, we want a motive power that will be as effectual and as powerful as steam, or more so, without requiring such costly, weighty, and cumbersome machinery to use it. The world is full of wants, which genius may reap a rich reward in supplying; and in the warehouse of nature there are mighty agencies sleeping, which at the touch of that arch-magician's wand, will leap forth living and obedient things. "He who would gain fame as an inventor must pry into the secrets of nature, and imitate her operations. It is the perfection of invention to *imitate* nature, the maturity of science and art to tread in her steps."

We have quoted the extract, at the commencement of this chapter, from a report made by an experienced officer of the patent department, as a word of warning, that those who are wasting their time and substance, and neglecting their business, in trifling experiments, may pause and reflect. It is impossible, in ordinary cases, for a man to tell whether his idea has not been thought of, again and again, and found impracticable; and to gain the necessary information, even if possible, would require an expenditure of time that would be more costly than an application for a patent. The study is more intricate than the study of the law. This, however, is another case in which warning is useless. Invention is a passion, and when indulged, becomes a master-passion. When, therefore, the disease becomes chronic, it is almost incurable, and the best that can be done is to apply cooling ointments, and let it take its course. Go on, then, thou second Fulton! Invent some new improvement in stoves, or churns, or washing-boards, or chicken-coops. These are necessary articles, and the world wants the best. It has its eyes intensely fixed upon you; they glisten with joy when your countenance gives signs of hope, and sink in despair when your face is dejected. It *may* be that you will obtain a patent, and it *may* be that it will pay its cost. If it does, invest the surplus in lottery tickets, and you *may* make *two* fortunes.

Akin to inventions, without partaking of any originality, is the *patent medicine business.* Like the former, the success of a few has excited the cupidity of the many. Men of all classes pronounce a eulogium on the "pill business." Mechanics contrast it with the results of their labor; the clerk sighs for a medical secret; the "regular" foams at the mouth; and even the merchant has an idea that it is a "mighty profitable thing."

Quackery is as old as the profession of which it is the offshoot, and will last as long. Paracelsus, who flourished in the sixteenth century, is regarded as the prince of quacks. The magistrates of Basle engaged him, at a high salary, to fill the chair at their medical university. At his first lecture he burned the works of Galen and Avicenna, and asserted that there was more knowledge in his *cap* than in the heads of all the physicians, and more experience in his *beard*, than in all the universities. Great and learned men were among his patients; and the noted Erasmus consulted him. He boasted that he had discovered a *panacea* which would cure all diseases at once, and even prolong life indefinitely; but, unfortunately for his reputation, he died at the early age of forty-eight, after a few hours illness, with a bottle of his panacea in his pocket. We would, however, by no means assert that all prepared remedies are valueless. Those that pretend to owe their virtues to great discoveries in medical science; the universal remedies or "cure-alls," and those which require improbable stories to bolster them up, are all probably valueless. There are few, if any specific remedies. Iodine has been regarded as a specific for scrofula; but it will not hold good in all cases. There is only *one* specific preventive known, and that is vaccination for smallpox. But many of the remedies are simply prepared prescriptions, in daily use by the profession, and these are salutary. Few that are valuable contain any thing new. Patent medicines are principally designed for country consumption. The idea is a good one, though the mode of management is wrong. It is certainly policy for every family, where an apothecary is not immediately at hand, to have a medicine-chest of simple remedies for simple diseases. To make this selection wisely, requires some knowledge and judgment; and all remedies which pretend to too much, or which are advertised too largely, should be avoided. All powerful medicines should only be administered by the profession.

We think it would be well for medical practitioners to abate a little in their dignity, in regard to prepared prescriptions. There can be nothing wrong in keeping common prescriptions prepared beforehand, or even putting them into circulation; and certainly there is nothing wrong in fairly advertising them, for, when an article is good, the public should know it. A set of remedies, agreed upon by a college of physicians, and certified by them as safe, and ordinarily used for certain simple diseases, would probably do away with all others, and prevent imposition. It would be a benefit to the public; and as patent medicines are now used where their remedies would then be used, it would not be injurious to the profession.

Dr. Rush was once asked, What per cent. had been added to human life by the art of medical practitioners. He answered, that it depended upon whether old women are to be included in the list —if *not*, the addition would be much less. The same may probably be said of patent medicines.

As a pursuit the patent medicine business is not more successful nor profitable, on an average, than any other. A few men, of distinguished tact, like Dr. Wright, of Philadelphia, proprietor of Wright's Indian Vegetable Pills, have met with deserved success: and a few others, with more boldness than skill, have drawn splendid prizes; but the majority of those who undertake the business without sufficient capital or calculation, suffer the usual penalties of reckless speculation. A writer in the *Tribune*, some time since, expressed what we regard as correct sentiments on the subject. "It is much overdone, even to an extent beyond almost any other. A few having realized a fortune, hundreds, thousands, have rushed into it, and lost the little means which they expected would so rapidly accumulate. It is an uncommonly flattering business considering *alone* the actual cost of the stock; hence thousands have been rashly invested in the manufacture and distribution of remedies without counting the tremendous cost of popularity: and it is obvious that, unless large sales are made, ruin will follow: so that, by a safe calculation, it is believed ninety in every hundred fail, who undertake the business. The manner of doing this remarkable business is invariably to manufacture large quantities, and establish agencies in every part of the country; it being almost without exception a commission business, and this is the only means of extending it. Of course, without a very large capital, nothing of late years can be done to compete with the already established remedies. Townsend labored two years, and accomplished nothing. Finally, Mr. Clapp, of Albany, who is wealthy, joined him, investing ample means; since which the sarsaparilla era soon reached its zenith. But, as every thing must have its day, it is rapidly declining.

"Many have been deluded into the belief that 'to come out largely' would bring customers from the four parts of the country, and have soon run out every dollar paying advertisements; then they fill the papers with 'wants' like this: 'Wanted, $1000, with a partner to engage in a business in which $5000 can be made in a month,' &c., &c. Despairing of ever obtaining a livelihood by such precarious means, they either go to work at something useful, or engage in a more desperate effort to humbug the sick.

"Nor is it now a simple matter to introduce a new curative, as besides the various popular nostrums, hundreds of respectable physicians in all parts of the country (and small druggists), seeing such a demand for patent medicines, and knowing that if they did not, others would sell, have made up 'cure-alls,' and distributed them in their vicinity; but, as they do not understand the business, and have but little capital, half of them resume their legitimate profession. When Dr. Brandreth began, a medicine could more easily work its way to fame with less means, as competition was not so strong as to keep it back; but even then without skill none could succeed.

"As a body there is equal talent engaged in the business to any other. It is noticed that medicines which are most extensively advertised by fulsome laudations, as rapidly decline as they go up; the proprietors thinking, if they make money at all, they will do it soon. Others, who have confidence in the intrinsic value of their remedies, pursue a different course, fearing that great excitement and exaggeration will impair the confidence of the public, and shorten their popularity.

"We copy the following from a late number of a medical paper:—

"'When a physician so far forgets the feelings of humanity that should always predominate in his practice, and uses his profession as a cloak to amass a fortune, he generally accomplishes his object like Dr. Morrison, of London, the inventor of the 'Hygeian Pills.' These pills were put up in packages of three boxes each, numbered one, two, and three, and to be taken in regular order; holding out the impression that they contained three different kinds of medicine. These pills became at one time quite popular in the United States, till the general agent's sale in New England was $100 a day, when he, becoming an extensive counterfeiter of them, had to leave the place. It was afterwards proved that these pills were made in New York; and that number one, two, and three, were all the same article. The medical faculty came out in London, and stated that Dr. Morrison was destroying much life by the recommendation of such quantities of medicine. He prosecuted the faculty for libel, and in every instance was beaten. In fifteen years, he amassed a princely fortune, and built himself a palace with the hope of enjoying his wealth; but an overruling Providence has called him to give an account of his doings, and to meet those from whom he extorted much of his wealth.

"Several physicians have adopted the course of Morrison, of London, by manufacturing many articles to be taken for the same complaint. A physician located in Broadway, New York, issues his handbills monthly, stating the day he would be in Boston, Lowell, Providence, Fall River, New Bedford, Norwich Town, New York, Troy, Albany, and Hudson, for consultation gratis. The secret of this doctor's success has grown solely out of his vituperation against the medical faculty; branding them with ignorance, as possessing no medical skill; intended to be understood by the afflicted that they all go in for making the most money out of the sick except himself, who is the only Good Samaritan, and filled with philanthropy for the distressed. Whilst the truth is, the most of his money is wrung out of the poor, who too often have to obtain through charity, the means to purchase his extravagant medicines; he telling them, in all cases, they have the liver complaint—that being curable—when he knows they are in a consumption, and no relief can be had for them.

"It is to be regretted that such a large number of our classical scholars run into the medical profession, as our large cities are crowded, and there are ten to do the practice that was formerly done by one; which has induced many to adopt the method of travelling from place to place, and give advice gratis, but charge extravagantly for their medicines, and relying upon excitement for their practice, as the opportunities to pronounce them sick when little or nothing ails them is too great to be resisted; and it would be well for persons to listen to these travelling doctors with both ears open, but with their hands on their pockets, for fear their money may be magnetized from them, as these travelling doctors are constantly increasing, and receive encouragement from persons attending their lectures, and other various modes of making their appearance known."

CHAPTER XIII.

HOW TO BECOME MILLIONAIRES—OPINIONS OF MILLIONAIRES.

Many of those who have risen to elevated positions by unlocking the golden gates of wealth, have favored the world with very valuable opinions which they regarded as the key to their success, and a recapitulation of them in a connected form, which was never done before, will afford us entertainment, and perhaps instruction.

Rothschild's Opinion.—The founder of this world-renowned house, whose immense transactions we may subsequently notice, is said to have ascribed his early success to the following rules:—

1. "I combined three profits; I made the manufacturer my customer and the one I bought of my customer; that is, I supplied the manufacturer with the raw material and dyes; on each of which I made a profit, and took his manufactured goods, which I sold at a profit; and thus combined three profits.

2. "Make a bargain at once. Be an off-handed man.

3. "*Never have any thing to do with an unlucky man or place.* I have seen," said he, "many clever men who had not shoes to their feet. I never act with them; their advice sounds very well, but fate is against them; they cannot get on themselves; how can they do good to me?

4. "*Be cautious and bold.* It requires a great deal of boldness and a great deal of caution to make a great fortune; and when you have got it, it requires ten times as much wit to keep it."

The continued prosperity of the eminent banking-house of the Rothschilds is ascribed, in the following biographical extract, to two principles: "He who does not delay for casualties, and has knowledge enough to perceive that in all great affairs the success not only depends on the choice and use of the favorable moment, but *especially on the pursuit of an acknowledged fundamental maxim,* will soon perceive that particularly two principles were never neglected by this banking-house; to which, besides to a prudent performance of its business and to advantageous conjunctures, it owes the greatest part of its present wealth and respectability.

"The first of these principles was that which caused the five brothers to carry on their business in a perpetual uninterrupted communion. This was the golden rule bequeathed to them by their dying father. Since his death, every proposition, let it come from whom it may, is the object of their common deliberations. Every important undertaking is carried on by a combined effort, after a plan agreed upon, and all have an equal share in the result. Though for several years their customary residences were very remote, this circumstance could never interrupt their harmony; it rather gave them this advantage, that they were always perfectly well instructed of the condition of things in the different capitals—that each of them, on his part, could the better prepare and initiate the affairs to be undertaken by the firm. The second principle in perpetual view of this house is, not to seek an excessive profit in any undertaking; to assign certain limits to every enterprise; and, as much as human caution and prudence can do, to make themselves independent of the play of accidents."

David Ricardo, the celebrated political economist, was born in London, of a Jewish family, in 1772. His character for probity, industry, and talent early procured for him the means of support; and becoming a member of the Stock Exchange, he accumulated an immense property. He is author of many works on finance; and in 1819 was elected to parliament. Died, 1823. He had what he called his own three golden rules; the observance of which he used to press on his private friends. These were:—

"*Never to refuse an option when you can get it.*

"*Cut short your losses.*

"*Let your profits run on.*"

By cutting short one's losses, Mr. Ricardo meant that, when a member had made a purchase of stock, and prices were falling, he ought to resell immediately. And by letting one's profit run on, he meant that, when a member possessed stock, and the prices were rising, he ought not to sell until prices had reached their highest, and were beginning again to fall. These are indeed golden rules, and may be applied with advantage to innumerable transactions other than those connected with the Stock Exchange.

Stephen Girard was born on the 24th day of May, 1750, within the environs of Bordeaux, in France. He sailed to the West Indies as a cabin-boy, when only twelve years of age; and, after residing there some time, removed to the United States. He followed the sea, as mate, captain, and part owner of a vessel for a while, and accumulated some money. He entered into partnership with Isaac Hazlehurst, of Philadelphia, and purchased two vessels to commence the St. Domingo trade; but they were captured, and that dissolved the firm.

During the war, he was at Mount Holly, in the business of bottling claret and cider. In 1779, he returned to Philadelphia, and entered upon the New Orleans and St. Domingo trade. He then tried a partnership with his brother, which, in the course of three or four years, exploded, as usual, in a rupture. Shortly after this, his prospects were materially aided by the acquisition of $50,000, deposited in one of his vessels during the insurrection at St. Domingo, and for which the owners never called. In 1791, he commenced ship-building, and from that time until his death was engaged in various mercantile speculations, and in banking. In 1811, he had $1,000,000 in the hands of the Barings, who were then in imminent danger of failure. Had they failed, it is very probable that the Girard College would never have been built. The effect on his peculiar constitution of mind would, most likely, have proved fatal. He died in 1832, estimated to be worth $12,000,000.

He never gave an opinion of the causes of his success, that I am aware of. When requested to furnish incidents for his life, he refused, replying, "My actions must make my life." We can probably glean his opinion from the following two or three *little* "actions."

A gentleman from Europe purchased a bill of exchange on Girard, to defray the expenses of a tour to this country. It was duly honored on presentation, but in the course of their transactions, it so happened, that *one cent* remained to be refunded on the part of the European; and on the eve of his departure from this country, Girard dunned him for it. The gentleman apologized, and tendered him a six and a quarter cent piece, requesting the difference. Mr. Girard tendered him in change *five* cents, which the gentleman declined to accept, alleging he was entitled to an additional quarter of a cent. In reply Girard admitted the fact, but informed him that it was not in his power to comply, as the government had neglected to provide the fractional coin in question, and returned the gentleman the six cent piece, reminding him, however, that he must still consider him his debtor for the balance.

"An acquaintance was invited to witness the improvements at his farm, and was shown to a strawberry bed, which had been in the greater part gleaned of its contents, and told that he might gather fruit in that bed, when the owner took leave. That friend, finding that this tract had been nearly stripped of its fruit by his predecessors, soon strayed to another tract, which appeared to bear more abundantly, when he was accosted by Mr. Girard: 'I told you,' said he, 'that you might gather strawberries only in that bed.'"

"We saw that remarkable man (Girard), after his head was white with the frosts of nearly fourscore years, and could not help noticing, even then, the minute attention which he gave to the most trivial thing that could affect his fortune. 'Take that lot of fowls away; the roosters are too many; they would keep the hens poor,' said the old merchant to a farmer, who had brought them for one of Girard's ships—'take them away—I will not buy them.'"

"Take care of the cents, and the dollars will take care of themselves," was evidently his fundamental maxim.*

* Girard was never less a prophet than when he said, "All that I have to say is, that no man will ever be a gentleman with my money." There

John Jacob Astor, I am informed by his son, W. B. Astor, is not known to have had any fundamental rule or favorite maxim, and the general outline of his career is too well known to need rehearsal.

Nicholas Longworth, the millionaire of Cincinnati, was born in Newark, N. J., January 16, 1783. Formerly a cobbler, as I have been informed, he removed to Cincinnati in 1804, studied law, and practised for some fifteen years. His earnings and savings he invested in lots around Cincinnati, the rise of which was the foundation of his fortune. He then turned his attention entirely to land or lot speculations, which, in a rising market, as that has always been, is a business in which all is gain and nothing loss. As an example of the facility with which small amounts, comparatively, secured what has since become of immense value, Mr. Cist, in his memoir of him, states that Mr. Longworth once received as a legal fee from a fellow who was accused of horse-stealing, and who had nothing else to give, two second-hand copper stills. The gentleman who had them in possession refused to give them up, but proposed to Mr. Longworth to give him a lot of thirty-three acres on Western Row, in lieu of them—a proposal which the latter, whose opinions of the value of such property were ahead of his time, gladly accepted. This transaction alone, taking into view the prodigious increase of real estate in that city, would have formed the basis of an immense fortune, the naked ground being now worth *two millions* of dollars.

What Mr. Longworth is worth is not known. The estimates vary greatly, and it is probable that after his death there will be considerable litigation. A gentleman recently has recovered land from him to the value of $500,000. In 1850, his taxes amounted to upwards of $17,000, which is the largest sum paid by any individual in the United States, William B. Astor excepted, whose taxes for the same year were $23,116. It must be remembered,

have been more gentlemen made with his money than with the money of any other twenty men.

however, that the taxes in Cincinnati are no trifle on any amount of property.

Mr. Longworth's opinion probably is that speculating in real estate, in a constantly rising market, is a very good business. I am informed, by a friend in that city, that he holds it to be an indispensable requisite, that a man who desires to get rich, should be from Jersey, where he himself hails from. I regard this as metaphorical language, meaning, probably, that he must have a *sandy* head, and a stony heart.

P. T. BARNUM, the noted exhibiter of natural curiosities, the distinguished manager and financier, the courteous gentleman, and future Governor of Connecticut, ascribes his success in accumulating a million of dollars in twelve years, as the newspapers inform us, to the unlimited use of "Printer's Ink." Whatever may be the valuable secret, aside from his own remarkable energy, talent, and knowledge of human nature, he is worthy of all the success that he has attained. May he never meet with less!

A MERCHANT OF BOSTON, of fifty years' standing, who is represented to have amassed a fortune, states some incidents in his early life which impressed upon his mind the utility of two maxims, which he ever afterwards adopted as guides of conduct. "Thence," he says, "I have had these Mentors before me,

"DO YOU WHAT YOU UNDERTAKE THOROUGHLY.
BE FAITHFUL IN ALL ACCEPTED TRUSTS.

"I am satisfied they have served me well *threescore* years."

JOHN FREEDLEY'S never-varying motto was, *self-dependence, self-reliance.*

"It is a mistaken notion," he writes, "that capital alone is necessary to success in business. If a man has head and hands suited to his business, it will soon procure him capital. My observations through life satisfy me that at least nine-tenths of those most successful in business start in life without any reliance except upon their own head and hands—hoe their own row from the jump. All professions and occupations alike give the field for talent, perseverance, and industry; and these qualities, whether in the East,

West, or South, sooner or later, will crown the aspirant with success. But to enable any new beginner to succeed, he must not be allured from his course by attractive appearances, nor be driven from it by trifling adverse gales. He must fit himself for the calling he adopts, and then pursue his course with a steady eye. The first and great object in business is to make yourself independent—to have the means of livelihood without being under obligations to any person; whatever more is acquired increases the power of doing good and extends influence."

JOHN GRIGG, of Philadelphia, the founder of the well-known publishing house of Grigg & Elliott, and G. E. & Co., of which Messrs. Lippincott, Grambo & Co., are the worthy successors, has favored us with some points which his experience has taught him it is important for men about commencing business to observe. His life, it may be remarked, is another encouraging example of what integrity, united to talent, energy, and good fortune, may hope to accomplish under our free institutions. Beginning the world an orphan farmer boy, he has accumulated, as public opinion says, a fortune, and though rich, he has shown that he understands what few rich men ever have understood—that is, the art of using money wisely, as well as getting it. In a conversation with him the other day, he expressed the opinion that endorsing is a cause of one-half the failures in business, and stated the remarkable fact that he had never asked a man to endorse a note for him in his life. One great reason of his success, I have been informed, among many others, was his power of inspiring confidence—confidence in his sincerity, honesty and ability. Many of his customers dealt with him for years without once inquiring the price of an article. He says of the complete business man, as Gen. Butler in his eulogy of Calhoun said of the statesman, "he should have in an eminent degree the self-sustaining power of intellect. He must possess energy and enterprise, with perseverance and great mental determination. *To inspire confidence, which after all is the highest of earthly qualities*, is a mystical something which is felt but cannot be described."

But to his opinion in his own language.

I. Be industrious and economical. Waste neither time nor money in *small* and *useless* pleasures and indulgences. If the young can be induced to *begin* to *save*, the moment they enter on the paths of life, the way will ever become easier before them, and they will not fail to attain a competency, and that without denying themselves any of the real necessaries and comforts of life. Our people are certainly among the most improvident and extravagant on the face of the earth. It is enough to make the Merchant of the old school who looks back and thinks what Economy, Prudence and Discretion he had to bring to bear on his own business, (and which are in fact the bases of all successful enterprize,) start back in astonishment to look at the ruthless waste and extravagance of the age and People. The highest test of respectability with me, is honest industry. Well-directed industry makes men happy. The really noble class—the class that was noble when "Adam delv'd and Eve spun," and have preserved their patent to this day untarnished, is the laborious and industrious. Until men have learned industry, Economy, and Self-control, they cannot be safely entrusted with wealth.

II. To industry and economy, add self-reliance. Do not take *too much advice.* The business man must keep at the helm and steer his own ship. In early life every one should be taught to think for himself. A man's talents are never brought out until he is thrown to some extent upon his own resources. If in every difficulty he has only to run to his principal, and then implicitly obey the directions he may receive, he will never acquire that aptitude of perception, and that promptness of decision, and that firmness of purpose which are absolutely necessary to those who hold important stations. A certain degree of independent feeling, is essential to the full development of the intellectual character.

III. Remember that punctuality is the mother of confidence. It is not enough that the Merchant fulfils his engagements, he must do what he undertakes precisely *at the time*, as well as in the way he agreed to. The mutual dependence of merchants is so great, that their engagements like a chain, which, according to the Law of Physics is never stronger than its weakest link, are oftener broken through the weakness of others than their own. But a prompt fulfilment of engagements is not only of the utmost importance, because it enables others to meet their own engagements promptly. It is also the best evidence that the Merchant has his affairs well ordered—his means at command, his forces marshalled, and "every thing ready for action"—in short that he knows his own strength. This it is which inspires confidence, as much perhaps as the meeting of the engagement.

IV. Attend to the *minutiæ* of the business, small things as well as great. See that the store is opened early, goods brushed up, twine and nails picked up, and all ready for action. A young man should consider capital, if he have it, or as he may acquire it, merely as tools with which he is to work, not as a substitute for the necessity of labor. *It is often the case that diligence in employments of less consequence is the most successful introduction to great enterprises.* Those make the best officers who have served in the ranks. We may say of Labor, as Coleridge said of Poetry, it is its own sweetest reward. It is the best of Physic.

V. Let the young Merchant remember that selfishness is the meanest of vices, and it is the parent of a thousand more. It not only interferes both with the means and with the end of acquisition—not only makes money more difficult to get, and not worth having when it is got, but it is narrowing to the mind and to the heart. Selfishness "keeps a shilling so close to the eye, that it cannot see a dollar beyond." Never be narrow and contracted in your views. Life abounds in instances of the brilliant results of a generous policy.

Be frank. Say what you mean. Do what you say. So shall your friends know and take it for granted that you mean to do what is just and right.

VI. Accustom yourself to think vigorously. Mental capital, like pecuniary, to be worth any thing must be well invested—must be rightly adjusted and applied, and to this end, careful, deep and intense thought is necessary if great results are looked for.

VII. Marry early. The man of business should marry as soon as possible, after twenty-two or twenty-three years of age. A woman of mind will conform to the necessities of the day of small beginnings; and in choosing a wife, a man should look at, 1st. The heart; 2d. The mind; 3d. The person.

VIII. Every thing, however remote, that has any bearing upon success must be taken advantage of. The business man should be continually on the watch for information, and ideas that will throw light on his path, and he should be an attentive reader of all practical books, *especially those relating to business, trade,** *&c.*, as well as a patron of useful and ennobling literature.

IX. Never forget a favor, for ingratitude is the basest trait of man's heart. Always honor your country, and remember that our country is the very best poor man's country in the world.

JOHN McDONOGH, the millionaire of New Orleans, whose death is yet recent, is accredited with what I consider one of the most valuable opinions on the subject on record. It was narrated by a lawyer of New Orleans, during some "idle moments" (?) in a court-room in that city, as a reminiscence of a personal interview with McDonogh, and is as follows:—

"I said to Mr. McDonogh, 'You are a very rich man, and I know that you intend to leave all your property to be expended in charitable purposes. I have been thinking over your singular life, and I want you to give me some advice in regard to the great success which has attended you; for I, too, would like to become very rich, having a family, so as to leave my heirs wealthy.' 'Well,' said he, 'get up, sir;' and as I rose from my arm-chair, he took my seat, and turning to me as if he was the proprietor and I his clerk, said, pointing to a common chair in which he had been sitting, 'Sit down, sir, and I will tell you how I became a rich man, and how, by following three rules, you can become as rich as myself.'

"'I first came to Louisiana,' continued Mr. McDonogh, 'when it was a Spanish colony, as the agent for a house in Baltimore and a house in Boston, to dispose of certain cargoes of goods. After I had settled up their accounts and finished their agency, I set up to do business for myself. I had become acquainted with the Spanish

* Mr. Grigg has sent me a note for this edition, that he would like to add that every merchant should have a copy of the *Merchant's Magazine*, *De Bow's Review*, and (ought I to mention it?) *Freedley's Treatise on Business*, an elementary treatise on the principles of Business. "Every counting-house, every private and public Library," he has been pleased to add, "should have a copy of them all."

governor, who had taken a fancy to me, although I had never so much as flattered him, and through his influence I obtained a contract for the army, by which I made $10,000. After this, I gave a splendid dinner to the principal officers of the army and the governor, and by it obtained another contract, by which I made $30,000.

"'This is what the French and the Creoles do not understand. I mean the spending of money judiciously. They are afraid of spending money. A man who wishes to make a fortune must first make a show of liberality, and spend money in order to obtain it. By that dinner which I gave to the Spanish authorities, I obtained their good-will and esteem, and by this I was enabled to make a large sum of money. To succeed in life, then, you must obtain the favor and influence of the opulent, and the authorities of the country in which you live. This is the first rule.'

"'The natural span of a man's life,' observed Mr. McDonogh, 'is too short, if he is abandoned to his own resources, to acquire great wealth, and, therefore, in order to realize a fortune, you must exercise your influence and power over those who, in point of wealth, are inferior to you, and, by availing yourself of their talents, knowledge, and information, turn them to your own advantage. This is the second rule.' Here he made a long pause, as if lost in thought, and seeing him remain silent, I asked, 'Is that all?' 'No,' said he, 'there is a third and last rule which it is all-essential for you to observe, in order that success may attend your efforts.' 'And what is that?' I inquired.

"'Why, sir,' said he, 'it is *Prayer*. You must pray to the Almighty with fervor and zeal, and you will be sustained in all your desires. I never prayed sincerely to God, in all my life, without having my prayer answered satisfactorily.' He stopped, and I said, 'Is this all?' He answered, 'Yes, sir; follow my advice, and you will become a rich man.' And he arose and left me.

"'Well,' asked one of the company, 'have you followed his advice?"

"'No,' said the counsellor. 'I have not, for certain reasons. I do not wish to be considered harsh in drawing the conclusions I did from Mr. McDonogh's advice. They were, that when a man desires to become rich, he must corrupt the high, oppress the poor, and look to God to sustain him.'"

This is the story, the moral of which has been recommended to our serious consideration. This is the story that has abashed the countenance, and turned the stomach of a New Orleans lawyer; that has been bandied through the country, and kicked at, and spurned by every newspaper, magazine, and periodical, whether religious or secular—" none so vile as to do it honor." Truly the satirist is right; our morality *is* excessive. There is no danger of another deluge. We think the angels, with their instinctive perception of what is holy, will soon be down here to take up their permanent residence amongst us.

In this world, then, " where men are gods and women angels," it would be a dangerous task to attempt its defence. We must leave it, as Bacon did his name and memory, " to men's charitable speeches, to foreign nations, and the next age." All that we can do in our limited space is, to earnestly beg those who are the leaders and guides of popular opinion on questions of morality and religion to reconsider their opinion; for, if it be not immoral, it is most valuable; and, by following its advice, thousands who are now in the " slough of despond" and the morasses of poverty, will be enabled to climb up to the firm land of happiness, influence, and independence.

In judging of an opinion, charity demands that of words which will bear two constructions, that most favorable to virtue and morality shall be adopted. In applying a rule to action, mixed with narrative and explanation, we must exclude what is personal and explanatory, and look only to that which is directory and abstract. A rule may be good, though the instance given to elucidate it may be faulty. A decision may be correct, though the reasons given for coming to it may be weak. Whether McDonogh " corrupted the high or oppressed the poor," we do not know, nor is it a part of our business to know. There is nothing in the story to show that he did; and if there were, it would not depreciate the value of the rules if abstractly good. An opinion is good or bad in itself, whether it comes from a slave or from a philosopher. Whether dinners are the most happy way to obtain favor is a matter of extreme doubt. It is a plan that, though harmless in itself, has lost its originality; and from abuse has fallen into discredit.

I. McDonogh's first abstract rule for success in life is " to obtain the favor and influence of the opulent, and the authorities of the country in which you live." Can this mean to "corrupt the high?" Quite the reverse. It is a rule given to a man who is poor in order to obtain the first start. A poor man has not the means to corrupt the high; and in nine cases out of ten, any attempt at corruption on the part of a man with small means and limited influence at least, would rebound on his own head, and defeat the end at which he aimed. It cannot mean corruption, because that would be inconsistent with the adoption of the third rule, prayer, which completes the system. A man cannot pray to the "*Almighty with fervor and zeal*," to bless an act which he knows to be bad. It means simply what it says, to obtain the favor and influence of the opulent, and to use the means which wisdom and a knowledge of human nature suggest as suitable to the end.

The first clause of this rule is applicable to every one who desires to improve his condition. The man born in the lower walks of life must improve his mind and conduct, and fit himself for admission into more influential circles, and then court admission; and the man who is already there must not sink himself by low associations. The mechanic or architect who wishes to make his fortune must not be contented with building *shantees*, but must endeavor to attract the attention and obtain the favor of the man who designs building a *mansion*. The scientific man who has not the means to perfect his plan must draw the notice of a man fond of scientific pursuits who has the means. In all cases, it implies the opposite of that fictitious independence which "cannot dig, and is ashamed to beg."

Perfect independence of feeling—the independence of the man in the time of the deluge who despised Noah and his "old boat"—has something in it that excites admiration. But independence, to be admirable, must be perfect. The man who aspires to the virtue of absolute independence must stand like an iceberg, isolated and alone, disdaining all connection with the mainland of humanity. He must trust to his own good right hand, spurning all assistance, and indulge in no complaints when he sees men of greater pliability getting ahead of him. This has ever been a fault in poets and literary men. They seem to think that the world, which knows little about them, should come cap in hand to do them service. They are too proud to ask for that which they need; and yet whine, like whipped hounds, because they do not receive. They disdain to mingle with men, or the herd as they call them, and solicit favor and influence; and yet sit in their rookeries and indite snarling epics on the baseness and ingratitude of the world. This is the affectation of independence; and, like all affectation, is contemptible.

It is man's birthright to ask of those who can give that which he needs. If it be reasonable—if it be done at opportune times and in a sincere, prayerful spirit, he will receive. Do you wish information? Court the favor, and influence, and society of the well-informed and the learned. Do you wish office? Court the favor of those who have offices to give. Do you wish chances to make money? Follow McDonogh's advice, and obtain the "favor and influence" of business men and the opulent.

There is much unnecessary and harsh feeling in the world—an apparent conflict between classes, that arises from a neglect of this very rule. Men fret themselves in secret; they suffer their minds to become soured against a whole class, because nobody will patronize them, because those who can aid them will not notice them. Let them ask themselves, first, what have they done to attract their notice? There is a powerful feeling in the breast of every man, worthy of the name, that makes him desirous of obliging whenever he can; and there is a vanity which makes it pleasing to patronize; but it must be sought after. All men, whether rich or poor, have enough to engage their attention without seeking out those to whom they can be serviceable. It is as little as a man can do, who desires a reasonable favor of another, to ask for it. Let him choose his time opportunely—let him avoid making himself obtrusive or troublesome—let him state his wishes frankly, fully, yet respectfully—let his request be moderate; and if he fails? 'Tis but in one case—pick your flint, and try elsewhere. Are you repulsed rudely? The man was a scoundrel, or an upstart, one of that dunghill breed, of which unfortunately there are some; but you were not a fool for attempting it.

As we make our beds so we must lie. If, then, we aspire to emulate Diogenes, trampling on the bed of Plato; if we are ambitious of the applause of foolish boys and silly men, we must rail at every thing which we have not, and are not, particularly at rich men, and run over a rigmarole of hard names, as pampered minions, purse-proud, unfeeling wretches, and we will get their applause. If we aspire to be revolutionists, and will run the risk of a traitor's fate, we should attempt insurrectionary movements, and denounce all government and authority, because it is government. But if we aim to become wealthy men and good citizens, our first step is to "obtain the favor and influence of the opulent;" "to *obey magistrates; to be ready to every good work; to speak evil of no man: to be no brawlers; but gentle, showing all meekness unto all men.*"*

II. Mr. McDonogh's second rule is, that "the natural span of a man's life is too short, if he is abandoned to his own resources, to acquire great wealth; therefore, in order to realize a fortune, you must exercise your influence and power over those who, in point of wealth, are inferior to you, and, by availing yourself of their talents, knowledge, and information, turn them to your own advantage." This, a distinguished counsellor of the New Orleans bar calls "oppressing the poor," and this a religious periodical pronounces "devilish."

> "Are these the breed of wits so wondered at?
> Well, better wits have worn plain statute caps."

I am of opinion that the distinguished counsellor, in transcribing this rule, used words that will bear a more unfavorable construction than those which Mr. McDonogh used, or intended to use. But, take them as they stand, what do they mean? Do they mean that a man who wishes to increase his fortune must use force to press poor but talented men into his service, as they impress seamen? Do they mean that a man should use his means in hiring agents to scour the country, and catch all the men of "talents, knowledge, and information" they can find, bind them hand and foot, drag them to his door, and there force them to reveal their information? A distinguished counsellor seems to think so, and all counsellors are wise as well as "honorable" men.

* Titus iii. 1--2.

We think it has a great deal of meaning in it, but does not embrace force or oppression. We think it means, in the first place, that as a man cannot carry on extensive operations, relying on his own resources or abilities alone, he must employ agents; and that, in employing agents, he should choose men of "talents, knowledge and information," in preference to those whose only recommendation is physical strength and stupidity. The business of clerking, or agendizing, in the United States, is, at the present time, overstocked by men who have no business there—by men whose proper occupation is farming; and, in consequence, there are thousands of talented men, well qualified for their duties, out of employment. Business men will find it greatly to their advantage to employ educated, talented assistants.

We think it means, in the second place, that, having employed able agents, the employer should make it a constant practice to consult and advise with them, and get their suggestions in his various operations. The rule, in this respect, is much needed. I have known instances in which men have persevered in a plan, to their own loss and inconvenience, merely because the improvement had been suggested by a subordinate. This is great weakness. We are never too old nor too wise to learn; and shrewd men, who are desirous of increasing their fortune, will endeavor to have constantly around them those who can advise them. The President has his cabinet; a general has his officers; a business man should also have his bureau. Self-conceit is a great stumbling-block in the way of continued prosperity, and has proved the ruin of many. The man who, because he has made a few fortunate speculations, considers himself infallible, or despises the opinion of all less wealthy or fortunate than himself, had better retire with what he has made immediately. Attention to McDonogh's rules is all that can save him, if he continues in business.

We think it means, in the third place, that whereas it is a well-known fact that men of talents and learning delight in the company of active, intelligent, business men, who possess more of the world's comforts than themselves, the man of business, who is desirous of increasing his fortune, should encourage their visits by polite, flattering attentions, all the while keeping both ears open to catch information or suggestions from them, which, though useless to themselves, he may appropriate to his own great advantage.

Fourthly: We think it means that, as there are many men of great abilities in their various pursuits, who have not the capital to make their ability available to themselves, the man who is desirous of increasing his wealth should employ them to carry out their ideas for his own benefit, paying them a fair price for their services; or should associate himself with them in a limited partnership, and divide the profits. Thus one capitalist may share the profits of a dozen different establishments, and yet be a great benefactor. There are hundreds of able men, in all countries, who are useless to themselves for want of capital, and whom capitalists should seek out; and there are thousands of men, of splendid talents in their way, who are utterly incompetent to manage a business for themselves, even if they had the capital, but who, associated with men of a different order of talents, commonly called business tact, can greatly promote the well doing of both parties.

This rule is applicable in many other cases than those I have mentioned; but I need not consume time and space to notice them. We, the common people can cipher it out for ourselves, and understand it, though lawyers may not. It is the wisest and most beneficent rule that has ever fallen from human lips. Were mankind to adopt it to-morrow, with some variations in the words used, in order to convey the meaning, there would be a change over the face of society like the wonderful transformations in magic. Every one would fall into his proper position, and each would receive his due. Those whom nature designed for laborers and producers would not usurp the place of distributors; and those who are qualified for intellectual pursuits would find abundance of employment; mind would receive a new impulse to improvement, and talent would find encouragement; capital would be associated with science, and science co-operate with capital; men of wealth would feel themselves honored and benefited by association with men of learning, and learned men would be made happy in the partial enjoyment of the comforts of wealth.

III. McDonogh's last rule is prayer. This is all that was want-

18

ing to perfect the system; to make it a system worthy of a better origin; yea, worthy of the authority of inspiration. Prayer is a powerful aid to success in two ways. It prepares the mind for great undertakings; it gives an earnestness and seriousness to the character; it curbs that levity and frivolity which trifle with important concerns, viewing every thing as a game; it gives a restraining power in the hour of temptation, and makes simple faith mightier than wisdom; it creates a subdued enthusiasm, a calm confidence in eventual success that no present danger can overthrow—a lofty reliance on an unseen power which the prayerless cannot comprehend; it fits the mind to conceive great thoughts, and the man to do great deeds. Secondly: It invokes to human exertions the favor and influence of the Most High. God will hear and answer sincere prayer. "He will regard the prayer of the destitute, and not despise their prayer." Ps. cii. 17. "Are not five sparrows sold for two farthings, and not one of them is forgotten before God? Fear not, therefore, ye are of more value than many sparrows."

Genius and revelation harmonize in commendation of the efficacy of prayer. The most splendid genius of the nineteenth century, in speaking of the French Revolution, says: "The despoilers of all that beautifies and hallows life had desecrated the altar and denied God; they had removed from the last hour of their victims the Priest, the Scripture, and the Cross. But Faith builds, in the dungeon and the lazar-house, its sublimest shrines; and up through roofs of stone that shut out the eye of heaven, ascends the ladder where the angels glide to and fro—prayer." * * * "When science falls as a firework from the sky it would invade—when genius withers as a flower in the breath of the icy charnel—the hope of a childlike soul wraps the air in light, and the innocence of unquestionable belief covers the grave with blossoms."

Revelation invites men every where, and in every thing, to place their trust in their Creator, and not on their own strength. "Trust in the Lord with all thine heart, and lean not on thine own understanding. In all thy ways acknowledge him, and he *shall direct thy paths.*" Prov. iii. 5, 6. "Call upon me in the day of trouble. I will deliver thee, and thou shalt glorify me." Ps. l. 15.

'He that diligently seeketh good procureth favor; but he that seeketh mischief, it shall come unto him. He that trusteth in his riches shall fall; but the righteous shall flourish as a branch." Prov. xi. 27, 28.

Sublime system! The wit of man has never conceived a better, and withal so practical as to be within the reach of the humblest individual in the land. What immense influences it centres upon one man and one business! On the one hand, the humble aspirant calls to his aid the powerful influence of money and the favor of the opulent; on the other he draws to himself the still greater power of talent and knowledge; and above all, he invokes, by prayer and an upright life, the blessing of "Him that sitteth on the circle of the earth; that stretcheth out the heavens as a curtain, and spreadeth them out as a tent to dwell in."

I must close this chapter, and the whole subject of "Getting Money;" and I cannot do so more appropriately than wi h the following truthful quotation:—

"If we were to consult the annals of commercial life, we should find that, in most instances, the men who have been distinguished for success in business are of the same stamp as those who have been eminent in the walks of literature and science. They have been characterized by self-denying habits, by simple tastes, and by unpretending manners; whilst the bold, the vain, the presumptuous, and the reckless have done immense mischief to themselves and others, in the department of trade, dissevering the bonds of confidence and good feeling, and often scattering havoc and ruin around them. The same principles and motives of action prevail in the good, the wise, and the prudent, among all sorts of men. It is that wisdom which is unpretending and boasteth not, and that quiet sort of penetration and sagacity, which is little deceived by self-flatteries and delusions, which are often more injurious and ruinous than all the worldly artifices and deceptions which are practised upon us."

CHAPTER XIV.

LOSING MONEY.

CHANCES OF SUCCESS—CAUSES OF FAILURE.

It was the custom of Napoleon, says Bourrienne, after a hard battle had been won, to ride over the field of contest, to see the extent of the destruction. That is our solemn task at this time. We have heard the shouts of the victorious; we have listened to the proud boasts of the conquerors, the Napoleons of wealth, and have recorded their wise sayings. Now, it is our painful duty to go over the field where their triumphs were won, and see how many, with minds as great, and aspirations as high, have fallen in the strife. Perchance, we may learn there greater lessons of wisdom; perchance, we may see our way clearer, and possibly discover the post of safety, if not of honor. "Wouldst thou be rich? Consult not the rich man, but the bankrupt. 'Tis more to know what to avoid than what to do."

We have chosen to consult both. We will inquire, first, *as to our chances of success;* and, secondly, *as to the causes of failures and their remedies, if any.*

CHANCES OF SUCCESS IN MERCANTILE LIFE IN BOSTON.

On the evening of the 28th of February, 1840, General Henry A. S. Dearborn delivered an address at an agricultural meeting of the members of the Legislature, which embraced a statement that startled many, and attracted the attention of business men in all parts of the country. Freeman Hunt, Esq., of the *Merchant's Magazine,* wrote to General Dearborn for a copy of his remarks, made in connection with that statement, which he placed at his disposal. General Dearborn was Collector of the Port of Boston for nearly twenty years, and was therefore enabled to notice the vicissitudes in trade, and his statements are confirmed by the remarks of a Boston merchant, which are here appended. He is speaking of the superior advantages of a residence in the country, and observes:—

"In England, the pleasures, and privileges, and blessings of the *country* seem properly understood and valued. No man there considers himself a freeman unless he has a right in the soil. Merchants, bankers, citizens, men of every description, whose condition of life allows them to aspire after any thing better, are looking forward always to retirement in the country—to the possession of a garden or a farm, and to the full enjoyment of rural pleasures. The taste of the nobility of England is eminently in that direction. There are none of them who, with all the means which the most enormous wealth can afford, even think of spending the year in London, or of remaining in the confinement, noise, and confusion of the city, a day longer than they are compelled to do by their parliamentary or other public duties.

"There is, in this respect, a marked difference between England and France. Formerly, the nobility of France were scattered broadcast over the territory, and had their villas, their castles, and chateaux in all the provinces of the kingdom. But the monarchs, anxious to increase the splendor of their courts, and to concentrate around them all that was imposing and beautiful in fashion, luxury, and wealth, collected the aristocracy in the capital. The natural consequence was that the country was badly tilled, and agriculture made no advancement, while England was making rapid and extraordinary progress in the useful and beautiful arts of agriculture and horticulture, and now, in her cultivation, presents an example of all that is interesting in embellishment and important in production. We are the descendants of England; yet on these subjects we have reversed the order of taste and sentiment which there prevails.

"Happy would it be for us if our gentlemen of wealth and intelligence would copy the bright example of the affluent and exalted men of England. If, after having accumulated immense fortunes in cities, they would carry their riches and science into the country, and seek to reclaim, to improve, and render it more productive and beautiful, Massachusetts might be transformed into a garden, and rival the best cultivated regions on the globe.

"It is an inexplicable fact that even men who have grown rich in any manner in the country should rush into cities to spend their wealth; and it is equally as remarkable, that those who have accumulated fortunes in the city shudder at the idea of going into the country, where wealth might be safely appropriated to purposes of the highest utility, pleasure, and refinement.

"There prevails, in this, rather too much ignorance, false sentiment, and unworthy prejudice. The city must, of course, be regarded as the proper seat of active business, in all the branches of commerce and navigation. But when a large portion of life has been spent in these harassing pursuits, and men have acquired the means of competence and independence in the country, why they should not seek to enjoy the refreshing exercise, the delightful recreations, and the privileged hours of retirement and reflection which a rural residence affords, was a mystery which it was impossible to solve.

"It was not merely the ungovernable influence of a city life upon health that was most deeply to be regretted. Many an uncorrupted young man from the country, impelled by a reckless passion for gain, has there early found the grave of his virtues. But too many instances might be pointed out, in which the acquisition of property has proved as great a curse as could have befallen them. The chances of success in trade are likewise much less numerous, and are more uncertain than men generally believe, or are willing to allow. *After an extensive acquaintance with business men, and having long been an attentive observer of the course of events in the mercantile community, I am satisfied that,* AMONG ONE HUNDRED MERCHANTS AND TRADERS, NOT MORE THAN THREE, IN THIS CITY, EVER ACQUIRE INDEPENDENCE. *It was with great distrust that I came to this conclusion; but, after consulting with an experienced merchant, he fully admitted its truth.* Infinitely better, therefore, would it be for a vast portion of the young men who leave the country for the city, if they could be satisfied with a farmer's life. How preferable would it have been for many of those who have sought wealth and distinction in cities, if they had been satisfied with the comforts, innocent amusements, and soothing quietude of the country; and, instead of the sad tale of their disasters, which must go back to the parental fireside, the future traveller, as he passed the humble churchyard in which they had been laid at rest with their laborious ancestors, might truthfully repeat these emphatic words of England's gifted bard:—

" 'Some village Hampden that, with dauntless breast,
The little tyrant of his fields withstood;
Some mute, inglorious Milton here may rest;
Some Cromwell, guiltless of his country's blood.' "

The following confirmatory remarks of of an intelligent gentleman from Boston appeared in the *Farmer's Library* :—

"The statement made by General Dearborn appeared to me so startling, so appalling, that I was induced to examine it with much care, and, I regret to say, I found it true. I then called upon a friend, a great antiquarian, a gentleman always referred to in all matters relating to the city of Boston, and he told me that, in the year 1800, he took a memorandum of every person on Long Wharf, and that, in 1840—which is as long as a merchant continues in business—only *five* in *one hundred* remained. They had all, in that time, FAILED, OR DIED DESTITUTE OF PROPERTY. I then went to a very intelligent director of the Union Bank—a very strong bank. He told me that the bank commenced business in 1798; that there was then but one other bank in Boston, the Massachusetts Bank, and that the bank was so overrun with business that the clerks and officers were obliged to work until twelve o'clock at night, and all Sundays; that they had occasion to look back, a year or two ago, and they found that, of the *one thousand accounts* which were opened with them in starting, only *six* remained; they had, in the forty years, either *failed or died destitute of property*. Houses, whose paper had passed without a question, *had all gone down in that time*. Bankruptcy, said he, is like death, and almost as certain; they fall single and alone, and are thus forgotten; but there is no escape from it, and he is a fortunate man who *fails young*.

"Another friend told me that he had occasion to look through the probate office a few years since, and he was surprised to find that over 90 per cent. of all the estates settled there *were insolvent*. And, within a few days, I have gone back to the incorporation of our banks in Boston. I have a list of the directors, since they started. This is, however, a very unfair way of testing the rule, for bank directors are the most substantial men in the community. In the old bank, over *one-third* had failed in forty years, and in the new bank a much larger proportion.

"I am sorry to present to you so gloomy a picture, and I trust you will instil into your sons, as General Dearborn recommends, a love of agriculture; for, in mercantile pursuits, they will fail to a dead certainty."

CHANCES OF SUCCESS IN BOSTON, PHILADELPHIA, AND NEW YORK.

NAHUM CAPEN, Esq., Editor of the *Massachusetts State Record*, makes some interesting statements on the subject in the following letter which he wrote to the Hon. Truman Clark, to be presented at one of the legislative agricultural meetings held weekly during the session of the Legislature at the Senate Chamber.

BOSTON, *March* 2, 1847.

HON. TRUMAN CLARK.

MY DEAR SIR: In accordance with your wishes, I send herewith such statistics in regard to failures in Massachusetts, as I received last year, in reply to a circular I sent to every town in the commonwealth, for the purpose of collecting information for the *Massachusetts State Record.* As these returns were imperfect, I deferred any publication of them till another year, when probably I should have the means of doing the subject ample justice.

Number of towns represented, 144; estimated population of ditto, 242,186: number of farming towns, 79; manufacturing and farming, 56; number engaged mostly in navigation, 9; number of failures reported, 357.

Business of Bankrupts.—Farmers, 59; manufacturers and mechanics, 182, including 70 boot and shoe manufacturers; laborers, 9; innholders, 1; speculators (farmers), 4; ministers, 1; traders, 63; business not stated, 48. * * *

It does not appear, from my returns, how many farmers failed in consequence of becoming speculators, intemperate, or indolent men. It seems to me that an industrious, temperate, and frugal farmer can hardly do otherwise than succeed. Small gains, gradually accumulated, are safer and surer than large profits and sudden fortunes. Their influence is favorable to the growth of good morals, and they do not endanger the habits of prudence.

If Governor Carver had invested £70 on his arrival in the country at compound interest, the accumulated sum at this time, would be sufficient to buy the whole State of Massachusetts, and it would exceed the banking capital of the United States.

If a young man at twenty-one were to lease a farm and make an annual profit of one hundred dollars, and invest both principal and interest, from year to year, for twenty-five years, his fund would amount to $5,000. If he were to own the farm, he might have a fund at interest of $10,000 in twenty-five years.

A trader, however, may begin with a capital of $10,000 on the credit system, as now managed, and in twenty-five years, there are ninety-seven chances to every one hundred, that he will be $10,000 in debt beyond his means to pay.

This percentage of success and failure has been alluded to, at your discussions, as being true of Boston. I believe it to be nearly correct. I have been advised by very intelligent gentlemen, who have the means of knowing, *that not more than* ONE *per cent. of the best class of merchants succeed without failing in* PHILADELPHIA, *and that not more than* TWO *per cent. of the merchants of* NEW YORK ULTIMATELY *retire on an independence, after having submitted to the usual ordeal of failure.* These calculations are based, it must be observed, upon periods of twenty-five and thirty years.

The lot of the merchant is one of great labor and anxiety, compared to that of the farmer. He labors harder, his life is shorter, and he is less sure of a competency in old age.

A contributor to the *Merchant's Magazine* states that it is said "that but *one* eminent merchant, and his death is still recent, has ever continued in active business, *in the city of New York*, to the close of a long life, without undergoing bankruptcy or a suspension of payments in some of the various crises of the country. It is also asserted by *reliable authority*, from records kept during periods of twenty to forty years, that, of every hundred persons who commence business in Boston, ninety-five at least, die poor; that of the same number in New York, not two ultimately acquire wealth, after passing through the intermediate process of bankruptcy; while in Philadelphia, the proportion is still smaller.

By the statistics of bankruptcy under the uniform bankrupt law in 1841,

The number of applicants for relief under that law were	33,739
The number of creditors returned . .	1,049,603
The amount of debts stated . . .	440,934,615
The valuation of property surrendered .	43,697,307

If this valuation were correct, nearly ten cents would have been paid on every dollar due; but what was the fact?

In the Southern district of New York, one cent was paid, on an average for each dollar due; in the Northern district, 13⅝, being by far the largest dividend. In Connecticut, the average dividend was somewhat over a half cent on each dollar.

In Mississippi, it was . .	6 cents to	$1,000
" Maine	½ cent "	100
" Michigan and Iowa . .	¼ " "	100
" New Jersey . . .	4 cents to	100
" Tennessee	4½ " "	100
" Maryland	1 dollar to	100
" Kentucky	8 dollars to	1,000
" Illinois	1 dollar to	1,500

" Pennsylvania, East Virginia, South Alabama, Washington, nothing.

Palmer's Almanac, 1849.

After making every possible allowance for the enhancement of this enormous amount of debt by inflation of values, speculative prices, &c., the proportion of $400,000,000, lost by those of the 1,049,603 creditors who were engaged in proper and legitimate business, must still have been immense, and may justly be charged against the profits of our regular commerce. These things being so, our system of trade should be characterized, not as a system of exchange, but as a system of bankruptcy, tending to the ruin of all who engage in it; the exceptions being only numerous enough to prove the rule."

CHANCES IN CINCINNATI.

C. Cist, of *Cist's Cincinnati Advertiser*, the statist of that city, published, some two or three years ago, the following result of his investigations :—

" The avidity with which young men crowd those avenues in life in which there is a chance of making money with rapidity, or of acquiring political or social distinction and eminence, is the more remarkable, when it is apparent, on the surface of the subject, that they are venturing in a lottery in which there are many blanks to one prize. A few acquire the object of their pursuit; the mass sink into obscurity and insignificance.

"Take, for example, mercantile pursuits. It is the experience and observation of intelligent persons in the East, that there is hardly a firm in existence now which did business twenty years ago; and that nine out of ten in mercantile life, in the long run, amidst the fluctuations of trade, are broken.

"Let me, however, bring the subject nearer home. I had prepared a list of the principal active business men who were in trade, twenty years ago, in Cincinnati, of which a brief extract is all that I have space for in these columns. In place of giving names, I shall distinguish them by numbers.

"No. 1. Broke; resumed business; has since left Cincinnati.
" 2. Broke; resides in Indiana.
" 3. Broke; and now engaged in collecting accounts.
" 4. Died.
" 5. Now captain of a steamboat.
" 6. Left merchandising to put up pork, which business he also quit in time to save his *bacon:* independent in circumstances.
" 7. Dead.
" 8. Broke; resides at St. Louis.
" 9. A firm; one of the partners dead; the other out of business; both insolvent.
" 10. Partners; both dead.
" 11. Partners; broke; one now a book-keeper, the other dead.
" 12. Became embarrassed, and swallowed poison.
" 13. A firm; broke.
" 14. A firm; broke; one of the partners died a common sot; the others left the city.
" 15. Broke, and left the city.
" 16. A firm; all its members out of business.
" 17. A firm; senior partner dead.
" 18. A firm; senior partner dead, junior resides at Toledo.
" 19. Is now a clerk, and left Cincinnati, after becoming intemperate.
" 20, 21, 22, 23. Died intemperate.
" 26. A firm; one of the partners in another business; one removed to New York, and one a clerk.
" 27. Broke; and drowned himself in the Ohio.
" 28 Broke; died of delirium tremens.
" 29, 35, 36, 37, 38. Broke, and removed to other cities.

" 32. Out of business, having broke three times.

" 33. Broke; now dealing in flour

" My list comprehends some 400 business men, of which the above is a sample. I know of but *five now in business who were so twenty years since.* Such is mercantile success."

We regret to say that our inquiry, as to the chances of success in mercantile pursuits, has resulted somewhat unfavorably. The reflections excited by the foregoing statements, from undoubted authority, are any thing but flattering to those embarking in business with the ardent desire of sudden acquisition, and indulging in golden visions of easily acquired affluence. Taking the experience of the past as a criterion, there are, indeed, many chances to one that he who to-day launches his bark on the troubled sea of mercantile speculation, will, in a very few years, find his vessel drawn within a maelstrom, or stranded upon a rock. The picture is discouraging, and we need all the philosophy we can muster. We must recollect that "partial evil is universal good."—We must remember that every man is the artificer of his own fortune, whether it be in the struggle for literary or political honors, or in the sharper strife for material wealth. We must hope that it was by departing from the plain and well-established maxims of common caution that men invited disaster upon their enterprises, and that with greater caution, prudence, and the aid of improved experience, we may escape their fate.

These statements come with a different meaning to different men. They are encouraging incentives to perseverance for those who have resolved on pursuing a steady, prudent course, without being allured from it by attractive appearances. They are homilies on humility for the attention of the proud—on kindness to the unfortunate, for the selfish—on the need of light and information, for all. They are fruitful of stern rebuke to those false teachers who preach up prodigality by preaching down economy, and to that fool Thompson who said that "'a penny saved is a penny got,' is a scoundrel maxim;" and they are a balm of consolation to the honest bankrupt, who is mourning over his failure, and will not be comforted, for he may see that he is in a goodly company, and can call upon immense numbers to unite with him in singing the chorus of the old song,

"Let us all be unhappy together."

As to the *causes of failures*, we are sorry to say that we have not been able to find any satisfactory statistics. We are surprised at this, because it is a subject that should engage the attention of the statist above all other subjects. Government even would not misapply their surplus funds in undertaking an extended and elaborate investigation of the matter, as it would probably conduce more to the general good than many of their investments. When the "death-shots fall thick and fast;" when a crisis comes, as it is called, men's minds become excited, and they anxiously inquire for some immediate cause; but when houses "fall single and alone," the business world wags on in presumptive security—though each, it seems, must take his turn—and no general investigation is had. Let us add our humble note of invitation to the patriotic and intelligent statisticians of the country that they attend to this matter.

We find the following in the "Report of his Majesty's Commissioners for inquiring into the Administration and Practical Operation of the Poor Laws, 1834."

Mr. Green, one of the official assignees in cases of bankruptcy, gave the subjoined return:—

"As far as I can recollect, from the books and documents furnished by the bankrupts, it seems to me that 14 have been ruined by speculations in things with which they were unacquainted; 3 by neglected bookkeeping; 10 by trading beyond their capital and facile means, and the consequent loss and expense of accommodation bills; 49 by expending more than they could reasonably hope their profits would be, though their business yielded a fair return; none by any general distress, or the falling off of any particular branch of trade."

Another officer states:—

"The new court has been open upwards of eighteen months, during which period 52 cases of bankruptcy have come under my care. To the best of my judgment, not one of them can be attributed to any general distress. It is my opinion that 32 of them have arisen from an imprudent expenditure, and 5 partly from that cause, and partly from a pressure on the business in which the bankrupt was employed—15 I attribute to imprudent speculations, combined, in many instances, with an extravagant mode of life. Among these fifteen I find a tailor, in a very small way of business, borrowing money to become the owner of a West India ship trading to Jamaica, a concern with which he was wholly unacquainted; consequently, he was cheated in every way and speedily ruined. A London publican, having a slight knowledge of science, neglects his business here and goes over to France, for the purpose of entering into a contract with the French authorities for the supply of Paris with water. A working goldsmith, never having had £10, takes Seville House, Leicester Square, and engages singers and musicians for the purpose of establishing concerts. The 32 classed as failing through imprudences in their mode of living, include many whose necessities, leading them to resort to accommodation bill transactions, have become the prey of money-lenders and their attendant harpies, the inferior class of solicitors."

We think—but we desire to know the fact by an extended investigation—that the causes of failure are as numerous and as varied as the follies and misfortunes of mankind; that there is no one deep-seated evil to which all can be ascribed. We think—but we would like to be certain of it—that the causes to which the majority of the failures above mentioned are ascribed, will be found to be the principal causes of failure in all countries and at all times.

In the most simple operation of commercial speculation, under our present system, there are more possible chances of failure than there are of success. We might illustrate this, and at the same time enumerate some of the causes of failure, by a supposition suggested by the following story, related by the Rev. J. W. Higgison, of Newburyport:—

"One of the most eminent literary men of this country once told me that, many years since, when a boy on a farm he had permission given him to sell for himself a calf of his own raising; and that he remembered so vividly the struggles of mind he went through, the bitter anxieties of hope and fear, the intense temptation to extort more than the animal was strictly worth, and contrive little plots to conceal its defects and exaggerate its merits, that the experience comes back to his mind to this day, when he felt especially indignant at the baseness of commerce, and made him more charitable to the offender, remembering that he also had been tempted."

We cannot stop to compliment "the most eminent literary man of this country" on his exquisite sensibility; nor to congratulate him on his good fortune in abandoning further thoughts of commercial ventures for literary pursuits; but must proceed to our supposition. Suppose that the nerves of this lad had been a little stronger—that he had felt himself able to manage more than one calf, and had purchased two others on, say three months' credit, at six dollars each, with a view of taking them to a distant market and selling them at a profit; what causes might have contributed to his failure, and what were his chances of success? First, Accident: As his calves dying, or escaping, or being stolen, would have caused his failure. Secondly: A want of judgment as to the value of calves; so that he finds the butchers will not give cost, will cost his failure. Trusting them to agents to sell who prove dishonest, or taking in a partner with him who cheats him, will ruin him. Suppose that his hotel expenses, in consequence of a failure of the crops, are unexpectedly greater than the profits—he must suspend. A failure, then, of the agricultural productions of the country, or a great and sudden expansion of the currency, and the consequent high prices of food, causes failures. A great depression in the market price, in consequence of an excess of supply, at a time when he must sell, will also compel him to suspend.

Suppose that he is induced to sell to a butcher on credit, and, in the mean time, low prices of produce, or a scarcity of money render the farmers unable to pay their debts to the country storekeepers—and they the city merchant—and the merchant the importer—and the importer the money borrowed from the butcher—and the butcher the lad—the lad must fail. A superabundance of the agricultural productions of the country, or a contraction of the currency, and the consequent low prices of produce, may cause a general failure. Suppose that he takes paper money in payment, and the banks explode, or having received gold and silver, he is agreeably elated, and attempts to keep it up by stimulants which result in difficulty and expense; he must fail. Bad morals, as well as bad currency, are a cause of failure. Extravagance in living—certain expenses while his profits are uncertain—will be certain to ruin him. The purchase of a lot with a view of selling it at a profit before his note falls due, and property falling, will compel him to make an assignment. Suppose, finally, that he sells his calves at a profit of two dollars each, over and above all expenses—gets safely home without being robbed, or losing his money—and pays his debt promptly—why he has made six dollars, and is a successful merchant.

> "Oh! if this were seen,
> The happiest youth—viewing his progress through
> What perils past, what crosses to ensue,
> Would shut the book, and sit him down and die."

Failures in general, I think, may be ascribed to four general causes: *Accidents; bad legislation; defective personal habits;* and *excessive use of credit.*

Accidents do not occur so frequently as we might suppose. Insurance will guard against loss from some, and prudence against others; but loss may occur in spite of both, and in such cases there is no remedy. A failure of the crops, or surplus production, causes a great inconvenience for a time, but it is soon over; and those who have conducted their business on certain sound principles, maintaining a due portion of liabilities to capital, can survive the pressure.

Bad and unstable legislation are frequent causes of serious embarrassment. Unstable legislation is as prejudicial to the business interests of a country as unjust laws. It causes difficulty in two ways. Men who have invested their capital on the faith of existing laws are liable to a serious loss from a change of the laws; and, on the other hand, capitalists, aware of this predisposition to change, are timid in their investments, preferring less profit and greater certainty. The consequence of this is that the profits of some kinds of business are reduced below the average, while other productive interests are only partially developed. In no country in the world is legislation so vacillating as in the United States; and no other country in the world could have borne an equal amount of it without entire prostration. It is a fault of both our National and State governments, and always will be a fault, while party interests predominate over patriotism. Men of both parties should unite in exempting the interests of trade, at least, from the operation of political influences. Wise laws will not prevent failures; but they will prevent those failures—and they are not a few—that arise from unwise or unstable laws.*

But legislation, in a representative government like our own, can be remedied by the choice of wise legislators. The remedy is entirely in the hands of those who are aggrieved by it. The prominent mental attribute of a good legislator is, *soundness of judgment.* He should also possess stern integrity and business habits. Ability in discussion is no recommendation, but a decided disadvantage; and is rarely associated with superior judgment. The man who can make a three hours' speech is *prima facie* incompetent for a legislator; and those who have spent a considerable portion of their life in the *practice* of the law are of the same category. They fall under Bacon's censure, subject of course to be rebutted by unquestionable testimony, of desiring "rather commendation of wit in being able to hold all arguments, than of judgment in discerning what is true, as if it were a praise to know what might be said, *and not what should be thought.*" But these men also have their place and their duties to discharge as good citizens; these are, to discuss questions before the people, and suggest arguments that should be duly considered by the legislators in forming their opinion. The acts of the legislature should be the embodied opin-

* "We have referred to convertible and inconvertible currency. Do you think that any system of currency, convertible or inconvertible, can be devised, in which occasional periods of commercial distress will not arise, as long as commercial transactions are entered into by parties almost without limitation beyond their means?" "I do not think it possible—I do not think that any system of currency that any human being can devise can correct the follies of mankind. There are always some people who will speculate beyond their means; *but under a proper system, there would not be whole rows of perfectly innocent people knocked down as there have been lately.*"—CHARLES TURNER. *Parliamentary Committee Rep.*

ion of the majority of disinterested jurors, who have taken but little part in the discussion, and who were chosen for the marked soundness of their judgment.

The Parliament of Great Britain, though not enlightened, and far from perfect, has points of superiority over our legislatures, as is evidenced in the stability of their legislation. They err, probably, in the other extreme. "The House of Commons wastes little, either of time or power. Its members are averse to rhetoric, and fiercely intolerant of abstractions. You will hear among them little fine speaking, but much sensible talking, What is once settled there is settled forever. They will endure no rigmarole about the rights of man, and the eternal fitness of things, and the shades of Hampden and Sydney. Many things are taken for granted, to the great saving of time and strength. Provided, too, that their work is done, they care very little how it looks. Acts of Parliament are often clumsily drawn, but they generally hit the grievance between wind and water. Every thing is for use, and nothing for show. Parliament is, in short, *a factory for the making of laws*, and they will no more listen to a professor's discourse on the principles of legislation, than the operatives in a mill at Lowell would leave off their work to hear a lecture on the force of gravity, or the pressure of fluids." Those men who have manifested the greatest judgment and prudence in the management of their private business should be selected as legislators, and their *votes*, not their speeches, should be the tests of their merit.

Defective personal habits can be remedied by "a remove of the impediments of the mind." Intemperance is a habit that is almost certain to result in failure Even the moderate use of alcoholic stimulants to the man whose business requires a clear intellect and constant prudence is attended with danger. It clouds the perception, and creates a feeling of boldness and recklessness, that may, in a moment, thwart the best laid plans of years. The business man who indulges at all in artificial stimulants can never be sure of himself. One glass at certain times will produce more intoxication than five at other times. Occasional periods of excess, though more disgusting, are less dangerous than habitual tippling, provided the debauchee takes the precaution to transfer his business in the mean time to another, and not to resume it until every drop is purged from the system. In all cases, however, the effect is gradually to undermine energy, to impair moral principle, to provoke an irritability of the system which renders us liable to be impolite to customers, and to quarrel in unguarded moments with those with whom it is our interest to be most friendly. Experience has shown that it was full of danger under the old plan of few sales and large profits, and common sense warns us against it, under the new plan of quick sales and small profits.

A *departure from regular business* is a personal matter that frequently results in failure. Men become dissatisfied with the slow gains of the calling with which they are acquainted, and suffer themselves to be enticed from it by stories of fortunes which have been acquired in other pursuits. There is scarcely a business that can be named, in which all have failed; and those who make the success of others their plea for change, may spend their lives in changing their plans.

Every business has its peculiarities and its mysteries, that cannot be acquired by intuition. Practice must make perfect. All who have followed a certain occupation for twenty years will readily perceive that, although they thought themselves wise when they began their career, they were exceedingly ignorant. The tendency of business, as civilization progresses, is to subdivision of employments; and those who attempt to resist it by a combination of several kinds in their own hands, even though apparently connected, are generally forced to regret it. In the dry-goods business, for instance, there seems to be a growing disposition to combine retailing, jobbing, and importing, in the same hands, and as it is a violation of the general law, it is likely to result unfavorably. The *Dry-Goods Reporter*, in 1848, made some appropriate remarks on this subject:—

"The position of the jobber and importer can be illustrated better by an anecdote, which we heard yesterday from undoubted authority. A jobber who, one year since, was affected with the inporting mania, and followed the business successfully during the year 1847, realizing therefrom over two thousand dollars, says he would willingly give all the money he made in '47, and five hundred dollars added thereto, to be rid of his imports for '48. Many will say this was all owing to circumstances, which probably might not happen again in years, and that the importers were all in the same boat. Softly, man; this is not exactly so. Upon inquiry you will find that but few of the present quantities of excess goods *belong* to our importers. They are merely the *factors;* the *ownership* rests elsewhere, and the heavy loss (for a heavy loss must be sustained on this spring's imports) will fall upon Europe, and not be sustained here.

"Importers, who are pecuniarily interested in the price at which goods are sold in this country have some connecting branch or resident partner in Europe, whose duty it is to watch the market there. The exports from thence is the barometer; and when such times as the present are upon us, we find that, although seemingly, and in reality have goods enough on hand, they belong to other parties, and in many instances have been shipped against their advice. So sensitively alive are these resident partners in Europe to the exports, that we have heard of £5 having been paid for the outward manifest of a ship bound to the United States.

"We have been frequently amused at the remarks of Zadock Pratt, Esq., ex-member of Congress—a man of strong common sense, who was originally a tanner by trade. A speculator was showing him a new method of tanning, by which he represented great quantities of money could be made. Pratt told him he did not doubt it, but he was making money enough; that he (the speculator) had better find some one who was not doing so well. He has resisted all attempts to allure him from his legitimate business, and by close application has amassed a quarter of a million.

"Our advice is to the retailer, do not attempt to job; to the jobber, leave importing alone; and to the importer, allow not the offer of an extra price induce you to break a package, for it is as completely unjust for you to rob the jobber of his legitimate profit as it would be for the jobber to retail goods. We say, emphatically, 'Stick to your regular business.'"

The division and subdivision of employments is favorable to the success of all, and "to depart from regular business is to lose money."

The last of the habits purely personal that we shall notice is —*extravagance in expenditure*. This seems to be the most serious in its results of all. According to our statistics, two-thirds at least of the failures are ascribed to an imprudent expenditure of "more than they could reasonably hope their profits would be, though their business yielded a fair return." This is a matter of astonishment. It conflicts with all our received ideas that men manifest great shrewdness in matters which affect their own interest. It is an indisputable truth, we think, that a man who, in collecting pebbles or pearls, will scatter with his left hand all that he collects with his right, cannot get a "heap;" that he who spends as much as he makes cannot increase his wealth; and that he who spends more than he makes will increase his poverty wonderfully. How shall we account for this ruinous propensity? To what cause shall we ascribe it? Have the feminine portion of the world any thing to do with it? It certainly cannot be that men of themselves are so weak as to allow a petty ambition for show, for expensive toys and trinkets, to derange the weightier matters of business. It must be that the devil is at his old tricks, working for the downfall of mankind, and, having succeeded so well with mother Eve, is still operating to the same end, through her daughters.

A writer in the *Providence Journal* makes "some calculations to show that the failure of nine-tenths is directly attributable rather to a profuse expenditure of their gains in living beyond their income, and to rashly extended operations, undertaken to sustain such a career, than to the generally unrequiting nature of business pursuits. It appears by a recent statistical report, that one-half of the whole property of Providence, with a population of 40,000, is in the hands of 175 individuals. It will be found, on investigation, that the large estates of the 175 individuals who possess one-half of the whole property in this city, have been solely acquired by persevering diligence and economy, rather than by bold enterprises; which, when successful, induce reckless habits, like success in drawing the prizes in a lottery.

Every one becomes surprised in examining the Annuity tables in familiar use in the offices of Life Insurance Companies, at the astonishing aggregate amount of the daily expenditures of small sums, compounded with interest, and finally summed up at the termination of a long life, as exhibited in the following abstract:—

TABLE SHOWING THE AGGREGATE VALUE, WITH COMPOUND INTEREST.

Daily Expenses				In 10 years.	In 20 years.	In 30 years.	In 40 years.	In 50 years.
2¾ cents a day	or	$10	a year	$130	$360	$790	$1,540	$2,900
5½	"	20	"	260	720	1,580	3,080	5,800
8½	"	30	"	390	1,080	2,370	4,620	8,700
11	"	40	"	520	1,440	3,160	5,160	11,600
13¾	"	50	"	650	1,860	3,950	7,700	14,500
27½	"	100	"	1,300	3,600	7,900	15,400	29,000
55	"	200	"	2,600	7,200	15,800	30,800	58,000
82½	"	300	"	3,900	10,800	23,800	46,200	87,000
$1 10	"	400	"	5,200	14,400	31,600	51,600	116,000
1 37	"	500	"	6,500	18,000	39,500	77,000	145,000

By reference to the preceding table, it appears that, if a laboring man, a mechanic, unnecessarily expends only 2¾ cents per day from the time he becomes of age to the time he attains the age of threescore and ten years, the aggregate, with interest, amounts to $2,900; and a daily expenditure of 27½ cents amounts to the important sum of $29,000. A six cent piece, saved daily, would provide a fund of nearly $7,000, sufficient to purchase a fine farm. There are few mechanics who cannot save daily, by abstaining from the disgusting use of tobacco, from ardent spirits, visiting theatres, &c., twice or thrice the above stated amount of a six cent piece. *The man in trade who can lay by about a dollar per day will find himself similarly possessed of* $116,000, *and numbered among the one hundred and seventy-five men who own one-half of the property of the city of Providence.*

Few people estimate the large sums to which the yearly saving in personal and household expenses will accumulate. Four thousand dollars a year is not an uncommon expenditure for merchants in this and other cities. Half a century ago, $500 would have been regarded as a sufficient expenditure. The difference between these two sums for fifty years, with the accumulation of compound interest, reaches the enormous amount of over one million of dollars. Extend the time eleven years, and this sum, great as it is, becomes doubled.

The preceding calculations are sufficient to encourage hope of eventual success and independence in the bosom of every young man, who, on commencing business, will maintain a determined resolution to combine industry with economy; and also to warn him that, without economy, the opposite result of bankruptcy is frightfully certain.

With the plain statements of actual results before us, it cannot, therefore, be a matter of surprise that the present general prevalence of an unrestricted indulgence in showy habits of dress and of living, should cause the failure of nine-tenths of the men who embark in business, and involve, also, the prudent and careful, on whom must fall the losses caused by recklessness and extravagance in every form.

The true value of money consists in the rational use of it. Economy becomes a vice in the miser, while extravagance becomes, on the other extreme, a vice in the spendthrift. The golden mean lies between these extremes. By applying available gains for the procurement of rational comforts and enjoyment, and for advancement in moral and intellectual culture, we fulfil the highest desire of our nature."

Excessive use of credit must bear a portion of the blame attached to extravagance of expenditure. They are intimately connected and interwoven with each other. The facilities for obtaining credit tempt men to an extravagance of living, and an imprudent expenditure compels them to resort to accommodation bills, and other means of supplying their necessities. Dr. Johnson has observed that "he that once owes more than he can pay is often obliged to bribe his creditor to patience by increasing his debt. Worse and worse commodities, at a higher and higher price, are forced upon him; he is impoverished by compulsive traffic, and at last overwhelmed in the common receptacles of misery, by debts which, without his own consent, were accumulated on his head."

The credit system is also chargeable with tempting the sanguine into "speculations in things with which they were unacquainted, and to trading beyond their capital and facile means." Men's ambition to get on faster than prudence will justify finds a ready means of gratification through the facilities for obtaining credit. Capital is not now the thing needful to effect any change; the ability to borrow or get credit is all that is necessary. The mechanic can become a tradesman or a doctor; the shopkeeper an importer; a stonecutter a mill owner; a tailor a ship owner; a working goldsmith can take Seville House to give concerts; a minister of the gospel may become a foreign merchant; and a foreign merchant, a land speculator, and act the capitalist.

"Some fifteen or twenty years ago, a great change took place here, in the management of foreign commerce. It was through an invention for substituting a bill of exchange on London, which would be accredited in distant countries, in place of the usual outfit of money or goods on which foreign voyages had been conducted before. It was no longer necessary for a man to gather up his property, and put it in hard money, or in a cargo newly purchased, on board ship. He was no longer reminded, by every difficulty that he met, in providing the requisite funds, that he was putting at risk—perhaps the accumulations of his life; and was led, therefore, to consider well what he was about. It was only necessary for him to satisfy the agent of some European banker that he was able to bear any positive loss that might occur at the end of a voyage; or, if not so, to give security for a small portion of the credit which would cover such loss, and the whole business of the outfit was done in an hour. The right to draw the bills was given, and he had only to hire a vessel, if he did not own one, and dispatch her; or to join, as one, in making up a voyage, although the whole business was new to him. The vessel might be sent to Canton, for instance, for teas or silks. To pay for them, bills or orders to receive money in London would be given. Although the Chinamen would not want such bills for their own use, the English, from whom they purchase manufactured goods, would readily take the bills in payment; and the parties here would receive their vessel back with a full cargo, for which they would have to make payment in London after it should be sold.

"The consequence was, that great facilities were offered to people to engage in business in which they had no previous experience, and for which they have, in many cases, suffered severely themselves, besides causing the downfall of several important banking-houses in Europe, who had injudiciously supplied the means, and tempted them to such dangerous folly.

"Within the same period there has been, on the other hand, a great expansion of the currency in this country. The value of real estate appeared to be increasing surprisingly, and men whose proper business is foreign commerce have been tempted to withdraw their capital from its previous uses, while this contrivance of bills enabled them to continue their usual trade, and make great speculations in lands, in hopes of sudden wealth.

"Failures have succeeded, and the unsuspicious creditor, who supposed that he had been selling his goods to a person employed solely in domestic manufactures, for instance, finds that it depended entirely upon the success of a Calcutta voyage, in which the purchaser had secretly engaged, whether he was ever to be paid. Or he finds that, while he supposed that he had sold his goods to a merchant whose attention was devoted to foreign trade, the real capital that was believed to be in that trade had beeen diverted to the purchase of prairies at the West, or cotton lands at the South; and that, in truth it depended upon the tide of emigration to some new settlement in a wild country, whether he was ever to get his payment.*

But these are not the only evils of the credit system. Men are not only enticed by it to forsake the business with which they are acquainted, or to combine with it imprudent speculations, but to extend their legitimate business beyond all bounds of prudence or calculation. They take upon themselves obligations, the extent of which they scarcely know; they connect themselves with houses in a virtual partnership, over whose affairs they can exercise no control; they suffer their business to grow upon them until it gets beyond their powers of management, and they are compelled to resign it to agents and to Providence. This is not all. They must live in a manner worthy of such an establishment; their business is as remote from their inspection as an Irish estate, and their amusements must be of the same princely order. In course of time, however, their dignity and business collapse together, carrying

* Hon. Thomas G. Cary.

havoc and destruction to the homes of innocent and unsuspecting creditors.

The anxiety to do an immense business, which a bloated credit system inordinately sharpens, also leads to investments in improper mercantile securities, of which we have before spoken, and to the conversion of floating into fixed capital. The reverses that befell the houses of Messrs. Palmer & Co., Messrs. Ferguson & Co., and Macintosh & Co., whose stoppage, in 1830, in England, inflicted a tremendous shock on the India trade, were immediately traceable to an error of this kind. They invested their own capital, and that intrusted to them by others, in indigo factories in India, conducting their home business on credit, and, as can be easily understood, when monetary affairs became unsettled, their securities were wholly unmarketable in London, and they were compelled to suspend. Recent failures there have been traced to the same cause. Messrs. Reed, Irving, & Co., who failed in '46 or '47, for an immense sum, sank in sugar plantations, in the Mauritius alone, three million dollars. Messrs. Gower, Nephews, & Co., sank, in the same island, upwards of a million, while Cochrane & Co. were implicated in indigo factories abroad.

In the investigations of the Parliamentary Committee, as to the causes of the failures in London in '46 and '47, much valuable information was elicited. Several distinguished merchants gave their opinion as to what constitutes overtrading. Charles Turner, a merchant of Liverpool, says: "The brokers have been in the habit, we all know now pretty well, not only of advancing upon goods after their arrival, to meet bills drawn against those goods, which is perfectly legitimate, and upon bills of lading, which to a certain extent, might also be done, but, beyond that, they have done what is perfectly illegitimate; they have advanced upon the produce before it was shipped, and in some cases before it was manufactured."

At another place he says: "I will just mention one fact; there is one house which failed in London the other day, and in examining their affairs, a transaction of this sort was found to have taken place. There is a house in Manchester, and another at Calcutta; they opened a credit account with a house in London to the extent of two hundred thousand pounds; that is to say, the friends of this house in Manchester, who consigned goods to the East India house from Glasgow and from Manchester, had the power of drawing upon the house in London to the extent of two hundred thousand pounds; at the same time there was an understanding that the corresponding house in Calcutta were to draw upon the London house to the extent of two hundred thousand pounds; with the proceeds of those bills sold in Calcutta, they were to buy other bills, and remit them to the house in London, to take up the first bills drawn from Glasgow. The whole of this was not carried out, but that was the arrangement; so that, if the arrangement had been fully carried out, there would have been six hundred thousand pounds of bills created upon that transaction. That I call over-trading."

This was unquestionably over-trading on a large scale. It is these kinds of operations, which are by no means confined to London, that do more harm to society than gambling saloons or lottery offices. They create false views of failure, and surround it with a species of meretricious dignity. A marble mason, who failed in Philadelphia about a year ago, for one hundred and thirty thousand dollars, without being able to pay any dividend at all, is considered to have elevated that trade above the ordinary mechanical standard. His failure too, it may be remarked, was not caused by any disasters in his trade; but to trading beyond his capital, an imprudent meddling with land speculations, bonus operations, and their consequent usurious interest.

What are the remedies for an excessive use of credit? The remedies are of two kinds, moral and legislative. The latter falls within the province of the political economists, and we will not meddle with it. We hope they will soon get through refining definitions, and attend to it. We venture, however, to predict that, in less than fifty years, gold and silver will not be the only legal tender; that Government, or a board of trade under Government will have power to issue an inconvertible paper money in quantities sufficient to facilitate exchanges—the only use of money; that banks will issue no bills, but act as comptrollers of credit—proportioning loans to capital, as experience has found to be safe; that all laws for the collection of debts, except banker's securities, and in case of wages, will be repealed, and transactions between individuals reduced to a cash standard. But, until the laws aid us in keeping aloof from danger, our only remedy is a *moral or personal one.* The leading causes of failure, which we have noticed, are *founded on a desire to get forward too fast*—an ambition, on the one hand, to get *rich without labor*, and, on the other, an impatient desire to enjoy *the luxuries of life before we have earned them.* We must check this ambition and desire; we must amend our minds, and curb our imaginations.

"As for the true marshalling of men's pursuits towards their fortune," says Bacon, "as they are more or less material, I hold them to stand thus: first, the amendment of their own minds; for the remove of the impediments of the mind will sooner clear the passages to fortune than the obtaining fortune will remove the impediment of the mind." The facts which we have given, and which cannot be disputed, afford us powerful arguments for regulating and moderating our desire for gain; and a careful observation of the world will confirm the resolution. It is certain that the inordinate, grasping anxiety for wealth which characterizes some men will be fatal to their ultimate success. The very ambition to be rich often defeats itself and leads to ruin. It blinds the judgment, and misleads into visionary schemes and ruinous speculations, so that men of the coolest and most deliberate habits, when they have yielded to a passion for wealth, are no longer capable of reasoning wisely. The passion is, in itself, a proof of bad judgment. Only a few can be rich, and the chances are too great against any one to make it wise in him to centre his hopes upon a result in which he is very likely to be disappointed. It may be said of wealth, as it has been of happiness, that when unsought it is often found; when unexpected, often obtained; while those who seek for her the most ardently, fail the most, because they seek her where she is not.

What course, then, shall we pursue? Are there no hopes of obtaining reasonable wealth? Certainly there are. But we must reject, without hesitation, the advice of those injudicious friends who argue that no one can get rich without assuming great risks—who urge us to plunge in where the business is most weighty and important. We must avoid that fated circle whose business and expenditures are of the dazzling, magnificent kind. The demon of bankruptcy presides there—we may rely upon it. Had we the Swedenborgian "inner light," and even without it, we could see him skulking around their stores—in their counting-houses, ay, riding as footmen on their equipages. We must place ourselves beyond the outer edge of this dashing circle, whence we can occasionally look over and note their downward progress. When their ruin comes, which is as certain as death, there will be excellent opportunities to improve our fortunes, by picking up pieces of the wreck at our own prices.

We must manage our own business as we would prosecute a science, for its own sake, and not solely with a view to wealth. We must study its principles; keep on the watch for information, which we may turn to advantage; assign certain limits to every enterprise; never seek for an excessive profit in any undertaking, and make ourselves, as far as human caution and prudence can do, independent of the play of accidents. If misfortune comes, as it may come, it has not been our fault. If a competency is the result, it is all that we expected; if wealth comes, we are prepared to make sure of it.

A course of prudent moderation in every thing, in the desire for gain, the amount of business, in personal expenses, will materially improve our chances of success, and at the same time strengthen the character and increase our happiness. The Hon. Thomas G. Cary, an eminent merchant of Boston, and formerly a director of the U. S. Bank in its palmy days, in an address delivered some years ago, has furnished us with some excellent incentives to the adoption of this course. He discourses thus:—

"The man who is prepared to work through life takes his labor with cheerful ease. The Saturday evening which brings repose to man and beast is not more agreeable to him than the renewal of his occupation on that Monday morning that lowers so gloomily over one who has before him a week of embarrassment in meeting obligations that have been entered into with the delusive hope of rapid gain, and which he would rejoice to cancel, by returning his purchases, if he could retrace his steps.

"The man of regular industry, too, and of principle, while he is free from deep anxiety for the future, usually gives it that due care which gradually improves his condition. As only a small portion of the world can ever be *rich*, he may not be likely to become so. Yet he has his chance. As he advances in life, he sees some of those who at times have almost excited his envy at their seeming prosperity, becoming involved in difficulty, and falling far behind him. When the crisis comes, perhaps he finds, to his surprise, that he is looked to as a strong man; for he has something *at command*, and appears at ease, when almost every one about him, who has been more ready to give promises than he, is straitened, and must sell at a loss.

"When property, then, seems to be losing its value and is neglected, opportunities rise around him of using what means he may have with an advantage that he had never anticipated, and his possessions begin to extend. Pursuing the same steady course, his strength increases. Without much calculation about it, he finds himself, perhaps, becoming comparatively rich. Causes are at work that may possibly make him quite so, without endangering his independence or tranquillity. If wealth comes, he makes sure of it. His spirit is not intoxicated, though his views expand with his acquisitions. The temptation to advance finds no treacherous ally within him, in a spirit of rivalry, ambition, or envy, urging him on to risk all that he may have in grand undertakings, that are to outdo all who are before him, and dazzle his little world with the magnitude of his operations."

* * * * * * *

Instances may certainly be found of men who disregard the rules of wisdom and virtue, and yet become rich and powerful. But where one such man can be pointed out, a score of others, who resemble him in every thing but shrewdness and energy, may be mentioned, who have disgracefully failed.

It may be, on the other hand, that among twenty men who act with strict regard to principle, not more than one of them would be found to have become rich. But the other nineteen have probably never failed. They have earned all that they have ever spent. They have performed their portion of the labor of the world. They have its confidence and respect. Be they mechanics, farmers, or professional men; be they merchants, seamen, or laborers on the wharves, they are known as men of independent spirit, who can neither be bought nor bent to improper designs; as men who fulfil the great purposes of life, and who are regarded and remembered for their worth.

But the man, be he good or bad, who begins with the determination to be rich early in life, is most likely to be disappointed. Let him select the best example of rapid success that can be found; let him, if he can, begin with the same means, and do precisely the same things, as did those who have become rapidly rich, and he is very likely to find, in the end, that although, *the same course pursued ten years sooner or ten years later, might have been successful, yet owing to causes entirely beyond his own control, it could not possibly succeed when he attempted it: and that it required all the skill that he possessed even to avoid ruin.*

In truth, the path that leads *speedily* to wealth is generally discovered, when found at all, by some accidental concurrence of circumstances. But the turnings that lead to failure and disgrace can be seen from afar; and may, in most cases, be avoided by seasonable care. The father can direct his son, when he begins the journey of life, where to observe them. The great Parent of men has set up the landmarks; and the mother can teach her boy how he is to avoid them when he enters on the highway of the world. She cannot instruct him by what means he may be enabled to ride onward, among the throng, in a luxurious equipage; but she may do much to save him from the humiliation and sorrow of those who are seen standing in tatters at the roadside, after straying in search of some imaginary short-cut to wealth, and scrambling back through the mud and briers of the swamp.

The difference to his future might be vast, if her aspirations for his greatness, which are, perhaps, sowing the seeds of selfish and fatal ambition in his mind, should be exchanged for the spirit of real affection, that would instruct him in the virtues of industry and truth. In a word, it does not lie with the young man, when he begins life, to say whether or not he is to be *rich;* but whether or not he will make a mischievous *failure*, is, in most cases, an affair that he can decide for himself.

There are some interesting questions connected with the subject of failure, to a few of which we must give a passing notice.

First: When should a man fail? In most cases, he has no choice as to the time; but no man has a right to fail who is not insolvent merely to save himself from loss. By doing so, he unnecessarily endangers the failure of those who rely upon him in order to meet their own payments; he unjustly creates distrust among business men in general, and destroys confidence. When, however, he discovers that he is insolvent, the sooner he fails probably the better. It is an old Shaksperian truth that "Sorrows come not single spies, but in battalions;" and when a train of unfortunate circumstances has so set upon a man as to reduce him below the line of solvency, the sooner he arrests it by a prompt winding up, the better for himself and his creditors. The catastrophe of failure seldom comes at once. The shadows of it are often cast before. As they deepen and thicken, they offer continual temptation, hard to resist. In this protracted agony, it is that men commit the greatest errors—errors, which, with sometimes perhaps an undue severity of judgment, fasten a stain upon their character that no time can efface.

What ought one to do under such circumstances? is another question. "The first thing a man has to do"—we quote the Hon. John Sargeant—"is to take honest counsel with himself; to state the case fairly; to examine it deliberately, and decide it justly; to go through with it as a work he is bound in conscience to perform; not slightingly, not carelessly, not deceitfully, but thoroughly, as if he were upon his oath to make a true inventory and appraisement. He is to look at his books, not to see the figures there set down, but whether the value is what they represent. Such a work is hard, very hard. Many a man closes his eyes, because he knows what they would see if they were opened. He perceives, but he voluntarily makes his perception indistinct, and persuades himself, or tries to persuade himself, that the truth is obscure when he knows it is clear. He cannot plead ignorance, and is therefore accumulating for himself a store of self-reproach; for finally he will be compelled to confess that he has sinned against knowledge. The next thing to be done is to consult *judicious friends*. If it be hard for a man to look steadfastly at a painful and humiliating truth, still harder is it for him frankly to make it known to others. Yet it must be done, if we would profit by the advice of friends. And, lastly, it is the duty of a man, in these circumstances, to counsel with his creditors; for it is their interest that is to be dealt with. Safe counsellors they will be found, and generous ones, too, if they are honestly treated."

Our duty, then, is comprehended in a few words: A fair disclosure, a full surrender, and an equal distribution.

Another consideration is the treatment of debtors. When creditors are notified of a failure, all opinion should be suspended until a thorough investigation is had. A clear distinction should then be made between the treatment of a *fraudulent* and of an *unfortunate* debtor. While the former should suffer all the punishment due to detected villany and outraged confidence, the latter merits, and should receive, all the kindness invariably due to misfortune. In fact, all failures, not plainly fraudulent, should be treated with a great deal of liberality. The creditor should never forget, as Dr. Johnson observed, that he has "shared in the guilt of improper trust; that he suffered the debt to be contracted with the hope of advantage to himself; that *he proportioned the profit to his own opinion of the hazard, and, that there is no reason why one should punish another for a contract in which both concurred.*" But a failure from evident misfortune merits not only liberal, but kind treatment. He who adds to the distress of an unhappy man by a rude word or a vindictive act puts himself beyond the pale of human sympathies, and should be "mocked at when *his* calamity cometh."

Finally, the world should remember that,

"They wha fa' in fortune's strife
  Their fate we should na censure;
For still the important end o' life
  They equally may answer:
A man may hae an honest heart,
  Though poortith hourly stare him;
A man may tak' a neebor's part,
  Yet hae nae cash to spare him."

CHAPTER XV.

SAVING, SPENDING, GIVING, TAKING, LENDING, BORROWING, AND BEQUEATHING MONEY.

We presume that it needs no demonstration to prove that the *saving* of money is as essential as getting, for the attainment of a permanent independence. This is one of those self-evident truths that meet with a ready and a universal assent. It is even a truism that it is as physically impossible for money to accumulate without saving, as for a leaking vessel to hold water. There is no income so large that cannot be got rid of, and no sum so small, that an able-bodied, industrious man may earn in this country, that will not suffice, so long as he remains single, to lay the foundation of an independent fortune. A young man who can earn a dollar a day has but to resolve to save a portion of what he earns towards capital to start business upon, and the difficulty is already half overcome. A capital acquired in this way is generally lasting, while capital acquired by loan or inheritance is too frequently lost. The industry and efforts used in acquiring capital train to habits of business which, as we have before shown, are necessary to success, and without which training, business is most apt to fail. In looking abroad, too, we generally see those who commence life by their own personal efforts, and by such efforts *start themselves* in the world, are the most successful. It is astonishing on how small a sum a man who is determined to save, may live comfortably. One of my predecessors in the "Art of money-catching," as he has entitled it, has given "directions for preparing fourscore good and wholesome dishes, on most of which a man may live for two-pence a day." Every thing depends upon the habits and associations formed in youth. A young gentleman of elegant tastes and expensive habits, especially a pet of the ladies, may as well fiddle jigs to a milestone as to hope to make headway in the world, or to retain it if thrust upon him by others. A particularly fast man, with an ardent admiration of "good stock," will very probably discover that his business and money took to flying when he took to riding. An excellent judge of good wines, or a connoisseur in rare dishes, may calculate with certainty that his pockets will become slim in exact proportion as his belly grows round. In a word, prosperity without economy is an impossibility.

But a man has only the right to commence the work of saving after all his just debts are paid; and *all* his debts are not merely those of which the evidence is a note, or a bond, or a mortgage, or a book account. If he is the head of a family, he is under obligations to his family which he must discharge. As a member of society, and one of the great family of man, he owes debts of brotherhood to those whom misfortune has visited, of which he must pay his proportion. As a Christian, the recipient of the bounty of God, he owes a portion annually for the enlargement of his Maker's kingdom upon the earth. Charity is not merely a politic virtue, in the exercise of which he may reap an inward satisfaction, but in the neglect of which he incurs no guilt. Charity is a solemn *debt*, which no one can fail to pay without moral bankruptcy. It is a debt so binding in its nature that physical impossibility to have the means to discharge it is the only sufficient excuse. It is a debt, nevertheless, in the discharge of which, when the proceeds are applied to the dissemination of education, morality, and religious truth, one may as justly be called a shrewd man as an honest and a charitable man; for no one of sound judgment, I think, will deny that if all men acted intelligently, and in accordance with the precepts of the gospel, all could attain twice their present ratio of prosperity with one-fourth the present anxiety, risk, and trouble.

It is in an awful reflection that in a land abounding in wealth, men willing to labor should seek the means of subsistence, and not find it. It *is* a sorrowful thought that in a Christian land they should ask for bread, and not receive it. It is a heart-sickening sight, as in the Old World, to see the extremes of unbounded affluence on the one hand, and miserable degraded poverty on the other. Truly, as I once heard an Irishman observe when speaking of a famished countryman who had begged at a nobleman's door for the meat that he was giving to his dogs, and was rudely turned away, "I wonder that God can look on these things, and keep his patience." It does prove that there is something radically wrong in society, but still the wrong, in my opinion, does not consist in the organization of society, nor in the fact that some men have obtained more than their share of the world's possessions, provided they got them legally, honestly, and honorably, but in the fact that they have not properly used what they rightfully obtained. They have not borne their share of the burdens of society. They have not contributed their proportion to its maintenance and the due preservation of its health. Until the world is a second Eden, it needs, and can profitably use the labor of all who are in it. Much less than one-tenth of the world's income, which was the quantum demanded under the old Jewish dispensation, would provide a capital to employ usefully and profitably all who needed work, and were willing to work, and also support all who were unable to work and needed assistance.*

* "Let us now consider the sums that might be raised, supposing only one-tenth of income to be set apart for the purposes of philanthropy and religion. Supposing the population of Great Britain to amount to 16,000,000, and reckoning only 2,000,000 heads of families, or the eighth part of the population to be connected with the Christian church; and supposing, farther, that only one-fiftieth of these, or 40,000, have incomes averaging £500; the tenth of these incomes would produce a sum of £2,000,000. Supposing the tenth part of the remaining population, 196,000, to have incomes of £200 a year, the annual tithe would be £3,920,000. Suppose the remaining 1,764,000 to have at an average £80 per annum, its tithe would amount to £14,112,000, so that the whole of this supposed annual tithe of income would amount to above *twenty millions of pounds*, which is more than forty times the amount of the annual funds of the Bible, Missionary, and other philanthropic societies in Great Britain, which do not amount to *half* a million. In this calculation, I have not taken into account a million or two of the grown-up individuals belonging to the different families of the kingdom, who have separate establishments from their parents, and who might be supposed to contribute several millions of pounds. Nor have I taken into the calculation several thousands of the nobility and gentlemen who occupy the highest places of society, some of whom could afford from

The totally different rules and principles that apply to the *getting* and to the *using* of money, are the rock on which theorists split. The distinction is one that they do not seem to perceive clearly. They pour out the vials of their indignation on the getting of money, when it should fall upon the improper use of money. They at one time contend that a man should not devote more of his time to the acquisition of property than will barely suffice for his wants, and then argue for an amount of charity that he could not possibly be able to give without unremitted industry. A preacher, on one Sabbath morning, will speak so disparagingly of the worldliness of men's nature, and the baseness of their strife after filthy lucre, that one, if he interpreted him literally, would be tempted to sell all that he has, and retire to a monastery. On the next, pro-

one to ten thousand pounds annually, and which would add a considerable number of millions to the sum above stated. If such sums could be raised without subtracting any substantial comfort from a single individual, how small is the number of Christians worthy of the name, to be found in our country, since the fiftieth or even the hundredth part of this sum can scarcely be raised among all the ranks and denominations of religious society. But much more than even the above-stated proportion ought, in numerous instances, to be devoted to religion and philanthropy. If, for example, a person has an income of £900 a year, I have no hesitation in saying that, if he wish to act as a steward under God, for the distribution of his bounty, he ought to consecrate £400 annually to the promotion of Christianity and general improvement. And will any one aver that the remaining £500 is not sufficient to procure every comfort that a rational or a Christian character ought to desire? But the whole £900, it may be said, is requisite for the individual to keep up the dignity of his station. If keeping up the pomp and dignity of a station is to be set up in competition with the demands of religion, then let the individual take the world on his back, and march off as far as he can from Christian society; for such persons have too frequently been a pest to religious associations. Verily, I say unto him, he shall have his reward, but a reward after which, I trust in God, I shall never aspire. Let such remember the Divine admonition: 'Ye cannot serve God and mammon.' There is an absolute incompatibility between the service of the one and of the other; and he who is not prepared to give up worldly maxims, pomp, and splendor, and to devote his influence and his superfluous wealth to the cause of religion, ought not to assume the Christian name."—*Thomas Dick, LL. D.*

bably, he will argue for an amount in charity—to say nothing of an increase of salary, which all ought to have—that one must have been active and industrious, and made a successful year indeed, to be able to meet his charity bill, without taking into account his other necessary expenses. Again, the Socialists, if I understand them correctly, with a right perception of the just claims of all who are born on the earth to the necessaries of life, but with a seemingly wrong conviction that we all are demented, would have the world a sort of well-regulated Lunatic Asylum, in which the inmates are to have certain hours to work, and a certain amount of work to perform, apparently with a view partly to support life, and partly to prevent the too frequent necessity of trepanning and strait waistcoating. Our doctrine would be totally different from this. We would say to the modern philosophers who sincerely desire to benefit and reform mankind: Admit that the choice of the mass of mankind, in devoting themselves energetically to the physical improvement of the world, is a wise one; search with a keen, sharpened inspection into the world's experience for facts and principles, that will enable them to be more successful in their undertakings; trace out accurately the bounds within which they can go safely, and beyond which there is danger; lay down, not merely general principles, but rules that will be applicable in individual cases as they arise; enlighten their consciences, and make wiser their heads; aim to remove as much as possible the load of anxiety that presses upon the mind of him who is travelling the thorny path of business, in view of future danger and evil; arouse men to greater energy, and to a more exalted enterprise, until the land is covered with a network of iron, and the ocean white with the sails of ten thousand argosies, bearing merchandise and civilization to all quarters of the globe; urge them to this for the sake of the glorious results that will follow, and not for the sake of individual wealth; denounce, with the withering fire of Juvenal, the aristocracy of wealth, which is fully as contemptible, if not more contemptible than the aristocracy of fashion, or of blood; arouse the people to a just appreciation of their power, that they may not bow down with truckling servility to the insignia of wealth, unaccompanied by merit, but pour forth their voice in one quick peal against those who deny the claims of the unfortunate to their assistance, in order to expend more in selfish gratification, and the "royal sound will shake the whole heaven." In a word, teach us how to get more money with less risk and anxiety, and then how to use it so as to increase our happiness here, and in view of a happy immortality hereafter. Then will the plague-spots disappear from the face of society, and the roseate hues of health bloom again on her faded cheek.

But there is a question of equal difficulty, and perhaps of greater practical importance, which honest men encounter, and that is, how can contributions be given so as to effect the greatest good? It is unquestionably true, that the present system is a defective one. At present, a man who gives nothing from year to year to any charitable purpose may have the reputation of being a liberal and a just man; while another, who gives perhaps more than his share, in proportion to his income, will have quite a contrary reputation. At present, a man so disposed may shirk all giving, under pretence of favoring some one or another of the numerous charities. At present, a man who pays much respect to the world's opinion must give to all and to every thing or to nothing, in order to escape villanous abuse. At present, if he once has the misfortune to be known as a charitable man, petitions will be thrust at him almost every hour of the day; preachers will preach at him, his door will be besieged by the loudest and fastest talking, if *not* the most beautiful of women, and he must constantly undergo the pain of refusal, or be beggared. If he gives to street beggars, he is liable to imposition; if he refuses, he has no place to direct them where their merits will be inquired into, and the deserving assisted. All this is wrong, but what is the remedy? My proposition would be to establish a *great National Society,* perhaps under the sanction of Government, and of which all the present charitable associations should be branches. The first object would be to ascertain what per cent. of the aggregate income would be sufficient to do all that should be done, and then to assess each individual's proportion as taxes are now assessed, and deliver to each his charity bill as regularly as his tax bill. The penalty for non-payment should be publication in the principal papers of the county, for a certain number of weeks, with the amount attached, as tax delinquents are published in some of the States. Then we would know who fulfilled his duty, and who did not; who were good citizens, and who were not. The management of this society should be in the hands of the ablest business men, and especially of those who, having accumulated wealth, are about to retire from business, in order to save them from the dreadful alternative of having nothing to do but nurse gouty legs, and fret over their past life and present inaction. The details and feasibility of this suggestion I leave to those who are intimately conversant with the best mode of organizing and managing great public bodies.

Henry Taylor, for many years connected with the British Government, has, in his celebrated essay, "Of Money," never before republished in this country, fully considered the important matters which form the snbject of this chapter, and, as variety is charming, he shall conclude it. The entire essay, with the exception of one or two pages of unpractical remarks on Getting Money, the substance of which is contained in the caption of our first chapter, is embraced in this volume.

As to the *saving* of money, he says: the saving, like the getting, should be intelligent of a purpose beyond; it should not be saving for saving's sake, but for the sake of some worthy object to be accomplished by the money saved. And there is to be especially guarded against that accumulative instinct or passion, which is ready to take possession of all collectors.

Some very small portion of a man's income may perhaps be justifiably saved to make provision against undefined and unforeseen contingencies, and also to assure himself that he *can* save. But in the case of most men, there will be a sufficiency of distinct and definable ends, whether certain or contingent, which will not only justify, but enjoin the laying by of a proportion of their income. A young man may very well lay by money to enable him to be more free in the choice of a wife. A middle-aged man may lay it by in order that his old age may have fewer labors and cares, or more comforts. A father may lay it by for his children. But in all these cases, if the end be not kept steadily in view from first to last, and the means kept no more than proportionate and subordinate, there is the risk that the saver may become a miser. The young may grow old without taking a wife, and save still when he no longer thinks of marrying; or he may think that what he has saved may entitle him to a rich wife, rather than enable him to choose. The middle-aged man may reach old age with no disposition to increase his comforts, and every disposition to increase his hoard. And finally, the father, though his motive for saving is the most warrantable of all, may yet be betrayed by the very largeness of the allowance which the world makes in such cases, into avaricious errors. His case, as being most common, and that in which men are least on their guard, deserves to be the more closely considered.

The prudent parent is less likely to be corrupted into a covetous parent, if he be saving for *several* children, than if it be for *one* only child, or for an eldest son; for avarice projects itself more readily in the singular number than in the plural; and saving for a provision is always to be distinguished from saving for aggrandizement, which is no other than a form of avarice. Saving for an only child or an eldest son may be defended when the father has means beyond the devisable patrimony, and when that patrimony is insufficient for the station to be inherited along with it. But, if the patrimony be insufficient, and the father has *no* extrinsic means, he must not make it more insufficient in *his* lifetime, in order that it may be less insufficient in his son's; he is not to be niggardly in order that his son may be liberal. He may indeed retrench in matters connected with the keeping up of appearances, that is, he may ostensibly retire from his station for a time, or for life; but he must not, whilst keeping up the appearances of his station, fall short in matters of bounty and liberality.

In saving for younger children, the parent has to consider what is a competency; and if he be wise, and can count upon an average share of health and ability in his younger sons, he will not relieve them from the necessity of earning the main part of their livelihood; for, unless a man's property be large enough to find him an occupation in the management of it, and in the discharge of the duties incident to it (which, generally speaking, can only be the case of the eldest son,) it will be essential to his happiness that he should have to work for his bread. And it is on this fact that the custom of succession according to primogeniture is to be defended; for, if any one is sacrificed by this custom, it is rather the eldest than the younger sons: the eldest being too often pampered into self-love, the most wretched inheritance of all, the younger being trained to self-sacrifice, fortified in self-reliance, and through industry and progress leading a wiser, a better, a more generous, and a happier life.

How much to save for a *daughter* is another question; and since a woman's life for the most part turns upon her marriage, it is her matrimonial prospects which are principally to be regarded. Let not her wealth be too tempting; an heiress has a large assortment of suitors, and yet an ill choice; and do not, if you can help it, let her poverty be an obstruction; for prudent men make good husbands, and in most cases a man cannot marry with prudence where there is not the fair facility of a moderate fortune. I have heard, indeed, of a father who stinted his daughters' dowries on purpose that poor men might not be able to marry them; whence he inferred that rich men would. He might be mistaken in his inference, for, though rich men can *afford* to marry poor maids, yet men are not found to wish less for money because they want it less, and in the making of marriages it is generally seen that "wealth will after kind." Even if he were not mistaken, however, the calculation was but a sordid one at the best; and considering how many requisites must be combined to make a good husband and a happy marriage, the father is likely to impose a cruel limitation of choice, who needlessly adds wealth to the number of essentials. Even the marriage which is poor through an improvident choice, is less likely to end ill than that which is rich through a constrained choice.

There is yet another domestic object which may be a fair ground for saving out of a patrimony. One of the incidents of the law and custom of primogeniture to which our natural feelings are the least easily reconciled is the effect of it upon the wife and mother when she passes into widowhood. She is deposed from her station, and deprived of her affluence at the moment of her greatest domestic calamity, and her own child is the person to whom they are transferred. It may be that the cares, duties and responsibilities of a large property and a high proprietary station are not suitable to a widow in the decline of life; but this is not left for her to determine, and very frequently the still less acceptable cares of a straitened income, and a total change in her mode of life, are fixed upon her. The force of custom has brought the feelings of mankind into more accordance than one would have thought possible with so unnatural an arrangement; but the husband needs not to be charged with parsimony who should save money with a view to mitigate the future contrast between his wife's position and his widow's.

As to the SPENDING of money. *The art of living easily as to money, is to pitch the scale of living one degree below your means.* Comfort and enjoyment are more dependent upon easiness in the detail of expenditure than upon one degree's difference in the scale.

Guard against false associations of pleasure with expenditure; the notion that because pleasure can be purchased with money, therefore money cannot be spent without enjoyment. What a thing costs a man is no true measure of what it is worth to him; and yet how often is his appreciation governed by no other standard, as if there were a pleasure in expenditure *per se.*

Let yourself feel a want before you provide against it. You are more assured that it is a real want; and it is worth while to feel it a little in order to feel the relief from it. When you are undecided as to which of two courses you would like best, choose the cheapest. This rule will not only save money, but save a good deal of trifling indecision.

Too much leisure leads to expense, because when a man is in want of objects, it occurs to him that they are to be had for money, and he invents expenditures in order to pass the time.

A thoroughly conscientious mode of regulating expenditure implies much care and trouble in resisting imposition, detecting fraud, preventing waste, and doing what in you lies to guard the honesty of your stewards, servants, and tradesmen, by not leading them into temptation, but delivering them from evil.

A man who should be justly sensible of the duties involved in expenditure and determined to discharge them, would find the burden of them heavy; and instead of having a pleasure in expense, he would probably desire, as much as might be, to avoid the trouble of it. We sometimes hear rich men charged with parsimony, because they look minutely to differences of cost; but, if they are spending their money in a right spirit, the question they have to consider is, not whether the sum is of importance to themselves, but whether it is right or wrong that it should be given or taken.

Young men, instead of undertaking the disagreeable office of checking accounts, are often inclined to lay out a good deal of money in the purchase of bows and smiles, which they mistake for respect. It is only right and just payment that commands real respect, and the obsequious extortioner, well understanding the weakness on which he practises, will often repay himself for his own servility, not only in money, but in secret contempt for his dupe.

Prodigality is indeed the vice of a weak nature, as avarice is of a strong one; it comes of a weak craving for the blandishments of the world which are easily to be had for money, and which, when obtained, are as much worse than worthless as a harlot's love is worse than none.

As to GIVING AND TAKING.—All giving is not generous; and the gift of a spendthrift is seldom given in generosity; for prodigality is equally with avarice, a selfish vice; nor can there be a more spurious view of generosity than that which has been often taken by sentimental comedians and novelists, when they have represented it in combination with recklessness and waste. He who gives only what he would as readily throw away, gives without generosity; for the essence of generosity is in self-sacrifice. Waste, on the contrary, comes always by self-indulgence; and the weakness and softness in which it begins will not prevent the hard-heartedness to which all selfishness tends at last. The mother of Gertruda

"In many a vigil of her sick bed
Bid her beware of spendthrifts, as of men
That seeming in their youth not worse than light,
Would not end so, but with the season change:
For time, she said, which makes the serious soft,
Turns lightness into hardness."

When you give, therefore, take to yourself no credit for generosity, unless you deny yourself something in order that you *may* give.

I have known a man who was never rich, and was indeed in a fair way to be ruined, make a present of several hundred pounds under what he probably conceived to be an impulse of generous friendship; but if that man had been called upon to get up an hour earlier in the morning to serve his friend, I do not believe that he would have done it. The fact was, that he had no real value for money, no real care for consequences which were not to be immediate; in parting with some hundreds of pounds, he flattered his self-love with a show of self-sacrifice; in parting with an hour's folding of the hands to sleep, the self-sacrifice would have been real, and the show of it not very magnificent.

Again, do not take too much credit even for your self-denial, unless it be cheerfully and genially undergone. Do not dispense your bounties only because you know it to be your duty, and are afraid to leave it undone; for this is one of those duties which should be done more in the spirit of love than that of fear. I have known persons who have lived frugally, and spent a large income almost entirely in acts of charity and bounty, and yet, with all this, they had not the open hand. When the act did not define itself as a charitable duty, the spirit of the God-beloved giver was wanting, and they failed in all those little genial liberalities towards friends, relatives and dependants, which tend to cultivate the sympathies and kindnesses of our nature quite as much as charity to the poor, or munificence in their contributions to public objects.

The kindness from which a gift proceeds will appear in the *choice* as well as in the cost of it. I have known a couple who married on £300 a year receive three carriages as wedding gifts, they being unable of course to keep one. The donors had been thinking rather of what would do credit to themselves than of what would be serviceable and acceptable.

When gifts proceed from public bodies, communities, or high functionaries, in the way of testimonials, and are to do honor to the party receiving them, they should, if possible, assume a shape in which they will be seen without being shown.

There is often as much generosity in accepting gifts as there can be in bestowing them—the generosity of a nature which stands too strong in its humility to fear humiliation, which knows its own independence, and is glad to be grateful.

Upon a very different sense of generosity are some of the practices of the present time founded. It is not an uncommon thing amongst some persons, with peculiar notions of doing things delicately, for contributions to be conveyed to some decayed gentlewoman under various pretences which are meant to disguise, more or less transparently, the fact that she receives money in charity. Some wretched products of her pencil, which would not command one penny in the market, are privately sold for five shillings a piece, and the proceeds paid to her as if she had earned them; or a few deplorable verses are stitched together, and disposed of in the same manner. It is surely impossible to take a more unworthy view of what should be the character of a gentlewoman than that which this sort of proceeding implies. If a gentlewoman be in want, she should say so with openness, dignity, and truth, and accept in the manner that becomes a gentlewoman, in all lowliness, but without the slightest humiliation or shame, whatever money she has occasion for and others are willing to bestow. The relations between her and them will in that case admit of respect on the one side, and gratitude on the other. But where false and juggling pretences are resorted to, no worthy or honest feeling can have place.—Delicacy is a strong thing; and whether in giving or taking, let us always maintain the maxim, that what is most sound and true is most delicate.

There are some other ways of the world in this matter of charity, which proceed, I think, upon false principles and feelings—charity dinners, charity balls, charity bazaars, and so forth; devices—not even *once* blessed—for getting rid of distress without calling out any compassionate feeling in those who give, or any grateful feelings in those who receive. God sends misery and misfortune into the world for a purpose; they are to be a discipline for His creatures who endure, and also for his creatures who behold them. In *those*, they are to give occasion for patience, resignation, the spiritual hopes, and aspirations, which, springing from pain when there comes no earthly relief, or the love and gratitude which earthly ministrations of relief are powerful to promote. In *these*, they are to give occasion for pity, self-sacrifice, and devout and dutiful thought, subduing, for the moment, at least, the light, vain, and pleasure-loving motions of our nature. If distress be sent into the world for these ends, it is not well that it should be shuffled out of the world without any of these ends being accomplished; and still less, that it should be made the occasion of furthering ends in some measure opposite to these; that it should be danced away at a ball, or feasted away at a dinner, or dissipated at a bazaar. Better were it, in my mind, that misery should run its course, with nothing but the mercy of God to stay it, than that we should thus corrupt our charities.

Let me not be misunderstood. Feasting and dancing, in themselves and by themselves, I by no means disparage; there is a time and a place for them; but things which are excellent at one time and occasion, are a mere desecration at another. It is much more easy to desecrate our duties, than to consecrate our amusements; and better not, therefore, to mix them up with each other.

Another modern mode is to raise a subscription by shillings or pennies, fixing the contribution at so low a sum that nobody can care whether they give it or not, and collecting it in the casual intercourse of society. This is a less vitiated mode than the others, being of a more negative character; but if the others are corrupted charity, this is no better than careless charity.

Lastly, there is a rule in giving which is often overlooked by those whose generosity is not sufficiently thoughtful and severe, Generosity comes too perverted from its uses when it ministers to selfishness in others; and it should be our care to give all needful support to our neighbor in his self-denial, rather than to bait a trap for his self-indulgence; in short, to give him pleasure only when it will do him good, not when sacrifice on our part are the correlatives of abuses on his; for he who pampers the selfishness of another, does that other a moral injury, which cannot be compensated by any amount of gratification imparted to him.

> "Give thou to no man, if thou wish him well,
> What he may not in honor's interest take;
> Else shalt thou but befriend his faults, allied
> Against his better, with his baser self."

As to BORROWING AND TAKING. *Never lend money to a friend, unless you are satisfied that he does wisely and well in borrowing it.* Borrowing is one of the most ordinary ways in which weak men sacrifice the future to the present; and thence it is that the gratitude for a loan is proverbially evanescent; for the future becoming present in its turn, will not be well pleased with those who have assisted in doing it an injury. By conspiring with your friend to defraud his future self, you naturally incur his future displeasure. To withstand solicitations for loans, is often a great trial of firmness; the more especially as the pleas and pretexts alleged are generally made plausible at the expense of truth, for nothing breaks down a man's truthfulness more surely than pecuniary embarrasment.

> "An unthrift was a liar from all time;
> Never was debtor that was not deceiver."

The refusal which is at once the most safe from vacillation, and perhaps as little apt to give offence as any, is the point blank refusal without reason assigned. Acquiescence is more easily given in the decision of a strong will than in reasons, which weak men, under the bias of self-love, will always imagine themselves competent to controvert.

Some men will lend money to a friend, in order, as it were, to purchase a right of remonstrance; but the right so purchased is worth nothing. You may buy the man's ear, but not his heart or understanding.

I have never known a debtor or a prodigal who was not in his own estimation an injured man; and I have generally found that those who had not suffered by them were disposed to side with them; for it is the weak who make the outcry, and it is by the outcry that the world is wont to judge. They who lend money to spendthrifts should be prepared, therefore, to suffer in reputation as well as in their purse. Let us learn from the son of Sirach: "Many, when a thing was lent them, reckoned it to be found, and put them to trouble that helped them. Till he hath received, he will kiss a man's hand, and for his neighbor's money he will speak submissively; but when he should repay, he will prolong the time, and return words of grief, and complain of the time. If he prevails, he shall hardly receive the half, and he will count as if he had found it; if not, he hath deprived him of his money, and he hath gotten him an enemy without cause; he payeth him with cursings and railings, and for honor he will pay him disgrace."

It is a common reproach with which mankind assails mankind, that those who fall into poverty are forsaken by their friends:—

> "Ay, quoth Jacques,
> Sweep on, you fat and greasy citizens;
> 'Tis just the fashion. Wherefore do you look
> Upon that poor and broken bankrupt there?"

But before the friends of the poor be condemned, it would be well to inquire whether their poverty have been honestly come by; and I believe it would be rarely found that a person in a fair condition of life is allowed to sink unassisted into extreme indigence without some serious fault and offence; and the person having so sunk, it will be found to be still more hardly the case that the pressure of poverty is not too strong for his character. It is when the character has given way, that poverty is deserted; for pity and affection, divorced from respect, lose the main element of their strength and permanency.

The ordinary course of things, then, is as follows: A becoming embarrassed, through some perhaps venial imprudence, is kindly assisted by his friends B, C, and D; who, however, do not altogether approve his conduct, but think it would be ungenerous in them, under the protection of the favors they are conferring, to assail him with reproaches. So far all goes smoothly between A on the one hand, and B, C, and D, on the other. But A having, by the loans he has received, staved off any immediate consequences of his imprudence, is under a rather stronger temptation than before to forego the severe self-denial which would set him right again. He has now broken the ice in the matters of asking favors; he has incurred whatever humiliation belongs to it; and having begged once, it costs him comparatively little to beg again. This process of begging and borrowing goes on, therefore, becoming continually more frequent and less efficacious; and as the borrower grows less and less scrupulous, he nourishes his pride, the ordinary refuge of those who lose their independence, and resents every repulse as an insult. B, C, and D then discover that they are not thanked for what they have lent, but rather reproached for not lending more and more; whereupon they withdraw their friendship; and those who ignorantly look on, or perhaps hear the story of A, whilst B, C, and D are silent out of consideration for him, make remarks on inconstancy in friendship and the manner in which men are forsaken in their adversity and distress.

The desertion of friends, however well merited, leads the embarrassed man to consider himself as a castaway, and throw himself into still more reckless and shameless courses, and on the part of men in this condition there is sometimes seen a perfect infatuation of extravagance, which seems to proceed from the delusions of a disordered mind and a sort of fascination in ruin. Such men come to have a repugnance to spare expense, because it brings the feeling of their difficulties home to them; and a relief in profuseness, because it seems for the moment to renounce the very notion of embarrassment. The end may be short of the gallows, for in our days the gallows has fallen out of favor, but it will scarcely be short of a punishment worse than death; for men will not tolerate in its necessary consequences that to which they are very indulgent in its inchoation, and the "unfortunate debtor" who was cockered with compassion whilst he was in that stage of his existence, is regarded with just indignation and abhorrence when he has passed into that of the desperate outcast; though it may be as much in the course of nature that the one stage should follow the other, as that a tadpole, if he lives, should grow to be a toad.

There remains to be considered the subject of BEQUEATHING.

To make a will in one way or another is, of course, the duty of every person whose heir-at-law is not the proper inheritor of all he possesses; and unless where there is some just cause for setting them aside, expectations generated by the customs of the world are sufficient to establish a moral right to inherit, and to impose a corresponding obligation to bequeath. For custom may be presumed, in the absence of any reasons to the contrary, to have grown out of some natural fitness; and at all events it will have brought about an amount of adaptation which is often sufficient, as regards individual cases to make a fitness where there was none. Unless in exceptional instances, therefore, in which special circumstances are of an overruling force, the disappointment of expectations growing out of custom is not to be inflicted without some very strong and solid reasons for believing that the custom needs to be reformed.

If there be such reasons, by all means let the custom be disregarded, all expectations to the contrary notwithstanding—

> "What custom wills in all things should we do,
> The dust on antique time would lie unswept,
> And mountainous error be too highly heaped
> For truth to overpeer."

But the presumption should be always held to be in favor of custom, and he who departs from it without the plea of special circumstances should be able to find in himself a competency to correct the errors of mankind.

If it be not well for the natural or customary heirs that they should be disappointed, neither is it for those to whom an inheritance is diverted, that wealth should come upon them by surprise. Sudden and unexpected accessions of wealth seldom promote the happiness of those to whom they accrue; and they are, for the most part, morally injurious, especially when they accrue by undue deprivation of another.

But some part of the property of most people, and a large part, or even the whole of the property of some people, may not be the subject of just or natural expectations on the part of customary heirs; and in respect of such property, there is a great liberty of judgment on the part of the testator, though it is to be a grave and responsible, not a capricious liberty. The testator has to consider to whom the property will bring a real increase of enjoyment, without increase of temptation, and in whose hand it is likely most to promote the happiness of others. In general, the rule of judgment should be to avoid lifting people out of one station into another; and to aim at making such moderate additions to moderate fortunes in careful hands as may not disturb the proportion of property to station; or, still better, may rectify any disproportion, and enable those who are living with a difficult frugality to live with a free frugality.

This rule is not, I fear, very generally regarded, for mere rectitude, and the observation of measures and proportions, do not much lay hold of the minds of men. On the contrary, there is a general disposition to add to any thing which affects the imagination by magnitude; and there is also in some people a sort of gloating over great wealth, which infects them with a propensity to feed a bloated fortune. Jacques took note of this when he saw the deer that was weeping in "the needless stream:'

> "Thou mak'st a testament
> As worldlings do, giving thy sum of more,
> To that which had too much."

Thus it is that in the most solemn acts which men have to perform in the management of their money; in those too from which selfish ends seem most removed, they will often appear to be as little sensible of moral motives and righteous responsibilities as in any other transactions; and even a *testator jamjam moriturus* will dictate his will with a sort of posthumous cupidity, and seem to desire that his worldliness should live after him.

LETTERS

AND

MISCELLANIES.

LETTERS FROM HON. JOHN FREEDLEY.

Mr. Freedley was born near Norristown, Montgomery Co., Pa., May 22, 1793. He was engaged in making brick for a while, but concluded to abandon "foot" work and try "head" work. He studied law, was admitted to the bar August 16, 1820, and rose rapidly in his profession. His knowledge of the German language, and his previous acquaintance with business, obtained for him at once an extensive practice. His earnings and savings he invested in real estate purchased at sheriff's sales, and at ordinary public and private sales, and gradually he became something of a land speculator. His purchases, however, were managed with such judgment that they invariably advanced in value, and in some cases largely. The first estimate of his property in his annual inventory, which he afterwards kept regularly, is dated April 1, 1822, and is $\$5,680\frac{57}{100}$.

In 1832 or 1833, he embarked in the marble business, and gradually withdrew from his profession. In 1838, he made the following memorandum: "I now find my debts about $50,000, and these too have grown upon me in ten years. It is one of the consequences of *too much* enterprise, too great a disposition to drive a business It is a rock on which many have split, and it is marvellous that, seeing the breakers ahead, and knowing the dangers of an onward course, we are not willing to avoid them. But ten years since I was a simple six per cent. man, and had never given a note or an obligation. I owned no real estate; now I have run on the opposite extreme; own lands every where, and rest easy under a debt of fifty thousand." The usual consequences of this "too much enterprise," in those times that tried men's pockets, he did not entirely escape, though the actual results to him were not more serious than the loss of a few thousands, and a great deal of anxiety and mental harassment. In 1844 or '45, he disposed of his marble business, and in 1846, though a Whig, was elected to Congress as Representative for the 5th Pennsylvania Congressional district, which usually gives from 500 to 600 Democratic majority. In 1848, he was re-elected. In Congress, an affection of the voice as well as a retiring nature prevented him from taking an active part in the debates of that turbulent body, but in his votes he always exercised his own independent and unsurpassed judgment. He died December 8, 1851. He was a man of kind heart, superior mind, simple tastes, and unpretending manners.

The following letters and memoranda will not possess much interest for the general reader; but to his constituents and friends, with whom he was deservedly considered high authority, they will not be altogether devoid of interest, especially to those whose attention has been directed to the subjects of which they treat.

March 19, 1848.

As to the *times*, I confess the prospects are dreary. The great manufacturing establishments of our country are stopping or keeping on at a sickly pace. Business seems to be approaching a stand-still, and the different branches of business are relatively like the members of the animal body. If one branch is paralyzed, it affects all the rest. It is not wise to suppose that merchandising and building will go on as usual when the factory, furnace, and the machine-shops are stopped. A paralysis in industrial pursuits affects the prices of property, real and personal, and makes the stock which was worth $1000 under the favorable circumstances, not worth more than $500 under the depression.

* * * * * *

So far I have been a silent observer in the legislative hall, and, perhaps, shall remain silent, unless the tariff question comes up, and I should get an opportunity on that. There is always difficulty to obtain the floor, on a question of importance, and I never was good at a scramble for precedence.

* * * * * *

As to the political horizon, I scarcely know what to say. The news this morning of a bloody revolution in France raises the curtain to new scenes for the imagination to dwell upon. Where is this to end? To what is it to lead? How is it to affect us? I cannot imagine an answer to either of these questions. It may be but a three days' commotion, and it may convulse the whole earth. The war with Mexico, I fear too, is not yet over. It has taught us, I trust, *that it is easier to get into a fight than it is to get out of it when you are in.*

WASHINGTON, *July* 1, 1848.

DEAR ——:

From your last letter, I could not tell whether you had received mine with the advertisement of the Webster Lands at the time you wrote it or not. I should like to have information specifically respecting those lands, and if there is chance for speculation, I possibly might buy; but I confess the chances of a *non-resident* to speculate in wild lands is not what it is cracked up to be, and yet with proper industry and attention it might be made a productive business, yielding at least 25 per cent. on the capital invested. I will tell you how. There are now, and will be for a year to come, a great quantity of land bounty warrants for sale here. They are selling at from $115 to $125 per warrant. Each of these is equal to $200 in paying for government land. Now my plan would be this, that I, or you and I, or brother Henry and you, should attend the land sales, and loan to actual settlers the money to redeem or purchase their lands, take the title, and give a bond to reconvey on repayment of the sum agreed on. Each land warrant would be equal to $200 in an operation of this kind, and the settlers will give 12 or 15 per cent. on this for two or three years. Thus the $115 paid for the warrant would be made to yield $300 in three years, or perhaps $400 in four years. I have an opportunity of the best of information on this subject. The two new members from Wisconsin are in our mess. The one, Mr. Lynde, is a lawyer, and speaks very discouragingly of investments in back lands, says it is the most unsafe and unprofitable investment you can make; that it requires constant watching, or you will lose your land. If there is timber on it, it will be plundered. That the feeling of the people is against non-residents, and in favor of burthening such land with heavy taxes, that the tax collector does not look up the owner, but the owner must call at the office and pay, or his land will be sold without notice for taxes; and even when the owner or his agent is careful to pay, his land will sometimes be sold on account of the carelessness of the officer to give credit. He further states that mortgages or titles from new settlers to secure money paid or loaned is equally unsafe, and requires the same kind of care; that when the non-resident comes to look for his security for the money he advanced, he finds that the occupant permitted the land to be sold for taxes, perhaps for the express purpose of cutting out your mortgage or title. On the other hand, Dr. Darling, the other member, says that money may now be invested in land which will produce from 25 to 100 per cent. per annum. He admits that care and attention are necessary. He is a shrewd discriminating Yankee, and knows "what is what." He and his son keep an office, and their special business is of the kind here designated. I think their office is at *Fond du Lac*, at the head of Winnebago Lake. They keep a surveyor out to look up advantageous locations—have maps of surveys, and keep a record of all that is located, and mark it on the map, so that they know how the current is setting, and what tracts will grow into value most rapidly. They also buy and sell these land warrants. Dr. Darling, living here, buys them at, say $118, and sends them out to his son, who sells them at $175 to $180, and I think he says they now sell on an average one a day. Thus managed, it may be to them a good business. It is for the reasons here stated, that I would remark that the only course for me would be the one marked out in the commencement. But whether there is any thing even in this worth pursuing, I submit to you as a question.

J. F.

To E. T. F.

July 29, 1848.

It is now pretty certain that Congress will finally break up on the 14th of August, and I shall be heartily glad of it. I am very tired of Washington, and of being a member of Congress. The business does not suit my taste; a large portion of the session I was laboring under severe colds, which rendered me unfit for business or for enjoyment. Since the warm weather has set in, I am in a measure free from colds, and enjoy good general health, but have an affection of the head or throat which affects my voice. It is of more than twelve months' standing, and I am now under medical treatment for it. I have hopes, but fear that my voice may be permanently affected, in which case I shall be incapacitated for public speaking, and shall decline being a candidate for a re-election.

The following is an extract from his "Address to the Free Electors of the Fifth Pennsylvania Congressional District," embracing his views on the tariff question.

* * * * * *

Sept. 27, 1848.

The famine in Europe during the past year, for a time, averted the evils, predicted from a repeal of the protective tariff, and gave a transient cause of gratulation to the friends of free trade. That has passed away—and while it served to postpone the predicted evils, it has also made the contrast the more glaring. The famine in Europe the past year enabled us to export breadstuffs and provisions to the amount of near forty millions, and turned the balance of trade in our favor, so that specie flowed into the country by millions, which stimulated every branch of industry. The present year those exports will not exceed the one-seventh of that amount, and those at prices which do not remunerate the shipper, while the imports continue quite as large as last year, thus not only absorbing the balance of last year, but showing a balance against us of some thirty millions, which must be paid in specie, These excessive importations still continue, and will continue under the present tariff so long as one dollar of money can be drawn from the country to pay for them. I have seen it stated that the imports into the port of New York alone, in the last week, exceeded two millions five hundred thousand dollars, while the exports do not exceed one-third of that amount.

The distress existing in Europe has reduced the amount of consumption and prices there, and leaves the market glutted and depressed. The manufacturer, rather than reduce his prices too much at home, for the purpose of raising the necessary funds, sends his surplus goods abroad, and sacrifices them in a foreign market. Hence goods are sent over, and oftentimes sold at prices much below their cost. The effect is to stop the manufacturer here, and to throw the operatives in an important branch of industry out of employ. It is this that has so suddenly paralyzed business at the present time, and caused the great scarcity of money. The wail of the farmer, the mechanic, the business man, and the laborer is daily and hourly sounding in our ears the change which has taken place within a few short months; the buoyancy and prosperity of the past season have disappeared—and why?—Because our country is flooded with foreign manufactures which come in competition with, and undersell our own, and thus deprive the manufacturing portion of our community of their accustomed labor and means of support. For this evil there is no remedy but a PROTECTIVE TARIFF. The present *ad valorem* duty is scarcely equal to the difference between the price of labor here and in Europe. It therefore leaves the manufacturer and the operative at the mercy of the foreign capitalist—the *cost of transportation* across the Atlantic is no protection. It is a mere nothing—not equal to fifty miles land carriage in our own country.

It must be admitted that in this country the condition of the laboring classes is superior to those of Europe—they are paid better prices for their labor, and *do* afford themselves more of the comforts of life. Capital also commands a higher rate of interest here than in Europe; hence with equal facilities goods can be produced cheaper in Europe than in this country. How then shall we counterbalance this advantage on the part of the European manufacturer, so as to give some security for capital invested in manufacturing establishments here? The opponents of a protective tariff say it must be by reducing *the wages of labor to the European standard.* Is this practicable? Is it desirable? The united voices of millions with one accord answer no, and they should consign to infamy the man who would propose it. The only other course is, to make that capital secure, by a tariff on imports—*a substantial protective tariff,* which will cause to be manufactured in our own factories and workshops, by our own artizans and operatives, the merchandize needed for our consumption. It is only by this policy that our country can be made prosperous and truly independent.

Nor is it true that protection is a tax upon the consumer. All experience proves it to be a mistaken notion that a protective tariff enhances the *regular* price of the goods so protected. It only protects the producer here against the sudden influx from a foreign glutted market, and thus renders his business more secure. That security invites competition, and that competition after a time gives the article to the consumer at a price below what he would obtain the foreign article at if there were no protective tariff. In determining upon the the expediency of *ordering* the goods, the merchant will take into consideration the duties which he will have to pay upon them, but having ordered them, or receiving a cargo on foreign account, he puts them into the market and sells them at the price at which that article is then selling, without regard to the amount of duties paid upon it. If the article is then at a high price, he makes a profit. If, on the other hand, the market is glutted and the article is at a low price, he "pockets the loss." The price of all merchandise is regulated by the supply and demand. The varying prices of the same description of goods under the same tariff will satisfy a careful observer that the cost of importation, or the amount of duty paid, has but little to do with regulating the price at which the goods are sold.

But suppose we admit, for the sake of the argument, that a protective tariff enhances the price of goods to the extent of that protection, still the prosperity of the whole people and the best interests of the country require the adoption of that policy. I aver that there never was a country truly independent and prosperous which did not protect its own industry. Our own country, in all instances, has been most prosperous when she had a protective tariff. It is for the benefit of all that the branches of industry should be multiplied. Each then assists the other, and the prosperity of one branch gives succor and sustenance to the other. The artisan, the manufacturer, and the mechanic are the legitimate customers of the farmer. Increase the business of these branches, and you in the same proportion increase the market and prosperity of the farmer. Depress or destroy any of these branches, and you injure or destroy his market to the like extent. That policy which tends to give the farmer good prices and a ready market tends to his prosperity, and with these he will care but little whether he has to pay six or eight cents per yard for the calico necessary for his family, or whether he has to pay five or four cents per pound for the iron he uses. It is then *disingenuous and untrue* to assert that the duty necessary to protect and preserve the manufacturer is a tax and burthen upon the farmer.

The industry of the country is, in part, made up of the agriculturist, the manufacturer, and the mechanic. Each branch is in a measure dependent upon the other, as each gives aid and support to the other. When the manufacturer is prosperous, that prosperity will be felt by the mechanic and by the farmer. When the business of the employer is profitable and prosperous, the operative and laborer will have plenty of work and good wages; but when the business fails to remunerate the employer, the workman will soon feel his dependence, and perhaps find himself out of work and without the means of a livelihood. It is not, then, the capitalist alone who is benefited by a protective duty, as is often asserted by the British presses in mercantile cities, but every man, woman, and child, dependent upon their own industry for support, is alike benefited by it.

To ascertain the correctness of the position here stated, I would ask my fellow-citizens to look back to the year 1842, when the protective tariff law was passed, and compare the state of the industrial classes and business of that year with 1847, when that tariff had been in operation but a little more than four years, and see the contrast. How many hives of industry have sprung up within that time? How have your cities and towns increased?—thereby affording additional markets to the farmer for his products. How many operatives and mechanics have, within that time, secured to themselves snug homes of their own?—and let them say, if they can, that a protective tariff benefits no one but the capitalist and employer. To exemplify and make the matter of a protective tariff more plain to the comprehension of every person, I would remark that, within my Congressional district, there are perhaps thirty cotton and woollen factories, employing each from sixty to four hundred operatives, and perhaps an equal number of furnaces, forges, rolling mills, and foundries, employing each from twenty to one hundred workmen.

I have obtained a statement of the operations of one of these cotton mills, by which it appears that at this one establishment there is paid *as wages to operatives*, every four weeks, the large sum of $6,100, amounting in the aggregate, in the course of a year, to about $75,000, which is again paid out by these operatives to the property holder as rent—to the storekeeper—to the market man—mechanic and tradesman. In its ramifications. it sustains the business and affords a livelihood to at least quadruple the number of the operatives to whom it is paid, and ultimately most of it gets into the purse of the farmer for his produce. There is paid annually for coal the sum of $8,337. This goes to give employment and support to the miner—the boatman—the boat-builder and machinist, and also ultimately comes to the farmer. The other expenses are for oil, for flour, for sizing, for hauling cotton and manufactured goods, and for incidental expenses —making the aggregate paid out *at this factory*, in the course of the year, $94,298 71! This is but one of the fifty or sixty establishments in this Congressional District to which I have already alluded, each exercising a like beneficial influence in its vicinity by the employment it gives. Now, let us suppose that the policy of our government should enable the European manufacturer so to flood our markets with goods of a similar description as to supply the demand at prices lower than it costs the manufacturer to produce them, and thus compel him to stop his factory. What would be the consequence? These four hundred operatives would be thrown out of employment, and deprived of their means of subsistence. The houses now occupied by them would be deserted. They would be driven to seek employment in other pursuits.—Every branch of industry throughout the neighborhood would at once feel its withering effect. Property and prices would droop. Those indebted would become bankrupt, and the poor be without support. This effect upon the neighborhood by the stoppage of a factory is but the type of the *general depression* upon the whole country where its manufacturing interests are paralyzed by excessive importations. Bankruptcy and widespread distress always have, and always will be the consequence.—This, fellow-citizens, is not a fancy sketch—it is plain common sense—it is but cause and effect.—The employer and the employed—the owner and the operative are mutually dependent upon each other. In most instances, the prosperity of the one is the prosperity of the other. Take from industry its employment, and you deprive the laborer of his bread. Lessen the wages of labor, and you deprive the operative of the *luxuries*, and perhaps even of the *comforts* of life. Take from the employer his fair profits on his business, and you *compel* him to lessen his expenses by *reducing wages*, and perhaps ultimately to stop his business, and thus to give up the market to his foreign competitor.

Allow me then to ask who is to be benefited by this *free trade* policy, to which the Democracy of Pennsylvania have so suddenly and so strangely become a convert? If the effect is to destroy the business of the manufacturer, or to *coerce the labor* of this country into a *copartnership* with the pauper labor of Europe—if its effect is to check and destroy that prosperity, that bounding forward which we have witnessed every where in our glorious State since the enactment of the tariff law of 1842, and more especially along the beautiful valley of the Schuylkill—if its effects are to deprive the farmer of his home market—to lessen the ability of his customers to buy or to pay, and consequently to lessen the value of his land and of all he has to sell—if its effects are to flood our markets with the product of foreign workshops, and thus to throw our own workmen out of employment; or to force them to work at wages which will afford them but a scanty subsistence: then where, I ask, are its benefits?—The drone who lives on the interest of his money, and the office-holder who lives on his salary or emoluments of office, may be benefited, as it tends to make things cheap. It may also tend to give increased business to the jobbers and agents of foreign houses. But besides these I know of no branch of industry or class of people that can be benefited by such policy. And yet we find farmers and those of other laboring classes, who do not aspire to or ever expect office, supporting those who espouse and advocate this fatal policy.

REED HOUSE, ERIE, PA., *July* 29, 1849.

DEAR ——:

My last letter to you was, I think, from Cleveland, and intimated a wish that you would write to me at Chicago, which place I expected to take in the circuit of my journeyings. From Cleveland I went to Detroit, and from thence to *Sault St. Marie*, where I regaled myself on white fish and brook trout. In looking around, I felt that I had got to the extreme of civilized society. I saw the Indian in his wigwam, and paddling his bark canoe. After spending two days there, I went to Mackinaw, where I again feasted on the fish of those waters. From thence I went by Green Bay to the village of that name. I then left the water, and had some *practical* knowledge of the staging of that country. I wént up the Fox River to Neenah at Lake Winnebago, where I again took steamboat and went by way of *Ashkosh* to *Fond-du-Lac*. Here I sold out my interest in the nine land warrants I had given Dr. Darling to locate for me. He allowed me 25 per cent. per annum on my investment, from the time he received the warrants until payment of the money, which is to be in 18 months from the time of his receipt of the warrants. When the bargain was completed and I had his notes, he informed me that he would make $1000 by the bargain, and have the money for the lands before the notes came due. I am satisfied he will, as he was about selling one of the tracts at 20 shillings an acre, whereas it only costs him about 90 cents per acre. But so be it. I do well enough, and he does much better. I find there is no difficulty in investing in Wisconsin on mortgage in considerable sums at from 15 to 18 per cent., and on small sums on land at from 25 to 50 per cent. A young man from the East came out there last spring with $3000 in money, and, with the assistance of Dr. Darling, invested the whole at about 40 per cent. I have some idea of selling off my Norristown lots and investing in the West.

On leaving *Fond-du-Lac*, I went through the interior of Wisconsin by stage to Watertown, and thence to Milwaukie. Wisconsin comes quite up to my expectations in fertility, and as a farming country, but it is no place to make or save money at farming. From Milwaukie I went to Chicago, where I found two letters, but was disappointed

soon be over for the present season: or it is, perhaps, now over, though note-brokers and private bankers continue to charge a large interest. But this is the business of broking and banking, and we are not in that business. and, unless the inducements were great, should not like to be. Then, as to loaning money in small sums on security of land in the way we spoke of, this requires vigilance, judgment, and close attention, and would be in connection with your professional business, and would be begun in a small way. That is, it would not require much capital at first. Wherever you locate in the West, I will authorize you to draw for a few thousand in this way.

To B. M. B.

The following letter will show that he did not escape the "Nicaragua" fever, though perhaps happily, the attack was light.

June 24, 1850.

YOUR favor of the 8th inst., came duly to hand, and I herewith send you an article from this day's *National Intelligencer*, on Central America, which has had the effect to raise the fever in me at least 30 per cent. It contains information of the greatest importance. The mind is dazzled at getting hold of some thousand acres of mahogany forest, or of getting hold of one of those farms on the plains of Nicaragua with from 10,000 to 40,000 oxen, bulls and cows upon them, and then getting Pennsylvania farmers upon them. For I tell you, in a very few years that country will be filled with Americans. They are now flocking there. Or the idea of having a few acres on the Island of *Manzanilla* in Navy Bay, in case that should be the eastern terminus of the Panama railroad; and then the richness of the forests, the mines and the soil, all combine to give it advantages over any other country now known, not excepting California itself. The climate, too, is said to be entirely healthy. I have letters from a young friend of mine who passed through last summer on his way to California, and was delayed some months in Central America; he writes that it is not only the most delightful, but the most healthy climate in the world. The necessaries of life are very cheap: oranges and bananas a shilling a hundred; eggs two cents per dozen, &c. It would also appear that the government, in some instances, gives large tracts of land with the view of having them settled or colonized. But the main object would be the business we propose to establish there. The nature and extent of this must be determined after a full and careful examination of all that is to be seen It would be best to begin on a small scale, and gradually expand. I wish to enter into a joint concern with you in this matter, and wish you to go to that country and make the necessary examination early after September next as may be. I know you have the knowledge and the discrimination, and I have perfect confidence in your judgment. I can invest $30,000 the first year from time to time, as it may be required, and I wish you during the same time to put in $20,000, which, with your additional services, will make us about even. And, in order to have every thing perfectly fair, every investment or business transaction must be for the *joint concern*. I will have to stick here at my post until the 4th of March next, when I will be free to take a hand in the business. I think it probable that our business would be that of banking and broking, loaning money at short dates, and dealing in exchange and general speculation, as opportunity offers. In short our object will be to make money by all fair means, and therefore a first object is to get a reputation for capital and for probity.

It will be necessary for you to make yourself acquainted with the Spanish, so as to speak it and write it. You must have a passport; and a letter of recommendation, or what else it is called, *from a Catholic bishop*, will be of great service, and is almost necessary.

The report of the geological survey of Wisconsin and Iowa, by Dr. Owen, has not yet been published, at least I have not seen it. I think there was an order the other day for printing 5000 copies of it, which will be out in three or four weeks. I will endeavor to remember to send you a copy when it comes out.

I remain truly yours,

J. F.

WASHINGTON, *Aug.* 24, 1850.

DEAR ——:

ON my return to this city on Monday last, after a short visit home, I received your letter of the 4th inst. from Harrodsburg. You no doubt had an interesting jaunt, and seem to have experienced the usual incidents of travel, much fatigue, and something still to interest. I am myself very desirous of taking a tour through the Southern States, particularly to visit the limestone valleys and regions of Alabama, Georgia, North Carolina, and Tennessee, and see their deposits of marble and of iron ore—their coal districts, and their water powers. I feel satisfied that upper or Western Georgia and Alabama afford better locations for all kinds of manufacturing than either the Eastern States, or Pennsylvania. There the loom and the spindle would be taken to the cotton. The plough, the loom, and the anvil would be then side by side.

In your former letter you did not seem to be taken with the idea of a residence in Central America, or in California, and further reflection and more recent information has tended to cool my ardor on this subject. There would be heavy drafts on a person's comforts there, even if the chances of making money were as great as I at first supposed them to be. To be candid, my advancing years, and the effect that *trouble* and *anxiety* have upon my spirits, admonish me that I would better sit down among my friends, and enjoy my few remaining days in quiet, divested of the anxieties and cares of business. This would be better accomplished at Philadelphia or at Norristown than in any other place. There are other places where I could make my investments a little more productive—where money would command a higher interest. But, then, the question arises, ought this to be an object with me, circumstanced as I am? At Chicago and Milwaukie, I could make permanent and safe investments at from ten to eighteen per cent., and last spring I seriously contemplated investing on mortgage there, at those rates, but have not yet determined when I will enter upon this matter, and one matter after another transpires to admonish me not further to strive at accumulation. So you will see I am not yet able to make to you a definite proposition on the subject of a future business.

J. F.

To E. T. F.

LETTERS FROM J. W. SCOTT, Esq.

GOOD LOCATIONS FOR INVESTMENT.

It is a peculiar characteristic of the Yankee, that when he "comes of age" he becomes dissatisfied with his paternal home, and his old associations, and must go a wandering; and it is still more peculiar that in his new situation he will endure contentedly and cheerfully, privations and hardships which he would pronounce unendurable in the old. Sometimes he does wisely and well by the change; and sometimes he sings "Home, sweet home," with a great deal of pathos. It is no doubt a mere "game of chance." A man who thinks of going to a new settlement, should ask himself the question which an old special pleader asked of a father who was anxious to apprentice his hopeful son to the law: "Can your son, sir, eat sawdust without butter?" and secondly, he should see that he has money enough to take him to his new destination, keep him as long as he chooses to stay, and bring him back when he wishes to return; and thirdly, he should answer satisfactorily the question, "What shall I do if that which I do account upon shall not turn out as I expect?" It is certainly the height of folly for a young man with little or no money to leave a fair situation with a view of seeking a better in the large cities or towns of the South or West. It was computed there were over 8000 persons seeking situations in New Orleans the winter preceding the last. It is questionable policy for a man who has reached middle life to cut himself loose from old ties, and go to new places in search of fortune. But to the young man of robust constitution and some capital, the younger States undoubtedly afford more abundant opportunities for the profitable use of his energy and capital than the older states, and to the man of capital, they offer inducements that are exceedingly attractive. Every thing, however, depends on the choice of a location, and reliable information on this subject is of great value.

J. W. Scott, Esq., whose statesmanlike mind can ascend to the loftiest generalization from a basis of the most carefully selected facts, and one of the obliging, big-hearted men of the West, gives a good deal of valuable information on this subject in the following letter and articles:—

ADRIAN, MICH., *Feb.* 2, 1852.

DEAR SIR:—

Yours of 9th January reached me after a slow progress, characteristic of this winter's mail hitherward.

If you will designate with more particularity on what branch of business you desire a letter from me, I shall be better able to say whether my knowledge can be made available for your purpose. My hobby, for many years, has been the developement of the West, including its increase in population, commerce, and arts. As connected with this, I have watched with deep interest the public improvements in progress to connect this region with the old States, and to develop our internal resources. At present, I feel more interest in the growth of the western foci of commerce than in any other public matter. In the November number of *Hunt's Merchant's Magazine*, is an article prepared with considerable labor, intended to show, in a bird's-eye view, the relative growth of the towns of the United States. This article would indicate the towns or cities which, having the most rapid relative growth, would seem to be the best for investment, with a view to rapid increase of value. My confidence in Toledo has induced me to invest chiefly in and around it, in preference to any other. By drainage and other improvements, it is becoming healthy; its position is handsome and commanding, on a harbor equalled, on the lakes, by none but that of Detroit. It is the lake terminus of a longer line of canals than is to be found, continuous, elsewhere in the world. This advantage may be considered permanent; for canals will not, hereafter, be built to any extent. These canals ("Wabash and Erie, and Miami and Erie") connect Toledo with the Ohio River at Cincinnati and Evansville. The first, which will be completed this year, will be 460 miles in length; the other, 247 between Toledo and Cincinnati. The common trunk of both, extending 70 miles westward to the junction, is over 60 feet wide, and 6 feet deep. From the junction to Fort Wayne, it is 50 by 5; thence to the Ohio River, 40 by 4 feet. It is hardly necessary to say that these canals penetrate the richest, and soon to be the most populous valleys of the West—the Miami and Wabash. The natural position of Toledo is as favorable for the concentration of railroads as for canals. It is now the practical terminus of the Southern Michigan railroad, now nearly finished to Chicago. Connecting with this at Toledo, is the Toledo, Norwalk, and Cleveland railroad in progress of construction, to be finished this year. A railroad is being constructed from Dayton northward, intended to reach the Michigan line through Toledo, in the direction of Detroit. Two charters are in existence for an air line railroad, directly west towards Chicago, probably to connect with the northern Indiana at Goshen. One of these charters is in the hands of the directors of the Southern Michigan Company, which has agreed to build that part in Indiana in five years. You will see by the map that this would be *the* route to connect Toledo and Chicago. The canal towns from Toledo southwestward, are now endeavoring to get up a line of railroad from Toledo to Terre Haute. Looking at the map, you will see that railroads *may* be made from Toledo towards nearly all the points of the compass. I say *may* be made, for you are doubtless aware that our whole West is so level, that no obstacle to the cheap construction of the railroad is any where presented. Their construction, therefore, is only a question of the ability of the country through which they pass to build and give them profitable employment. With a soil and climate equal to any, the country around Toledo for one hundred or two hundred miles, is in a state of improvement, as progressive as any other region of the West. Next year it will be accessible to the whole eastern system of railroads.

Plank roads are becoming quite common in the lake portion of the West. They are made for from $1200 to $1800 per mile. Toledo has upwards of 100 miles made and in progress, of which about sixty is completed.

In regard to the investment of capital, the West, generally, in her rapidly growing towns, holds out sufficient inducements. I say in her *towns*, for both reason and experience told me, years ago, that investments in mere farming lands was something like a purchase of fresh air or water, too little of a monopoly to be made profitable. Accessible farming lands are too abundant to be worth more than the cost of converting them into farms. It is not so with the best town locations. These have been marked out by nature, and are but few in comparison with the immense fertile country surrounding them. Such are Cincinnati, Chicago, St. Louis, and Toledo. These, taken together, will double their population every five or six years. Wealth, it is well known, increases faster than population—take the country through. In towns or cities, it is most rapidly progressive.

I think scarcely a month passes when a person in Toledo, with money, may not buy real estate, that may be sold again within one year on contract, say one-fourth down, and balance in three annual payments, for double the cost. Sometimes this may be done in much less time. Supposing the currency of the country to remain in its present proportion to population, it seems to me that the real estate in Toledo will double about once in three years. If the currency becomes more plethoric, the duplication might be much sooner, and *e converso*. All our lake towns of promise are now growing very fast. Some of them will overtake the largest river towns within the lives of many now living. Among the most prosperous now, are Cleveland, Sandusky, Toledo, Detroit, and Chicago. All afford good society. There is less form and etiquette than in eastern towns, but *I* think there is more intelligence, and not less real refinement. In the appearance of all, there is a want of finish, as compared with older towns, on the Atlantic. This is most apparent in Toledo, where the high bank has been, and is being brought to a pleasant grade. This, of course, exposes much raw earth, and gives a rawness to every thing around. The exports of Toledo, by lake, last season were valued at ($12,000,000) twelve millions. They exceed those of any lake port above Buffalo. The imports may be worth seven millions. Population over 5000. What more shall I say, and about what?

Respectfully,

J. W. SCOTT.

To E. T. Freedley, Esq.

The following is an extract from that valuable article in the November number of *Hunt's Merchants' Magazine*, to which Mr. Scott above refers, and which I have the permission of the courteous and gentlemanly proprietor of that magazine to give.

I cannot omit this opportunity, as an act of justice to Mr. Hunt, who has done as much as any man in America to raise the reputation of American books in England, and in justice to all who may favor this book with a perusal, to commend Mr. Hunt's Magazine to their especial attention and patronage, as one of the most certainly profitable investments they can make. Every business man should as certainly subscribe for it as he should insure his property. In the case of insurance, if his property does not burn down, he loses his money, but in the case of subscription to that magazine he will not lose his money in any event, and may reap an advantage as great as the restoration of property destroyed In the first place, he will increase his stock of useful and practical ideas, which in itself is worth more than the cost; secondly, he will possess the most comprehensive work of the age for present and future reference; and thirdly, he will take the best possible means to put himself in the way of meeting with suggestions and ideas that may happen to just suit his circumstances, and which he may turn to his advantage to the tune of hundreds or thousands of dollars. Let every one be watchful, for he knows not the day nor the hour when the good idea may come.

"The following table gives the average period of duplication, *for the last thirty years*, in the order of most rapid growth:—

AVERAGE TIME OF DUPLICATION.

	Years.		Years.		Years.
Lowell	4	Zanesville	13	Richmond	24
Buffalo	6½	Springfield, Mass.	13	Baltimore	25
St. Louis	7	New Orleans	15	Savannah	25
Rochester	7	Boston	15	Portland	25
Cincinnati	7½	Albany	15½	Wilmington, Del.	25
Louisville	8	Philadelphia	16	Lancaster, Pa.	25
Detroit	8	Hartford, Ct.	16	Newburg	26
Columbus, Ohio	8½	Nashville	17	Taunton	26
Pittsburg	8½	Reading	17	Hudson, N. Y.	27
Bangor	9	Chillicothe	17	York, Pa.	30
Erie	9	Providence	18	Charleston, S. C.	40
Wheeling	9½	Augusta, Me.	18	Carlisle	40
Mobile	10	Schenectady	19	Norfolk	42
Newark	12	New Haven	19	Salem, Mass.	60
Worcester	12	New London	25	Newport	70
New York	13	Washington	20	Newburyport	80
Troy	13	Harrisburg	20	Portsmouth	85
Utica	13	Bath, Me.	20		

The order of growth, and the average period of duplication, for the twenty years, from 1830 to 1850, are shown, with an approach to accuracy, in the following table :—

AVERAGE TIME OF DUPLICATION.

	Years.		Years.		Years.
Cleveland	5	Erie	9	Nashville	14
Columbus	5	Louisville	9½	Lynn	14½
St. Louis	5½	Pittsburg	10	New York	15
Sandusky City	6	New Albany	10	Troy	15½
Detroit	6	Madison	10	Chillicothe	16
Indianapolis	7½	Rochester	10½	Wheeling	16
Mobile	7½	Worcester	11	Philadelphia	17
Lowell	8	Newark, N. J.	12	Providence	17½
Cincinnati	8½	Zanesville	12	Hartford	17½
Marietta	8½	Syracuse	13	Washington	18
Dayton	8½	Lockport	14	New Orleans	18
Bangor	8½	Springfield, Mass.	14	New Haven	18½
Buffalo	8½	Fall River	14	New London	18½

	Years.		Years.		Years.
Portland . . .	18½	Richmond . .	21	Salem, Mass. . .	37
Baltimore . .	19	Reading, Pa. .	21½	Newburyport . .	40
New Bedford .	19	Lancaster . .	24	Carlisle	40
Bath, Me. . .	19	Savannah . .	24	Charleston, S. C.	50
Utica	19	Harrisburg . .	24	Norfolk . . .	50
Boston . . .	20	Natchez . . .	25	Portsmouth, N. H.	90
Albany . . .	20	Taunton . . .	26	Hudson, N. Y. .	100
Wilmington, Del.	20	Poughkeepsie .	28	Newburg, N. Y. .	100
Schenectady . .	20	York, Pa. . .	29	Newport, R. I. .	100

The following table exhibits the average period of duplication on the increase of the ten years, from 1840 to 1850 :—

AVERAGE TIME OF DUPLICATION.

	Years.		Years.		Years.
Milwaukie . .	3	Springfield . .	10	Troy	14½
Chicago . . .	3½	Fall River . .	10	Wilmington, Del.	15
St. Louis . . .	4	Hartford . . .	11½	Lancaster, Pa. .	15½
Manchester, N. H.	4	Reading . . .	11½	Patterson . . .	16
Sandusky City .	5½	New York . .	12	Bath, Me. . . .	16
Columbus, Ohio	6	Boston . . .	12	Albany	16½
Cleveland . .	6	Washington . .	12	York, Pa. . . .	20
Toledo . . .	6	Rochester . .	12	Utica	24
Cincinnati . .	6	Chillicothe . .	12	New Bedford . .	26
Marietta . . .	7	Philadelphia .	12½	Lockport . . .	27
Indianapolis .	7½	Savannah . .	12½	Schenectady . .	28
Pittsburg . .	8	Portland . . .	12½	Newburyport . .	28
Newark, N. J. .	8	Providence . .	12½	Norfolk	30
Oswego . . .	8	Lynn	12½	Petersburg, Va. .	32
Dayton . . .	8	New Haven . .	13	New Orleans . .	34
New Albany .	8	Columbia, S. C.	13	Charleston, S. C. .	35
Buffalo . . .	8½	Baltimore . .	13½	Portsmouth . .	40
Nashville . . .	8½	Wheeling . .	13½	Salem	42
Detroit . . .	9	Lowell . . .	14	Newport, R. I. .	65
Zanesville . .	9	Mobile . . .	14	Natchez	85
Louisville . .	9½	New London .	14	Poughkeepsie . .	90
Worcester . .	9½	Bangor . . .	14	Hudson . . .	100
Madison . . .	9½	Richmond . .	14½	Carlisle . . .	180
Syracuse . .	10				

Having laid before our readers the facts in relation to the growth of the principal centres of population of the United States, they may now proceed with us to deduce a law of growth from their average times of duplication, for a period of sixty years, as to those existing previous to 1790, bringing in the new places as they come forth from the wilderness, and take a place on the census list, in successive decennial enumerations. The figures represent, with an approach to accuracy, the number of years each place has required, on the average, to double the number of its people.

	AVERAGE FOR					
	60 Years.	50 Years.	40 Years.	30 Years.	20 Years.	10 Years.
New York	15	14½	15	13	15	12
Philadelphia . . .	18	20	18½	16	17	12½
Baltimore	17	21	21	25	19	13½
Boston	21	23	18½	15	20	12
Albany	16	15	16	15½	20	16½
Salem, Mass. . . .	50	50	85	60	37	42
Worcester	21	18	17	12	11	9½
Charleston, S. C. . .	45	45	50	40	50	35
Providence	...	23	19½	18	17½	12½
Washington	...	13	16½	20	18	12
Richmond, Va. . .	...	24	29	24	21	14½
Lancaster, Pa. . .	...	40	35	25	24	15½
Alexandria, Va. . .	...	50	200	450	440	400
Cincinnati	...	6½	7	7½	8½	6
Pittsburg	...	9	9½	8	10	8
St. Louis	...	9½	9	7	5½	4
New Orleans . . .	...	...	14½	15	18	24
Louisville	...	...	8	8	9½	9½
Buffalo	...	...	8½	6½	8½	8½
Detroit	...	...	8½	8	6	9
Bangor	...	...	10	9	8½	14
Wheeling	...	...	10½	9½	16	13½
Utica	...	...	12	13	19	24
Wilmington, Del. . .	...	...	17½	25	20	15
Newark	...	...	17½	12	12	8
Reading	...	...	19	17	21½	11½
Hartford, Ct. . . .	...	...	19½	16	17½	11½
Providence	...	...	19½	18	17½	12½

	60 Years.	50 Years.	40 Years.	30 Years.	20 Years.	10 Years.
Savannah	...	...	21	25	24	12½
Portland, Me. . . .	...	...	21	25	8½	12½
New Haven . . .	...	...	21	19	18½	13
Harrisburg	...	...	22	20	22	27
Schenectady . . .	...	...	30	19	20	28
York, Pa.	...	...	32	30	29	20
Lancaster, Pa. . .	...	...	35	25	24	15½
Carlisle	...	...	45	40	40	180
Norfolk, Va. . . .	...	...	50	42	50	30
Portsmouth . . .	...	...	106	85	90	40
Newport, R. I. . .	...	...	150	70	100	65
Newburyport . . .	...	...	160	80	40	28
Lowell	...	...	...	4	8	14
Rochester	...	...	...	7	10	12
Columbus, Ohio . .	...	...	...	8½	5	6
Bangor	...	...	...	9	8½	14
Erie, Pa.	...	...	...	9	9	12
Mobile	...	...	...	10	7½	14
Zanesville	...	...	...	13	12	9
Springfield, Mass. .	...	...	...	13	14	10
Nashville	...	...	...	17	14	8½
Chillicothe	...	...	...	17	16	12
Augusta, Me. . . .	...	...	...	18	18	15
Schenectady . . .	...	...	...	19	20	28
Hudson	...	...	...	27	100	100
New London . . .	...	...	...	25	18½	14
Bath, Me.	...	...	...	20	19	16
Newburg, N. Y. . .	...	...	...	26	100 decrease.	
Taunton, Mass. . .	...	...	...	26	26	16
Syracuse.	...	...	...	...	13	10
Poughkeepsie . . .	...	...	...	...	28	90
Lockport	...	...	...	...	14	27
Lynn	...	...	...	...	14½	12½
New Bedford . . .	...	...	...	...	19	26
Fall River	...	...	...	...	14	10
New Albany, Ia. . .	...	...	...	...	10	8
Natchez	...	...	...	...	25	85
Madison	...	...	...	...	10	9½
Indianapolis . . .	...	...	...	...	7½	7½
Cleveland	...	...	...	...	5	6

	60 Years.	50 Years.	40 Years.	30 Years.	20 Years.	10 Years.
Columbus	...	...	...	...	5	6
Marietta	...	...	...	...	8½	7
Sandusky City . .	...	...	...	...	5	5½
Dayton	...	...	...	...	5	8
Chicago	...	...	...	...	...	4
Manchester, N. H. .	...	...	...	...	...	4
Milwaukie	...	...	...	...	...	3
Toledo	...	...	...	...	...	6

NOTE. Lawrence, Mass.; Racine, Wis.; Kenosha, Wis.; and several other places of importance, came into existence within ten years.

It will be observed that the growth of our towns, during the last ten years, has, in general, been decidedly greater than that of any ten preceding years. This goes to prove the great influence of railroads, canals, and other facilities to commercial movement.

In respect to all those places which are favorably located for the concentration of internal commerce, the law of growth may be fairly deduced from the foregoing tables. Their progress, it will be seen, has, in the main, been in proportion to the command of this internal commerce. Salem, Newport, and some others, which have exhibited the slowest growth, have but a slight hold on the surrounding soil. On the other hand, Cincinnati, St. Louis, New York, and Boston are in the midst of a rich country, and have extensive and easy channels of intercourse with the interior.

The cities of the Atlantic border, below the Chesapeake, and of the Gulf of Mexico to New Orleans, have the disadvantage of being far removed from the country which yields their chief commercial aliment. The pine barrens extend from the coast some fifty to one hundred and fifty miles. This has to be past, in connecting Charleston, Savannah, &c., with the country, on whose internal resources they depend.

The institution of slavery has also, an unfavorable influence in the growth of towns situated in States where slaves are most numerous. Whether this is inherent, or owing to the profits of planting being greater than manufacturing, it is not for us to decide.

It has been said, that speculation on the future probable growth of our towns has no practical value. Can this be so? Is it of no practical value to the man of business, seeking a place for the exercise of his talents, to have the means provided of judging of the relative advantages for commerce, and its future expansion, of the places between which he has to choose his future home? Is it of no moment to the mechanic seeking a permanent location of his factory or shop? Tens of thousands are every day invested in real estate, whose only value depends on the growth of the places in which and near which it is situated. Many of these investments are made with a view to their value many years in the future. Ought they to be made with or without knowledge of all the circumstances that may be reasonably expected to bear on their future value? In this country, growth in numbers generally represents increase of capital and business.—It may, therefore, answer as a tolerable basis for a calculation of the relative value of real estate.

In 1860, New York, with its suburbs, may be expected to contain half a million more than her present numbers. Where will these be located, and what will be the value of the lots to be covered with buildings for their accommodation? These inquiries will be resolved in the mind of any man about to invest in real estate there, and expecting to turn the investment into money in nine or ten years. But, perhaps, he will first desire to ascertain whether New York, or some other commercial point, offers the best prospect of a good profit on his investment. Our last table gives a scale of growth. In the cases embracing forty, fifty, and sixty years, the past may be considered a safe guide for the future. A nearly uniform high rate of increase, through so many decades, may be relied on with much confidence, in calculations for the future.

In relation to places of recent origin, although their law of growth may not be deduced from an experience of the past of sufficient duration to warrant a decision from that alone, yet there may be causes in operation, sufficiently obvious, to force a conviction of a future increase, corresponding to the past. Such seems to be the case of Chicago and other western cities. In less than twenty years, that place has grown from a mere station to contain thirty thousand. Troy, N. Y., contains about the same number. Who would say that the prospective value of real estate surrounding each should be estimated equal?

New Orleans and Cincinnati are now nearly equal in population. In ten years the former will scarce gain forty thousand, while the latter will increase not less than one hundred and fifty thousand. Who would give the same for vacant lots on the borders of the former as on those of the latter—other things being equal?

On account of the permanency of the record afforded by the *Mer-*

chant's Magazine, the opinion is here repeated that, within one century, the largest cities of America will be in the interior, and that Cincinnati, Chicago, St. Louis, and Toledo will be the four largest.

J. W. S.

CENSUS OF CITIES OF THE UNITED STATES IN 1850.

List of Cities and Towns in the United States whose population, by the Census of 1850, *is* 10,000 *and upwards.*

1	New York,	N. Y.	515,507
2	Philadelphia,	Penn.	408,815
3	Baltimore,	Md.	189,048
4	Boston,	Mass.	136,871
5	New Orleans,	La.	116,348
6	Cincinnati,	Ohio,	115,436
7	Brooklyn,	N. Y.	97,838
8	St. Louis,	Mo.	64,252
9	Albany,	N. Y.	50,763
10	Pittsburg,	Penn.	50,519
11	Louisville,	Ky.	43,196
12	Charleston,	S. C.	42,985
13	Buffalo,	N. Y.	42,261
14	Providence,	R. I.	41,512
15	Washington,	D. C.	40,001
16	Newark,	N. J.	38,894
17	Rochester,	N. Y.	36,403
18	Lowell,	Mass.	33,383
19	Williamsburg,	N. Y.	30,780
20	Chicago,	Ill.	29,963
21	Troy,	N. Y.	28,785
22	Richmond,	Va.	27,482
23	San Francisco,	Cal.	25,000
24	Syracuse,	N. Y.	22,271
25	Alleghany,	Penn.	21,262
26	Detroit,	Mich.	21,019
27	Portland,	Maine,	20,815
28	Mobile,	Ala.	20,513

29	New Haven,	Conn. . . .	20,345
30	Salem,	Mass. . . .	20,264
31	Milwaukie,	Wis. . . .	20,061
32	Roxbury,	Mass. . . .	18,384
33	Columbus,	Ohio, . . .	18,183
34	Worcester,	Mass. . . .	17,367
35	Utica,	N. Y. . . .	17,565
36	Charleston,	Mass. . . .	17,216
37	Cleveland,	Ohio, . . .	17,034
38	New Bedford,	Mass. . . .	16,443
39	Reading,	Penn. . . .	15,748
40	Cambridge,	Mass. . . .	15,215
41	Savannah,	Ga. estimated . .	15,000
42	Bangor,	Maine, . . .	14,432
43	Norfolk,	Va. . . .	14,326
44	Lynn,	Mass. . . .	14,257
45	Lafayette,	Indiana, . . .	14,211
46	Petersburg,	Va. . . .	14,010
47	Wilmington,	Del. . . .	13,979
48	Poughkeepsie,	N. Y. . . .	13,944
49	Manchester,	N. H. . . .	13,932
50	Hartford,	Conn. . . .	13,555
51	Lancaster,	Penn. . . .	12,369
52	Lockport,	N. Y. . . .	12,323
53	Oswego,	N. Y. . . .	12,205
54	Springfield,	Mass. . . .	11,766
55	Newburg,	N. Y. . . .	11,415
56	Wheeling,	Va. . . .	11,391
57	Patterson,	N. J. . . .	11,341
58	Dayton,	Ohio, . . .	10,977
59	Taunton,	Mass. . . .	10,441
60	Norwich,	Conn. . . .	10,265
61	Kingston,	N. Y. . . .	10,233
62	New Brunswick,	N. J. . . .	10,019
63	Nashville,	Tenn. estimated .	10,000
64	Lexington,	Ky. do. .	10,000

GETTING AND LOSING MONEY BY STOCK-JOBBING—ROTHSCHILD.

The amount of business sometimes transacted in one day at the Stock Exchange is very great. On some occasions, property, including time bargains, to the amount of £10,000,000 has there changed hands in the short space of a few hours. The late Mr. Rothschild is known to have made purchases in one day to the extent of £4, 000,000. The influence which that great capitalist exercised over the funds may be said to have been omnipotent. He could cause a rise or a fall, to a certain extent, whenever he pleased. He was a singularly skilful tactician. To those who know any thing of the Stock Exchange it cannot be necessary to state that he never went into it himself. That, indeed, would have defeated his objects. Had he transacted his business in the funds in his own person, every body must have seen what he was doing, and consequently others, knowing his general good for tune, would have sold out when he sold out, and purchased when he purchased. One great cause of his success was the secrecy in which he contrived to shroud all his transactions. He had certain men whom he employed as brokers on ordinary occasions; but whenever it suited his purpose, or when he supposed that by employing them it would be ascertained that he wished to effect a rise or a fall, he took care to commission a new set of brokers to act for him. His mode of doing business, when engaging in large transactions, was this: Supposing he possessed exclusively, which he often did a day or two before it could be generally known, intelligence of some event which had occurred in any part of the continent sufficiently important to cause a rise in the French funds, and through them on the English funds, he would empower the brokers he usually employed to sell out stock, say to the amount of £500,000. The news spread in a moment in Capel Court that Rothschild was selling out, and a general alarm followed. Every one apprehended he had received intelligence from some foreign part of some important event which would produce a fall in prices. As might, under such circumstances, be expected, all became sellers at once. This of necessity caused the funds, to use Stock Exchange phraseology, "to tumble down at a fearful rate." Next day, when they had fallen, perhaps, one or two per cent., he would make purchases, say to the amount of £1,500,000; taking care, however, to employ a number of brokers whom he was not in the habit of employing, and commissioning each to purchase to a certain extent, and giving all of them strict orders to preserve secrecy in the matter. Each of the persons so employed was, by this means, ignorant of the commission given to others. Had it been known the purchases were made for him, there would have been as great and sudden a rise in the prices as there had been in the fall, so that he could not purchase to the intended extent on such advantageous terms. On the third day, perhaps, the intelligence which had been expected by the jobbers to be unfavorable, arrives, and instead of being so, turns out to be highly favorable. Prices instantaneously rise again; and possibly they may get one and a-half, or even two per cent. higher than they were when he sold out his £500,000. He now sells out at the advanced price the entire £1,500,000 he had purchased at the reduced prices. The gains by such extensive transactions, when so skilfully managed, will be at once seen to be enormous. By the supposed transactions, assuming the rise to be two per cent., the gain would be £35,000. But this is not the greatest gain which the late leviathan of modern capitalists has made by such transactions. He has on more than one occasion made upwards of £100,000 on one account.

Repeated efforts, but always without effect, and generally to the ruin of the party making them, have been made to overthrow the power of Rothschild in the money-market. It was clear that the only way in which this could be done, if it was to be done at all, would be by the party attempting it engaging in transactions of corresponding magnitude. By far the boldest of these attempts was made some years ago by a young gentleman, a Mr. James H——. He made a number of most extensive purchases, and sold out again to a very large amount, all in a very short period of time; and so far from imitating the conduct of the rival whose empire on the Stock Exchange he sought to subvert, in the secrecy of his transactions, he deemed it essential to the success of his schemes that his operations should be performed as openly as possible. Mr. H—— was the son of a wealthy country banker, and held, at the time of his introduction, money stock in his own name, though it actually was his father's, to the extent of £50,000. The reputation of being so rich invested him at once with great importance in the house. The £50,000, after Mr. H—— had been some time a member, was privately re-transferred to his father, the real owner of it. For some time, and until he became perfectly master of the rules and usages of the house, he acted with great prudence and caution confining his transactions to small amounts, but he eventually began to astonish "the natives"—for so the members are often called—by the boldness of his manœuvres. In a very short time he became the dread of all parties: the Bulls* and Bears were anxious to follow him; but like Rothschild, he evinced a disposition to act independently of every person and every party. About this time consols were as high as 96 or 97. In a few months afterwards symptoms of a coming panic began to manifest themselves; and a well-known writer on money matters, having at the time, for reasons best known to himself, began to deal out his fulminations against the Bank of England in an influential newspaper, the unhealthy state of the market was greatly aggravated, though high prices were still maintained. Mr. H—— watched the state of things with great attention; and being satisfied in his own mind that a leader was only wanting to commence and carry on a successful war against Rothschild, he determined himself to become that leader; and it must be admitted that he acquitted himself as an able general. Going into the house one afternoon, he accosted one of the most respectable jobbers thus:—

"What are consols?"

"Ninety-six and eight," was the answer.

"In £100,000?" continued he.

"Yes," said the Jobber. "You have them. £100,000 more?"

"I'll take £100,000 more."

"They are yours."

"Another £100,000?"

"No: I don't want any more."

On this transaction being finished, the adventurous young gentleman immediately turned round and announced aloud that "£200,000 had been done at 96, and more offered." Then walking backward and forwards "like a tiger in a den," he followed up the bold tactics he had commenced by offering any part of a £1,000,000 at 94. For a great part of this amount he at once found purchasers. But he was not yet content with the extent of his transactions, great as they were; nor would he wait for buyers at 94. He offered them, viz., consols, at 93, at 92, and eventually as low as 90, at which price they left off that day. Next day he renewed his exertions to depress the market, and

* Those who have purchased more stock than they can pay for, with the hope of selling it at a profit before pay day, are the Bulls, and those who have contracted to deliver more stock than they have, in the hope of purchasing it at less price before delivery day, are the Bears. It is the interest of the former to raise the price; of the latter to depress it.

he succeeded to the utmost of his wishes; for consols did not stop in their descent till they reached 74. As was to be expected, contemporaneous with this sudden and extraordinary fall in the price of consols, there was a run on the Bank of England which almost exhausted it of its specie. He then purchased to so large an extent that, when a reaction took place, he found that his gains exceeded £100,000.

It can scarcely be necessary to say that all eyes were fixed with amazement on the boldness of the young gentleman's operations. Many fancied they saw in those operations the dynasty of Rothschild tottering to its fall. With what feelings the "Jew" himself regarded the adventurous conduct of his new and unexpected rival, no one had an opportunity of knowing; for in nothing was Rothschild more remarkable than in the reserve he maintained on all matters relating to the money-market. The rivalry of Mr. H—— was however, of short duration: he very soon fell a victim to an enterprise which, both in conception and execution, evinced much more of the quality of boldness than of judgment. In about two years after the above extensive "operation," he attempted another on a scale of corresponding magnitude; but in this case Rothschild, anticipating the tactics he would adopt, laid a trap for him into which he fell, and became a ruined man. He was declared a defaulter, and his name stuck up on the blackboard. It was only now that the discovery was made that the £50,000 money-stock, supposed to be his own, was in reality his father's, and that it had been retransferred in his name. A deputation from the committee waited upon Mr. H—— immediately after his failure, at his own house in the neighborhood of Regent's Park, when one of the most rapacious of the number suggested a sale of his furniture, and a mortgage of annuity settled on his wife. He received the suggestion with the utmost indignation, and ringing the bell for his servant, desired him to show the deputation down stairs, adding that he would be—I shall not say what—before he would pay a sixpence after the treatment he had met with from them. "As for you, you vagabond, 'My son Jack,'* who have had the audacity to make such a proposal to me—as for you, sir, if you don't make haste out of the room, I'll pitch you out of the window." It is scarcely necessary to say that "My son Jack" was the first who reached the bottom of the stairs.

But though no person, during the last twelve or fifteen years of

* The designation by which one of the members always went, his father having been accustomed to speak of him as his "son Jack."

Rothschild's life, was ever able for any length of time to compete with him in the money-market, he on several occasions was, in single transactions, outwitted by the superior tactics of others. I will give one instance. In that instance Rothschild had to contend not only with a man of more than ordinary ability, but one in the soundness of whose judgment all who were acquainted intimately with him reposed the most implicit reliance. Hence they, and especially his moneyed connections, were ready to follow him in any operation. The gentleman to whom I allude was then and is now the head of one of the largest private banking establishments in town. Abraham Montefiore, Rothschild's brother-in-law, was the principal broker to the great capitalist, and in that capacity was commissioned by the latter to negotiate with Mr. —— a loan for £1,500,000. The security offered by Rothschild was a proportionate amount of stock in consols, which were at that time 84. This stock was of course to be transferred to the name of the party advancing the money—Rothschild's object being to raise the price of consols by carrying so large a quantity out of the market. The money was lent, and the conditions of the loan were these—that the interest on the sum advanced should be at the rate of 4½ per cent., and that if the price of consols should chance to go down to 74, Mr. —— should have the right of claiming the stock at 70. The Jew, no doubt, laughed at what he conceived his own commercial dexterity in the transaction; but ere long he had abundant reason to laugh on the wrong side of his mouth; for no sooner was the stock pawned in the hand of the banker, than the latter sold it, along with an immensely large sum which had been previously standing in his name, amounting altogether to a little short of £3,000,000. But even this was not all: Mr. —— also held powers of attorney from several of the leading Scotch and English banks, as well as from various private individuals who had large property in the funds, to sell stock on their account. On these powers of attorney he acted, and at the same time advised his friends to follow his example. They at once did so; and the consequence was that the aggregate amount of stock sold by himself and his friends conjointly exceeded £10,000,000. So unusual an extent of sales, all effected in the shortest possible time, necessarily drove down the prices. In an incredibly short time they fell to 74—immediately on which Mr. —— claimed of Rothschild his stock at 70. The Jew could not refuse; it was in the bond. This climax being reached, the banker bought in again all the stock he had previously sold out, and advised his friends to repurchase also. They did so, and the result was that in a few weeks consols reached 84 again, their original price, and from that to 86. Rothschild's losses were very great by this transaction; but they were by no means equal to the banker's gains, which could not have been less than £300,000 or £400,000.

Since Rothschild's death, no one can be said to have taken his place on the Stock Exchange. There are several gentlemen who engage in very large transactions, but they can scarcely be said to approximate in amount to his. Neither do they stand out, as capitalists, with any very great pre-eminence. Rothschild's sons are, of course, severally rich, even when compared with those who are regarded among the most affluent; but when compared with him, they can only be considered poor, his wealth being divided amongst them. But, independently of this, they have neither the spirit of enterprise nor the financial knowledge or skill of their late father.

It is to the transactions of speculators in the funds, such as those I have described in the case of Rothschild, and to others of a smaller amount by less affluent parties, and not to any purchases effected or sales made by the public, that the sudden rise or fall of consols is to be ascribed. Were the funds left to the operation of the public alone, there would be scarcely any fluctuation in them at all.

* * * * * *

Fortunes are lost or gained on the Stock Exchange with a rapidity unknown in any other place. It is no uncommon thing—it was still less uncommon in time of the war—for a man to be worth £20,000 or £30,000 one day, and to be a beggar the next. There are also many instances, in the annals of the Stock Exchange, of parties who could not command a farthing one day, being worth £20,000, £30,000 £40,000, or £50,000 the next. As illustrative of the sudden and singular vicissitudes of fortune which men sometimes undergo in that place, I may mention a curious instance in the case of Mr. F——, the present proprietor of one of the most extensive estates in the county of Middlesex. He had been for some years a member of the Stock Exchange, when, on becoming unfortunate, he had to suffer the indignity of having his name chalked on the blackboard; an indignity to which poverty more frequently than dishonorable conduct is subjected. The loss of a handsome fortune, coupled with the treatment he had received from the committee, worked his feelings up to such a state of frenzy that, chancing to pass London Bridge a few days after the battle of Waterloo, he, in his despair, threw the last shilling he had in the world over the bridge into the water. For a few moments afterwards he stood motionless on the spot, leaning over the parapet, and gazing vacantly into the water. The emotions which then passed through his mind were of a nature which no second party could describe; and which, indeed, even he himself could not by possibility convey, with any thing like their vividness or power, to the minds of others. His predominating feelings—but no idea can be formed of their burning intensity—were those of envy of the insensate stones, and of a wish that he himself were, like his last shilling, at the bottom of the river. That moment, but for the crowds of persons who were passing and repassing, he would have thrown himself over the parapet of the bridge, and ended his woes by ending his existence. From that instant, he formed the purpose of committing suicide; and he began to move slowly towards home with that view. Before he had reached the other end of the bridge, he was met by a Frenchman with whom he had been on terms of great intimacy. He would have passed by the Frenchman, so absorbed was he with the wretchedness of his condition, without recognizing him. The latter, however, advancing towards Mr. F.——, seized him by the hand, and inquired how he was. He managed to lisp out an "O, how are you?"

"This is a most important affair to both countries," said the Frenchman.

"What affair?" inquired the other, partially recovering himself from the frightful reverie to which he had been giving way.

"Why, the great battle," observed monsieur.

"The great battle! What great battle?"

"The battle of Waterloo."

"You are surely dreaming. I have not heard a word about it: the newspapers make no mention of any battle having been lately fought."

"I dare say they do not. How could they? Intelligence of it has only reached town within the last two hours. The foreign secretary and the French ambassador alone know any thing of it. Government have received the tidings of it: it is not an hour since I parted with the French ambassador from whom I had the information. Napoleon is signally defeated."

Mr. F—— felt as if he had started from a deep sleep. He felt as if he had become a new man. The advantage to which such important intelligence might be turned on the Stock Exchange, the scene of so many disasters and so much degradation to him, immediately shot across his mind.

"And the battle was an important one?"

"*Most* important," said the Frenchman, with great emphasis. "It will prove fatal forever to the prospects of Bonaparte. His usurpation is at an end," he added, with evident joy, being a great adherent of the Bourbon family.

"Were the numbers on either side great?"

"I have no idea of the exact numbers; but the battle was the greatest which has been fought in modern times, and it lasted a considerable part of three days."

Mr. F—— cordially shook the Frenchman by the hand, and said he would call on him in a day or two. Hastily returning to the city, he hurried to a certain firm on the Stock Exchange, informed them that he had just become exclusively possessed of most important information, and expressed his readiness to communicate it to them on condition that he should receive the half of whatever profits they might realize on any operation they might have in the Stock Exchange in consequence of that information. They agreed to his proposal: he told them the result of the battle of Waterloo: they rushed into the market, and purchased consols to an enormous amount. In the mean time, Mr. F—— proceeded to another large house, and told them also that he possessed information of the most important character, of which he was sure they had heard nothing. They admitted they knew of nothing that was not in the public prints. He made the same proposals to them he had done to the other firm: they also, not supposing Mr. F—— had spoken to any other party on the subject, at once closed with the offer, and on the intelligence being communicated to them, one of the partners called the other aside—there were only two in the counting-house at the time—and whispered to him not on any account to let Mr. F—— out of his sight, lest he should allow the important intelligence to transpire to some one else—adding that he would that instant hurry to the Stock Exchange, and employ various brokers to purchase consols to a large amount. "You'll recollect what I have said?" he observed to his partner, as he hastened out of the counting-house. "I'll take special care of that," said the other. "Leave such matters to me," he added in his own mind. A thought struck him. "Mr. F——, will you just step into the parlor," pointing the way, "and have a lunch?" Mr. F—— assented. They both proceeded to an apartment in another part of the house. A lunch was brought. Mr. F——, whose state of mind had deprived him of all appetite for some days past, now ate rather heartily. While busy with the things set before him, the other, rising from his seat, said, "You'll excuse me for a moment, Mr. F——, while I transact a small matter in the counting-house." "Certainly," said Mr. F——; "take your time." The other quitted the room, and on getting to the outside, locked the door, unknown to Mr. F.——, and put the key in his pocket. In about half an hour, the first partner returned from the Stock Exchange, and stated that the funds had already, from some cause or other, risen in an hour two or three per cent. The cause, it is unnecessary to say, was the immense amount of consols which had been purchased by the first house to whom Mr. F—— gave the information. Both partners proceeded to the apartment in which they had shut up their prisoner, and apprised him of the rise which had taken place, adding that they did not think it advisable to purchase at the advanced price. He urged them to do so, expressing his firm belief that when the news of so important a victory by the Allied Powers had been received, the funds would rise at least 10 or 12 per cent. The parties acted on his advice, and made immense purchases. The event justified the soundness of Mr. F——'s counsel, and the accuracy of his opinion; for, on the day on which intelligence of the battle was made general, the funds rose to the amazing extent of 15 per cent.—which is the greatest rise they were ever known to experience. Mr. F——'s share of the profits between the two houses in one day exceeded £100,000. He returned next day to the Stock Exchange, and very soon amassed a large fortune, when he had the wisdom to quit the place forever, and went and purchased the estate I have alluded to which he still possesses.

The funds experienced a greater fluctuation, as well as greater rise, on the day on which the result of the battle of Waterloo was made known, than they ever did at any previous or subsequent period. The average rise in the course of the day, as just stated, was fifteen per cent.; but taking all their different variations, up and down, and down and up together, the fluctuation was fully 100 per cent.

It can scarcely be necessary to say that, during the time of the war, the fluctuations of the funds were much greater than they have been since the peace. The news of every succeeding battle sent them up, or drove them down, according as the results of such battle were supposed likely to affect this country. As might have been expected, all sorts of rumors as to new battles were got up to serve the purposes of individuals. Many a battle was fought, and many a victory gained and lost on the Stock Exchange, which were never heard of any where else. So accustomed, indeed, had the members become to false intelligence in one or two of the leading papers, given with all the solemnity and positiveness of truth, that they frequently found themselves in the predicament of the persons who had been so often groundlessly alarmed by the cry of "Wolf" from the shepherd's boy, that they did not believe it when true. On one occasion, a blunt, honest member, who had an immense stake depending on the aspect of the war on the continent, having heard a rumor that a certain battle had taken place, but not knowing whether to credit it or not, determined on waiting personally on Lord Castlereagh, then foreign minister, with the view of endeavoring to get at the truth. He sent up his name to his lordship, with a note stating the liberty he had taken in consequence of the amount he had at stake, and begging as a favor to be informed whether the news of the battle in question was true. The noble lord desired the gentleman to be sent up stairs. He was shown into his lordship's room. "Well, sir," said his lordship, "I am happy to inform you that it is perfectly true this great battle has been fought, and that the British troops have been again victorious."

"I am exceedingly obliged to your lordship for your kindness in giving me the information: I am a ruined man," said the Stock Exchange speculator, making a low bow and withdrawing. He had calculated on the triumph, at the next conflict, of Napoleon's army. He had speculated accordingly; a contrary issue at once rendered him a beggar.

MERCANTILE TRANSACTIONS IN SCOTLAND.

It is not as in England, where, when an article is offered for sale, it is immediately purchased, or at once rejected as being too dear; but here there is a long haggling and cheapening of every article successively offered. The relation of my transactions with a man will show the general mode of doing business. He bids me call again, which I do several times without doing any thing He wishes to be the *last* I do with; but *all* cannot be *last,* and *all* have wished to be so. After a few days, I get him to proceed to business: he objects to the price of the article I offer. He will not buy. I try to induce him, but do not offer to make any reduction. Says he, "You are over dear, sir; I can buy the same gudes 10 per cent. lower; if ye like to tak' off 10 per cent., I'll tak' some of these."

I tell him that a reduction in price is quite out of the question, and put my sample of the article aside; but the Scotchman wants it.

"Weel, sir, it's a terrible price; but as I am out o' it at present,

I'll just tak' a little till I can be supplied cheaper, but ye maun tak' aff 5 per cent."

"But, sir," says I, "would you not think me an unconscionable knave to ask 10 per cent., or even 5 per cent., more than I intended to take?"

He laughs at me. "Hoot, hoot, mon, do ye expect to get what ye ask? Gude Lord! an' I was able to get half what I ask, I would soon be rich. Come, come; I'll gie ye within twa an' a half per cent. of your ain price, and gude faith, mon, ye'll be well paid."

I tell him that I never make any reduction from the price I first demand, and that an adherence to the rule "saves much trouble to both parties."

Weel, weel," says he, "since ye maun hae it a' your ain way, I maun e'en tak' the article; but really I think ye are over-keen."

So much for buying and selling: then comes the settlement. "Hoo muckle discount do ye tak' aff, sir?"

"Discount! You cannot expect it. The account has been standing a twelvemonth."

"Indeed, but I do expect discount—pay siller without discount! Na, na, sir, that's not the way here; ye maun deduct 5 per cent."

I tell him that I make no discount at all. "Weel, sir, I'll gie ye nae money at a'."

Rather than go without a settlement, I at last agree to take 2½ per cent. from the amount, which is accordingly deducted

"I hae ten shillings doon against ye for short measure, and fifteen shillings for damages."

"Indeed, these are heavy deductions; but if you say that you shall lose to that amount, I suppose that I must allow it."

"Oh, ay, it's a' right; then, sir, eight shillings and four pence for packsheet, and thirteen shillings for carriage and portage."

These last items astonish me. "What, sir," says I, "are we to pay all the charges in your business?" But if I do not allow these to be taken off, he will not pay his account; so I acquiesce, resolving within myself that, since these unfair deductions are made at settlement, it would be quite fair to charge an additional price to cover the extortion. I now congratulate myself on having concluded my business with the man; but am disappointed.

"Hae ye a stawmpe?" asks he.

"A stamp, for what?"

"Just to draw ye a bill," replies he.

"A bill, my good sir! I took off 2½ per cent. on the faith of being paid in cash." But he tells me it is the custom of the place to pay in bills, and sits down and draws me a bill at three months after date, payable at his own shop.

"And what can I do with this?"

"Oh, ye may tak' it to Sir William's, and he'll discount it for you, on paying him three months' interest."

"And what can I do with his notes?"

He'll gie ye a bill in London, at forty-five days."

"So, sir, after allowing you twelve months' credit and 2½ per cent. discount, and exorbitant charges which you have no claim on us to pay, I must be content with a bill which we are not to cash for four months and a half."

"Weel, weel—and now, sir," says he, "if you are going to your inn, I'll gang wi ye, and tak' a glass o' wine."

A HAMBURGH MERCHANT IN HIS COUNTING-HOUSE.*

It was not six o'clock, yet I was already pacing my room with hasty and anxious strides, and my fellow lodgers must certainly have regretted my vicinity, in that I was the indiscreet disturber of their morning repose. Was ever poor author, through unforeseen circumstances, betrayed into a more vexatious dilemma than was I at that moment, in the free Hans Town of Hamburgh? My exchequer was exhausted, and my departure yet to be effected, with not a red cent left in my pocket. Mr. Marr, my friendly host, is good and kind-hearted, and not the man to cut an unpaid account immediately from one's skin; but the Prussian Schnellpost takes no passengers on credit, and on the next day, without fail, I must forth to Berlin. For the twentieth time had I rummaged through my letter-case, in the hope that some shrinking treasure-certificate, some modest letter of credit, might have crept into a corner, but in vain! Stop! what paper is that? It is a letter which a well-wishing patron has given me, and which I have negligently omitted to present. The address is quite simple—"Herr Mohrfeld, Deich Street." I breathed aloud, "Perhaps this is the man from whom help is to reach me." I remembered that my patron had described him as the head of a very eminent mercan-

* Translated from the German by T. P. Kettle for the *Democratic Review*.

tile house, whose acquaintance would greatly advantage me. Speedily did I come to a decision—dressed myself, and with the stroke of eight left the hotel for Deich Street, where I expected my rescuing angel to appear to me. Stop! here, at the hop-market, I must pause a moment. Yonder is a short, thick-set man, in a blue overcoat, with a badly-combed brown hair, and whose ruddy face has a blunt and taciturn expression. He has bought a good fish, sent a porter away with it, and pursues his walk. He has his hands crossed behind him—his eyes cast upon the ground—and with a low humming, turns into the Deich Street. Without his taking any notice of me, we strode together, and at last both stood still before the same house. There he recovered from his thoughtful manner, and, looking steadily at me, asked in a suppressed tone, "Do you wish to speak with any one here?" Vexed that so ordinary-looking a man should address me with so little ceremony, I answered with some haughtiness, "I have business with the house of Mohrfeld." He smiled, and then said earnestly, "I am Mohrfeld!" What! and from this man, who buys his own fish, and appears in a threadbare coat, am I to expect help? Is this mean looking personage the only dependence, in respect of his purse, of his novel-writing guest? But he was the only anchor of hope to which I could cling. With lightning haste I removed my hat, and said, with a most respectful air, "Pardon me!—I had till now not the honor—I have"—here I drew the letter from my pocket—"a commission to deliver this letter." Herr Mohrfeld interrupted me. "Not now; by and by I will speak with you in the counting-room; you must, however, wait awhile. Come"—he stepped into the house, and I followed. In the great hall all was activity. There were two great scales, on which workmen were weighing coffee, as a clerk stood by with his memorandum-book. Mr. Mohrfeld looked on silently for a few moments, and was passing on, when a laborer threw down a bag of coffee in a manner to burst it and scatter the berries upon the floor. "What gross carelessness!" tartly exclaimed the merchant; and stooping to collect the scattered coffee, continued, "Gather it all up, and put it again in the sack. Then have it properly mended; and you, Mr. Moller, see that the bag is weighed afterwards, and if there is a loss, charge the amount to this improvident man. It shall be deducted from his week's pay."

That is hard," said the man. "Only a little coffee"—

"Only a little coffee!" answered the merchant quickly. "He who despises trifles is not worthy of great things; out of eight-and-forty shillings is composed a thaler; and to one good vintage many warm days are necessary. So! not worth the trouble? Negligence is a great failing, and ruinous to ordinary business. Mr. Moller, when this man again, even in the smallest particular, displays his carelessness, discharge him on the spot. I make you answerable."

"Great God!" thought I, "for a handful of coffee, will he deprive a man of his bread? How hard! how cruel! how will it go with me?"

A young man, dressed with great elegance, came now out of the office, bowed to the merchant, and was about to pass out of the door, but at a look from his employer, stood still.

"What an appearance you make!" said Mohrfeld, disdainfully. "Is there to be a ball in my counting-house? and where were you yesterday evening? If I am not in error, you were curvetting on a palfrey out at the Damn Door, and had no time to observe your employer, who passed you on foot."

"I beg a thousand pardons," answered the young man, turning blood-red in his face. "I"—

"So good!" interrupted Mohrfeld. "I have nothing to do with that which my people do out of business hours, if they perform their duties punctually. But with you it is different. You have a poor mother who suffers for necessaries; three uneducated brothers, two of whom I met yesterday barefoot, and that at a time of life when they should be in school. It would be more honor to you to attend to that, and to take care of your brothers, instead of dressing in the latest fashion, and capering upon a saddle-horse. Go to your business, sir."

The young man became purple in the face, withdrew himself backwards like a crab, and vanished through the door. The merchant strode through the store, and entered the counting-room, where I followed him. What a sight! A long and rather gloomy hall presented itself, with numerous desks, behind each of which stood a person busily writing or reckoning, and of whom I counted thirty. In an adjoining room sat many more. Not far from the door sat a rather elderly man at a counter, and near him stood several iron chests, and the association drew from me a deep sigh.

"Well, Mr. Caston," said the merchant, as he approached his cashier, "what news?" "But little," answered he quietly. "There is a demand for bills. We have, however, nothing to spare. In Livonia we have nothing, and on Genoa and Venice we have not more than our three ships loading for those ports require. Two value on New York, and one on Havana, that will be wanted, and I have notified them. Can you use any Copenhagen or Swedish paper at the current rates?" "No; there must be as little funds as possible locked up in paper. I shall need a large cash balance. Remember that." He passed on, and stood before a desk. "Were the goods sent yesterday on board the Artemisia, Mr. Kohler?" he asked. "Are the policies for the Pleil taken out, and has Captain Heysen got his papers?" "It is all attended to," said the clerk. "Here is the bill of lading; here the policy, and the receipt of the captain." "Good; your punctuality pleases me. Go on; method is the soul of business. Take care of that sand, however. It has a slovenly appearance to see it so scattered as on your desk."

Mr. Mohrfeld had now arrived at his desk, which was secluded from the main hall by a rail. He pointed me to a chair, and began to examine some letters that had waited his coming. A deep silence now pervaded the room, which was broken only by the monotonous scratching of many quills. No loud word was spoken, and seldom a suppressed whisper was heard. No notice was taken of me; not a word was addressed to me, nor was a curious glance directed towards me. The merchant read through his letters, and called several young men to him, giving directions, but receiving no answers. "At one o'clock, all must be ready for signature. You, Mr. Becker, must take care that no more errors creep into your French letters. You are too quick, too hasty. Take example of Mr. Hart—his English letters are a master correspondence. Above all, I observe lately in your letters a worthless innovation. You use a pompous, verbose style, and employ three lines where three words are sufficient. Abandon that. A flowery style is always a folly, and especially so in mercantile letters; but it comes from the senseless novels and romances that you are eternally reading, and which will yet incapacitate you for every useful employment. I have warned you—take care for the future."

This was a brilliant prospect? What reception could a novel-writer expect from a man possessed of such views? At this moment Mohrfeld turned to me, and said rather short, "Well, sir, about our business?" "At your service," I stammered, and reached him my letter; but he had not opened it ere we were again interrupted. "See there! good-morning, Captain Heysen," said the merchant, with animation. "You come, probably, to take leave; a lucky voyage to you, and bring yourself and crew back in good health. Pay good attention to ship and cargo, and make me no 'general average' Your wife, say you? Why, in any circumstances, let her apply to me at once. If you have a good opportunity, and avail yourself skilfully of it, you may be back by Christmas. Well, adieu, Captain: you have"—here he glanced at the almanac—"no time to lose. It is now high water; you may lose the tide, and I am not pleased to have the ship anchored at Blankenese. Lucky voyage." The captain vanished, and another man took his place. "Good-morning, Mr. Flugge; what have you to say?" asked the merchant; "I am well pleased with that last purchase of wood. You earned your commission with honor. When you have such another lot on the same terms, let me know. My ships must be employed. There are already three lying idle. As soon as the new stock arrives, let me know. Adieu." "I beg your pardon, sir"—this was directed to me—"that I keep you so long waiting; but the current business takes precedence." "Good-morning, Pilot! Already back. Is my 'Hope' gone to sea safely?" "All as you wish, Mr. Mohrfeld," answered a robust Elbe pilot. "The ship is a fast sailor, and not afraid of a breeze. Here is a letter from the captain. But I must to day on board another vessel. Perhaps I can take my pilotage with me?" "That's of course, Pilot; and for the quick pilotage, ten thalers more. Go to my cashier; he will make it all right." "What do you want?" This was addressed to a meagre-looking little man, with a bald head and snuffy nose, who, in a threadbare black coat and stooping posture, stood before the wealthy merchant.

"I beg a thousand pardons," he answered; "I am Doctor Eck, from Frankfort. I have for a long time had in consideration the peculiar procreation of mankind, and at last have succeeded in the formation of a brilliant theory, that I intend to promulgate in a series of lectures; and I would therefore solicit—"

"I am sorry," interrupted the merchant; "but I am opposed to all theories that cannot be promptly applied to the concerns of life. Away with your air-castles, fog-projects, and chimeras! I am very sorry."

The poor doctor perspired with anxiety; and, scarcely able to speak, he looked pitiably at the subscription-list in his hand, and stammered out something of patrons and down-trodden sons of Minerva; but his voice faded into an indistinguishable murmur. The merchant regarded him for a moment with a sarcastic smile, then took the list, and wrote a line. It must have been a very important line, for the face of the doctor brightened with a heartfelt laugh as he busied himself to lay more papers upon the desk. The merchant motioned him away, saying, "No matter! It is a pleasure to me when my signature can be of use to a meritorious and learned man, even if personally I derive no profit from his talents. Your theory and my practice are very different; an interchange of ideas that are so directly opposed leads only to endless confusion. Farewell!"

The doctor retired, and made room for a man who pressed close up, and without further ceremony began: "Mr. Mohrfeld, your 'Fortuna' is quite ready, and can be launched at any moment. I wish to know what time you will appoint?"

"Monday morning, Mr. Reich," answered the merchant. "I am well pleased with your prompt and efficient mode of business. Now, as young beginners should be encouraged, you may lay the keel of a new ship on my account. Try yourself at that. I passed your yard yesterday, and observed the order and industry with which it is conducted. Persevere in that manner. Well! remember Monday morning. Farewell! Who are you?"

This was addressed to a poorly-clad woman, with pallid cheeks and eyes red with weeping, who now stood before him. At this-nearly harsh address of the merchant, she looked anxiously up, and answered, "I am the wife of Bodmer, the man who was so unfortunate as to fall from the loft and break his leg."

"Shocking! very shocking! I am very sorry for Bodmer; he was an orderly man, and ever cheerfully performed his duties. But my surgeon visited him; what did he say?"

"He gives the best hope of saving my husband's life, but it will be a tedious sickness; and who knows if the poor man will ever again be able to work! What, then, shall we, with our five poor children, do?"

"Have confidence in the man in whose service you have met the misfortune," answered the merchant. "What the patient needs of wine and strengthening food shall be furnished from my kitchen The weekly wages you will receive regularly on Saturday. Now go home, and remember me to your husband, whom I will soon visit."

The woman through her tears rendered speechless thanks, and the merchant began reading my letter.

"Your letter has rather an old date," said he, suddenly; "I have long expected it. Your circumscribed time has probably prevented an earlier call?"

I stammered out a lie, something about my indisposition to disturb so active a business man, and that at the moment I was in great necessity. He did not let me finish, but went on:—

"You are here highly recommended to me. If I can do any thing for you, speak freely. Persons away from home frequently stand in need of aid."

This was the moment to speak of the deep ebb of my purse; but oh! the false shame—the words would not leave my lips.

"Nothing?" he proceeded. "Well, on another occasion, perhaps. Come, however, on Sunday to my cottage before the Damn Door, and take a spoonful of soup with me. Men of business have on week-days but small leisure to bestow on mere conversation."

Here was my dismissal; but without money, however, I could not go. I was completely cleaned out, and must travel. At this moment, there came to my rescue a clerk, who handed between the desk and myself a letter brought by an express, addressed to Mr. Mohrfeld. It was instantly opened and read, and was probably of a favorable nature, as a pleasing smile played round the lips of the merchant; but suddenly, as if betraying a weakness, it again vanished, and he laid the letter with accustomed unconcern on one side. As he did so, his glance again fell on me.

"Any thing further to command, sir?"

Now must I speak, cost what it will. I stepped close to his chair, bowed my lips to his ear, and poured forth a multitude of words, among which the most emphatic were, "want of money." To an elegant construction of sentences at such a moment, would even Demosthenes have given no thought. The merchant stared at me with wondering eyes, then took my letter in hand, and again read it through with close attention; after which he wrote a line under it and handed it to me, saying, "Here, sir; have the goodness to hand this to my cashier. I shall depend on seeing you at my table on Sunday; for the present you will excuse me."

I bowed silently, and soon stood before the man surrounded with iron chests. He took the letter, and said, "You have to receive one hundred marks courrant. Will you please give a receipt? Here is the money."

"And here, sir, is your receipt," cried I, with a lightened heart, as I thrust the fifty-one thalers, nineteen and two-thirds shillings into my pocket, hurried out of the office into the free air of heaven, and turned towards the Alster Hall, in the elegantly-decorated rooms of which I speedily enjoyed a substantial breakfast.

LEAVES FROM A MERCHANT'S EXPERIENCE.

In compliance with the "Request to the Reader," (to which I respectfully invite the attention of all,) a merchant of twenty years' standing has kindly sent me the following interesting leaves from the note-book of his own experience, illustrative of certain sound mercantile principles.

I recollect a circumstance that occurred to me at the commencement of my business life, nearly twenty years ago. I had purchased the stock, goodwill, &c. of a large wholesale establishment, in a city not a thousand miles from your present residence. A few days after my induction into this establishment, an old merchant, who had in past time, been a formidable competitor of my predecessor, called to see me. He had on several occasions manifested an interest in me, and now came to proffer his advice.

"You have commenced business," said he, "under favorable auspices, and, under God, your success depends upon yourself. I am an old man, and have been intimately acquainted with all the mysteries of your trade for more years than you have lived. And now I tell you, you are doing wrong in selling to Goodman & Prompt."

"Why?" said I in astonishment, "there are no men buying in this market who have a better reputation, and I have exerted myself immensely to get them to make this bill."

"It is true," replied my interlocutor, "but they are not the sort of men you ought to sell to—they *buy too largely*. My advice to you is, *do not sell more than* $ 2000 *worth of goods to any one man or firm at one time.* If you have ten such customers, it is probable that nine of them will pay you, but one in the ten will give you trouble; and should one of them fail to pay you, you will lose all the profit made on the goods sold to the other nine."—So saying the old gentleman left me.

I was convinced of the truth and justice of his remarks, but I could not now do otherwise than send the goods. Mr. Prompt had bought the bill, given his note, and gone home. I had "drummed" him more assiduously than I ever drummed afterwards. I had sold him $ 2200 worth of goods—by far the largest bill I ever sold before or since. My profit was small, it is true; but it was my first large sale. and I hoped I had made a customer. So the goods were sent.

Six months afterwards, Mr. Prompt again appeared in our city He paid me $2200 in par funds, bought a bill amounting to $1200, and thirty days thereafter remitted me a check for this amount, less the discount. Goodman & Prompt were *very* desirable customers, and my doubts and fears were given to the winds. They dealt with me regularly, sometimes paying cash, sometimes buying on six months—but always paying—until one fatal year they failed, owing me $2500, of which I never received a dollar. They had "over-traded,"—and in their assignment to cover confidential debts, they gave up every cent they were worth. I believe they were perfectly honest and upright men, and I would sell either of them a small bill to day, if I were in business. They were *very* unfortunate, and *so was I.* I should mention that they owed me for *two* bills—the first $1800, I had extended for them, and assured Mr. Goodman that "it made no difference," as I could easily get the money for his note with my endorsement; and I sold him another bill of $700 without fear or doubt. At this time I had not learned that it is always bad policy to "*lap bills.*"

* * * * * * *

My esteemed mentor, to whom I referred in a former letter, frequently gave me the following advice: "*Attend,*" said he, "*to your legitimate business.* You will find that it requires all your energies to keep *that* under your own control: so that you cannot afford to give time and attention to mere speculations. Moreover you will almost inevitably lose in the long run, if you encourage a speculating spirit. But above all, I warn you against going out of your *own line* of business. If you *do* venture, let it be in articles in which you constantly deal."

This was the substance of advice with which Mr. B. in his kindness and friendship frequently favored me. But it required a little experience to teach me the value and sound wisdom of his counsel.

One of my Tennessee customers sent me 3000 lbs. of beeswax, with instructions to sell it, on arrival, and credit his account with the proceeds. I had frequently received similar remittances, but the lots had heretofore been small, and the product trifling, and the sales had been confided to one of my clerks. But this shipment was worth nearly $1000, and I determined to give it my personal attention—especially as it came from a valuable customer whom I was anxious to please.

Therefore, when the beeswax arrived, I had it hoisted to the fourth floor of my warehouse, and all the barrels opened; and then I called on several dealers and invited them to examine the article and give me an offer for the lot. Alas! beeswax happened to be very "dull" just at that time, and of all the parties I invited, only one came to see the wax. He was a shipping merchant, engaged largely in the South American trade, and appeared to be better informed in *beeswax statistics* than any of the other dealers. I well remember his offer and his remarks on the subject. He said, "I will give you 22½ cents cash, for the lot. This is rather above the market; but the article is very fine, and I think it may be higher some day." I enquired where he sold it, and found that he was in the habit of shipping it occasionally to South America. After a little deliberation, I declined taking his offer, and suddenly resolved to keep it myself, and wait for the advance in price. I argued, that "it did not really cost an *outlay*, as my customer's account was not due, and would not mature for nearly four months; and before that time, I would doubtless be able to sell it at such an advance as would repay me for waiting."

Accordingly I sent an account sales at 22½ cents, having first ascertained that I could not get this price for it from any other house than the one referred to above. The wax was headed up, and I eagerly watched for the expected rise. I examined old price-currents, and found it sometimes quoted at 26, and once, I think, at 28 cents. I talked about beeswax to all the wholesale druggists I knew; and was surprised to discover that they did very little with the article: in fact, in the whole city, I could not find one who would invest 600 or 700 dollars in it at 20 cents; that is for their regular sales; as the market price was about 22 cents for six months after I received it; and I suppose I could have sold it at that price, any day, to the shippers.

I kept that horrid beeswax on hand *thirty months!* At last there was a slight advance. It was quoted at 24½ cents. I went immediately to my South American friend, and asked for another offer. Imagine my disgust, when he informed me that "he was not in the market. The price was too high, and it would probably be down to 22 or 22½ cents again in a week."

I assure you that I was heartily sick of the very name of beeswax; and when he offered me 23½ cents, "on account of the extra quality of the lot," I accepted at once, and the wax was delivered to him the same day. I should remark, that the quotation 24½ cents was in a Boston paper, and I would have made nothing by shipping it there, as freight, brokerage, &c., would have more than swallowed the difference. My loss, in interest, loss of weight, &c., was very nearly $100. After all I got the experience at a moderate price.

E. B. D.

WASHINGTON, D. C., *January* 7, 1853.

P. T. BARNUM'S RULES FOR SUCCESS IN BUSINESS

I HAVE delayed the further progress of this book some three weeks, to obtain the opinion of one who is known all over the world as the ablest tactician, and one of the most successful business men of the age, and I am happy to say it is worth waiting for. Had I received it earlier, I would have been tempted to affix it to the encomium which I passed upon McDonogh's, as the "most valuable opinion upon record." It is certainly a volume within itself. I am sure my friends the editors will, after a while, be wanting a slice of it for the benefit of their readers, and they are most welcome to it; but, gentlemen, do not, I pray you, forget to mention the source from which you obtained it, or to tell your readers that "there are a few more of the same sort left." Amidst the multiplicity of books, there is danger that those which may have the best effect will be unheard of by the public without your fostering care. In the following letter, Mr. Barnum has given me authority to make alterations, &c., which I have not made, because I see no need of any, and for fear of spoiling it. It is possible that his remarks on advertising should be slightly qualified, to be good advice to all men—for a man should be first certain that his articles are really good in themselves, and would be popular if generally known; and, secondly, he should be certain of his own strength—that is, he should be a Barnum before he attempts to rival a Barnum.

BRIDGEPORT, *June* 28, 1852.

EDWIN T. FREEDLEY, ESQ.

DEAR SIR: Upon receiving your telegraph dispatch on Saturday, that you are waiting at an expense for my letter, I telegraphed you that you should receive it on Wednesday, but on reflection I determined to keep you no longer waiting, so I sat right down and wrote the inclosed. I fear that it is not what you want—but such as it is, I send it. Very likely the grammar may need correcting, and I also give you full liberty to curtail and leave out any thing you please, and make any alterations and additions that you please, provided you do not alter the general meaning and spirit of the article.

I hope you will be successful in your publication, and I shall be glad to purchase a copy of the work when it is completed.

Truly yours,

P. T. BARNUM.

I can scarcely expect to offer any thing new on the subject proposed, but will name a few rules that I am convinced, from experience and observation, must be observed in order to insure success in business.

1st. *Select the* KIND *of business that suits your natural inclinations and temperament.*—Some men are naturally mechanics; others have a strong aversion to any thing like machinery, and so on; one man has a natural taste for one occupation in life, and another for another. "I am glad we do not all feel and think alike," said Dick Homespun, "for, if we did, every body would think my gal, Sukey Snipes, the sweetest creature in all creation, and they would all be trying to court her at once."

I never could succeed as a merchant. I have tried it unsuccessfully several times. I never could be content with a fixed salary, for mine is a purely speculative disposition, while others are just the reverse, and therefore all should be careful to select those occupations that suit them best.

2d. *Let your pledged word ever be sacred.*—Never promise to do a thing without performing it with the most rigid promptness. Nothing is more valuable to a man in business than the name of always doing as he agrees, and that to the moment. A strict adherence to this rule gives a man the command of half the spare funds within the range of his acquaintance, and always encircles him with a host of friends, who may be depended upon in almost any conceivable emergency.

3d. *Whatever you do, do with all your might.*—Work at it, if necessary, early and late, in season and out of season, not leaving a stone unturned, and never deferring for a single hour that which can just as well be done *now*. The old proverb is full of truth and meaning, "Whatever is worth doing at all, is worth doing well." Many a man acquires a fortune by doing his business *thoroughly*, while his neighbor remains poor for life, because he only *half* does his business. Ambition, energy, industry, and perseverance, are indispensable requisites for success in business.

4th. *Sobriety. Use no description of intoxicating drinks.*—As no man can succeed in business unless he has a *brain* to enable him to lay his plans, and *reason* to guide him in their execution, so, no matter how bountifully a man may be blessed with intelligence, if his brain is muddled, and his judgment warped by intoxicating drinks, it is impossible for him to carry on business successfully. How many good opportunities have passed, never to return, while a man was sipping a "social glass" with his friend! How many a foolish bargain has been made under the influence of the *nervine*, which temporarily makes its victim so *rich!* How many important chances have been put off until to-morrow, and thence for ever, because the wine-cup has thrown the system into a state of lassitude, neutralizing the energies so essential to success in business. The use of intoxicating drinks as a beverage is as much an infatuation as the smoking of opium by the Chinese, and the former is quite as destructive to the success of the business man as the latter.

5th. *Let hope predominate, but be not too visionary.*—Many persons are alway kept poor, because they are too visionary. Every project looks to them like certain success, and therefore they keep changing from one business to another, always in hot water, and always "under the harrow." The plan of "counting the chickens before they are hatched," is an error of ancient date, but it does not seem to improve by age.

6th. *Do not scatter your powers.*—Engage in one kind of business only, and stick to it faithfully until you succeed, or until you conclude to abandon it. A constant hammering on one nail will generally drive it home at last, so that it cannot be clinched. When a man's undivided attention is centered on one object, his mind will continually be suggesting improvements of value, which would escape him if his brain were occupied by a dozen different subjects at once. Many a fortune has slipped through men's fingers by engaging in too many occupations at once.

7th. *Engage proper employees.*—Never employ a man of bad habits, when one whose habits are good can be found to fill his situation. I have generally been extremely fortunate in having faithful and competent persons to fill the responsible situations in my business, and a man can scarcely be too grateful for such a blessing. When you find a man unfit to fill his station, either from incapacity or peculiarity of character, or disposition, dispense with his services, and do not drag out a miserable existence in the vain attempt to change his nature. It is utterly impossible to do so. "You cannot make a silk purse, &c." He has been created for some other sphere; let him find and fill it.

8th. *Advertise your business. Do not hide your light under a bushel.*—Whatever your occupation or calling may be, if it needs support from the public, *advertise* it thoroughly and efficiently, in some shape or other, that will arrest public attention. I freely confess that what success I have had in life may fairly be attributed more to the public press than to nearly all other causes combined. There may possibly be occupations that do not require advertising, but I cannot well conceive what they are. Men in business will sometimes tell you that they have tried advertising, and that it did not pay. This is only when advertising is done sparingly and grudgingly. Homœopathic doses of advertising will not pay, perhaps—it is like half a potion of physic—making the patient sick, but effecting nothing. Administer liberally, and the cure will be sure and permanent. Some say "they cannot afford to advertise;" they mistake—they cannot afford *not* to advertise. In this country, where every body reads the newspapers, the man must have a thick skull who does not see that these are the cheapest and best medium through which he can speak to the public. where he is to find his customers. Put on the *appearance* of business, and generally the *reality* will follow. The farmer plants his seed, and while he is sleeping his corn and potatoes are growing. So with advertising. While you are sleeping or eating, or conversing with one set of customers, your advertisement is being read by hundreds and thousands of persons who never saw you, nor heard of your business, and never would, had it not been for your advertisement appearing in the newspapers. The business men of this country do not, as a general thing, begin to appreciate the advantages of advertising thoroughly. Occasionally the public are aroused at witnessing the success of a Swaim, a Brandreth, a Townsend, a Genin, or a Root, and express astonishment at the rapidity with which these gentlemen acquire fortunes, not reflecting that the same path is open to all who *dare* pursue it. But it needs *nerve* and *faith*—the former to enable you to launch out thousands on the uncertain waters of the future; the latter to teach you that, after many days, it shall surely return, bringing an hundred or a thousand fold to him who appreciates the advantages of printers' ink, properly applied.

9th. *Avoid extravagance; and always live considerably within your income, if you can do so without absolute starvation!*—It needs no prophet to tell us that those who live fully up to their means, without any thought of a reverse in life, can never attain a pecuniary independence. A brief reference to my own history may, perhaps, serve to illustrate this part of the subject. By the death of my father in

1826, I was thrown upon the world at the age of sixteen, dependent solely upon my own resources for support. I never found any difficulty in *making* money, but the thought did not occur to me (during fifteen years), of trying to *save.* At one time, when lotteries were lawful in my native State (Connecticut,) I was extensively engaged in the sale of tickets, and my profits were enormous, sometimes as high as five hundred dollars per day—but I thought very little of trying to lay up money; I could always easily manage to expend my income, let it be ever so great.

In 1841, I purchased the American Museum in New York, without a dollar, for I was not worth a dollar in the world. But I was never disheartened; I always felt that I could make money fast enough, if I only set my mind to it. I remember meeting a friend in Broadway a few weeks before I came in possession of the Museum.

"Well," says I, "Mr. A., I am going to buy the American Museum."

"*Buy* it!" says he, for he knew I had no property. "What do you intend buying it with?"

"Brass," I replied, "for silver and gold I have none."

It was even so. Every body who had any connection with theatrical, circus, or exhibition business, from Edmund Simpson, manager of the Old Park Theatre, or Wm. Niblo, down to the most humble puppet-showman of the day, knew me perfectly well. Mr. Francis Olmsted, the owner of the Museum building (now deceased), a noble, whole-souled man as one often meets with, having consulted my references, who all concurred in telling him that I was a "good showman, and would do as I agreed," accepted my proposition to give security for me in the purchase of the Museum collection, he appointing a money-taker at the door, and crediting me, towards the purchase, all the money received after paying expenses, allowing me fifty dollars per month, on which to support my family, consisting of a wife and three children. This was my own proposition, as I was determined so to live, that six hundred dollars per annum should defray all the expenses of my family until I had paid for the Museum; and my treasure of a wife (and such a wife *is* a "treasure") gladly assented to the arrangement, and expressed her willingness to cut the expenses down to $400 per annum if necessary. One day, some six months after I had purchased the Museum, my friend Mr. Olmsted happened in at my ticket-office, at about 12 o'clock, and found me alone, eating my dinner, which consisted of a few slices of corned beef and bread that I had brought from home in the morning.

"Is this the way you eat your dinner?" he inquired.

"I have not eaten a warm dinner since I bought the Museum, except on the Sabbath," I replied, "and I intend never to eat another on a week day, until I get out of debt."

"Ah! you are safe, and will pay for the Museum before the year is out," he replied, slapping me familiarly on the shoulder, and he was right, for in less than a year from that period I was in full possession of the Museum as my own property, every cent paid out of the profits of the establishment. Had I been less economical, and less *determined*, my expenses would have kept pace with my income; I should have lost much valuable time in going home every day to my dinner; and my present situation would probably have been very different from what it is.

Men and women, accustomed to gratify every whim and caprice, will find it hard at first to cut down their various unnecessary expenses, and will feel it a great self-denial to live in a smaller house than they have been accustomed to, with less expensive furniture, less company, less costly clothing, a less number of balls, parties, theatre-goings, carriage-ridings, pleasure excursions, cigar-smokings, liquor drinkings, &c. &c. &c.; but, after all, if they will try the plan of laying by a "nest-egg," or, in other words, a small sum of money, after paying all expenses, they will be surprised at the pleasure to be derived from constantly adding to their little "pile," as well as from all the economical habits which follow in the pursuit of this peculiar pleasure. The old suit of clothes, and the old bonnet and dress, will answer for another season; the Croton or spring water will taste better than champagne; a brisk walk will prove more exhilarating than a ride in the finest coach; a social family chat, an evening's reading in the family circle, or an hour's play of "hunt the slipper," and "blind man's buff," will be far more pleasant than a fifty or a five hundred dollar party, when the reflection on the *difference in cost* is indulged in, by those who begin to know the *pleasure of saving*.

Thousands of men are kept poor, and tens of thousands are made so after they have acquired quite sufficient to support them well through life, in consequence of laying their plans of living on too expensive a platform. Some families in this country expend $20,000 per annum, and some much more, and would scarcely know how to live on a smaller sum. Prosperity is a more severe ordeal than adversity, especially sudden prosperity. "Easy come, easy go," is an old and true proverb. *Pride*, when permitted full sway, is the great undying canker-worm which gnaws the very vitals of a man's worldly possessions, let them be small or great, hundreds or millions. Many persons, as they begin to prosper, immediately commence expending for luxuries, until in a short time their expenses swallow up their income, and they become ruined in their ridiculous attempts to keep up appearances, and make a "sensation."

I know a gentleman of fortune, who says that, when he first began to prosper, his wife *would have* a new and elegant sofa. "That sofa," he says, "cost me thirty thousand dollars!" The riddle is thus explained. When the sofa reached the house, it was found necessary to get chairs "to match," then sideboards, carpets, and tables, "to correspond" with them, and so on through the entire stock of furniture, when at last it was found that the house itself was quite too small and old-fashioned for the furniture, and a new one was built "to correspond" with the sofa and *et ceteras;* "thus," added my friend, "running up an outlay of $30,000 caused by that single sofa, and saddling on me, in the shape of servants, equipage, and the necessary expenses attendant on keeping up a fine 'establishment,' a yearly outlay of eleven thousand dollars, and a tight pinch at that; whereas ten years ago, we lived with much more real comfort, because with much less care, on as many hundreds. The truth is," he continued, "that sofa would have brought me to inevitable bankruptcy, had not a most unexampled tide of prosperity kept me above it."

10th. *Do not depend upon others.*—Your success must depend upon your own individual exertions. Trust not to the assistance of friends, but learn that every man must be the architect of his own fortune; and with proper attention to the foregoing rules, and such observations as a man of sense will pick up in his own experience, the road to competence will not, I think, usually be found a difficult one.

P. T. BARNUM.

BRIDGEPORT, CONN., *June* 28, 1852.

A REQUEST TO THE READER.

I WILL be greatly indebted, and make due acknowledgments to all who will favor me with any facts in their possession, derived, from their experience or observation, not to be found in books, that will enhance the interest and usefulness of this book. I should like to have a large number of letters for insertion, under the head of "Letters and Miscellanies," with the names of the writers to be appended or without them—with a mention of their business, and thus make it of pecuniary benefit to them, or without it, as they choose. There is not one man in a million whose experience would fill a book or a pamphlet, that would be worth the reading; but, I believe that one out of every five has some fact—some peculiar incident of history—some anecdote illustrative of a principle, or giving an insight into human nature—some adventure that caused trouble or loss through a neglect that others should be warned against—some thought, opinion, or fact, that would be interesting and important for all to know. In conversation we frequently hear them detailed, and this is an excellent opportunity to collect them together. By united co-operation we can make the most interesting, and, perhaps, really useful book that has been published lately. On the subject of failures in business, I have no doubt that a great many valuable facts could be elicited, if we knew where to apply.

I beg leave to state, that it is not general rules, nor general advice that we *now* want—for Franklin, McDonogh, Grigg, and Barnum have, perhaps, exhausted the subject—but it is a condensed statement of *special facts* as they occurred in the course of an individual's business experience, with the important lesson they taught him; as, for instance, "At such a time I neglected so and so, and the consequence was, I involved myself in trouble and lost money: At another time, I managed thus, and made money, or recovered a doubtful debt," &c. I respectfully solicit from a few of those who are known as first-rate salesmen, an analysis of the mode by which they appreciate character so quickly, and accommodate themselves thereto, and will guarantee them against all harm in revealing secrets, or danger that the world will ever become too wise. I also assure them that the few who are continually on the watch for information, and have the sense to take advantage of hints, are worth all the trouble.

Have the kindness to mention this to your friends, and may prosperity attend you!

LEGAL ADVICE

AND

USEFUL SUGGESTIONS

FOR THE

PURCHASERS OF THIS BOOK.

LEGAL ADVICE AND USEFUL SUGGESTIONS.

As the public has been disposed to treat this book with unmerited kindness—two editions having been sold in a few weeks, and a third called for—I feel under obligations to make it, if possible, a profitable investment to all who purchase it; and I have thought that some LEGAL ADVICE, in matters of daily concern, would be acceptable to all and useful to many. Though not a lawyer by profession, I had the advantage some years ago, of "delving in its mines," at the law school of Harvard University, and I give these remarks and advice as the teachings of Simon Greenleaf, late Royal Professor of Law at that institution.

The starting-point of the majority who engage in business, is the situation of Clerk or Agent; and we commence with some remarks applicable to the relation of

AGENCY.

It is a general rule of law, that whenever a person has power to do a thing, he may consequently, as incident to his right, do it by attorney or agent.

If a person be appointed a *general* agent, as in the case of a factor for a merchant residing abroad, the principal is bound by all his acts: but an agent constituted for a particular purpose, and under a *limited* and *circumscribed* power, cannot bind the principal by any act exceeding his authority.

Every general power necessarily implies the grant of every matter necessary to its complete execution. An attorney who has power to convey land has necessarily the power to receive the purchase-money.

In the appointment of a general agent, as he *is bound by all his acts,* a man *should take particular care whom he authorizes, or it may be* of the *most fatal consequence to him.* If a person on a former occasion, in the principal's absence, usually accepted bills for him, and the latter on his return approved thereof, he would be bound in a similar situation on a second absence from home; and it has been held that if a person usually subscribes an instrument with the name of another, proof of his having done so in many instances, is sufficient to charge him whose name is subscribed without producing any power of attorney.

When a clerk who has been empowered to draw or accept the bills of exchange in his employer's name, leaves his service, it is always prudent in the latter to give express notice of such facts to all his correspondents individually, for he may be bound by the acts of such clerk subsequently to leaving his service. A general notice in a newspaper is not sufficient to affect a former customer, unless he had express notice thereof.

When an agent has deviated from his orders, and you do not intend to assent to it, give immediate notice of your dissent.—Silence is considered in law an equivalent to a ratification.

Be cautious in sanctioning acts unauthorized by you, even if they are apparently insignificant or to your advantage.—Permitting a man to act as agent, and repeatedly adopting such acts, confers an implied authority upon the supposed agent, and gives the public a right to suppose him clothed with authority.

To agents we say: 1. *Never employ the funds of your principal, either his property or credit in your own behalf, for you expose yourself if the adventure is a losing one to bear the loss, and if a gaining one to lose the profit.* It is optional with the principal to disavow such transactions of agents, or to claim the benefit of them. It is also a general principle of law, that if the agent attempt to buy the goods he has on sale for his principal, without the express consent of the latter, after full knowledge, the latter may at his election either hold him to the bargain as purchaser, or refuse it and hold him to account for any greater price or value which has been or can be obtained for it at the same time.

2. *Always disclose your character as agent.*—If this be not done, a person with whom you deal has the right to hold you as the actual party; and has also the right, on discovering your principal, to resort directly to him. Yourself and principal are both bound.

3. *Be careful, in signing obligations as agent, not to use language im-*

porting personal obligation on your part.—The mere use of the word "Agent," will not relieve from personal responsibility, unless the principal's name appear on the face of the paper. The agent should always in his own signature, express both the principal's name and his own.

4. Verbal communication is in most cases valid authority for the appointment of an agent, but he should in all cases demand some written evidence of his authority, as he is always responsible, that he is authorized to do such acts as he professes to execute. An agent who acts without or beyond his authority, binds himself and not his principal. There should be two parts of a power of attorney—one kept by the person to whom it is given, the other kept by the person interested.

5. *Where the authority is not discretionary, obey orders strictly whatever may be the consequence to your principal. For a deviation from orders there is no excuse.* If goods be consigned to sell on arrival, the agent must sell on the first opportunity, and cannot wait for a change in the market, whatever may be his knowledge or desire to benefit his principal. By saying, however, that he must sell at the first opportunity, is not meant that he must close with the first offer, be it what it may; but it is meant that the agent must not in such case attempt to wait any change of times, but must make the sale without delay, at the best price, and on the best terms he can then do.

6. Where the language of your principal is obscure, ambiguous, or contradictory, *construe it strictly;* that is, do not infer that it contains more than it clearly implies. If you err by strict construction, you are on the safe side, and not exposed to exceed your power.

7. *Always keep your principal constantly instructed as to your proceedings.* The duty of keeping up correspondence is considered in law a part of the reasonable diligence due the principal, for the consequences of a want of which the agent must suffer; but aside from law, it is a duty which the agent owes to himself as a true man of business. There are few things more annoying than not to receive advices concerning matters in which one is interested, and not to receive prompt answers to letters is a downright insult. A neglect of business correspondence is *prima facie* evidence of incapacity.

In dealing with an agent, always demand satisfactory evidence of his authority to act for his principal. By a neglect of this—as the act of an agent who exceeds his authority does not bind his principal—your contract may be an invalid one.

BILLS OF EXCHANGE AND PROMISSORY NOTES.

Bills of Exchange are either foreign or inland. They are foreign when drawn by a person residing in one country upon a person residing in another; as where a bill is drawn in Philadelphia upon a merchant residing in Liverpool; and inland, when both the drawer and the drawee reside within the same State or kingdom. The latter are usually called *drafts.*

A Promissory Note is defined to be a direct engagement in writing to pay a sum specified, at a time therein limited, or on demand, to a person therein named, or his order, or to the bearer.

Checks nearly resemble bills of exchange, and differ from them in this respect, that they are mostly made payable to bearer, and should be drawn upon regular bankers.

Bills of exchange and negotiable promissory notes are distinguished from all other parol contracts, by the circumstance that they are *prima facie* evidence of valuable consideration, both between the original parties and against third persons.

In an action by the *bona fide* holder of a negotiable note, received before due, against the maker, the consideration cannot be inquired into, if the instrument be not in its creation void.

The holder of a bank check is *prima facie* the rightful owner, and is not bound to prove a consideration unless circumstances of suspicion appear.

Whenever the holder of negotiable paper has notice, either positively or constructively, of any equity subsisting between the original parties, he takes it subject to such equity.

The parties concerned in a draft or bill of exchange are the *drawer*, or the party who draws the bill; the *drawee*, or the party on whom it is drawn; and the *payee*, or party in whose favor it is drawn. When the drawee has accepted the bill he becomes the *acceptor*. When the payee assigns his right, by writing his name on the back, he becomes an *indorser.*

Indorsements are made either in *blank*, in *full*, or *restrictive*. An indorsement in *blank* is by far the most common, and is made by the mere writing of the indorser's name on the back of the bill, without any mention of the name of the person in whose favor the indorsement is made. A blank indorsement makes a bill transferable to the indorsee by mere delivery; and its negotiability by that method cannot be restrained by any subsequent indorsement in full, because the holder, by delivery, may consider himself as the indorsee of the payee, and strike out all the subsequent indorsements, whether special or not.

An indorsement in *full* is so called, because the indorser expresses therein in whose favor he makes the indorsement; as, "pay the con tents to A. B. or order."

A *restrictive* indorsement gives a bare authority to receive the money, without power of transfer; as "pay to A, for my use," or to "J. S. only."

In drawing a bill or note, attention should be paid to the following matters: 1. That it be properly dated. 2. That the time of payment be clearly expressed. 3. That it contain an order, at least a request to pay. 4. That in case of a foreign bill, drawn in sets, each set contain a proviso that it shall be payable only in case the others are not paid. 5. That it be clearly expressed to whom the bill is payable. 6. That where the instrument is intended to be negotiated, words of transfer be inserted. 7. That the money to be paid be distinctly and intelligibly expressed. 8. That in certain cases "value received," be inserted. 9. That the drawer's name be clearly signed. 10. That the bill be properly addressed to the drawee. 11. That where the bill is to be paid at a certain place, that place be properly described.

I. *Where there is danger of loss, have the bill, note, or check made payable "to order;" and in such cases, it is advisable for the indorser to fill up blank indorsements, so as to make it an indorsement in full.*—If the holder of a foreign or inland bill of exchange, check, &c., transferable by *mere delivery*, lose or be robbed of it, while in his possession, and it get into the hands of a person who was not aware of the loss, for a sufficient consideration, previously to its being due, such person, notwithstanding he derived his interest in the bill, &c., from the person who found or stole it, may maintain an action against the acceptor, or other parties, and the original holder, who lost it, will forfeit all right of action; and, if a person who has not given a consideration for a lost or stolen bill, transferable by mere delivery, presents it to the drawee, at the time it is due, and he pay it before he has notice of the loss or robbery, such drawee will not, in general, be liable to pay it over again to the real owner. (CHITTY *on Bills*, 171.)

But, where a bill is assignable, by *indorsement*, no interest can be conveyed, otherwise than by that act; and a person getting possession of it, by a forged indorsement, will not acquire any interest in it, although he was not aware of the forgery. Consequently, the original holder, when he has regained possession of the bill, can recover against the acceptor and drawer, although the acceptor may have paid the bill.

If the *bona fide* owner of a bank note cut it into two parts, and send the parts in different letters, and one of them be stolen or lost, he may recover the whole amount from the bank, on producing the other; and, a notice by the bank, that notes voluntarily cut by the owner, would not be paid unless all the parts should be brought together, does not alter the law, although the notice was seen by the party by whom the notes were cut. (*Martin* vs. *U. S. Bank.*)

No person should refuse to pay a bill which he has accepted to the loser, on the ground of its having been lost, if he has sufficient security and indemnification offered to him; and a court of equity has jurisdiction to enforce payment of the amount of a *negotiable* note so lost, upon sufficient indemnity being given.

It is said that if one part of a foreign bill of exchange, drawn in sets, be lost by the drawee, or be by him given to a wrong person; or if, by any other means, the holder cannot have a return of the bill, either accepted or not accepted, the drawee must give to the holder, or to his order, a promissory note for payment of the amount of the bill, on the day it becomes due, on delivery of the second part, if it arrive in time, or if not, upon the note; and if the acceptor refuse to give the note, the holder must demand the money, though he have neither note nor bill; and if payment be refused, a protest must be regularly made for non-payment. (Bul. *Nisi Pri.* 271.)

In all cases, if a bill of exchange be lost, and a new one cannot be had from the drawer, a protest may be had on a copy.

II. *Always present bills for acceptance as soon as possible; and presentment should, in all cases, be made during the usual hours of business.*—It is clearly established, that a valid acceptance may be in writing, on the bill itself, or on *another paper*, as by a letter undertaking to accept bills already drawn, or it may be *verbal*. Where a bill, payable after sight, is accepted, it is usual and proper, also, to write the day on which the acceptance is made.

An acceptance, may be implied as well as expressed; and it may be inferred, from the *drawee's* keeping the bill a great length of time, or by any other act which gives credit to the bill, and induces the holder not to protest it.

A verbal or written promise to accept at a future period a bill *already* drawn, or that a bill then drawn shall meet due honor, or a promise of the same nature, as "leave the bill and I will accept it," amounts to a complete and absolute acceptance in the hands of a *bona fide* holder, although the drawee had no consideration for the promise.

The holder of a bill is not bound to receive an acceptance, which varies in any respect from the tenor of the bill; but if he do receive a *partial* or *conditional* acceptance, and mean to avail himself of the acceptance, he should immediately give notice to the other parties to the bill of the fact, and express in his notice the nature of it.

The doctrine is well established, that the acceptor is bound to know the hand-writing of the drawer, and cannot defend himself from payment by a subsequent discovery of forgery. (10 *Wheat.* 333.)

If acceptance be refused, it is always advisable to have a bill regularly protested, and to give notice to the parties interested: and it is advisable for each party, immediately on receipt of notice, to give a fresh notice to such of the parties who are liable over to him, and against whom he must prove notice; and the notice should be given by an agent or servant who will be competent to prove it, and not by the holder in person.

If the drawee, on presentment of a bill for acceptance, dishonor it, wholly or partially, the holder may insist upon immediate payment, by the parties liable to him, as well of the drawee as of the prior indorsers, or in default thereof, may instantly commence an action against them. (CHITTY *on Bills*, 244.)

Where a foreign bill is protested for non-acceptance, or for better security, any person, with the consent of the holder, may accept it for the *honor* of the drawer, or any of the indorsers; and such acceptance is called an *acceptance supra protest.*

The method of accepting supra protest, is said to be as follows: The acceptor must personally appear before a notary public, with witnesses, and declare that he accepts such protested bill in honor of the drawer or indorser, and that he will satisfy the same at the appointed time; and then he must subscribe the bill, with his own hand, thus: "Accepted supra protest in honor of J. B.;" or, as is more usual, "Accepts S. P." (*Bayl,* 48.)

III. *Never make any alteration even of the most trivial character in any bill, note, due-bill, or check.*—If a bill be altered in any *material* respect, as for instance in the date or sum without the consent of the drawer, it will at common law discharge him from liability, though it may afterwards come into the hands of an indorsee not aware of the alteration, and if it be altered after acceptance or indorsement without the acceptor's or indorsee's consent, such alteration will have the same effect as to their liability. The effect of an alteration will be the same, although the day of payment be thereby retarded. But an alteration in a part *not material*, as, for instance, the insertion in the acceptance of the place where the bill is to be presented for payment, will not discharge the acceptor. It is, however, advisable never to make any alteration after a bill has been executed, for it might possibly subject an innocent holder or negotiator to an indictment for forgery, at the prosecution of a fraudulent or vindictive party. If, upon a bill being presented for acceptance the drawee alters it as to the time of payment and accepts it so altered, he vacates the bill as against the drawer and indorsers. But if the holder acquiesce in such alteration and acceptance, it is a good bill as between him and the acceptor.

IV. *Never pay drafts or checks before the day on which they are dated.*—Where a banker paid a check the day before it bore date, which check had been lost by the payee, it was held that he was liable to pay the amount to the loser, it being proved to be contrary to the usual course of business to pay drafts before the day on which they are dated.

The entry of a check as cash, made by the officer of a bank in the private bank-book of the holder, is equivalent to a payment. If a forged check be credited as cash in the bank-book of the holder, who, on being informed of the forgery, agrees under a mistake of his right that if the check be really a forgery it is no deposit, he is not bound by his agreement.

V. *Never take a note or bill over due without inquiring into the reasons why it has not been paid.*—There is a material distinction between the transfer made *before* a bill is due, and one made *after* that time. In the first case it is said the transfer carries no suspicion on the face of it, but when a transfer of a bill is made *after it is due*, whether by indorsement or mere delivery, the presumption is that the indorsee had notice of the circumstances which would have affected the validity of the bill in the hands of the person who was holder thereof at the time it became due.

VI. *Always present a bill or note for payment at the time when due, when a time of payment is specified and when no time is expressed, within a reasonable time, after receipt of the bill.*—Even the bankruptcy, insolvency, or death of the acceptor of a bill, or the maker of a note, however notorious, will not excuse the neglect to make due presentment, but in the case of death it should be made to the executor or administrator, and if none has been appointed, at the house of the deceased, otherwise the drawer and the indorsers will be discharged.

It is advisable always to present checks for payment the same day on which you receive them, or, at farthest, on the morning of the next day, unless prevented by distance, or some inevitable cause or accident, which in all cases will excuse the neglect to make presentment as soon as it would otherwise be necessary. (*Kyd*, 46.)

The presentment for payment of a bill should be made within the usual hours of business, and the holder of a bill is not bound to wait till the last moment of the last day of grace; for the undertaking of the acceptor is to pay the bill on demand on any part of the last day of grace. (4 *Term Rep.* 173.)

The drawer and indorsers of a bill would be discharged by the holder's taking a check from the acceptor, and delivering the bill to him, in case the check be not paid; but, if a creditor, on any other account than a bill of exchange, be offered cash in payment of his debt, or a check upon a banker from an agent of his debtor, and prefer the latter, this does not discharge the debtor if the check be dishonored, although the agent fail with a balance of his principal in his hands to a much larger amount. (2 *Camp.* 515.)

If you wish to hold the drawer and indorsers of a bill on non-payment by the drawee, do not agree to give the drawee time, or take a bond or any security payable at a future day, without the assent of the other parties thereto, for that would discharge them from liability, although due notice had been given of its non-payment. Whenever a new credit is given to the drawer, the holder takes it upon himself, and the drawer is discharged. (1 *Bay*, 177.) Where the holder of a bill of exchange discharges a party who is liable to the payment, all other parties to it, whose liability is subsequent to that of the party discharged, are thereby discharged also. (6 *Mass.* 85.)

It is always advisable for the drawer or indorser who pays a bill to take a receipt in the holder's own handwriting—on the back of the bill stating by whom it was paid—for the legal presumption is that it was paid by the acceptor. (2 *Camp.* 439.)

GUARANTEE AND SURETYSHIP.

A *guarantee* is a contract whereby one man obligates himself for the acts of another who is dealing for his own benefit. As consideration is necessary to all contracts not under seal, no contract of suretyship is valid without sufficient consideration. Where the guarantor's promise is made *before* the credit is given, it is requisite that the creditor give trust upon *the faith* of that promise; and where the promise is made *after* the credit has been given, there must be some new inducement, as giving longer time to pay, or a premium for the guarantee to make it binding upon the guarantor. Hence our advice is,

I. *Place no dependence on promises of guarantee of a credit already given, unless there is a consideration for the promise.*—If A purchases goods of B, and I promise to guarantee the debt, it is not binding upon me in law without some consideration, no matter in what express words my promise was made, nor what the fulness of proof of the promise may be. The only exception to this rule is where the credit was originally given *at the surety's request*, though without promise of guarantee, and he afterwards expressly promises to become liable for it.

II. *When you have acted upon or availed yourself of the guarantor's promise, given in letters of credit or otherwise, use reasonable diligence to notify him of your acceptance of his guarantee.*—There are numerous instances on record in which persons have been most egregiously deceived by a neglect of this precaution.—A notice to the surety of acceptance has, in many cases, been considered essential to the validity of the guarantee. But aside from this, it is an act of justice to the surety, so that he may know to what extent he is bound, and be able to watch over his debtor, and in season take such counter securities as may be useful to him.

III. *If you intend to rely upon a guarantee, do not be satisfied with any thing less than a positive promise of guarantee.*—A mere declaration of confidence or intentions, however favorable to the debtor, or saying that if such a one should wish to purchase, you would be willing to guarantee, does not amount to a guarantee. A promise of guarantee to be valid, by the statute laws of most of the States, must be in writing, and signed by the surety.

IV. *In determining contracts of suretyship, always adopt a strict construction, that is, do not suppose that they contain any thing more than the words plainly and clearly express.*—It is frequently important to know whether a guarantee be a temporary or a continuing one. A surety engages to become responsible for another to the amount of five hundred dollars: Is this guarantee terminated after that amount is trusted, or does it continue as long as that amount, credited from time to time, remains unpaid? The rule is that you are not to construe any guarantee to be a continuing one, unless it be so in express terms, or by necessary implication. If a guarantee be made to A, B, & Co., for the payment of a debt or the faithful behavior of a clerk, it is not binding upon the surety in the hands of A and B after the copartnership of A, B, & Co. has been dissolved. Adopt a strict construction.

V. Creditors should always use diligence in collecting the debt from the debtor, and should be especially careful that they do not, by giving time to the debtor, or releasing his debt, or destroying any of the collateral securities they may have, impair the right of immediate redress by the surety, or he will be discharged.

VI. *When, as surety, you take a bond of indemnity as counter security, see that it contains two stipulations—one that the debtor shall pay or perform the obligation required, and another, that you shall be indemnified against loss.*—If it contain only the indemnity, and not the performance clause, it cannot be made available until after you have paid the suretyship contract; but if it contain both these stipulations, you can proceed against the debtor as soon as the creditor can proceed against you.

Amongst the most common forms of suretyship are

LETTERS OF CREDIT.

Letters of credit are of two sorts, general and special; and both are given to furnish persons, when travelling, with cash, as their occasions may require. They are commonly open or unsealed, and contain an order from the writer to his correspondent, to furnish the bearer with a certain or an unlimited sum. The difference between them is, that the former is directed to the writer's friends at all the places where the traveller may come; the other to some particular friend, making himself responsible for the payment of whatever moneys shall be advanced, in compliance with the credit given on producing a receipt or a bill of exchange, which he thinks proper to have from the person credited. If any money be advanced on either species of these letters, and bills of exchange given for the sum on the person who wrote them, he is obliged to accept and pay the same. As the giver of these letters is thus responsible for the punctual repayment of the money advanced, he ought to be very cautious to whom he gives them, as in the hands of a dishonest person they may prove his ruin; and, as the person who requests can easily calculate what amount of cash he is likely to want, I think the compliment, for it can be nothing else, of an unbounded credit, should be excused, being really of no service either to him that pays or him that receives it. Advice by post, should always follow a letter of credit, and a duplicate of it accompany such advice; and it would be prudent therein to describe the bearer, with as many particulars as may be requisite, lest he should lose or be robbed of his credentials, and a stranger reap the benefit of them.

These letters are written in various forms, and though a copy may be superfluous to most persons, yet it may be serviceable to some:—

PHILADELPHIA, *August* 25, 1852.

SIR—This is to accompany Mr. Asher M. Wright, and to request you will furnish him with two hundred pounds sterling (*or with as much cash as he shall require of you,* if you give an unlimited credit); for which, please take his bills on me, or on any other upon whom he shall think proper to draw them: and I hereby engage for their punctual discharge, and remain, Sir,

Yours, respectfully,

ENOS M. JONES.

To Mr. SAMUEL F. PRINCE,
Merchant, *Liverpool.*

In a case, where A and B addressed a letter of credit to C, saying: "If D wishes to take goods from you on credit, we are willing to lend our names as security for any amount he may wish," and D took goods from C, on credit several times, for which he paid; but about a year afterwards, took another parcel of goods on credit, for which he gave his note to C, which was not paid: It was held that the letter of credit did not extend beyond the first parcel of goods delivered to D, and that A and B were not liable for an indefinite time, but only for an indefinite amount for one time. (8 *Johns. Rep.* 119.)

Where a person gives a letter of credit to A, addressed to B & Co., by which he authorizes A to draw bills to a certain amount on B & Co., and B & Co. having dissolved their partnership, A draws a bill on B, who accepts it, the guarantor is not liable to B on his letter of credit. (16 *Johns. Rep.* 100.)

A, of New York, gave a letter of credit to B, addressed to C in Albany, requesting C to deliver goods to B on the best terms, to a certain amount. C, instead of delivering the goods himself, gave B a letter to D in Geneva, requesting him to deliver goods to the amount, and engaging to be responsible, and D accordingly delivered the goods to B. In an action brought by C against A for the amount, it was held, that the engagement of A to C did not make him answerable for goods furnished by any other person. A surety is not answerable beyond the scope of his engagement. (10 *Johns. Rep.* 180.)

LAW OF PARTNERSHIP.

Partnership is a contract of two or more persons to place their money, effects, labor, and skill, or some or all of them, in lawful commerce or business, and to divide the profit and bear the loss in certain proportions. The two leading principles of the contract are, a common interest in the stock of the company, and a personal responsibility for the partnership engagements. The common interest of the partners applies to all the partnership property, whether vested in the first instance by their several contributions to the common stock, or afterwards acquired in the course of the partnership business: and that property is first liable for the debts of the company, and after they are paid, and the partnership dissolved, then it is subject to a division among the members or their representatives, according to agreement. If one person advances funds, and another furnishes his personal services or skill, in carrying on a trade, and is to share in the profits, it amounts to a partnership. But each party must engage to bring into the common stock something that is valuable: and a mutual contribution of that which has value and can be appreciated, is the essence of the contract. There must be a communion of profit to constitute a partnership as between the parties. They must not be jointly concerned in the purchase only, but jointly concerned in the future sale.

A participation in the loss or profit, or holding himself out to the world as a partner, so as to induce others to give credit on that assurance, renders a person responsible as a partner.

There is a just and marked distinction between partnership as respects the public, and partnership as respects the parties; and a person may be liable as a partner to third persons, although the agreement does not create a partnership between the parties themselves. It is a fundamental doctrine of the law, that though the person to be charged contributes neither money nor time, nor receives any part of the profits, yet, if he lends his name as partner, or suffers his name to continue in the firm after he has ceased to be an actual partner, he is responsible to third persons as a partner. *Dormant partners*, when discovered, are equally liable as if their names had appeared in the firm, although they were unknown to be partners at the time of the creation of the debt. Each individual member of a firm is answerable, *in solido*, for the whole amount of the partnership debts, without reference to the proportion of his interest, or to the nature of the stipulation between him and his associates; but special partners in a limited partnership, established in conformity with the statute law of the States where it is allowed, are liable only to the extent of the funds furnished.

It is a general and well-established principle, that when a person joins a partnership as a member, he does not, without a special promise, assume the previous debts of the firm, nor is he bound by them. To render persons jointly liable upon a contract as partners, they must have a joint interest contemporary with the formation of the contract. If, however, goods are purchased in pursuance of a previous agreement between two or more persons, that one of them should purchase the goods on joint account, in a foreign adventure, they are all answerable to the seller for the price as partners, even though their names were not announced to the seller; for the previous agreement made the partnership precede the purchase, and a joint interest attached in the goods at the instant of the purchase. (3 *Kent*, 36.)

I. Our advice is, first—*Be cautious in the selection of a partner.*—By entering into partnership each party reposes confidence in the other, and constitutes him his general agent as to all the partnership concerns: hence, the act of one, whenever it has the appearance of being on behalf of the firm, is considered as the act of the rest.

One partner can buy and sell partnership effects, and make contracts in reference to the business of the firm, and pay and receive, draw and indorse, and accept, bills and notes.

The act of one partner, though on his private account, and contrary to the private arrangement among themselves, will bind all the partners if made without knowledge in the other party of the arrangement, and in a matter which, according to the usual course of dealing, has reference to the business transacted by the firm.

In all contracts concerning negotiable paper, the act of one partner binds all; and even though he signs his individual name, provided it appears on the face of the paper to be on partnership account, and to be intended to have a joint operation. (1 *Camp. N. P.* 384.) But if a bill or note be drawn by one partner, in his name only, and without appearing to be on partnership account, the partnership is not bound by the signature, even though it was made for a partnership purpose. If, however, the bill be drawn by one partner, in his own name upon the firm, on partnership account, the act of drawing has been held to amount, in judgment of law, to an acceptance of the bill by the drawer, in behalf of the firm, and to bind the firm as an accepted bill. (5 *Day's Rep.* 511.) Even if the paper was made in a case which was not in its nature a partnership transaction, yet it will bind the firm if it was done in the name of the firm, and there be evidence that it was done under its express or implied sanction. But if partnership security be taken from one partner, without the previous knowledge or consent of the others, for a debt which the creditor knew at the time was the private debt of the particular partner, it would be a fraudulent transaction, and clearly void in respect to the partnership. So if from the subject-matter of the contract, or the course of dealing of the partnership, the creditor was chargeable with constructive knowledge of that fact, the partnership is not liable.

If, however, the negotiable paper of a firm be given by one partner on his private account, and that paper issued within the general scope of the authority of the firm, passes into the hands of a *bona fide* holder, who has no notice, either actually or constructively, of the consideration of the instrument; or if one partner should purchase, on his private account, an article in which the firm dealt, or which had an immediate connection with the business of the firm, a different rule applies, and one which requires the knowledge of its being a private and not a partnership transaction to be brought home to the claimant. (3 *Kent,* 44.)

One partner may *pledge* as well as sell the partnership effects in a case free from collusion, if done in the usual mode of dealing, and it has relation to the trade in which the partners are engaged, and when the pawnee had no knowledge that the property was partnership property. And if one partner acts fraudulently with strangers in a transaction within the scope of the partnership authority, the firm is nevertheless bound by the contract.

It is a general principle of law that one partner cannot bind a firm by deed, but nevertheless, he may by deed execute the ordinary release of a debt belonging to the copartnership, and thereby bar the firm of a right which it possessed jointly.

II. It is always advisable, though not essential that articles of copartnership should be formally drawn up, and they should specify the commencement and intended duration of the partnership; the kind of business to be pursued; the proportion of capital to be brought in; the manner in which the gains and losses are to be divided: whether interest is to be charged on capital, and at what rate: the allowance which the copartners may withdraw yearly for their private use and the disposition which is to be made of the joint property in the event of a dissolution.

III. *Insert in your copartnership agreements an article against the copartners becoming bound as surety or otherwise during the copartnership, except for the business of the firm.*—A violation of this stipulation gives the right to dissolve the copartnership.—This stipulation is exceedingly useful; not that any such contracts of suretyship bind the firm, for ordinarily they do not, and, being private stipulations between the parties, they do not affect the public; but this article acts as a salutary restraint upon the copartners, especially the younger members of houses, from the indulgence of a heedless kindness, and relieves them from solicitations for favors which it is often difficult to refuse and always wrong to grant.

IV. *Be certain to specify in your articles of copartnership what disposition is to be made of the joint property in the event of a dissolution.*—This is the most important of all the stipulations, and it is one of the first dictates of prudence to provide at the commencement of the union, when there is mutual confidence and good feeling between the parties, and when the uncertainty as to which party shall fall under the adverse operations of any stipulations, insures the adoption of such as are mutually and reciprocally just for the disposition of the property in the event of a dissolution; an event upon which it becomes so peculiarly situated, from the equal and conflicting rights of dissenting owners that the only administration of it which the law can sanction, is to take it from all.

V. *When the partnership is dissolved, give due notice of its dissolution in one of the usual advertising gazettes of the place where the business was carried on, and an actual and express notice to all who previously had dealings with the firm.*—Without this the partners may still act in the name of the firm, and create liabilities on its members in favor of all who shall not be actually proved to have had notice of dissolution.

If a partnership be formed for a single purpose or transaction, it ceases as soon as the business is completed. A partnership may be dissolved by the *voluntary act of the parties, or of one of them,* and by the *death, insanity, or bankruptcy of either,* and by *judicial decree,* or by such a change in the condition of one of the parties as disables him to perform his part of the duty.

It is an established principle in the law of partnership, that, if it be without any definite period, a partner may withdraw at a moment's notice, when he pleases, and dissolve the partnership; and even if the partners have formed a partnership by articles, for a definite period, it is now considered that each party may, by giving due notice, dissolve the partnership, as to all future capacity of the firm to bind him by contract. The only consequences of such a revocation of the partnership power, in the intermediate time, would be that the partner would subject himself to a claim of damages for a breach of the covenant.

When a partnership is actually ended, by death, notice, or other effectual mode, no person can make use of the joint property, in the way of trade, or inconsistently with the purpose of settling the affairs of the partnership, and winding up the concern. One partner cannot indorse bills and notes previously given to the firm, nor accept a bill previously drawn on it, so as to bind it. If the paper was even indorsed before the dissolution, and not put into circulation until afterwards, all the partners must unite in putting it into circulation, in order to bind them.

LAW OF INTEREST.

Where there is no contract, express or implied, for the payment of interest, it is not allowed on the price of goods sold, even though a certain day is fixed for payment—nor on the price of work and labor—nor on money lent—nor on money paid for the use of another—nor on money received for the use of another—nor on a balance struck on an account for goods sold. Interest is not due on a written instrument, unless it is expressed in the instrument that interest was intended to be paid, or such interest is implied. Interest may be implied from the usage of trade, or the dealings between parties; and it is always implied in mercantile instruments, as bills and promissory notes, after the time they ought to have been paid. If a note or bill, payable at a given time after date, be for a specified sum, "bearing interest," these entitle the holder to interest from date Without these words, the holder is entitled to interest from the day of maturity. Interest, however, is not then allowed, if the delay in payment is caused by the default of the holder.

If a bill be by the acceptor, payable at a particular place, the acceptor will not be liable for interest without proof of presentment at that place.

With regard to the time to which interest is to be computed—it is, in general, to be carried down to the time when final judgment may be signed.

Interest may be recovered from a banker, on money deposited in his bank by a customer, on its being proved to be the custom of the bank to allow it. (8 *Taunt.* 250.)

A man who holds money as an agent or banker, bound to produce it at a moment's notice to the depositor, is not liable to pay interest, if he makes it. But an agent who makes interest from money that it is his duty to pay over, is liable for interest.

A stakeholder is answerable for the loss, and hence entitled to any advantage; and it has been decided, that an auctioneer is a mere stakeholder. (5 *Burr*, 2639.)

If the purchaser pay part of the purchase-money to an auctioneer, and the vendor is not able to complete the contract, the purchaser is entitled to recover interest from the latter on the deposit, from the time the purchase should have been completed. (1 *Esp.* 268.)

The payment of interest on a legacy, commences, generally, *from a year* after the testator's death. (7 *Ves. Jr.* 96.)

A Rule for computation of Interest when partial payments have been made—Compute the interest on the principal to the time of the first payment, and if the payment exceed this interest, add the interest to the principal, and from the sum subtract the payment: the remainder forms a new principal. But if the payment be less than the interest, take no notice of it until other payments are made, which in all shall exceed the interest computed to the time of the *last* payment: then add the interest so computed to the principal and from the sum subtract the sum of the payments: the remainder will form a new principal, on which interest is to be computed as before. (2 *Johns. Chan. Rep.* 209.)

MISCELLANEOUS ADVICE.

I. If you receive an account current, from your creditor, and intend to dispute it, make your objections within a reasonable time after its receipt.

In the mercantile world, an account current, not objected to in the course of two or three posts after it is received, is deemed to be agreed to, and this understanding is regarded in the investigation of mercantile accounts in a court of equity. (Sherman *v.* Sherman, 2 *Vern.* 276.)

II. Never make advances on a bill of lading without an inspection of the letter of advice which accompanied it.

It is a well-established principle in law that a factor cannot pledge the goods of his principal; and the best evidence that one can have, whether he is dealing with a factor or a vendee, is the letter of advice which accompanies the bill of lading.

III. If you are the creditor in cases of guarantee or suretyship, it is your interest that the surety should unite with the debtor in a joint obligation. Under this form of contract, you can immediately proceed against both parties in the same legal proceeding. But if you are the surety, it is to your interest to enter into a separate contract, stipulating that the debtor shall do the act in question. Here notice must be given you of the debtor's default, and the creditor will have to enforce the obligation by two independent proceedings.

IV. If you are appointed executor or administrator, deduct the charges of administration from the amount of assets in your hands; for if you pay out all the money arising from the personal estate, you cannot obtain a licence to sell the real estate to pay the expenses of administration.

V. If two or more persons enter into an agreement for the purchase of an estate, an article should be inserted as between themselves, that in case default is made in either to pay his part of the purchase money, and the other pay it for him, he shall be entitled to call upon the vendor for a conveyance of the entire estate to hold as security for repayment—as it is considered he will not otherwise have a lien on the estate for his money.

VI. In purchasing an estate where the principal lives at a distance, the purchaser should take a covenant from the attorney, that the power is not revoked—that covenant to remain in force until the deed be confirmed by the principal.

VII. A partner assigning his share to the other, on dissolution of partnership, must—as they are joint tenants—use the word "*release.*" It is considered that word alone can pass the whole interest.

VIII. In an action to recover money due on a bond, the action must be brought in the name of the original obligee, notwithstanding the assignment, therefore, a power of an attorney to sue in his name should always be inserted in the assignment.

IX. On an assignment of a *chose in action* notice of the assignment by a copy, or a full and clear statement of it, should be given to the debtor.

FUNDAMENTAL LEGAL PRINCIPLES.

1. That which is originally void, does not by lapse of time become valid.

If an infant or married woman make a will and publish the same, and die of full age or single, it is still void. A will of a married woman made before marriage will not survive on the husband's death.

2. A personal right of action dies with the person.

3. The law compels no one to do impossibilities.

4. No one shall be twice vexed for one and the same cause.

5. The greater contains the less.

In an action for battery, and maiming is proved, it is well, because it is battery and more.

6. The law favors things which are in the custody of the law.

7. The husband and wife are one person.

8. Every act shall be taken most strongly against the maker.

If I plant land with corn, and lease it for years, the corn belongs to the lessee if I do not except it.

9. When two titles concur, the elder should be preferred.

10. Agreements overrule the law.

11. He who derives the advantage ought to sustain the burden.

12. No man shall take advantage of his own wrong.

13. Where the right is equal, the claim of the party in actual possession shall prevail.

14. He has the better title who was first in point of time.

15. A right of action cannot arise out of fraud.

16. It is fraud to conceal fraud.

17. The law assists those who are vigilant and not those who sleep over their rights.

18. Ignorance of the law excuses no one.

19. Who does not oppose what he might oppose, seems to consent.

20. When contrary laws come in question, the inferior law must yield to the superior; the law general to the law special; an old law to a new law; man's laws to God's laws.

A LIST

OF A FEW OF

THE WHOLESALE HOUSES.

A 1 IN THEIR RESPECTIVE BRANCHES IN THE CITY OF PHILADELPHIA.

Compiled for the Convenience of Country Merchants, Young Men Commencing Business, and all desirous of having their orders faithfully filled.

Also, Architects, Hotels, Insurance Companies, &c.

To make this partly a Reference Book for purchasers, I have compiled the following list embracing a *few* of the *best* houses in the respective branches of business mentioned, and I think that country merchants and purchasers generally will consult their own interests by noting them on their memorandum, and giving them a call before purchasing, as I have confidence they will find them not only able to supply a wide public demand for the articles in which they deal, and on the most favorable terms, but also *liberal, polite, and possessing the qualities that constitute good merchants.*

Importers.

STUART & BROTHER, (British Dry-Goods by the Package), 13 Bank St., and 14 Strawberry St.

CHARLES COLLADAY (Buttons, Trimmings, Bindings, &c., Agent for the Manufacturers), 35 Church Alley.

WRAY & GRAHAM (British and French Dry-Goods by Package,) 14 Church Alley.

NICHOLAS WOLFF (German Dry Goods, Cloths, Velvets, Hosiery, Gloves, &c.), 20 Church Alley.

Importers & Commission Merchants.

F. V. KRUG & CO. (Agents for Cohoes, N. B., Saxony Mills, Troy and Philadelphia Woollen Shirts and Drawers; Germantown Woollen Hosiery, Comforts, Hoods, &c.), 6 and 8 Church Alley.

HART & MITCHELL, (Shirts, Drawers, Cravats, &c.,) 32 and 34 Bank Street.

WRAY & GILLILAN, (British, French, and Scotch Goods,) 41 Chestnut Street.

Importers.

P. BRADY & CO. (British & French Goods), N. W. corner of Front and Chestnut Sts.

E. M. DAVIS & CO. (French and India Silk Goods, Gloves, &c.,) 183 Broadway, New York, and in Philadelphia, at 16 Strawberry st. and 15 Bank St.

ROBERT EWING, (Importer of Britsh Dry Goods, and Commission Merchant), 31 Chestnut St.

HENRY FARNUM & CO. (Foreign Dry Goods), 12 Chestnut St.

LEWIS, BROTHERS & CO. (French, Italian, and Swiss Goods), 80 Chestnut St.

LEWIS & CO. (British Dry Goods), 68 and 70 Market St.

LOTTIMER, LARGE, ELLERY & CO. (White Goods, Laces, Hosiery, Embroideries, and French Goods), 80 Chestnut St. (Jayne's Building.)

WILLIAM McKEE & CO. (Irish Linens and British Dry Goods,) 20 S. Front St.

GEORGE PEARCE & CO. (Lace Goods, Embroideries, &c.) 85 Chestnut St. Philadelphia, and 58 Broadway New York.

GEORGE B. REESE, (British Dry Goods), 70 Chestnut St.

STEEGMANN, BRITTAN & CO. (Laces, White Goods, and Embroideries,) 70 Chestnut St.

THOMPSON, POTTER & KEMBLE, (Lace Goods and Embroieries), 179 Market St.

WM. WATSON & CO., (British and Irish Dry Goods by the Package,) 8 Chestnut St.

Commission Merchants. Dry Goods.

DAVID S. BROWN & CO. (American Manufactured Goods), 38 & 40 S. Front st.

BROOKS & ROACH, (Philadelphia Manufactured Goods), 24 Chestnut

H. L. CARSON, (Philadelphia and Rhode Island Linseys), 12 S. Front

C. W. CHURCHMAN, (Foreign and Domestic Goods), 30 S. Front St.

FARNHAM, KIRKHAM & CO., (American Cotton and Woolen Goods), 34 S. Front st.

J. C. HOWE & CO. (Manchester Print Works, M. de Laines, Prints,) 82 Chestnut St

HACKER, LEA & CO. (American Manufactured Goods), 32 and 34 Chestnut st.

LAWRENCE, STONE & CO. Chestnut st. below Third.

MANDERSON & LAMMOT, (Foreign and American), 17 Chestnut st.

JOSEPH RIPKA, (Manufacturer of Fancy Cottonade, and a variety of other Pantaloon Stuffs), Warehouse 32 South Front st.

THOMAS P. REMINGTON, (American Manufactured Goods), 22 S. Front st.

SILL, ARNOLD & CO. (Woolen Dry Goods), 52 Chestnut st.

TREDICK, STOKES & CO. (Cotton and Woolen Goods), 18 S. Front st.

D. & J. TATEM, 23 Chestnut St.

THOMAS & MARTIN, (American Manufactured Goods), 10 North Front st.

TINGLEY, CALDWELL & ENGLISH 10 Chestnut st.

CHARLES H. WELLING, 18 Chestnut St.

WEST, FOBES & LLOYD, 41 Chestnut St.

WILSON, BROWN & CO. (American Manufactured Goods), 19 Chestnut St.

WOOD & ERRINGER, 37 Chestnut St.

WOOD, FULLER & WELLS, (Foreign and American), 88 Chestnut.

BANGS & MAXWELL, 14 S. Front.

Commission Merchants. General.

THOMAS ALLIBONE & CO. (Naval Stores and Cotton), 63 N. Water St., and 32 N. Wharves.

BUCKNOR, McCAMMON & CO. (Tobacco Warehouse), 41 N. Water St.

A. G. CATTELL & CO. (Grain, Seed, and Iron), 13 N. Wharves.

DANENHOWER & HARRIS, (Tobacco), 45 N. Front St.

LE FEVRE, BLACK & CO. (Flour, Grain, and Western Produce), 71 S. Wharves.

McCUTCHEON & COLLINS, (Provisions and Produce generally), S. W. corner of Front and New Sts.

GEORGE McHENRY & CO. (Shipping and General), 37 Walnut St.

ROWLEY, ASHBURNER & CO. (Oils, and Naval Stores), 14 N. Wharves, and 25 N. Water St.

A. & J. WRIGHT, (Flour Factors, and Salt Dealers), Vine St. Wharf.

Commission Merchants. Wool.

EDWARDS & JENNESS, 6 N. Front St.
COATES & BROWN, 43 Market St.
BENJAMIN BULLOCK & CO. 32 N. Third St.
KIMBER, HENRY & CO. 74 N. Front St.
REECE & SEAL, 18 N. Front St.

Importers and Jobbers. Dry Goods.

BARCROFT, BEAVER & CO. (also CLOTHING), 163 Market St.
BUCK, MORGAN & STIDFOLE, 113 Market St. below Third.
DEAL, MILLIGAN & CO. (also CLOTHING), S. W. corner of Market and Sixth Sts.
FITHIAN, JONES & CO. (FOREIGN AND DOMESTIC), 77 Market St. and No. 4 Church Alley.
FASSITT & CO. 48 Market St.
HAMMAN, SNYDER & CO. 146 Market St.
HOOD & CO. 189 Market St., 5th door below Fifth St.
HOSKINS, HIESKILL & CO. N. W. corner of Market and Fifth Sts.
LIPPINCOTT & PARRY, (CLOTHS, CASSIMERES, VESTINGS, &c.), S. W. corner of Market and Second Sts.
JAMES, KENT, SANTEE, & CO. (FOREIGN AND DOMESTIC), 147 N. Third St.
MILLER & LYON, (BRITISH, FRENCH, AND AMERICAN), 95 Market St.
McFARLAND, EVANS & CO. (FOREIGN AND DOMESTIC DRY GOODS), 105 Market St., and 34 Church Alley, between Second and Third Sts.
REED, BROTHERS & CO. (also CLOTHING), 177 and 177½ Market St., above Fourth, (north side).
RAIGUEL & CO. 128 and 130 N. Third St.
SEXTON, SEAL & SWEARINGEN, (also FANCY DRY GOODS), No. 11 S. Fourth St.
SMITH, MURPHY & CO. 97 Market.
T. SHARPLESS & SONS, 32 S. Second and 21 Strawberry St.
SIEGER, LAMB & CO. 49 N. Third St.
SPARHAWK, DUNTON & WURTS, 92 Market St.
SCOTT, BAKER & CO. 150 Market St.
TAYLOR & PAULDING, 96 Market.
TEMPLE & BARKER, 161 Market.
WAINWRIGHT, HUNTINGDON, & FLOYD, 152 Market St., and 23 Merchant St.
J. T. WAY & CO. 81 Market St., and 10 Church Alley.
WOOD, BACON & CO. (also CLOTHING), 127 Market St.
WOOD & OLIVER, 131 Market St.

Importers and Jobbers of Silks and Fancy Dry-Goods.

BUNN, RAIGUEL & CO. (FOREIGN AND AMERICAN DRY GOODS), 91 N. Third St.
INSKEEP, SHAKELFORD & McKEE, 124 Market St.
SIBLEY, MOLTEN & WOODRUFF, 118 Market St.
WOOD, COREY & WOOD, N. W. corner of Fourth and Market Sts.
YARD, GILMORE & CO. (FANCY DRY GOODS, WHITE AND LACE GOODS) 12 N. Third St.

Importers of Fancy Dry-Goods.

McFADDEN & GASS, (RIBBONS, LACE GOODS, EMBROIDERIES, HOSIERY, TRIMMINGS, &c.), 7 Bank St.
E. GRUNDY, (DRY GOODS, SMALL WARES, &c.), 16 Church Alley.
THOMAS MELLOR, (IMPORTER OF HOSIERY, GLOVES, AND TRIMMINGS,) 4 N. Third St.

MARPLE, ELLIS & McCLURE, (Hosiery and Trimmings,) 15 N. Third.
MECKE & LEPPIEN, (German Dry Goods, Belgian Cloths, &c.), 26 S. Second, and 17 Strawberry Sts.
R. G. ORWIG, (Fancy Dry Goods, Hosiery and Trimmings), 108 N. Third St.

Importers and Jobbers. Fancy Goods.

BEDELL & PEARCE, (Hosiery, Gloves, Trimmings, &c.), 57 N. Third St., one door below Arch, (lower side).
LIND, BROTHER & CO. 10 S. Fourth St., corner of Merchant.
OLIVER MARTIN & CO. (also Hosiery, Gloves, Trimmings, &c.) 24 N. Fourth St.
W. H. HORSTMANN & SONS, (also Manufacturers), 51 N. Third St.
POWELL, HAZLETT & CO. 140½ Market St., and 9 Merchant St.
SCHAFFER, ROBERTS & CO. 187 Market St.
SELLERS, SITER & CO. (also Hosiery, Gloves, Trimmings, &c.), 135 Market St.
JAMES SMITH & SONS, (Genuine Needles; Henry Walton, the Agent), 83 Market St.
R. & G. A. WRIGHT, 23 S. Fourth St., below Market.

.SHNELL & TULL'S Children's Velocipede, Coach, Gig, and Barouche Manufactory, 64 Dock St., above Second.
LOUIS C. BAUERSACHS, (Importer of French, English and German Fancy Goods and Toys,) 170 Market St.
FRANCIS, FIELD & FRANCIS, (Manufacturers of Tin Toys, Block-tin Ware, Plain and Japanned), No. 80 N. Second St.
VOGT & ZOLLIKOFER, (Importers of French China, Glass Ware, Fancy Goods, Toys, &c.), 205 Market St., (up stairs).

F. H. SMITH, (Manufacturer of Pocket Books, Porte Monnaies, Rose Wood Writing Desks, Dressing Cases, and Work Boxes), 205 Arch St., one door below Sixth.

Importers and Dealers in Foreign and Domestic Hardware and Cutlery.

MARTIN BUEHLER, BROTHER & CO. 195 Market St. (north side) secone door below Fifth.
CONRAD & ROBERTS, 123 North Third St.
JAMES J. DUNCAN & CO., 177½ Market St., between Fourth & Fifth.
FIELD & LANGSTROTH, 166 Market St.
FAUST & WINEBRENER, 68½ N. Third St., above Arch.
HEATON & DENCKLA, (American and Foreign Hardware Commission Merchants), 33 Commerce St.
JUSTICE, STEINMETZ & JUSTICE, Fifth and Commerce St.
KAY & DEHAVEN, 185 Market St., (north side), between Fourth and Fifth.
NEWLIN & MARSHALLS, (Importers of Hardware and Guns, and Dealers in Domestic Hardware), 151 Market St.
ERASMUS C. PRATT & BROTHER, (Importers of Needles, Fish Hooks Steel Pens, &c.), 28 Bank St.
SHIELDS & MILLER, 79 N. Third St.

S. H. BIBIGHAUS, (Manufacturer of Planes), 166 N. Third St.
WILLIAM M. McCLURE & BROTHER, (Building Hardware and Tools, Exclusively), 287 Market
TRUMAN & SHAW, (Housekeeping and Builders' Hardware, also, PLATFORM SCALES), 333 Market St., below Ninth.

Grocers.

BAGALEY, WOODWARD & CO., 221 Market St.
JOHN BROCK, SONS & CO. 97 and 99 N. Third St.
J. HARDING, Jr., 29 and 31 S. Front St., 28 and 30 S. Water St.
JAMES H. & THOMAS HART, 229 N. Third St.
GEO. LIPPINCOTT & CO. 17 North Water St., and 10 N. Wharves.
ROSS & DARLING, 129 N. Third St.
WATERMAN & OSBOURN, N. W. corner of Second and Arch (or Mulberry) Sts.

CALEB CLOTHIER, (FAMILY FLOUR DEALER), 35 N. Fifth St.

Drugs. Importers and Wholesale Dealers.

FREDERICK BROWN, (COMPOUNDER OF PHYSICIANS' PRESCRIPTIONS, AND ALL PHARMACEUTICAL PREPARATIONS and sole Manufacturer of BROWN'S ESSENCE OF JAMAICA GINGER), N. E. corner of Fifth and Chestnut.

BULLOCK & CRENSHAW, (IMPORTERS OF ENGLISH, FRENCH, AND GERMAN DRUGS, CHEMICALS, AND CHEMICAL WARES), N. E. corner of Sixth and Arch Sts.

G. W. CARPENTER & CO. 301 Market St.

COLLINS & ANDERSON, 27 South Fourth St., below Market.

CHARLES ELLIS & CO. (DRUGGISTS AND MANUFACTURING CHEMISTS), 56 Chestnut St. LABORATORY Sixth & Morris St.

FRENCH & RICHARDS, (also IMPORTERS OF FRENCH PLATE, and Agents for American Window Glass), N. W. corner 10th and Market Sts.

B. A. FAHNESTOCK & CO. (PROPRIETORS OF B. A. FAHNESTOCK'S VERMIFUGE), 52 Market St.

THOMAS P. JAMES, 212 Market St., (a few doors above the Red Lion Hotel).

JENKS & OGDEN, (IMPORTERS AND WHOLESALE DEALERS IN DRUGS, ACIDS, DYE STUFFS, AND CHEMICALS), No. 106 N. Third St., 3 doors below Race.

CHARLES D. KNIGHT, (WHOLESALE AGENT FOR TILDEN & CO.'S VEGETABLE EXTRACTS, and Dealer in HERBS, ROOTS, PLANTS, and BOTANIC MEDICINES), No. 7 S. Sixth St.

LINN, SMITH & CO. 8 S. Third St.

D. L. MILLER, JR., (also ACIDS, AND CHEMICALS GENERALLY), 56 South Front St.

JOHN M. MARIS & CO. (DRUGS, MEDICINES, DYE STUFFS, &c.), 9 S. Third St.

MOYER & HAZARD, (SUCCESSORS TO A. FULLERTON), 174 Market St.

T. MORRIS PEROT, (DRUGS, MEDICINES, CHEMICALS, &c.), 19 N. Fourth St., above Market.

GEORGE K. SMITH & CO. (also IMPORTERS OF SALTPETRE AND SULPHUR), 294 and 296 N. Second St.

JAMES H. SPRAGUE, (also IMPORTER AND DEALER IN WINDOW AND PICTURE GLASS OF EVERY DESCRIPTION: Zinc and other Paints), 33 and 35 N. Fourth St., (east side).

C. & J. L. SCHAFFER, 215 Market.

ROBERT SHOEMAKER & CO., (WHOLESALE DRUGGISTS, AND IMPORTERS OF FRENCH, ENGLISH AND BELGIAN, COLORED, ENAMELED, PLATE, AND CROWN GLASS, FRENCH WHITE ZINC, &c.), No. 354 North Second St. corner of Green.

WETHERILL & BROTHER, 65 N. Front St.

GEORGE D. WETHERILL & CO. (IMPORTERS OF DRUGS AND CHEMICALS, AND DEALERS IN PAINTS, OILS, GLASS, &c.), 56 N. Front St.

ALFRED WILTBERGER, (also PURE GROUND COLORS, VARNISHES, &c. Country Dealers supplied on reasonable Terms), 169 N. Second St.

BREINIG, FRONEFIELD & CO. (Proprietors of the only genuine and scientific vegetable CATTLE POWDER and LINIMENT), 187 N. Third St.

Boots, Shoes, and Straw Goods.

BOKER, BROTHER & JONES, 82 Market St.

BRODHEAD & ROBERTS, 135 N. Third St.

CONRAD, THOMPSON & CO., 60 Market St.

WILLIAM DULTY, 98 Market St.

HADDOCK, REED & CO. 164 and 166 Market St.

HENDRY, COOPER & CO., Third and Arch Sts.

D. RODNEY KING, (MANUFACTURER OF LADIES', MISSES', AND CHILDREN'S SHOES), 152½ Market St., S. side, between Fourth and Fifth.

LEVICK, BROTHER & CO., 160 Market St.

J. C. &. J. LEVIS, 60 N. Third St.

J. W. McCURDY & SON, (WHOLESALE MANUFACTURERS OF LADIES', MISSES', AND CHILDRENS' BOOTS, SHOES AND GAITERS,) 111 Chestnut St. (up stairs).

J. MILES & SON, (WHOLESALE MANUFACTURERS OF LADIES', AND GENTLEMEN'S, FINE BOOTS AND SHOES,) 37 S. Fourth St.

RORER, GRAEFF & DARLING, 126 N. Third St.

RUCKMAN & PRICE, 144 N. Third.

J. & M. SAUNDERS, 28 N. Fourth St.

BENJAMIN STRATTAN, (LADIES' FANCY BOOT AND SHOE MANUFACTURER), 21 S. Fourth St.

WHELAN & CO. 175 Market St.

B. P. WILLIAMS & CO. 14 S. Fourth.

Clothiers.

BENNETT & CO. (TOWER HALL), 182 Market St.

GANS, LEBERMAN & CO. (WHOLESALE, (only); Merchants supplied on the most liberal terms), N. W. corner of Third and Market.

A. T. LANE & CO. (MEN AND BOYS' CLOTHING AT WHOLESALE), No. 171 Market St., above Fourth, (N. side).

JACOB REED'S (WHOLESALE AND RETAIL CLOTHING ROOMS), S. W. corner of Fifth and Market Streets. Country Merchants supplied on liberal terms.

REED, BRO'S. & CO. (U. S. CLOTHING EMPORIUM. MEN AND BOYS' CLOTHING), 177 and 177½ Market St, north side, above Fourth St.

WOLF, ARNOLD & NUSBAUM, 70½ N. Third St.

THE CRESCENT ONE PRICE CLOTHING STORE, (JONES & Co. PROPRIETORS), Market St., above Sixth.

WILLIAM CURTIS, (MASONIC AND ODD FELLOWS' REGALIA), Odd Fellows' Hall, Sixth St., below Race.

Architects.

S. D. BUTTON, 23 Merchants' Exchange.

JOSEPH C. HOXIE, 24 Merchants' Exchange.

NICHOLSON & WADSKIER, (AUTHORS AND PUBLISHERS OF THE "PRACTICAL SCULPTOR), Johnson's Building, 103 Walnut St.

Agricultural Implements Seeds, &c.

R. BUIST, (SEEDS AND TREES), 97 Chestnut St. above Third.

THOMAS F. CROFT & CO. (VEGETABLE, FLOWER, GRASS, AND FIELD SEEDS, FRUIT AND ORNAMENTAL TREES), 309 Market St.

H. A. DREER, (GARDEN, GRASS, AND FLOWER SEEDS, PLANTS, FRUIT TREES, GARDEN IMPLEMENTS, AND BOOKS), 59 Chestnut St.

PROUTY & BARRETT, 194½ Market.

C. B. ROGERS' SEED AND AGRICULTURAL WAREHOUSE, 29 Market St., Manufacturer and Dealer in all the most approved Agricultural and Horticultural Implements: Imported,and American Field and Garden Seeds: Fruit, Shade, and Ornamental Trees: Guano, Sup. Phos. Lime, Poudrette, &c.; Inventor and Manufacturer of the Cast Steel Extending Point Surface and Sub-soil Plough.

Books. Publishers.

LIPPINCOTT, GRAMBO & CO. (also BLANK BOOKS), 14 N. Fourth St.

THOMAS, COWPERTHWAIT & CO. 253 Market St.

CLARK & HESSER, (BOOKSELLERS, PUBLISHERS, AND BLANK BOOK MANUFACTURERS), 18 S. Fourth St. below Market.

C. G. HENDERSON & CO., SUCCESSORS TO G. S. APPLETON, (BOOKSELLERS, PUBLISHERS, AND IMPORTERS), Corner of Fifth and Arch Streets. Have always on hand and offer to the Bookbuying community upon the best terms, the largest assortment of American and Foreign Books, in every department of Literature.

⁂ Public and private Libraries, as well as Bookbuyers generally, supplied at low rates.

PARRISH, DUNNING & MEARS, (BOOKSELLERS AND STATIONERS), 30 N. Fourth St.

T. K. COLLINS, JR., (BOOKSELLER, AND PUBLISHER; FAMILY BIBLES AND MUSIC BOOKS), 8 N. Sixth St.

JOHN LOCKEN, (PUBLISHER OF BIBLES AND PRAYER BOOKS OF ALL SIZES), 311 Market St.

WM. G. MENTZ, (PUBLISHER OF GERMAN AND ENGLISH BOOKS). Also, Blank Book Manufacturer, No. 53 N. Third St.

MILLER & BURLOCK, (PUBLISHERS OF FAMILY AND POCKET BIBLES, in various styles of Binding; SOUTHERN HARMONY, etc.; also, BOOK-BINDERS), 22 N. Ninth St.

JOHN H. SIMON, (BOOKSELLER AND PUBLISHER,) 114 N. Third St. Also, Paper and Rag Warehouse, 234 N. Third St.

SOWER & BARNES, (BOOKSELLERS, STATIONERS, AND PUBLISHERS OF PELTON'S OUTLINE MAPS AND KEYS), 81 N. Third St.

Blank Book Manufacturers.

JAMES B. SMITH & CO. 207 Market St., above Fifth.

S. L. ADAMS, Manufactory 56 N. Third St., Stationery Store Callowhill St., above Eighth.

WM. M. CHRISTY, 65 S. Third St. opposite Girard Bank.

PARRISH, DUNNING & MEARS, 30 N. Fourth St.

PERRY & ERETY, (also STATIONERS), 63 N. Third St. (up stairs).

WM. PIERSON, (also STATIONER), 52 N. Fourth St.

Book-Binders.

JOHN F. DUCOMB, No. 7 Hart's Building, Sixth St. above Chestnut.

GEO. W. DONOHUE, (also BLANK BOOK MANUFACTURER), S. W. corner of Fourth St. and Appletree Alley.

JOHN LOCKEN, 311 Market St.

PAWSON & NICHOLSON, No. 23 Minor St. between Fifth and Sixth, below Market St.

BOOK-BINDERS' DIES, ROLES & STAMPS.

GASKILL, COPPER & FRY, (ENGRAVERS OF), 18 Minor St. Philadelphia. Book Binders' stock always on hand.

Blacking and Ink.

JOHN ANNEAR, (MANUFACTURER OF WOOTTEN & ANNEAR'S PREMIUM BLACKING,) 94 Spruce, & 13 N. 3d St.

WM. CURREY, (MANUFACTURER OF WELLAR'S PATENT JAPAN BLACKING, 8 Premiums received), 50 Chestnut St.

JAMES S. MASON & CO. (MASON'S BLACKING), 108 N. Front St.

RUSHTON & MEYERS, (ORIGINAL MAGIC BLACKING. Also, DRUGGISTS' TINWARE), 39 Strawberry St.

WELPLY & HILL, (BLACKING AND INK MANUFACTURERS), 61 S. Fifth St.

Brass Cock Manufacturers and Brass Founders.

H. BELFIELD, Willow and Ridge Road; also, Broad above Willow.

FRICK & GAUL, 364 N. Third St.

McCAMBRIDGE & FRY, 15 Cherry St below Fourth.

J. & H. JONES, 93 and 95 Arch St., below Third.

H. HOMER, 77 Race St. below Third.

BRASS KETTLES AND SHEET BRASS.

SAMUEL CROFT, (MANUFACTURER, 53 Commerce St.

Britannia Ware.

HALL & BOARDMAN, (MANUFACTURERS), 93 and 95 Arch St. below Third.

Bricks.

WHARTON & MATLACK, (MACHINE AND HAND-MADE: also Agents for Patent Rights of Culbertson & Scott's Brick Machine), 110 S. Front St.

Burning - Fluid, Camphene, and Alcohol.

HENRY C. CORFIELD, (MANUFACTURER OF BURNING FLUID, PINE OIL, AND LAMPS), No. 454 N. Second St. below Poplar.

EDWARD F. CORFIELD, (also IMPORTER AND DEALER IN FANCY GLASSWARE), 152 S. Second St, above Spruce.

DAVIS & CULIN, (also LAMPS, LANTERNS, CHANDELIERS, &c.), N. E. corner of Fourth and Cherry Sts., Phila.: Front St. above Market, Camden, N. J.

MURPHY'S, (also LAMPS, LANTERNS, CHANDELIERS, &c.), 311 Market St., and 27 South St.

LEWIS L. PECK, No. 15 Dock St.

R. W. PLUMMER & CO. (also DEODORIZED ALCOHOL, VINEGAR, &c.), 116 and 118 Queen St., Southwark.

JOHN W. RYAN, (also DEODORIZED ALCOHOL), Washington and Swanson Sts., Southwark. All articles warranted. Orders from the city or country promptly attended to.

YARNALL & CORFIELD, (MANUFACTURERS), 274 and 280 N. Third, above Noble St.

Manufacturing Chemists.

POWERS & WEIGHTMAN, (SULPHATE OF QUININE, &c.), S. W. corner of Ninth and Parrish Sts.

POWERS, WEIGHTMAN & HARRISON, (OIL OF VITRIOL, &c.), Office at Powers & Weightman's Ninth and Parrish Sts.

ROSENGARTEN & DENIS, (SULPHATE OF QUININE, &c.), N. W. corner of Vine and Schuylkill Seventh.

J. P. & WM. WETHERILL, (WHITE-LEAD AND CHEMICAL WORKS), West Philadelphia.

Collecting Agencies.

C. R. HAWES & CO. (PARTICULAR ATTENTION PAID TO DOUBTFUL CLAIMS), 136 Market St.

WM. GOODRICH & CO. (MERCANTILE AGENCY), 116 Market St.

DAVID B. BIRNEY, (COMMISSIONER OF DEEDS FOR 29 STATES), 116 Market St.

Cigars, Tobacco, &c.

FRISHMUTH & BROTHERS, 105 N. Third St.

E. & A. KERN, N. E. corner of Third and Market Sts.

REINHOLD, DASH & CO. (WHOLESALE TOBACCO AND SEGAR WARE HOUSE), S. W. corner Third and Race.

A. STEVENSON, JR., 73 N. Third St.

Dental Depots.

JONES, WHITE & McCURDY, 116 Arch St. Philadelphia; 136 Broadway New York; 3½ Tremont Row, Boston.

Engravers.

WM. B. GIHON, (ENGRAVER ON WOOD) N. E. corner of Sixth and Chestnut.

C. T. HINCKLEY, (ENGRAVER ON WOOD), 66 S. Third St. (3d Story.)

WILLIAM G. MASON, (BUSINESS CARDS, SEALS, STOCK CERTIFICATES, AND ENGRAVING OF ALL DESCRIPTIONS), 46 Chestnut St. above Second.

J. & C. E. MAAS, (SEAL AND PLATE ENGRAVERS), 80½ Walnut St.

E. D. MARSHALL & CO. (CALICO ENGRAVERS), 6 Lagrange Place.

BANK NOTE ENGRAVERS AND PRINTERS.

DANFORTH, BALD & CO., No. 95½ Walnut St. Philadelphia; No. 1 Wall St. New York; No. 1 Gray's Building, Boston; Fourth St. near Walnut, Cincinnati. Original designs for Vignettes, and other embellishments furnished without charge.

TOPPAN, CARPENTER, CASILEAR & CO. 76½ Walnut St. Philadelphia; 29 Wall St. New York; Liberty Tree Building, corner of Washington and Essex Sts. Boston; N. W. corner of Third and Walnut Sts., Cincinnati.

Furniture Manufacturers.

W. & J. ALLEN, 136 S. Second St., below Dock.

GEORGE J. HENKELS, (PATENT EXTENSION DINING TABLE), 173 Chestnut St.

HART, WARE & CO. (COTTAGE) Store 280 Chestnut St.: Factory Twelfth and Buttonwood.

JAMES IRVINE, (STEAM TURNING, FANCY CABINET MAKING ESTABLISHMENT), 25 and 27 Dock St.

Furnishing Goods.

C. A. WALBORN & CO. (also GENTLEMEN'S FURNISHING), 7 and 9 N. Sixth Street.

WINCHESTER & SCOTT (GENTLEMEN'S FURNISHING) 172 Chestnut St. above Seventh.

THOMAS S. MOORE (IMPORTER AND DEALER) 5½ N. Second St., up stairs.

Gas-Fixtures, &c.

CORNELIUS, BAKER, & CO. (also LAMPS, CHANDELIERS, &c.), 176 Chestnut Street; Manufactory 131 Cherry Street.

HEIDRICK, HORNING & BROTHER, 221 N. Second Street, above Vine, Manufactory 86 Noble St.

Hardware, Guns, Cutlery, &c.

R. & W. C. BIDDLE & CO., 47 Market Street, Philadelphia, have constantly on hand Genuine Mouse-hole and W. Foster's Anvils, Blacksmith's Bellows, Vices, English and American Wagon-Boxes, Ames's & Rowland's Spades and Shovels, Beatty's and Butcher's Edge Tools, Butcher's and Greaves's Files and Tools, Pugh's Auger Bits, Rose & Son's Trowels, Wostenholm's and other Cutlery; which, with a full assortment of Hammered Pans, Brass Kettles, Horse Nails, Wrought Nails, Horseshoes, Hinges, Screws, Bolts, Locks, Planes, Rules, Tacks, Brads, Sparables, and Shelf Goods generally, will be sold at the lowest market prices, either by the Package or from the Shelves.

SPANG & WALLACE (FISHING AND FOWLING TACKLE of every description), 94 N. Third Street.

Glue, Sand-Paper, Hide-Whips, &c.

BODINE, BAEDER, & CO. (also EMERY AND SAND-PAPER, CURLED HAIR, &c.), 86 Market Street, Philadelphia; 235 Pearl Street, New York.

GERKER & BEEHLER (also CURLED HAIR, ISINGLASS AND BRISTLES), No. 20 Commerce Street, Philadelphia; 47 Vesey Street, New York.

GEORGE J. SCOTT (also CURLED HAIR, WAGON-WHIPS, CHAIR AND SOFA SPRINGS; Importer of Music Wire, and Piano Hardware), No. 9 N. Fifth Street, Philadelphia; 2 Platt Street, New York.

Gold Pens.

JONES & MORGAN (PROPRIETORS AND MANUFACTURERS OF WILLIAM FIFE'S PATENT OBLIQUE-POINTED GOLD PENS), 87 Tammany Street, and Corner of Third and Chestnut Sts.

CHARLES B. PEDDIE (MANUFACTURER OF GOLD PENS, GOLD AND SILVER PENCIL-CASES), S. E. Corner of Third and Chestnut Street.

OSMON REED (MANUFACTURER), 74 Market Street.

Hats and Caps.

BOWEN, COWELL, & CO., 176 Market Street.

C. H. GARDEN, 196 Market Street.

HENDERSON & TRIEBELS, 144 Market Street.

LASELL & BROTHER, 20 N. Fourth Street.

J. J. KOHLER, 138 N. Third Street (opposite the Eagle Hotel).

PRICE I. PATTON & CO., 118 Market Street.

JOHN C. YEAGER, 163 N. Third St.

Hotels.

GIRARD HOUSE, PRESBURY AND BILLINGS, Chestnut below Ninth Street.

JONES'S HOTEL, 152 Chestnut.

UNITED STATES, Chestnut between Fourth and Fifth.

FRANKLIN HOUSE, B. H. WOOLMAN (Terms $1 50 per day), Chestnut above Third.

AMERICAN HOTEL, WILLIAM HART CARR (Agent for the Proprietor, JOHN FATZINGER), opposite the Hall of Independence, Chestnut Street.

EAGLE HOTEL, DAVID STEM (Terms $1 per day), 139 North Third Street.

THE RIDGWAY HOUSE, M. WILLIAMS, foot of Market Street (upper side), fronting the Delaware.

MADISON HOUSE, J. OTTENKIRK, 37 and 39 N. Second Street.

BALD EAGLE, DANIEL DALBY, 234 N. Third Street.

MERCHANTS' HOUSE, William H. Bush, 237 N. Third Street.
BLACK BEAR, Wm. Fry (Terms 75 cents per day), 241½ N. Third Street.
WHITE SWAN, Weaver & Baldwin, 108 Race Street.
UTAH HOUSE, On the European Plan (similar to Lovejoy's, New York), Robert Miller, Proprietor, 188 Chestnut Street.
JONES'S EXCHANGE HOTEL, 77 Dock Street, opposite Exchange and Post-Office.

House, Hotel, and Steamboat Furnishing.

ISAAC S. WILLIAMS, 256 Market Street, between Seventh and Eighth.

Ink.

A. W. HARRISON Columbian Inks and Hair-Dye), 10 S. Seventh Street below Market.
JOSEPH E. HOVER (Manufacturer of Hover's Ink, &c.), 144 Race (Sassafras) Street.

Iron.

COLWELL & CO., 111 N. Water Street, and 53 N. Wharves.
GEO. EARP, Jr. (General Commission Merchant), 56 N. Wharves.
FISHER, MORGAN, & CO. (Bar-Iron and Cut Nails), 117 N. Water St., and 56 N. Wharves.
MORRIS, JONES, & CO. (Commission Merchants and Dealers in all descriptions of Iron, Nails, Copper, &c.), Market and Schuylkill Seventh Streets.
NATHAN TROTTER & CO. (also Metals), 36 N. Front Street.
JOS. & G. P. WHITAKER (Manufacturers of Principio, Rough and Ready, and Durham Pig-Iron; also sell Burden's Railroad, Ship, and Boat-Spikes, Horseshoes, and Rivets), 147 N. Water Street and 70 N. Wharves.

Iron Founders.

ABBOTT & LAWRENCE (Liberty Stove Works and Hollow-Ware Foundry), Brown St. above Fourth.
WM. P. CRESSON & CO. (Stoves; also, Tinned, Enamelled, and Ton Hollow-Ware, &c. &c.), Willow Street above Thirteenth.
NORTH, CHASE, & NORTH (Stoves, Ranges, Hollow-Ware, Machinery, &c.); Foundry corner of Second and Mifflin Streets; Warerooms 145 N. Second Street.
JAMES YOCOM & SON (Iron Fronts for Buildings, and Machine Castings generally), Foundry No. 11 Drinker's Alley; Office 125 N. Second Street below Race.

Iron Railing.

COLEMAN'S ORNAMENTAL IRON WORKS, No. 48 S. Fifth Street below Walnut.
HOOD & CO. (Manufacturers of Ornamental Iron Work) in all its branches, at the City Works), 121 N. Tenth Street above Race.
MORE & GALLAGHER, Corner of Ridge Road and Broad Street.
WOOD'S Ornamental Iron Railing Works, Ridge Road and Buttonwood Street.

M. WALKER & SONS (Wrought-Iron and Patent Wire Railing, Farm Fencing, Patent Wire Sacking Bedsteads, &c.), N. E. Corner of Market and Sixth Streets.

Jewelry, Watches, &c.

BUTLER & M'CARTY (Manufacturers of Thimbles, Spectacles, Spoons, and Importers of Watches), 105 N. Second Street above Arch.
CONRAD BARD & SON (Manufacturing Silversmiths, and Importers of Watches and Plated Ware), 116 Arch Street.
E. G. A. BAKER (Manufacturer and Dealer in Jewelry), Corner of N. Fourth and Branch Streets; Office 55 N. Third Street.
JAMES BARBER'S (Wholesale and Retail Clock Establishment); also, Sole Agent for A. W. Rapp's celebrated Patent Scientific Niche Gold Pen, wholesale and retail, South-East Corner of Second and Chestnut Streets.

DUBOSQ, CARROW, & CO. (WHOLESALE MANUFACTURERS OF, AND DEALERS IN JEWELRY), No. 5 Bank Alley, lower side of Pennsylvania Bank.

FARR & THOMPSON (IMPORTERS OF WATCHES AND JEWELRY, also GOLD PEN MANUFACTURERS), 112 Chestnut Street.

THOMAS C. GARRETT & CO. (IMPORTERS OF WATCHES AND MANUFACTURERS OF JEWELRY AND SILVER WARE), 122 Chestnut Street.

JOHN M. HARPER (IMPORTER OF ENGLISH AND SWISS WATCHES), No. 3 Bank Alley near the Exchange.

LEWIS LADOMUS (IMPORTER OF, AND WHOLESALE AND RETAIL DEALER IN WATCHES, JEWELRY, SILVER WARE, AND GOLD PENS), 106 Chestnut Street.

OWEN & DUBOSQ, (MANUFACTURERS AND DEALERS IN JEWELRY), 76 North Second Street.

OSMON REED (IMPORTER AND DEALER IN WATCHES, JEWELRY, GOLD PENS, FANCY GOODS, TOOLS AND MATERIALS), 74 Market Street, below Third.

STAUFFER & HARLEY (IMPORTERS OF WATCHES AND JEWELRY, AND MANUFACTURERS OF SILVER WARE), 06 North Second Street, corner of Quarry.

J. A. STODDART (IMPORTER OF WATCHES AND MANUFACTURER OF JEWELRY, WATCH-TOOLS, AND MATERIALS IN VARIETY), N. E. corner of Market and Third Streets.

TAYLOR, LAWRIE, & WOOD (SILVER WARE), 114 Arch Street. Manufacturers for Bailey & Kitchen, and Bailey & Co., 19 years.

C. & E. TRACY (MANUFACTURERS OF WATCH-CASES AND DIALS; also ASSAYERS AND DEALERS IN GOLD AND SILVER BULLION—CALIFORNIA GOLD BOUGHT), Goldsmith's Hall, Library Street.

WILSON'S SILVER PLATE, SPOON AND FORK MANUFACTORY, S. W. corner of Fifth and Cherry Streets. Also Importers of Plated Ware.

SHOW-CASE MAKERS.

BEAL & FORMAN (SILVER AND GERMAN SILVER MOUNTINGS), rear of No. 7 Cherry, between Third and Fourth.

FREDERICK HAFNER (GERMAN SILVER AND BRASS MOUNTINGS, NEW STYLE), 60 Vine Street below Second.

Leather, Morocco, &c.

FRITZ, WILLIAMS, & HENDRY (MOROCCO MANUFACTURERS, CURRIERS, IMPORTERS, COMMISSION AND GENERAL LEATHER DEALERS), 29 North Third Street.

GEORGE S. ADLER (MOROCCO AND PATENT LEATHER MANUFACTURER), 21 Margaretta Street.

CHAMBERS & CATTELL (MANUFACTURERS AND IMPORTERS OF LEATHER), 67 Chestnut below Third.

EVELAND & MAHARG (MANUFACTURERS OF MOROCCO AND FANCY LEATHER, FRENCH CALF, BOOK-BINDERS, BINDINGS, LININGS, &c.), 65 Willow Street, between St. John and Third Streets.

J. K. GAMBLE & BROTHER (MOROCCO AND FANCY LEATHER MANUFACTURERS), 5 Margaretta Street.

WM. T. McNEELY (MANUFACTURER OF MOROCCO, FANCY LEATHER, BUCKSKIN, CHAMOIS, AND PARCHMENTS), 46 N. Fourth Street.

MIDDLETON & CO. (TANNERS, CURRIERS, AND MOROCCO MANUFACTURERS), Store, 281 N. Second St.; Tannery, Crosswicks, N. J.

Locomotive Builders.

M. W. BALDWIN, Corner of Broad and Hamilton Streets.

RICHARD NORRIS & SON, Schuylkill Sixth Street above Railroad.

Looking-Glasses, &c.

JOSHUA COWPLAND (WHOLESALE DEALER IN LOOKING-GLASSES), 27 S. Fourth Street below Market.

THOMAS J. NATT & CO. (WHOLESALE AND RETAIL LOOKING-GLASS WAREHOUSE AND PLATE-GLASS DEPOT), 117 Chestnut.

JOSEPH S. NATT (FRENCH LOOKING-GLASS AND PLATE-GLASS DEPOT), 182 Chestnut Street, between Seventh and Eighth Streets.

CHARLES N. ROBINSON (also CARVED GILT BRACKETS, GILT PORTRAIT AND PICTURE-FRAMES, ENGRAVINGS, &c.), 248 Chestnut Street.

CHARLES S. SWAIN, 225 N. Second Street.

ISAAC J. CRESSWELL (also CLOCKS, WHOLESALE AND RETAIL, BRITANNIA WARE, AND FANCY HARDWARE), 299 Market Street, below Eighth.

Marble Dealers.

JOHN BAIRD (MANTLES, TOMBS, SLABS, &c.), Ridge Road and Spring Garden Street.

JOSEPH MAPLES (SCULPTOR AND MARBLE MASON), Arch Street near Broad.

ADAM STEINMETZ, Ridge Road above Willow Street.

J. E. & B. SCHELL, S. E. Corner of Tenth and Vine Streets.

H. S. TARR (MANUFACTORY OF CARVED AND ORNAMENTAL MARBLE WORK), Green Street above Seventh.

Medicines. Valuable.

SWAIM'S PANACEA, for the Cure of Scrofula, or King's Evil, and all Diseases arising from Impurity of the Blood.

SWAIM'S VERMIFUGE, a Valuable Family Medicine in Diseases arising from Debility of the Digestive Organs. (See Pamphlets, to be had gratis.) Prepared at Swaim's Laboratory, South Seventh St. below Chestnut.

WRIGHT'S INDIAN VEGETABLE PILLS, N. W. Corner of Fifth and Race Streets.

Millinery Goods and Ribbons.

M. BERNHEIM, 11 S. Second Street.

THOMAS MORGAN (Manufacturer of Bonnets and Millinery Goods), 88 North Ninth Street, above Cherry.

JOHN STONE & SONS, 45 S. Second.

A. H. ROSENHEIM & CO., 23½ South Second Street.

J. C. & W. E. TABER, 19 S. Second Street.

Military Furnishing Goods.

W. H. HORSTMANN & SONS,
51 NORTH THIRD ST.
(Manufactory Fifth and Cherry),
MANUFACTURERS OF
MILITARY GOODS,
Ladies' Dress Trimmings,
Carriage Laces and Trimmings,
Upholsterers' Trimmings,
Blind Trimmings,
Tailors' Trimmings,
Masonic and other Regalia.
IMPORTERS OF
Hosiery, Gloves,
Cotton Fringes, Yarn, &c.
Combs, Brushes, Fans,
French, English, and German
Fancy Goods, and
Manufacturers' Materials.
SOLE AGENTS FOR
RYLE'S SPOOL SILK.

Military Equipments.

LAMBERT & WHITE, 103 N. Third.

Importer of Mosaic Flooring Tile.

S. A. HARRISON (also AGENT AND IMPORTER OF TERRA COTTA WARE, ARCHITECTURAL ORNAMENTS), 146 Walnut Street.

Perfumery, Fancy Soaps, &c.

R. &. G. A. WRIGHT, 23 S. Fourth Street below Market.

XAVIER BAZIN, 114 Chestnut Street.

A. W. HARRISON, 10 South Seventh Street, above Chestnut.

W. SCHOLLENBERGER & CO., 26 Merchant Street, first street below Market, between Fourth and Fifth.

SAMUEL F. PRINCE (DOMESTIC MARBLE AND SOAPSTONE), Chestnut and Schuylkill Front Streets.

A FEW

OF THE

FIRST-CLASS WHOLESALE HOUSES IN CINCINNATI.

Agricult'ral Implements.

J. M. M'CULLOUGH (Fruit and Ornamental Trees, Garden, Field, and Flower Seeds, Horticultural and Agricultural Implements), 162 Main Street. Nursery and Seed Farm, Pleasant Ridge.

Exchange Brokers and Bankers.

T. S. GOODMAN & CO.
(Exchange and Banking House),
101 Main Street.
Stocks bought and sold on commission; collections made on all points throughout the country, and returns made with current rates of exchange without charge, and all other business appertaining to Banking.

J. S. DYE (Dye's Exchange Office), S. E. Corner Third and Walnut Sts., opposite Masonic Hall.

Book Publishers.

APPLEGATE & CO.

Booksellers, Publishers, Stationers, Printers, and Blank-Book Manufacturers,

No. 43 Main Street, West Side, below Second Street, Cincinnati.

SMITH & FAIRMAN (Book-Binders and Blank-Book Manufacturers), 141 Main St.

J. C. & H. L. TUMY (Book-Binders and Blank Book Manufacturers), 43 Main St.

H. B. PEARSON & CO., 17 E. Fourth Street.

Cigars, Tobacco, &c.

NEILSON & CHURCHILL (Importers and Manufacturers of Havana and Domestic Cigars, and Dealers in Tobacco, Snuff, &c.), 23 Main St.

B. VETTERLEIN & CO., N. W. cor. of Columbia St. and Broadway. Constantly on hand an assortment of Havana, Principe, and Domestic Cigars; Havana, Cuba, St. Domingo, and Spanish Seed Leaf Tobacco; Maccoboy, French, Fine and Coarse Rappee and Scotch Snuffs. The most approved brands of Virginia Manufactured Tobacco.

SIMEON B. WILLIAMS,
Manufacturer of Fine-cut Chewing and Smoking Tobacco, and dealer in Imported and Domestic Cigars, 88, 90, and 92 Pearl St. First Premiums, 1852, awarded at American Institute, N. Y., Mechanics' Institute, Cincinnati, Ohio State Fair, Cleveland, Michigan State Fair, Detroit.

China, Glass, & Queensware.

SAMPSON & CO. (Importers and Dealers in China, Glass, and Queensware), 92 Main Street, three doors below Third.

Commission Merchants.

CINNAMON & KERR (COMMISSION MERCHANTS AND DEALERS IN PRODUCE), 11 Water Street.

STRAIGHT & DEMING (WESTERN RESERVE CHEESE & BUTTER, FLOUR, BACON, LARD, DRIED FRUITS, SEEDS, SALÆRATUS, POT AND PEARL ASHES, FISH, HEMP, COTTON, and all kinds of PRODUCE, GROCERIES, and Manufactured Articles), 31 Sycamore Street. Particular attention given to the purchase of goods on orders.

Clothiers.

AMBERG & STACHEL (WHOLESALE CLOTHING DEPOT), 209 Main Street, 4 doors above Fifth.

FECHHEIMERS,GOLDSMITH, & CO. (WHOLESALE CLOTHIERS AND DEALERS IN DRY GOODS), No. 72 Main St., fifth door below Lower Market St.

T. W. SPRAGUE & CO. (FASHIONABLE TAILORS: also FINE CLOTHING READY MADE), 113 Main St. Amount of stock on hand, $75,000.

A. H. GUTHRIE & CO.
(DRAPERS, TAILORS, AND GENTLEMEN'S FURNISHING STORE),
34 Fourth St., N. side, between Main and Walnut.

WILLIAM ADDIS (MASONIC AND ODD-FELLOWS' FURNISHING STORE), Sixth Street, Bacon's Building, under Magnolia Hall, Manufacturer of Costumes and Regalia of every description, for Masons, Odd-Fellows, and Sons of Temperance.

☞ Being a member of the above orders, I am prepared at all times to furnish everything appertaining thereto with punctuality and dispatch.

Cocoa and Chocolate.

LAMBE & CO. (MANUFACTURERS), 130 Columbia Street, between Race and Elm.

Confectioners.

MYERS & CO. (WHOLESALE CONFECTIONERS), 40 Main Street.

Drugs. Importers and Wholesale Dealers.

BURDSAL & BROTHER, N. W. Corner of Main and Front Streets, is a FIRST-CLASS WHOLESALE DRUG HOUSE, AND IMPORTERS AND DEALERS IN ALL ARTICLES IN THE DRUG TRADE. (Motto—Large Sales and Small Profits.)

C. S. BURDSAL & CO. (DEALERS IN DRUGS, MEDICINES, PAINTS, OILS, DYESTUFFS, GLASSWARE, &c.), 228 Main Street, between Fifth and Sixth Streets.

CONKLING, WOOD, & CO. (MANUFACTURERS OF CASTOR-OIL, WHITE AND RED LEAD, LITHARGE, WHITING, PUTTY, CHROMES GREEN, RED, AND YELLOW, ASSORTED COLORS, DRY OR IN OIL, AND IMPORTERS OF COARSE PAINTS), North side of Court Street, East of Broadway, Cincinnati, Ohio.

ROBERT FLETCHER, AGENT FOR LANDRETH'S (Philadelphia) GARDEN-SEEDS; BAZIN'S (Roussel) PERFUMERY; NEW JERSEY ZINC PAINT, N. E. Corner Sycamore and Lower Market.

R. MACREADY (WHOLESALE DEALER IN DRUGS, MEDICINES, PAINTS, OILS, VARNISHES, DYES, BRUSHES, GLASSWARE, &c.), S. W. corner Front and Walnut Sts.

J. & C. REAKIRT (also DEALERS IN SATINET WARPS, STEEL REEDS, SHUTTLES, PICKERS, HARNESS TWINE, ROLLER CLOTH, PRESS PAPERS, TENTER HOOKS, CARD CLEANERS, COMB PLATES, &c.; and Agents for SMITH, WOODCOCK, & KNIGHT'S MACHINE CARDS), 21 Pearl Street.

ABIA ZELLER (WHOLESALE DRUGGIST), N. E. Corner of Main and Columbia Streets.

KOST, BIGGER & CO., Publishers of "Kost's Materia Medica and Therapeutics." Kost's "Domestic Medicine," Kost's "Pharmacy and Organic Chemistry," "Howard's Practice." "Howard's Midwifery," and "Howard's Physiology;" wholesale dealers in Foreign and Domestic Medicines (warranted pure and fresh), Perfumery, and Surgical Instruments, 45 E. Fourth St.

Dental Furnishing Depot.

S. WARDLE & CO. (MANUFACTURERS OF SINGLE TEETH), 256 Walnut St. Block Work made to order; Dentist's Instruments, Lathes, Tools, Operating Chairs, Spittoons, Material, &c. &c. Orders with remittances promptly attended to.

Daguerreotype Stock.

PETER SMITH (DEALER AND IMPORTER OF DAGUERREOTYPE STOCK, FANCY AND MILITARY GOODS), 36 Fifth St.

Dry Goods.

D. & R. BROWN (MANUFACTURERS OF HOSIERY, IMPORTERS AND WHOLESALE DEALERS IN RIBBONS, GLOVES, LINENS, LACE, SILK GOODS, SMALL WARES, &c.), 253 Main Street, three doors above Sixth.

GEORGE WHITE (WHOLESALE AND RETAIL DEALER IN EVERY DESCRIPTION OF FOREIGN AND DOMESTIC DRY-GOODS), No. 56 and 58 Fifth Street, North side.

Engravers.

H. C. GROSVENOR (ENGRAVER ON WOOD), N. E. corner of Fourth and Walnut Sts.

H. H. SHIPLEY, & BRO. (MANUFACTURERS OF EMBOSSED BUSINESS CARDS AND ENVELOPS), 22 W. Fourth Street.

ENGRAVERS ON WOOD.

FRAZER & DENIS, Gazette Building, 120 Main Street. Every description of WOOD ENGRAVING executed in superior style.

☞ Orders from abroad punctually attended to.

J. R. TELFER, 7 Gazette Building, 120 Main Street. Landscapes, Views of Buildings, Newspaper Headings, &c. engraved to order.

H. H. SHIPLEY & BROTHER, Nos. 6 and 22 W. Fourth Street. Engraving on Wood done in the best style.

BANK-NOTE ENGRAVERS AND PRINTERS.

RAWDON, WRIGHT, HATCH, & EDSON, S. E. corner Fourth and Main Sts. Also engraved in a style corresponding in excellence to that of *Bank Notes*, Railroad, State, and County Bonds, Bills of Exchange, Checks, Drafts, Certificates of Stock and Deposit, Promissory Notes, Bill and Letter Heads, Diplomas, Visiting and Professional Cards, Notarial, County, and Hand Seals, &c. Constantly on hand, *Bank-Note Paper*, of various tints, made to order, of very superior quality. The above office is under the supervision of GEO. T. JONES, Practical Engraver.

Fancy Goods.

DORR & ARNOLD (WHOLESALE DEALERS IN FANCY GOODS), 6 Sixth Street, between Main and Walnut. Manufacturers of various brands of Cigars.

TAYLOR, FRENCH, & WYNNE, 79 Main and 3 Pearl Streets.

F. SCHULTZE & CO. (IMPORTERS OF FANCY GOODS, TOYS, FRENCH CHINA, AND GERMAN GLASSWARE, COMBS, WORK-BOXES, MUSICAL INSTRUMENTS, &c.), 64 Main Street.

Furniture. Fashionable.

JOHN GEYER (WESTERN CHAIR AND FURNITURE MANUFACTORY) Nos. 8 and 10 East Fourth Street.

MITCHELL & RAMMELSBERG (WHOLESALE AND RETAIL FURNITURE WAREROOMS), 23 and 25 E. Second St., between Main and Sycamore.

L. M. CRANE,

MANUFACTURER OF FASHIONABLE

CABINET FURNITURE,

SOFAS, CHAIRS, ETC.

Warerooms, 81 Sycamore St., one door above Third.

☞ Work done to order; Furniture repaired; Upholstering done with neatness and dispatch, at moderate terms.

AARON SHAW, 18 East Fourth St. The subscriber keeps constantly on hand the richest PARLOR, CHAMBER, AND COTTAGE ENAMELLED FURNITURE. AARON SHAW.

Grocers.

BISHOP, WELLS, & CO.,

R. M. BISHOP, W. W. WELLS, G. W. BISHOP, } Wholesale Grocers, Forwarding and Comm'n Merchants,

Front St., five doors east of Main, opposite the Steamboat Landing.

JOSEPH C. BUTLER & CO. (WHOLESALE GROCERS AND COMMISSION MERCHANTS), 47 Main Street.

Albert G. Richardson,
GENERAL COMMISSION MERCHANT
AND
WHOLESALE GROCER,
Corner of Walnut and Columbia Streets.

SMITH & GRAHAM (WHOLESALE GROCERS AND PRODUCE MERCHANTS, AND DEALERS IN FOREIGN AND DOMESTIC LIQUORS, WINES, &c.), 4 and 5 Commercial Row.

SPRINGER & WHITEMAN, 16 and 18 Columbia Street.

Hardware and Cutlery.

R. W. BOOTH & CO. (CARPENTERS' AND COOPERS' TOOLS, ENGLISH SINGLE AND DOUBLE BARREL GUNS; also AGENTS FOR FAIRBANKS'S PLATFORM SCALES), S. W. Corner of Walnut and Pearl Streets.

LATIMER, COX, COLBOURNE, & LUPTON (JOBBERS OF HARDWARE), New Store, 74 Main St., near Pearl.

TYLER, DAVIDSON, & CO., 140 and 142 Main Street.

J. L. WAYNE (DEALER IN HARDWARE, PLUSH, HAIR CLOTH, SOFA SPRINGS, BURLAPS, CANVAS, TWINE, GIMP, VENEERS, GLUE, LOOKING-GLASS PLATES, &c. &c.), 124 Main St.

M'GREGOR, LEE, & CO. (MANUFACTURERS OF POWDER-PROOF BANK LOCKS, PRISON, STORE, AND HOUSE LOCKS; also HOTEL AND STEAMBOAT BELL WORK, &c., and DEALERS IN BUILDING HARDWARE), Western Row, between Sixth and Seventh Sts.

EVENS PERCUSSION PRESS, with SEAL, complete for $5. C. F. HALL, ENGRAVER, 14 W. Fourth Street, and corner of Fifth and Walnut, General Agent for the United States.

This unique invention is now used and highly recommended by Bankers, Merchants, Editors, Lodges, Notaries Public, Bodies Corporate, &c. &c.

U. S. ENGRAVING ROOMS, 14 W. Fourth Street, next door west of Firsf Presbyterian Church; sign, Arms ot the U. S. Seals (Arms) Designed and Engraved for Bodies Corporate, Civil and Ecclesiastical Courts, Lodges, Notaries Public, Bankers and Merchants, &c. Seal Presses, Copper and Steel Plate Engraving and Printing; Marriage, Business, and Address Cards; Self-Sealing Advertising Envelops and Colored Embossed Cards all executed in the best style of the art. C. F. HALL.

Hats. Fashionable.

L. H. BAKER & CO. (FASHIONABLE HATTERS), S. W. Corner of Main and Fourth Streets.

Hotels.

BURNET HOUSE, Third and Vine Sts.

DENNISON HOUSE (W. & E. B. DENNISON), Corner of Main and Fifth Streets.

GIBSON HOUSE (O. H. GEFFROY), Walnut Street, between Fourth and Fifth.

HORSES AND CARRIAGES TO HIRE.

ISAAC D. JOHNSON, East side of Walnut, between Eighth and Ninth Streets.

India Rubber Goods.

BART & HICKCOX (also UMBRELLAS, HOSE, STEAM PACKING, AND MACHINE BELTING, at Factory Prices), N. W. corner Fifth and Main Sts.

Iron Founders.

J. H. BURROWS & CO., COLUMBIA FOUNDRY, Columbia Street, between Elm and Plum; Office, 23 W. Front

St., between Main and Walnut: also Manufacturers of J. H. Burrows's Patent Grist Mills, French Burr Mill Stones, of all sizes, Steam Engines, Grist and Saw Mill Irons, and Castings of all descriptions: also Dealers in Bolting Cloths, Plaster of Paris, &c.

WM. C. DAVIS. WM. C. BARNARD.

W. C. DAVIS & CO., Proprietors of the ANCHOR IRON WORKS, and Manufacturers of Fisk's Patent Metallic Burial Cases, and every description of Cooking and Heating Stoves, Hollow Ware, Dog Irons, Sad Irons, Tea Kettles, Caldron, Potash, and Sugar Kettles, and Castings in general, and Dealers in English and American Steel; Juniata Iron, and Nails of all sizes and of a warranted quality. Sales Rooms corner of Ninth and Main; Foundry on Hunt Street.

Lard Oil.

BURCKHARDT & CO. (MANUFACTURERS AND WHOLESALE DEALERS IN LARD OIL, STEARINE, CANDLES, SOAP, &c.) N. E. Corner Sixth and Walnut, and 12 Hammond Street.

HENRY GOOCH, LARD OIL MANUFACTURER, 130 Columbia Street, between Race and Elm.

PROCTER & GAMBLE (also CANDLES, SOAP, PEARL-STARCH), 252 Main St., between Sixth and Seventh.

Looking-Glasses, &c.

BOWN & HARTIGAN (GILDING AND LOOKING-GLASS ESTABLISHMENT), 16 East Fourth Street. Steamboats and Storerooms decorated with Composition, Portrait, Picture, and Looking-glass Frames, and Window Cornices of every Description, made to order. Fine Engravings, Lithographs, &c.

WILLIAM WISWELL, JR. (LOOKING-GLASSES, PORTRAIT, AND PICTURE-FRAMES OF EVERY PATTERN; WINDOW, PLATE, AND OTHER FRENCH CRYSTAL GLASS OF ALL SIZES), 129 Main Street, between Third and Fourth Streets. Looking-glass Plates of every Size put into Old Frames.

Lithographers and Engravers.

MIDDLETON & WALLACE (RAILROAD BONDS, CERTIFICATES, MAPS, &c., VIEWS OF BUILDINGS, SHOW CARDS, CIRCULARS, &c.), Odd Fellows' Building, 115 Walnut St.

Marble Dealers.

D. BOLLES (ARTIFICER AND DEALER IN MARBLE), East side of Vine, between Fifth and Sixth Sts.

CHARLES RULE (LATE LOWRY AND RULE), corner of Broadway and Fifth. Monuments, Tombs, Grave Stones, Mantels, &c. constantly on hand and furnished to order.

The Trade supplied with Marble in Block and Slab, or sawed to order.

Mathematical Instruments.

T. F. RANDOLPH & BROTHER, N. W. corner of Fifth and Walnut Sts. (second story Apollo Building), Manufacturers of Surveyors' Compasses, Theodolites, Transits, Levels, &c. ☞ Repairing and adjusting Instruments done to order.

Mercantile Colleges.

BACON'S MERCANTILE COLLEGE, N. W. corner Sixth and Walnut Sts. The Course of Instruction consists of Double Entry Bookkeeping, embracing every department of Trade and Mercantile Accounts, Penmanship, Commercial Calculations, Lectures on Commercial Law, Political Economy, the Science of Accounts, Customs of Merchants, &c.

R. S. BACON, Principal.

GUNDRY'S MERCANTILE COLLEGE, Incorporated 1848. This institution qualifies individuals for the Counting-room and business pursuits. Terms for the full course $40.

JOHN GUNDRY, Principal.

THOMPSON'S PENMAN'S INSTITUTE, S. E. cor. Walnut and Eighth Sts. Open Day and Evening.

House and Sign Painters.

J. M. HUSTON (PLAIN AND ORNAMENTAL), 67 W. Third, between Walnut and Vine Sts. Fresco and Kalsomine Painting, in all their various branches, Imitations of Woods and Marbles, Plain, Ornamental, and Stained Glass, Damask, Tapestry, and Morocco. Specimens of each may be seen by calling at the Store. Wall Painting in Oil, Turpentine, and other Composition Colors. Zinc, Lead, Paints, Oils, and Glass, constantly on hand and for sale. Block Letters cut to order.

H. CUMMINGS (PLAIN AND ORNAMENTAL), 126 Walnut St., between Third and Fourth Sts. Fresco and Kalsomine Painting, in all their various branches; Imitations of Woods and Marbles, Plain, Ornamental, and Stained Glass, Damask, Tapestry, and Morocco. Specimens of each may be seen by calling at the Store. Wall Painting in Oil, Turpentine, and other Composition Colors. Paints, Oils, and Glass constantly on hand and for sale. Block Letters cut to order.

ROBINSON & CARLIN (PLAIN AND ORNAMENTAL), S. W. corner of Third and Race Sts. Sign Writing, Gilding, Graining, Glazing, and Wall Coloring done in Distemper with neatness and dispatch.

TEASDALE'S NEW YORK DYE HOUSE is a four story building with stone front, opposite the Walnut St. House, between Sixth and Seventh Streets. This is the only house in the West that ever received a premium for colors: it has no connection with any other New York Dye House in Cincinnati, and is the only house of the above name where first-rate work is done.

Millinery Goods.

J. SHUMARD & CO. (DEALERS IN FASHIONABLE STRAW GOODS, SILK BONNETS, RIBBONS, FLOWERS, SILKS, TRIMMINGS, &c.), 187 Main St.

Printers, Stereotypers, and Publishers.

I. HART & CO., 41 and 43 Columbia St. All kinds of JOB AND CARD PRINTING neatly executed at this establishment.

Perfumery and Fancy Articles.

KOHL & THORNE (IMPORTERS AND DEALERS IN PERFUMERY, FANCY ARTICLES, AND ALL THE POPULAR GENUINE FAMILY MEDICINES). Western Agents for Myer's Extract of Rock Rose, Kendall & Taylor's Thermometers, &c., N. E. Corner Fourth and Vine Streets. Chas. A. Dexter, Travelling Agent.

Paper Box Factory.

D. B. JORDAN, S. E. corner Main and Fifth Sts. The oldest establishment of the kind in the West. A good stock constantly on hand.

Piano-Fortes.

DAVID A. TRUAX (PIANO-FORTE AND MUSIC WAREROOMS), 80 Fourth St., between Walnut and Vine. A splendid assortment of SHEET MUSIC kept constantly on hand.

Rifles and Pistols.

GRIFFITHS & SIEBERT (RIFLE AND PISTOL MANUFACTURERS; WHOLESALE AND RETAIL DEALERS IN DOUBLE AND SINGLE BARREL SHOT-GUNS, REVOLVERS AND SINGLE PISTOLS, AND SPORTING APPARATUS), 279 Main St., between Sixth and Seventh. Guns, &c. neatly repaired. Gunmakers furnished with Gun materials at the lowest prices.

Pork and Beef Packers.

CHAS. DAVIS & CO., PORK AND BEEF PACKERS, Sycamore Street, between Eighth and Ninth.

Saddlery.

MOORES & BUTTERFIELD (SADDLE, HARNESS, AND TRUNK MANUFACTURERS), 89 Main St.

Stationers.

H. B. PEARSON & CO.,

WHOLESALE AND RETAIL

Cheap Book, Periodical, and Stationery Dealers,

17 East Fourth Street.

Tea Dealers.

MOORE & CHESTER (WHOLESALE TEA DEALERS), Seventh and Walnut Streets.

L. F. HARTER (TEA DEALER), 42 Fifth Street, one door west of Walnut, Apollo Building.

Trunks, Valises, Carpet Bags, &c.

G. W. SCHOLL & BROTHER (MANUFACTURERS), W. Row and Plum Sts., between Everet and Mason, and 57 N. W. corner of Walnut and Columbia, keep constantly on hand the largest stock.

Wines, Liquors, &c.

HAWTHORN & DUNN (IMPORTERS AND DEALERS IN WINES AND LIQUORS, VIRGINIA, MISSOURI, AND KENTUCKY TOBACCOS, TEAS, &C.), 50 Pearl Street.

Window-Shades.

THOS. J. ERNST (NEW YORK WINDOW-SHADE DEPOT), 2 College Hall. Manufacturer and Dealer in all kinds of Transparent Window-Shades; also Cords, Tassels, Brass-Mountings, &c. Shades of every Description made to Order.

Wool and Cotton Carding Machines.

A. C. BROWN (CINCINNATI MACHINE WORKS), 37 Walnut St. Machine Cards, Wool, Cotton, and Hair Picking Machines, Portable French Burr Mills, Steam-Engines, French Burr Mill Stones, Bolting Cloths, Reaping and Mowing Machines, Horse Powers and Thrashers, Stock Mills, Corn Shellers, Straw Cutters, Tobacco Screws, Mill Screws, Lard and Wine Press Screws, Machinery Castings, &c. for sale.

PENNSYLVANIA RAIL ROAD.

NOTICE TO WESTERN TRAVELLERS.

A CONTINUOUS RAIL ROAD

From PHILADELPHIA to PITTSBURGH, Penn'a.,

Massillon, Wooster, Cleveland, Cincinnati, O., Indianapolis, La Fayette, Terre Haute, Ind., and Chicago, Ill.

THROUGH	from	PHILADELPHIA	to PITTSBURG	in 19	Hours.
"	"	"	" CLEVELAND	in 26	"
"	"	"	" CINCINNATI	in 38	"
"	"	"	" CHICAGO	in 42	"

Being the Shortest and Quickest Route from the Atlantic Cities to the Great West.

FARE	from	PHILADELPHIA	to PITTSBURG	by Railroad,	$9 50
"	"	"	MASSILLON	"	10 00
"	"	"	CLEVELAND	"	10 00
"	"	"	CINCINNATI	"	16 30
"	"	"	CHICAGO	"	20 00
"	"	"	CINCINNATI	S. Packet from Pittsburg to Cincinnati.	11 00

On or about the Middle of MARCH, the Road from WOOSTER to CRESTLINE will be opened, and Time between PHILADELPHIA and CINCINNATI REDUCED to 34 Hours.

NOTICE.—In case of Loss, the Company will hold themselves responsible for personal baggage only, and for an amount not exceeding $100.

THOS. MOORE, *Passenger Agent,* Philadelphia.
February, 1853. **J. MESKIMEN,** *Passenger Agent,* Pittsburg.

PENNSYLVANIA RAIL ROAD.

This Road being now completed, it opens a direct Railway communicating between

PHILADELPHIA, PITTSBURG, AND THE WEST;

By which Freight can be transported quicker, and at cheaper rates, than by any other route; it also connects Daily with the

PACKETS AT PITTSBURG, FOR

WHEELING, CINCINNATI, LOUISVILLE, ST. LOUIS,

AND ALL THE DIFFERENT POINTS ON THE WESTERN LAKES.

Cars run through between Philadelphia and Pittsburg without transhipment of Freight, an advantage that can be appreciated by all shippers.

In case of obstruction of Navigation by Ice or Low Water, Freights can be forwarded from Pittsburg to Cincinnati, or Towns in the interior, by Rail Road.

RATES OF FREIGHT BETWEEN PHILADELPHIA AND PITTSBURG.

	Winter Rate.		Summer Rate.
First Class.			
Dry Goods, Books and Stationery, Boots, Shoes, Hats, and Carpetings, Furs and Peltries, Feathers, Saddlery, &c. . .	$1	per 100 lbs.	75c.
Second Class.			
Brown Sheetings and Shirtings in Bales, Drugs, Glassware, Groceries, except Coffee, Hardware, Hollow-ware, Machinery, Oil Cloth, Wool, &c., ...	85c.	"	60c.
Third Class.			
Butter in Firkins and Kegs, Candles, Cotton (in Winter), Queensware, Tallow, Tobacco in leaf or manufactured, (Eastward) &c. &c., ...	75c.	"	50c.
Fourth Class.			
Bacon, Cotton (in Summer), Coffee, Lard & Lard Oil (through), Pork, fresh, in full car loads at Owner's risk, . . .	65c.	"	40c.

E. J. SNEEDER, *Freight Agent,* Philadelphia.
GEO. C. FRANCISCUS, *Freight Agent,* Pittsburg.

PENNSYLVANIA RAIL-ROAD, WITH ITS CONNECTING LINES.

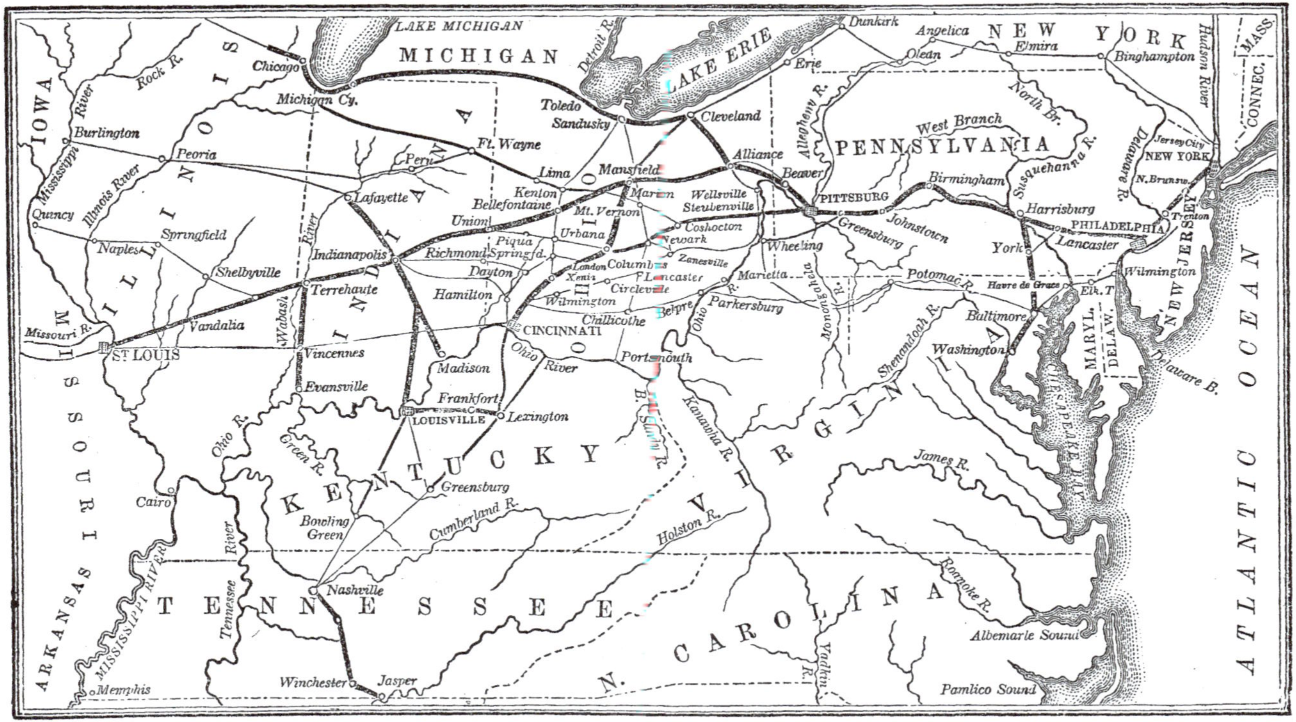

EXCELLENT INSURANCE COMPANIES.

Few at this day need arguments on the advantages of Life Insurance, but there are many who should be *cautioned to exercise greater care in the selection of an office.* The following is the Company mentioned p. 143, as an excellent instance of those doing business on the mutual principle. It requires all premiums to be paid in cash, and consequently its losses are paid wholly in cash. The advantages of the note system in part payment of premiums it considers questionable, inasmuch as the main object of insurance is to secure a certain sum *in cash*, to surviving relatives *beyond contingency*, but those Companies that take notes must pay their losses partly in notes. I have every confidence in its management—its past prosperity has been almost unprecedented—and I recommend those who think of insuring their lives on the *mutual* principle to obtain from the Agents a copy of their last Report containing full statements and particulars, or address

THE MUTUAL LIFE INSURANCE COMPANY

OF NEW YORK, 35 WALL STREET.

Net Accumulated Cash Fund, 1,800,000 Dollars,

Securely invested in Bonds and Mortgages on Real Estate, chiefly in New York and Brooklyn, the Real Estate, in each and every case, being worth double the amount loaned thereon.

All the Profits are divided among the Insured, and on Policies for the Whole of Life, will be made available in part payment of Premiums, after the dividend of 1853.

ISAAC ABBATT, *Secretary*,
CHARLES GILL, *Actuary*.

JOSEPH B. COLLINS,
President.

CAUTION.

Having determined to get your life insured, look well to the character of the Company in which you are invited to take a Policy. Examine the Charter. See that it has a fair chance of continuing to exist 25 to 50 years, or more. How must its funds be invested? Can the Trustees lend all the property to themselves? or on other personal security? or in any kind of stock which may become worthless? Do the Trustees make statements that are plain, and easily understood? and do their statements agree with the sworn accounts made to the State authorities? Are the rates of premium those of Companies known to have been successful?

You may live 15, 20, 30, even 50 years. Your object is to *secure*, beyond all reasonable doubt, a certain sum to your survivors. You do not wish even to trust yourself! You therefore desire to have every possible guaranty that the sum insured will be paid, as certain, not as *life*, but as *death!* What is the trifling accommodation of giving a note, (which must after all be paid,) or an annual dividend, or a less rate of premium, in comparison with the certainty of final payment?

Are you satisfied, that before making their dividend, they have ascertained by a most careful calculation, and by a competent and experienced Actuary, that they had actually made the profit they divide? And did they reserve a sum sufficient to insure *all* risks not terminated? It is easy to make a gross error in this matter, but one most fatal to the insured.

It can be shown to be mathematically true, that an annual dividend of 40 per cent. paid out in CASH to the insured, or the interest only of which should be annually paid in CASH, would eventually render the Company INSOLVENT, although for a number of years their assets would increase.

REMEMBER, you are not about to make a contract for a month, or a single year, but for a series of years! and should you discover, some time hence, that you have been misled into an unsound or worthless Company, you may then have become uninsurable from sickness. Therefore *begin* right, lest your good intentions be thrown away.

[*For the advantages of Mixed Life Insurance Companies, see page* 142. *The following are good ones.*]

THE GIRARD LIFE INSURANCE ANNUITY AND TRUST COMPANY OF PHILADELPHIA.

Office, No. 132 *Chestnut Street, the first door east of the Custom House.*

Charter perpetual—Capital $300,000 paid in and invested, which, together with the accumulated premium Fund, afford ample Security to the Insured—continue to make Insurance on Lives on the most favorable terms. They act as Executors, Trustees, and Guardians under last Wills and Testaments, and as Assignees and Receivers.

The premium may be paid yearly, half-yearly, or quarterly.

The Company add a BONUS periodically to the Insurances for Life. The first Bonus was appropriated in December 1844, and the second Bonus in December, 1849.

MANAGERS.

Thomas Ridgway,	John A. Brown,	George Taber,
Armon Davis,	Thomas P. James,	John R. Latimer,
John Jay Smith,	Joseph T. Bailey,	Wharton Lewis,
Robert Pearsall,	D. Danner,	John R. Slack.
Joseph Yeager,	Frederick Brown,	

Pamphlets containing tables of rates and explanations, forms of application, and further information, can be had at the Office.

JNO. F. JAMES, *Actuary.* THOMAS RIDGWAY, *President,*

THE UNITED STATES LIFE INSURANCE, ANNUITY, AND TRUST COMPANY OF PHILADELPHIA.

(Mixed) Charter Perpetual. Capital $250,000.

Office, South East Corner of Third and Chestnut Streets.

FRANKLIN FIRE INSURANCE COMPANY OF PHILADELPHIA.

Capital paid in, $400,000. Invested Fund, $1,250,000.

Office 163½ *Chestnut below Fifth Street. Charter Perpetual.*

Make Insurance, permanent or limited, against Loss or Damage by Fire, on Property and Effects of every description in Town or Country, on favorable terms.

DIRECTORS.

Charles N. Bancker,	George W. Richards,	David S. Brown,
Tobias Wagner,	Mordecai D. Lewis,	Morris Patterson,
Samuel Grant,	Adolphe E. Borie,	Isaac Lea.
Jacob R. Smith,		

CHARLES G. BANCKER, *Secretary.* CHARLES N. BANCKER, *President.*

THE MONARCH FIRE INSURANCE COMPANY OF LONDON.

CAPITAL $1,500,000, and Surplus Fund of $700,000.

PHILADELPHIA AGENT.

John G. Holbrooke, 56 Walnut Street (Farquhar Building). Losses adjusted and promptly paid in Philadelphia.

REFERENCES.

In Philadelphia—Messrs. Lawrence & Stone, Waln, Leaming & Co., Slade, Gemill & Pratt, M. L. Hallowell & Co., William Peter, Esq., H. B. M. Consul, Charles H. Welling, Esq., and Edward Frith, Esq.

In Baltimore—Messrs. Tiffany, Ward & Co., Wyman, Appleton, & Co., and Josiah Lee & Co.

In Washington, D. C.—Messrs. Corcoran & Riggs.

DIRECTORS IN BOSTON.

Nathaniel Thayer, Esq.	James Murray Howe, Esq.	James Sturgis, Esq.
Samuel Hooper, Esq.	Charles H. Mills, Esq.	Chas. F. Shimmin, Esq.
Farnham Plummer, Esq.		

GEORGE ADLARD,
Resident Secretary in Boston, and General Agent for the United States.

www.ingramcontent.com/pod-product-compliance
Lightning Source LLC
LaVergne TN
LVHW010145110826
845151LV00002B/430

* 9 7 8 1 4 2 5 5 3 7 4 6 3 *